Environmental Border Tax Adjustments and International Trade Law

NEW HORIZONS IN ENVIRONMENTAL AND ENERGY LAW

Series Editors: Kurt Deketelaere, *Professor of Law, University of Leuven, Belgium and University of Dundee, Scotland* and Zen Makuch, *Reader in Law, Barrister, Imperial College, London, UK*

Environmental law – including the pressing considerations of energy law and climate change – is an increasingly important area of legal research and practice. Given the growing interdependence of global society and the significant steps being made towards environmental protection and energy efficiency, there are few people untouched by environmental and energy lawmaking processes.

At the same time, environmental and energy law is at a crossroads. The command and control methodology that evolved in the 1960s and 1970s for air, land and water protection may have reached the limit of its environmental protection achievements. New life needs to be injected into our environmental protection regimes – perhaps through the concept of sustainability in its environmental, economic and social forms. The same goes for energy policy and law, where liberalization, environmental protection and security of supply are at the centre of attention. This important series seeks to press forward the boundaries of environmental and energy law through innovative research into environmental and energy law, doctrine and case law. Adopting a wide interpretation of environmental and energy law, it includes contributions from both leading and emerging international scholars.

Titles in the series include:

Regulation of the Upstream Petroleum Sector
A Comparative Study of Licensing and Concession Systems
Edited by Tina Hunter

Regional Environmental Law
Transregional Comparative Lessons in Pursuit of Sustainable Development
Edited by Werner Scholtz and Jonathan Verschuuren

Earth Governance
Trusteeship of the Global Commons
Klaus Bosselmann

Waste Policy
International Regulation, Comparative and Contextual Perspectives
Alexander Gillespie

Shale Gas and the Future of Energy
Law and Policy for Sustainability
Edited by John C. Dernbach and James R. May

The Privatisation of Biodiversity?
New Approaches to Conservation Law
Colin T. Reid and Walters Nsoh

Aquaculture Law and Policy
Global, Regional and National Perspectives
Edited by David L. VanderZwaag, Nigel Bankes and Irene Dahl

Charting the Water Regulatory Future
Issues, Challenges and Directions
Edited by Julien Chaisse

Shale Gas, the Environment and Energy Security
A New Framework for Energy Regulation
Ruven Fleming

Environmental Border Tax Adjustments and International Trade Law
Fostering Environmental Protection
Alice Pirlot

Environmental Border Tax Adjustments and International Trade Law

Fostering Environmental Protection

Alice Pirlot

F.N.R.S. Postdoctoral Research Fellow, Université catholique de Louvain, Belgium

NEW HORIZONS IN ENVIRONMENTAL AND ENERGY LAW

Edward Elgar PUBLISHING

Cheltenham, UK • Northampton, MA, USA

Published by
Edward Elgar Publishing Limited
The Lypiatts
15 Lansdown Road
Cheltenham
Glos GL50 2JA
UK

Edward Elgar Publishing, Inc.
William Pratt House
9 Dewey Court
Northampton
Massachusetts 01060
USA

A catalogue record for this book
is available from the British Library

Library of Congress Control Number: 2017939828

This book is available electronically in the **Elgar**online
Law subject collection
DOI 10.4337/9781786435514

MIX
Paper from
responsible sources
FSC® C013056

ISBN 978 1 78643 550 7 (cased)
ISBN 978 1 78643 551 4 (eBook)

Typeset by Columns Design XML Ltd, Reading
Printed and bound in Great Britain by TJ International Ltd, Padstow

Contents

Foreword

> Particular intelligent beings may have laws of their own making, but they have some likewise which they never made. Before there were intelligent beings, they were possible; they had therefore possible relations, and consequently possible laws. Before laws were made, there were relations of possible justice. To say that there is nothing just or unjust but what is commanded or forbidden by positive laws, is the same as saying that before the describing of a circle all the radii were not equal.
>
> Montesquieu, *The Spirit of Laws*, 1758, translated by Thomas Nugent

International taxation presently lies at the crossroads between two fundamental – yet contradictory – developments.

The first one is the progressive emergence of a supranational legal order in tax matters, under the initiative of global or regional organizations, such as the WTO, the OECD and the European Union. In the last century, states have agreed upon a set of common rules, with the aim of facilitating cross-border activities and removing obstacles, such as double taxation or discriminatory taxation, while safeguarding their taxable base and their power to use tax instruments to carry out effective policies in the economic, social and environmental areas. The main effect of these rules is to establish a level playing field, by eliminating (or, at least, strongly reducing) taxes which are targeted at imported products or foreign taxpayers and ensuring equality of treatment between domestic and cross-border taxpayers and transactions in the framework of a general system of taxation. At the same time, in order to avoid some taxpayers taking undue advantage of this situation, states have adopted cooperation instruments, whether on a bilateral or multilateral basis, in particular in the field of exchange of information and administrative assistance between tax authorities. Moreover, they have entered into agreements to address issues of global concern, such as the protection of the environment, which illustrates that the international legal order has broadened its objectives beyond the preservation of peace and the development of international trade.

The second development is more recent, and more preoccupying. We are indeed witnessing, in various parts of the world, a shift towards political nationalism and economic protectionism, which also impacts tax policy. Some are now openly advocating the return of tax borders as an adequate instrument to safeguard economic wealth and social cohesion, while questioning the need or the opportunity to address global issues at the international level, when not in some cases openly challenging the very existence of those issues, such as climate change. These renewed ambitions inevitably clash with, if not the words, at least the spirit of the existing international (tax) rules.

In this context, the research of Alice Pirlot is extremely timely. Based on a thorough investigation of the existing law, and a deep understanding of its historical and economic rationale, it offers a remarkably sound and well-balanced analytical framework to define the exact limits in international law to the application of cross-border taxes, namely for environmental purposes. The research manages to stay resolutely away from (unfounded) ideological reasoning, which would either blindly support interpretations rejecting the very idea that cross-border trade should be the object of specific taxes, or systematically support sovereignty arguments, which would undermine the legitimacy of supranational rules. One of its most original features is the reconstruction of the concept of 'border tax adjustment', which has been often misunderstood by the general public, by lawmakers and even in the scholarly literature. The research indeed unfolds into a policy analysis of the legal controversies surrounding the notion of border tax adjustment in environmental taxation. This analysis shows that it is often easier to hide behind legal arguments than to oppose the very principle of a measure. From that perspective, the book calls for legal experts to adopt a societal perspective when interpreting the law and its limits, acknowledging that the difference between action and passivity is more a question of political will than of respect for the law. A very stimulating lesson for a piece of research that makes an important contribution to the comprehension of the conundrum faced by states wishing to develop their tax policies while remaining open to trade with the rest of the world.

Professor Edoardo Traversa
Université catholique de Louvain

Acknowledgements

> Interdependence obliges us to think of one world with a common plan.
>
> Pope Francis, *Encyclical on Climate Change and Inequality: On Care for Our Common Home* (2015)

> What we need now is a holistic approach towards problems combined with a genuine sense of universal responsibility based on love and compassion.
>
> His Holiness the 14th Dalai Lama of Tibet (21 October 1991)

I would like to acknowledge the support of the National Fund for Scientific Research ('Fonds de la Recherche Scientifique'). The Fund provided me with a research mandate of four years (from October 2012 to October 2016), which allowed me to conduct the research that served as a basis for this book.

I express my gratitude to Professor Edoardo Traversa (Université catholique de Louvain) for his valuable input and guidance, his academic enthusiasm, openness and humanity.

I also would like to thank the members of my scientific committee, Professor Charles-Hubert Born (Université catholique de Louvain) and Professor Kurt Deketelaere (Katholieke Universiteit Leuven), for encouraging me during the four years of my research mandate. My thanks go as well to the distinguished professors who agreed to critically assess my research and provided me with useful comments: Professor Henri Culot (Université catholique de Louvain), Professor Nicolas de Sadeleer (Université Saint-Louis and Université catholique de Louvain), Professor María Amparo Grau Ruiz (Universidad Complutense de Madrid), Professor Alan Hervé (Université de Bretagne Occidentale), Professor Janet Milne (Vermont Law School) and Professor Geert Van Calster (Katholieke Universiteit Leuven). My thanks also to the professors who welcomed me in their research institutes: Professors Yariv Brauner and Michael K. Friel (University of Florida Levin College of Law), Professor Cécile Brokelind (Lund University School of Economics and Management), Professor Michael Lang (Wirtschaftsuniversität Wien), Professor Pasquale Pistone (International Bureau of Fiscal Documentation),

Professor Wolfgang Schön (Max-Planck-Institut für Steuerrecht und Öffentliche Finanzen) and Professor Marta Villar Ezcurra (Universidad San Pablo-CEU).

Finally, I would like to thank all the professors and colleagues whom I had the great honour to encounter before and during my early research years.

This research project was not only an academic experience; it was also a personally enriching path. Many thanks to my dear friends and to my family: *Merci*!

Abbreviations

ASCM	Agreement on subsidies and countervailing measures
ASEAN	Association of Southeast Asian Nations
BEPS	Base Erosion and Profit Shifting
BTA	Border tax adjustment
BTU	British thermal unit
CAT	Carbon-added tax
CBDR	Common but Differentiated Responsibilities
CITES	Convention on International Trade in Endangered Species of Wild Fauna and Flora
CSR	Corporate Social Responsibility
DCS	Directly competitive or substitutable
DSU	Dispute Settlement Understanding
ECJ	Court of Justice of the European Union
ETS	Emissions trading system
EU	European Union
GATS	General Agreement on Trade in Services
GATT	General Agreement on Tariffs and Trade
GHG	Greenhouse gas
HCFC	Hydrochlorofluorocarbons
ICAO	International Civil Aviation Organization
ICJ	International Court of Justice
IPCC	Intergovernmental Panel on Climate Change
LCA	Life cycle assessment
MEA	Multilateral environmental agreement
MFN	Most-favoured-nation (principle)
NT	National treatment (principle)
ODC	Ozone-depleting chemicals
ODS	Ozone-depleting substances

OECD	Organisation for Economic Co-operation and Development
OEEC	Organisation for European Economic Co-operation
PPM	Process and production method
PTA	Preferential trade arrangement
RCT	Retail carbon tax
RTA	Regional trade agreement
TBT	Technical Barriers to Trade
TEU	Treaty on European Union
TFEU	Treaty on the Functioning of the European Union
SGG	Synthetic greenhouse gases
SPS	Sanitary and phytosanitary (measures)
UK	United Kingdom
UN	United Nations
UNCTAD	United Nations Conference on Trade and Development
UNEP	United Nations Environment Programme
UNFCCC	United Nations Framework Convention on Climate Change
UN GA	United Nations General Assembly
US	United States of America
VAT	Value added tax
WTO	World Trade Organization

Table of cases

Note: The case law is classified in chronological order. GATT/WTO cases are cited in the text in full. After their first citation, they are then referred to in simplified forms.

EUROPEAN COURT OF JUSTICE (ECJ)

GATT PANEL REPORTS

WORLD TRADE ORGANIZATION REPORTS

Introduction

Taxation is a powerful policy instrument. Though the primary purpose of taxes is to raise revenue, taxation often reflects policy choices. Moreover, taxes sometimes serve as a direct tool for pursuing non-budgetary objectives. A good example of this is environmental taxes.

Taxation is a powerful policy instrument not only at the domestic level, but also at the international level. The phenomenon of harmful tax competition highlights how one state's decision to design harmful tax policies (for example, by lowering tax rates or refusing to exchange information) may have an impact on other states. Bilateral tax agreements through which two states agree as to the allocation of taxing rights on cross-border income also illustrate the role of taxation in international relations. A third example concerns border taxation on 'internationally traded goods', such as taxes on imported products. To a certain extent, each of these three examples give states the opportunity to impact on situations that take place beyond their national borders.

This book focuses on the third example, namely border tax adjustments (BTAs) in respect to internationally traded goods. The objective is to determine the extent to which countries may use such taxes to foster environmental goals at the international level. In other words, this book aims to demonstrate that it is legally possible to develop the environmental dimension of taxes imposed on internationally traded goods despite the legal limits that constrain countries in their design of border tax policies.

Both scholars and political figures have shown a growing interest in the potential role of border taxes to foster global environmental goals. This may be explained by the difficulties and limits in adopting ambitious environmental policies at the domestic level as well as the complexity in reaching international agreements on global environmental challenges.

In the literature, the concept of environmental BTAs is one of the most studied models of environmental tax imposed on internationally traded goods.[1] The concept of BTAs – defined in 1968 by the Organisation for

[1] The most significant works on environmental BTAs include: Madison Condon & Ada Ignaciuk, 'Border Carbon Adjustment and International Trade. A

Economic Co-operation and Development (OECD) – reflects the idea that countries may both tax imported products in the same way as they tax domestic 'like' products and relieve exported products from domestic taxes. The concept of environmental BTAs has been developed in the scholarship as a legal instrument to mitigate cross-border environmental issues, usually based on a two-fold rationale, both economic and political. First, in contrast to domestic environmental policies that only apply to domestic products and domestic producers, environmental BTAs apply to internationally traded goods and are therefore supposed to limit the risks of loss of competitiveness and pollution leakage. Second, environmental BTAs – which may be adopted unilaterally as opposed to international agreements – would be politically sound in that they could encourage third countries to follow suit by adopting new environmental standards at the domestic level. No consensus exists, however, in the economic literature on the validity of these arguments and on the exact effects of environmental BTAs.[2] This book does not take a stance on the

Literature Review' (2013) 6 OECD Trade and Environment Working Papers, OECD Publishing; Aaron Cosbey, Susanne Droege, Carolyn Fischer, Julia Reinaud, John Stephenson, Lutz Weischer & Peter Wooders, 'A Guide for the Concerned: Guidance on the Elaboration and Implementation of Border Carbon Adjustment' (2012) 3 Entwined Policy Report; Felicity Deane, *Emissions Trading and WTO Law. A Global Analysis* (Edward Elgar Publishing 2015), in particular chapter 7 ('The Border Adjustments of Emissions Trading Schemes'); Paul Demaret & Raoul Stewardson, 'Border Tax Adjustments under GATT and EC Law and General Implications for Environmental Taxes' (1994) 28(4) Journal of World Trade 5–65; Olivier De Schutter, *Trade in the Service of Sustainable Development. Linking Trade to Labour Rights and Environmental Standards* (Hart Publishing 2015), in particular chapter 3 ('The Special Regime of Border Tax Adjustments: Levelling the Playing Field'); Kateryna Holzer, *Carbon-Related Border Adjustment and WTO Law* (Edward Elgar Publishing 2014); Gary Clyde Hufbauer, Steve Charnovitz & Jisun Kim, *Global Warming and the World Trading System* (Peterson Institute for International Economics 2009); Joost Pauwelyn, 'Carbon Leakage Measures and Border Tax Adjustments under WTO Law', in: Geert Van Calster & Denise Prévost (eds.), *Research Handbook on Environment, Health and the WTO* (Edward Elgar Publishing 2013), 448–506; Geert Van Calster, *International and EU Trade Law. The Environmental Challenge* (Cameron May 2000), 414–485; Richard A. Westin, *Environmental Tax Initiatives and Multilateral Trade Agreements: Dangerous Collisions* (Kluwer Law International 1997).

[2] See i.a. Condon & Ignaciuk, *supra* n. 1; Warwick J. McKibbin & Peter J. Wilcoxen, 'The Economic and Environmental Effects of Border Tax Adjustments for Climate Policy' (2008–2009) Brookings Trade Forum 1–34; Marco Sakai &

validity of this literature, which is only used as an element of factual background.

In addition to their differences with pure domestic and international legal instruments, environmental border taxes should also be distinguished from 'non-economic (border) regulations'. First, regulations may be formulated in terms of voluntary standards, such as labelling requirements to provide consumers with better information on the environmental impact of the products that they consume. In contrast to such labelling instruments, taxes are a more direct tool to internalise the cost of pollution into products' prices. Second, regulations can serve to ban access to products that do not meet certain environmental standards. In contrast, taxes and other market-based instruments offer more possibilities for integrating environmental considerations into internationally traded goods.[3] With non-market-based regulations, the legislator may choose between two possibilities: to ban or not to ban the products. With taxes, the legislator has the same two possibilities: to impose a tax or not to impose a tax. However, the possibility of imposing a tax offers more alternatives than a ban. For example, the legislator may impose differentiated taxes, with different tax rates based on the environmental impact of the products.

This book aims to analyse environmental BTAs from a three-fold perspective, referring to the rationale of BTAs, their tax design and their legal framework.

Despite the highly political character of border taxation, the literature only contains a few references to the history and rationale of taxes imposed on internationally traded goods. However, the analysis of the rationale behind border taxes is key to determining the extent to which traditional BTAs allow the pursuit of environmental goals. The reason for this key role relates to the fact that the main legal provisions surrounding traditional BTAs have been drafted taking into consideration the objectives that these measures were aimed at pursuing. In other words, analysis of the rationale underlying traditional models of BTAs allows us to better understand the extent to which such tax models may be compatible with – and even integrate – environmental considerations (Part I). Academic literature appears fragmented: various tax and international trade law

John Barrett, 'Border Carbon Adjustments: Addressing Emissions Embodied in Trade' (2016) 92 Energy Policy 102–110.

[3] Quota restrictions could also serve to exert pressure on non-environmentally friendly countries to adopt environmental policies. Such measures would, however, be unlikely to comply with WTO law.

concepts are used inconsistently. Though legal concepts may be appealing from a rhetorical viewpoint, the inconsistent use of legal terms makes the literature confusing. Indeed, when a policy measure is mistakenly named after a legal concept, the legal analysis that follows will also be wrong.

Moreover, the legal scholarship has not yet analysed in detail the tax design of environmental BTAs.[4] The analysis of the tax design of such taxes is nevertheless necessary to assessing how – and to what extent – environmental criteria could be integrated into traditional BTAs, taking account of the practical implementation of these taxes. Therefore, the analysis explains how BTAs are designed by means of illustrative examples such as the EU VAT and excise duties systems and the US sales tax (Part II). Analysis of the design of BTAs is largely based on practical questions: 'How are these taxes applied in practice?'; 'How could environmental criteria be included in their tax mechanism?'; 'Should the tax rate be modulated based on environmental factors?'; 'Should the tax only be imposed on polluting products?', etc.

Finally, regarding the legal framework of BTAs, the academic literature has mainly focused its attention on the World Trade Organization (WTO) law compatibility of environmental BTAs. This research looks beyond WTO law's mainstream interpretations and highlights that WTO law provisions surrounding (environmental) BTAs may be interpreted in such a way to permit their development (Part III).[5] The approach is inspired by Critical Legal Studies, a movement that considers that law is 'indeterminate' and intrinsically linked to politics.[6] Based on this critical approach, this book highlights the conflicting views on the legal provisions

---

[4] Few tax scholars have analysed the interactions between tax and WTO law. See Jennifer E. Farrell, *The Interface of International Trade Law and Taxation* (26 IBFD Doctoral Series 2013); Michael Lang, Judith Herdin & Ines Hofbauer (eds.), *WTO and Direct Taxation* (Linde Verlag 2005); Michael Lang, Judith Herdin-Winter & Ines Hofbauer-Steffel (eds.), *The Relevance of WTO Law for Tax Matters* (Linde Verlag 2006); Marilyne Sadowsky, *Droit de l'OMC, droit de l'Union européenne et fiscalité directe* (Larcier 2013).

[5] This research nevertheless acknowledges the argument that a dispute settlement body is unlikely to distance itself from interpretations considered to be mainstream.

[6] On Critical Legal Studies, see Andrew Altman, 'Legal Realism, Critical Legal Studies, and Dworkin' (1986) 15(3) Philosophy & Public Affairs 205–235; Olivier De Schutter, 'Les Critical Legal Studies au pays du droit international public' (1992) 22 Droit & Société 585–605; Mike McConville & Wing Hong Chui, *Research Methods for Law* (Edinburgh University Press 2007), 155; Mark Tushnet, 'Critical Legal Studies: A Political History' (1990–1991) 100 Yale Law

surrounding environmental BTAs and demonstrates that room exists for supporting their adoption.[7] Consequently, it argues that the alleged incompatibility of environmental BTAs with international (trade) law cannot serve as a legal excuse not to adopt environmental policies at the national level.

Ultimately, this book seeks to bring some coherence to the legal literature, which is – given the interdisciplinary nature of the topic – necessarily a little chaotic.[8]

Journal 1515–1544; Roberto Mangabeira Unger, 'The Critical Legal Studies Movement' (1983) 96(3) Harvard Law Review 561.

[7] Critical Legal Studies often assume that law is the result of a constant struggle between social classes (see the critical race and feminist theories). Environmental tax law could also be analysed from the perspective of the struggle between 'market forces' and 'environmental forces'. See also McConville & Chui, *supra* n. 6, 155. Among the authors who have analysed tax law from the perspective of Critical Legal Studies, see Karen Brown, Mary Louise Fellows & Bridget Crawford, 'The Past, Present, and Future of Critical Tax Theory: A Conversation' (2012) 10(59) Pittsburgh Tax Review 13–49; Anthony C. Infanti & Bridget J. Crawford (eds.), *Critical Tax Theory: An Introduction* (CUP 2009); Anthony C. Infanti & Bridget J. Crawford, 'Critical Tax Theory: An Introduction' (2009) 4 University of Pittsburgh Legal Studies Research Paper; Lawrence Zelenak, 'Taking Critical Tax Theory Seriously' (1997) 76 North Carolina Law Review 1521–1580.

[8] Westin introduced his book with a similar idea. He wrote as follows:

> This writer cannot hope to do more than to raise the level of confusion. The reason is that this work covers numerous subjects: international trade treaties, microeconomics, tax policy concepts, and environmental taxes. None of these subjects is tidily stowed away. When one combines them, the outcome can only be organized chaos. Still, there is need for the study, because the pressures are urgent.
>
> (Westin, *supra* n. 1)

PART I

From economic to environmental objectives: looking back at the rationale of traditional BTAs and looking ahead to new paradigms

Initially, the concept of BTAs was unrelated to environmental issues. It was only in the 20th century, with countries' increasing awareness of environmental concerns, that proposals in favour of 'environmental BTAs' were developed, both in the academic literature as well as in political fora.

This first part comes back on the rationale of traditional (non-environmental specific) BTAs and looks ahead to the new theories that seem to underlie proposals in favour of environmental BTAs.

The history of BTAs has been largely unexplored by the literature. Nevertheless, the historical analysis of the development of traditional BTAs – from David Ricardo's theory of comparative advantage to the OECD and GATT reports issued in the 1960s/1970s – may contribute to a better understanding of BTAs' main purpose and WTO legal limits to their adoption (Chapter 1).

In comparison to traditional BTAs, environmental BTAs have had a much more recent history. The analysis of political proposals in favour of environmental BTAs illustrates that they are based on theoretical foundations that slightly differ from traditional BTAs, namely Ricardo's theory of comparative advantage and the theory of absolute advantage. Environmental BTAs' political history also shows that some steps have already been taken in support of the development of the environmental dimension of BTAs (Chapter 2).

1. History and theoretical foundations of traditional BTAs

This chapter discusses the historical development of BTAs against the background of the removal of tariffs, from Ricardo's economic theory on free trade to more recent views expressed at the political level since the middle of the 20th century.

Although Ricardo's theory on comparative advantage is at the heart of BTAs' rationale, later discussions on BTAs have not always given due credit to BTAs' historical development. The two main official reports on BTAs – the OECD 1968 and GATT 1970 reports – illustrate how national and regional practices vary between countries. These two reports – issued following the US claim that BTAs may not be economically sound – also highlight the main controversies as to BTAs' theoretical grounds in the 1970s. More than 40 years later, controversies remain, adding up to the uncertainties and questions surrounding BTAs' legal framework. The analysis of BTAs' negotiating history contributes to provide a better understanding of WTO law provisions surrounding their adoption. Indeed, the legal limits to the adoption of BTAs very much translate the original objectives that BTAs were intended to pursue. Moreover, BTAs' negotiating history can be used to clarify BTAs' legal framework as one 'supplementary means of interpretation' recognised by the Vienna Convention.[1]

This chapter first analyses BTAs' economic foundation (Section 1.1). Second, BTAs' political history is discussed (Section 1.2). Finally, this chapter offers an overview of BTAs' main theoretical foundations (Section 1.3).

---

[1] See Articles 31§1 & 32 of UN Vienna Convention on the Law of Treaties, Vienna, 23 May 1969, UN Treaty Series (1980), Vol. 1155, 1-18232, 332. On the role of the legislative history in interpreting WTO law, see Felicity Deane, *Emissions Trading and WTO Law. A Global Analysis* (Edward Elgar Publishing 2015), 56–57; Asif H. Qureshi, *Interpreting WTO Agreements* (CUP 2015), 52–54; Isabelle Van Damme, *Treaty Interpretation by the WTO Appellate Body* (OUP 2009), 309–320 (on the role of the negotiating history in the interpretation of WTO law).

1.1 BTAs' ECONOMIC FOUNDATION

1.1.1 BTAs' Historical Development in Light of the History of Tariffs

The oldest taxes imposed on imported products are tariffs, i.e. taxes imposed on imported products for the simple reason that they have entered the national territory. Though the exact origin of tariffs is difficult to locate, Asakura considers that the world history of customs duties started in ancient times.[2] In his book on the *World History of the Customs and Tariffs*, he writes: 'Since the Customs is one of the oldest fiscal mechanisms, it would seem reasonable to assume that the Customs also originated in these cradles of human civilization.'[3]

Over the years a variety of objectives were pursued by means of tariffs and tariff policy instruments, from discouraging the import of certain goods to providing protection to merchants in exchange for payment.[4] In the 13th century some cities mutually agreed to remove the tariffs imposed across their respective borders, practically forming the first free trade areas of the time.[5] Reduced tariffs on imports were also adopted in favour of imported products that were lacking in the domestic economy.[6]

In the 18th century economists started to criticise mercantilism, proposing alternative trade models. Adam Smith, David Ricardo and John Stuart Mill – who are among the most famous economists of the time – introduced free trade theories to improve welfare among nations. Under these new economic theories, customs duties became barriers to free trade. Roughly speaking, under free trade theories, tariffs could no longer serve to control international trade. Consequently, countries sometimes linked the removal of tariffs to regulatory prerequisites in order to prevent the import of undesirable products.[7] For example, the 1935 International Convention concerning the Export and Import of Animal

---

[2] Hironori Asakura, *World History of the Customs and Tariffs* (WCO 2003), 24.

[3] *Ibid.*, 20.

[4] *Ibid.*, 19.

[5] Ferdinand H.M. Grapperhaus, *Tax Tales From the Second Millennium* (IBFD 2009), 15. Asakura notes that preferential tariff rates already existed as early as the 10th century under the Byzantine Empire (see Asakura, *supra* n. 2, 115).

[6] Grapperhaus, *supra* n. 5, 15 & 19.

[7] See Steve Charnovitz, 'The North American Free Trade Agreement: Green Law or Green Spin?' (1994–1995) 26 Law & Policy in International Business 1, 60–61.

Products (other than meat, meat preparations, fresh animal products, milk and milk products) limited the free traffic in certain animal products to countries that have ratified the International Convention for the Campaign against Contagious Diseases of Animals.[8] This example illustrates that the removal of tariffs has been linked to regulatory requirements to guarantee that free trade policies do not conflict with other policy objectives, such as health policies, sanitary measures or environmental protection.

In other words, the call of free trade theorists did not necessarily amount to fully free and unrestricted international trade with a complete removal of barriers (including tax barriers) on imported products. This call rather introduced a distinction between undesirable barriers imposed on imported products (e.g. tariffs) and desirable measures (e.g. some regulatory barriers that are deemed necessary for health reasons) imposed on imported products. BTAs are another example of desirable measures imposed on imported products that have been approved by some free trade theorists. Ricardo argued that tax measures that raise domestic products' prices should also be imposed on imported products. This mechanism – latter called BTAs on imports – is supposed to level the playing field between domestic and foreign products, not to raise tariff barriers against foreign products.

In the middle of the 20th century, states gathered to negotiate a multilateral trade agreement that would provide for general rules to limit the adoption of tariffs. The General Agreement on Tariffs and Trade (GATT) was adopted in 1947 after the first round of tariff negotiations in Geneva. Rapidly, the GATT became the 'international trade treaty'.[9]

The GATT translated into formal legal rules the idea that the adoption of tariffs should be limited and strictly regulated to foster free trade. Primarily, WTO law requires member states to bind their tariffs at reduced levels, which means that they accept not raising their tariffs over the bound levels they have committed to. WTO law also requires that the most favourable treatment be applied to all member states, meaning that all WTO members should benefit from the advantages that are granted to another WTO member. This general requirement is called the 'most-favoured-nation principle' (MFN).[10]

---

[8] *Ibid.*, 60–61, referring to Art. 1, International Convention concerning the Export and Import of Animal Products (other than meat, meat preparations, fresh animal products, milk and milk products), Geneva, 20 February 1935.

[9] Jennifer E. Farrell, *The Interface of International Trade Law and Taxation* (26 IBFD Doctoral Series 2013).

[10] GATT Art. 1.

Despite the general WTO objective of reducing barriers to trade among all member states, WTO law recognises the possibility of maintaining (or adopting) certain taxes (or trade measures) on imported products in order to achieve objectives that do not directly (or primarily) relate to free trade. BTAs are one of these examples.

1.1.2 The Origin of BTAs' Economic Rationale

In contrast to tariffs, WTO law does not encourage member states to remove their BTAs. The reason is that BTAs are based on a different rationale than tariffs. BTAs are not imposed on imported products for the simple reason that national borders are crossed. BTAs rather aim to guarantee that the tax treatment that applies to domestic products is neutral vis-à-vis internationally traded goods, meaning imported and exported products.

The economic underpinning for BTAs is generally attributed to David Ricardo.[11] According to Ricardo, 'just competition' requires that imported products are taxed the same way as domestic products and that a drawback of the same amount as domestic taxes is allowed on exported products.[12] In his book entitled *On Protection to Agriculture*, Ricardo explains:

---

[11] Paul Demaret & Raoul Stewardson, 'Border Tax Adjustments under GATT and EC Law and General Implications for Environmental Taxes' (1994) 28(4) Journal of World Trade 6; Gary Clyde Hufbauer, *Fundamental Tax Reform and Border Tax Adjustments* (Institute for International Economics 1996), 21–23; Robert Ireland, 'Implications for Customs of Climate Change Mitigation and Adaptation Policy Options: A Preliminary Examination' (2010) 4(2) World Customs Journal 21, 25; John Snape & Jeremy de Souza, *Environmental Taxation Law, Policy, Contexts and Practice* (Ashgate Publishing 2006), 9; Terence P. Stewart, Eric P. Salonen & Patrick J. McDonough, 'More than 50 Years of Trade Rule Discrimination on Taxation: How Trade with China is Affected' (2007) Trade Lawyers Advisory Group, 24. See also OECD, Environment Policy Committee and Committee on Fiscal Affairs. Joint Sessions on Taxation and Environment. 2nd Session. Environmental Taxes and Border Tax Adjustments, COM/ENV/EPOC/DAFFE/CFA(94)31, 27 April 1994, 5, para. 9 (hereafter, 'OECD 1994 note on Environmental BTAs, COM/ENV/EPOC/DAFFE/CFA(94)31') and the *Zenith* Case (US Supreme Court, *Zenith Radio Corporation v. United States*, 437 US 443 (1978)), where a direct reference was made to David Ricardo.

[12] David Ricardo, *The Works and Correspondence of David Ricardo* (Pamphlets and Papers 1815–1823, ed. Piero Sraffa with the Collaboration of M.H. Dobb, Liberty Fund 2005, Vol. 4), available at <http://oll.libertyfund.org/title/205/38614/885295> (accessed 21 January 2014).

> A tax … which falls exclusively on the producers of a particular commodity tends to raise the price of that commodity, and if it did not so raise it the producer would be under a disadvantage as compared with all other producers; he would no longer gain the general and ordinary profits by his trade. … If no protecting duty is imposed on the importation of a similar commodity from other countries, injustice is done to the producer at home, and not only to the producer but to the country to which he belongs. It is for the interest of the public that he should not be driven from a trade which, under a system of free competition, he would have chosen, and to which he would adhere if every other commodity were taxed equally with that which he produces. A tax affecting him exclusively is, in fact, a bounty to that amount on the importation of the same commodity from abroad; and to restore competition to its just level, it would be necessary not only to subject the imported commodity to an equal tax, but to allow a drawback of equal amount on the exportation of the home-made commodity.[13]

From Ricardo's writings, it is usually understood that BTAs should only be applied to taxes 'which fall[] exclusively on the producers of a particular commodity' and not to income taxes or taxes that 'equally affect[] all classes of producers', which are assumed not to affect the relative value of goods.[14]

The distinction between specific and general taxes was later replaced by the distinction between indirect taxes (eligible for adjustments) and direct taxes (ineligible for adjustments). Moreover, the assumption that income taxes should not be compensated with adjustments has been called into question. In the 20th century authors indeed called into question the relevance of the distinction between consumption and production taxes (or indirect and direct taxes) as a valid eligibility criterion for BTAs (Chapter 5).

The fact that BTAs allow compensating for the impact of specific domestic consumption taxes on the relative value of goods should be put in perspective with Ricardo's most important legacy: the theory of comparative advantage.[15] This theory – often described as the classic

---

[13] *Ibid.*, section iii: 'On the Effects of Taxes Imposed on a Particular Commodity'. See also David Ricardo, *On the Principles of Political Economy and Taxation* (John Murray 1817), chapter 16.42, available at <http://www.econolib.org/library/Ricardo/ricP.htlm> (accessed 21 January 2014); David Ricardo, *On Protection to Agriculture* (London William Clowes John Murray, Albermarle-Street 1822), 15.

[14] Ricardo, *supra* n. 12, section iii.

[15] The theory of comparative advantage is not only attributed to David Ricardo but also to Robert Torrens and James Mill. See John Aldrich, 'The Discovery of Comparative Advantage' (2004) 26(3) Journal of the History of

economic rationale for free trade – is a refinement of Adam Smith's theory on the absolute advantage, which explains international trade by reference to the differences in absolute costs of production between countries.[16]

In contrast to the theory of absolute advantage, the theory of comparative advantage is based on the idea that any country may benefit from international trade given that all countries have a relative advantage in the production of certain goods.[17] The theory on comparative advantage is best illustrated by Ricardo's famous example of trade between Portugal and England. Though the production of cloth and wine is – in absolute terms – less efficient in England than in Portugal, England may have a comparative advantage in producing cloth when the ratio of the price of cloth between England and Portugal is lower than the ratio of the price of wine between England and Portugal.[18] In this example, the relative advantage of producing wine in Portugal is based on differences in labour

---

Economic Thought 379; Leonard Gomes, *The Economics and Ideology of Free Trade: A Historical Review* (Edward Elgar Publishing 2003), 40; Andrea Maneshi, *Comparative Advantage in International Trade. A Historical Perspective* (Edward Elgar Publishing 1998); Roy J. Ruffin, 'David Ricardo's Discovery of Comparative Advantage' (2002) 34(4) History of Political Economy 727–748.

[16] Daniel Bethlehem, Donald McRae & Rodney Neufeld, *The Oxford Handbook of International Trade Law* (OUP 2009), 7–9; Raj Bhala, *International Trade Law: Interdisciplinary Theory and Practice* (Lexis Law Publishing 2008), 201–240; Daniel C.K. Chow & Thomas J. Schoenbaum, *International Trade Law: Problems, Cases and Materials* (Wolters Kluwer Law & Business 2013), 32–33; Simon Lester, Bryan Mercurio & Arwel Davies, *World Trade Law: Text, Materials and Commentary* (Hart 2012), 21–24; Peter Van den Bossche & Werner Zdouc, *The Law and Policy of the World Trade Organization* (CUP 2013), 17–19. See also Reinhard Schumacher, 'Adam Smith's Theory of Absolute Advantage and the Use of Doxography in the History of Economics' (2012) 5(2) Erasmus Journal for Philosophy and Economics 54–80. See also Adam Smith, *An Inquiry into the Nature and Causes of the Wealth of Nations* (Edwin Cannan, Methuen & Amp, 1776 Library of Economics and liberty 1904), IV.2.12, available at <http://www.econolib.org/library/Smith/smWN13.htlm> (accessed 23 January 2014).

[17] Ruffin, *supra* n. 15. See also OECD, Trade Principles and Concepts, 1995, OECD/DG(95)141, 5.

[18] Gomes, *supra* n. 15, 36–37. See also the original work of Ricardo (Ricardo, *On the Principles of Political Economy and Taxation*, *supra* n. 13, chapter 7.7.16).

cost: it requires relatively less 'men' (i.e. labour) to produce wine in Portugal than in England.[19]

The theory of comparative advantage entails a normative message: countries will benefit from trade when production takes place in accordance with the comparative advantage theory.[20] As far as taxation is concerned, the normative message of the comparative advantage theory is the following: trade in accordance with the comparative advantage principle is only possible when tax neutrality prevails. Here, tax neutrality means that tax systems should not influence economic decisions.[21] To ensure tax neutrality, two main principles should be followed. The first principle – very intuitive – requires that countries refrain from using tax measures with trade-restrictive effects (i.e. tariffs).[22] In contrast, the

---

[19] Note, however, that the neo-classical understanding of comparative advantage uses other factors to explain countries' comparative advantage in producing certain goods, such as differences in technology and factor endowments such as land, labour and capital. See Bernard Lassudrie-Duchêne & Deniz Ünal-Kesenci, 'L'avantage comparatif, notion fondamentale et controversée', L'Economie Mondiale en 2002 (La découverte 2001), 90–104. On the Eckser–Ohlin theory, see Theo S. Eicher, John H. Mutti & Michelle H. Turnovsky, *International Economics* (Routledge 2009), 66–106.

[20] A. Lans Bovenberg & Jocelyn P. Horne, 'Taxes on Commodities. A Survey', in: George Kopits (ed.), *Tax Harmonization in the European Community: Policy Issues and Analysis* (1992) 34 IMF Occasional Papers, 22; Eicher, Mutti & Turnovsky, *supra* n. 19, 13–33; Gomes, *supra* n. 15, 39. See also Ricardo, *On the Principles of Political Economy and Taxation*, *supra* n. 13, chapter 7, para. 6.

[21] On the concept of 'tax neutrality' in other contexts, see Catherine Brown & Jack Mintz, 'On the Relationship between International Tax Neutrality and Non-Discrimination Clauses under Tax Treaties for Source-Based Taxes', in: Michael Lang, Pasquale Pistone et al. (eds.), *Tax Treaties: Building Bridges between Law and Economics* (IBFD 2010), 581; George Kopits, 'Overview', in: George Kopits, *Tax Harmonization in the European Community: Policy Issues and Analysis* (1992) 34 IMF Occasional Papers, 6; Cees Peters, 'International Tax Neutrality and Non-Discrimination: Plea for a More Explicit Dialogue between the State and the Market', in: Michael Lang, Pasquale Pistone et al. (eds.), *Tax Treaties: Building Bridges between Law and Economics* (IBFD 2010), 607. In the specific context of VAT, see Thomas Ecker, *A VAT/GST Model Convention* (IBFD Doctoral Series 2013), 103 et al.; Charlène Adline Herbain, *VAT Neutrality* (Promoculture Larcier 2015); Ben Terra & Julie Kajus, *A Guide to the European VAT Directives. Introduction to European VAT 2012* (IBFD 2013, Vol. 1), 289–293. See also OECD, OECD International VAT/GST Guidelines, Draft Consolidated Version. Invitation for Comments, February 2013.

[22] Ricardo, *On the Principles of Political Economy and Taxation*, *supra* n. 13, chapter 7, para. 34.

second principle requires that countries adopt tax adjustments to ensure that specific consumption taxes do not affect international trade. In other words, BTAs are a condition to guarantee that international trade takes place in accordance with the theory of comparative advantage.

Under Ricardo's model, taxation only – in contrast to other policies or situations – seems to call for compensating measures to ensure 'fair competition' between countries. In chapter 7 of his book *On the Principles of Political Economy and Taxation*, Ricardo distinguishes between the trade effects of taxation and other elements such as climate and manufacturing skills. He writes as follows:

> These [i.e. climate and skill/machinery] I believe to be the only two causes which regulate the comparative value of money in the different countries of the world; for although taxation occasions a disturbance of the equilibrium of money, it does so by depriving the country in which it is imposed of some of the advantages attending skill, industry and climate.[23]

Besides taxation, Ricardo does not discuss in much detail the effect of non-tax elements such as climate, skill and machinery. The question therefore arises as to the trade impact of non-fiscal policies: in addition to climate and manufacturing skills, non-fiscal policies, such as environmental standards, could also affect the relative cost of products.[24] Ricardo's model does not elaborate on the impact of these policies and on the potential need to compensate for their trade effects. One possible explanation is that Ricardo assumes that regulatory measures are – by definition – general measures, which means that they affect all producers equally without having an impact on the relative price of goods. This hypothesis is likely to be true for most domestic policies (education, labour standards, infrastructure, etc.).[25] Environmental standards, however, may arguably affect the relative value of goods as soon as they are applied to a limited number of goods.

---

[23] *Ibid.*, para. 44.

[24] See Alexander Gillespie, 'The Contradiction between Comparative Advantage in International Trade and Environmental Protection' (1995) 3 Waikato Law Review 129. See also OECD, Working Party No. 4 of the Council on border tax adjustments, Remarks on the United States Member of the Working Party at the 2nd Session on 2nd July 1965, Paris, 8th July 1965, C/WP4(65)3, 5.

[25] This distinction is particularly interesting as it has often been argued that adjustments for environmental purposes could lead to unlimited adjustments for any other purpose (e.g. in the field of social policies).

In the literature the concept of 'comparative advantage' is often confused with the concept of 'competitive advantage'.[26] The two concepts, however, rely on fundamentally different assumptions and should therefore be distinguished. The notion of competitive advantage cannot be captured in one single definition.[27] In legal scholarship, the term is usually defined by reference to absolute differences in the price of goods.[28] In other words, the concept is based on the assumption that trade flows are explained by the absolute advantage that a country has for producing certain goods.[29] The distinction between the two concepts also appears in the normative message that they entail. Under the concept of comparative advantage, BTAs are only necessary in respect of specific taxes. In contrast, it could be derived from the theory on competitive advantage that BTAs should be adopted in respect of any tax (and any policy) that is assumed to be shifted into products' prices. Indeed, the theory of competitive advantage assumes that trade flows are distorted as soon as a tax is passed into a product's price, which would explain the need for BTAs (Section 1.3).

---

26 Donald H. Regan, 'How to Think about PPMs (and Climate Change)', in: Thomas Cottier et al. (eds.), *International Trade Regulation and the Mitigation of Climate Change. World Trade Forum* (CUP 2009), 5. What Regan calls 'normative comparative advantage' seems to be closer to the notion of absolute advantage. See also Gillespie, *supra* n. 24, 130; Gilbert E. Metcalf & David Weisbach, 'The Design of a Carbon Tax' (2009) 33 Harvard Environmental Law Review 499, 540; Eckhard Siggel, 'The Many Dimensions of Competitiveness' (2007), CESifo Venice Summer Institute; Chris Wold, Sanford Gaines & Greg Block, *Trade and the Environment. Law and Policy* (Carolina Academic Press 2005), 31–32.

27 See Satya Dev Gupta, 'Comparative Advantage and Competitive Advantage: An Economics Perspective and a Synthesis' (2009), available at <http://economics.ca/2009/papers/0534.pdf> (accessed 28 October 2015).

28 Robert Howse, *The WTO System: Law, Politics & Legitimacy* (CUP 2007), 115. See also, in the economic literature: John C. Dunmore, 'Competitiveness and Comparative Advantage of US Agriculture', Paper presented at the 1986 National Public Policy Education Conference, Denver, Colorado, 16 September 1986; Harry Johnson & Mel Krauss, 'Border Taxes, Border Tax Adjustments, Comparative Advantage, and the Balance of Payments' (1970) 3(4) Canadian Journal of Economics 595–602.

29 Howse, *supra* n. 28, 115. See also Wold, Gaines & Block, *supra* n. 26, 31–32.

1.2 BTAs' POLITICAL HISTORY

The economic analysis of BTAs has largely influenced their long political history. References to the economic debate introduced by Ricardo have often accompanied BTAs' political developments. Nevertheless, later political views on BTAs have not always mirrored Ricardo's theoretical contribution (Section 1.2.1). Moreover, the OECD 1968 and GATT 1970 reports illustrate that important political claims have been expressed against BTAs' economic rationale (Section 1.2.2). Subsequent international, regional and national developments similarly highlight the controversial issues surrounding current BTA practices (Section 1.2.3). Proponents of the introduction of environmental BTAs should be aware of this controversial legal context to be prepared for answering criticisms of their proposals. Indeed, the integration of environmental considerations is likely to make BTAs even more controversial.

1.2.1 First BTAs

The first BTAs date back to the 18th century.[30] As early as 1791, the US had an excise tax that was border adjusted, at least upon exports.[31] In the 'Whiskey Act', the adjustment on exports aimed at 'the encouragement of the export trade of the United States'.[32]

Interestingly, the legislative rationale given at the time to explain the adoption of border adjustments on exports (i.e. the 'encouragement of exportation') seems to be contrary to its supposed economic rationale (i.e. achieving free trade in accordance with the theory of comparative advantage). Other later examples show that BTAs were not always justified based on the 'trade neutrality' argument. For example, the Danish Minister of Finance advocated the introduction of a value-added tax in the 1960s, considering that 'for the sake of Danish ability to compete, it would be no doubt to be to our advantage if we could act as pioneers in this field …'.[33]

---

[30] Hufbauer, *supra* n. 11, 21–22. See also OECD 1994 note on Environmental BTAs, COM/ENV/EPOC/DAFFE/CFA(94)31, 4, para. 7.

[31] *Ibid.*

[32] Stewart, Salonen & McDonough, *supra* n. 11, 23 quoting Sec. 51 of US, Act of 3 March 1791.

[33] Paul Gersman, 'Value-Added Tax' (1965) 19 The OECD Observer 39. This document is referred to by Leontiades in: Milton Leontiades, 'The Logic of Border Taxes' (1966) 19(2) National Tax Journal 173, 183.

1.2.2 International Fora on BTAs: The OECD and GATT Reports on BTAs

In the 20th century, two important fora discussed the issue of BTAs in an international context: the OECD in 1968 and the GATT in 1970. These discussions can be understood in the context of US criticisms against European tax systems increasingly relying on indirect taxes and related BTAs.[34]

1.2.2.1 Role of the OECD and the GATT in tax matters

The OECD was established on 14 December 1960 in Paris, replacing the Organisation for European Economic Co-operation (OEEC) created in 1948.[35] Neither the Convention of 1948 nor the Convention on the OECD contains provisions directly referring to taxation. It is, however, not surprising that taxation plays a significant role in the OECD in the light of the main objectives of the organisation: 'to achieve the highest sustainable economic growth', 'to contribute to sound economic expansion' and 'to contribute to the expansion of world trade on a multilateral, non-discriminatory basis in accordance with international obligations'.[36] Moreover, as early as 1956, a Fiscal Committee was established within the OEEC.[37] Nowadays, in tax matters, the OECD – in particular, the Committee on Fiscal Affairs and the Centre for Tax Policy and Administration – is well known for its work on transfer pricing and the OECD Model Tax Convention on Income and Capital.[38] In recent years the

---

[34] Rosendahl gives a very good summary of the political debate surrounding BTAs in the 1970s (Roger W. Rosendahl, 'Border Tax Adjustments: Problems and Proposals' (1970) 2 Law & Policy in International Business 85). See also Johnson & Krauss, *supra*, n. 28, 595 ('US public opinion has been very critical of the decision of certain Common Market and other European countries to move to a system of value added taxes on the destination principle, which change has been seen as harmful to the United States balance of payments position').

[35] Convention on the Organisation for Economic Co-operation and Development, Paris, 14 December 1960 (hereafter, 'OECD Convention').

[36] Article 1 of the OECD Convention.

[37] See Farrell, *supra* n. 9, 25. This Committee is now named the Committee on Fiscal Affairs.

[38] The Centre for Tax Policy and Administration can be described as one of the 'departments' of the OECD. Other 'departments' listed on the OECD website are i.a. the 'Development Co-operation Directorate', the 'Economics Departments', the 'Directorate for Education and Skills', the 'Directorate for Employment, Labour and Social Affairs', the 'Environment Directorate', the 'Trade and

OECD has been working on aggressive tax planning, including the BEPS ('Base Erosion and Profit Shifting') action plan.

The tariff negotiations that preceded the adoption of the GATT may explain its role, as an organisation, in tax matters.[39] The text of the GATT contains direct references to taxation, mainly customs duties and other indirect taxes, including provisions that define the legal framework surrounding the adoption of BTAs.[40] In contrast to the Convention for European Economic Co-operation, which was intended to 'create the conditions and establish the institutions necessary for the success of European economic cooperation …', the GATT introduced substantive legally binding obligations upon its members.[41] The different purposes of the two organisations may explain the lack of cooperation between the actions undertaken at the OECD and GATT levels. One of the few exceptions concerns the topic of BTAs, where information was exchanged between the OECD and the GATT Council in the late 1960s.[42] On 1 January 1995, the GATT was replaced by the WTO.[43] The organisation is now made up of 164 countries.[44]

1.2.2.2 Background of the reports

In the 1960s the US started to express concerns about the potential effects of BTAs on international trade, considering that the proposals to

---

Agriculture Directorate', etc. See the website of the OECD at <www.oecd.org> (accessed 11 November 2015).

[39] Farrell, *supra* n. 9, 24.

[40] See i.a. GATT Arts. I, II, III, VI, VII, VIII, X, XI. Farrell, *supra* n. 9, 24. Farrell considers that 'notwithstanding the narrow focus of the GATT 1947 and the failure of the ITO, the GATT 1947 contracting parties did not automatically assume that matters relating to direct taxation would fall outside the scope of the Agreement' (p. 24).

[41] See Convention for European Economic Co-operation, preamble.

[42] See Farrell, *supra* n. 9, 27, footnote 91. See also GATT, Minutes of Meeting held at the Palais des Nations on 27–28 March 1968, 5 April 1968, C/M/46, 11 (hereafter, 'GATT, C/M/46'); OECD, Council, Relations with the G.A.T.T. Report by the Trade Committee, Paris, 31 October 1961, OECD/C(61)45; OECD, Council, O.E.C.D. Documentation on Border Tax Adjustments. Request from the Director-General of the GATT (Note by the Secretary-General), Paris, 3 May 1968, C(68)60.

[43] WTO, Marrakesh Agreement Establishing the World Trade Organization, 15 April 1994; WTO, 'The 128 countries that had signed GATT by 1994', available at <http://www.wto.org> (accessed 27 January 2014).

[44] WTO, 'Members and Observers', available at <https://www.wto.org/english/thewto_e/whatis_e/tif_e/org6_e.htm> (accessed 4 July 2017).

modify the turnover tax systems in Europe – in particular, the German turnover tax – could have a negative impact on free trade.[45] According to the US:

> Tax systems had changed considerably since the GATT provisions on border tax adjustments had been drafted and a more sophisticated view of the effects of these would be taken today. Border tax adjustments had been expanded and developed in response to changes in tax systems at a time when tariffs and other barriers to trade were being progressively reduced. Border tax adjustments had, therefore, come to have relatively greater importance.[46]

In other words, BTAs – which were not considered an important issue at the time of the adoption of GATT provisions – became a policy issue for the US at the end of the 1960s.[47] Consequently, the US requested the OECD Council and the GATT to study the situation of tax adjustments.[48] Following this request, the OECD Secretariat released in 1964 a 'fact-finding report on border tax adjustments applied by member countries to exports and imports'. This report is organised in two parts: the first part analyses the various forms of BTAs as well as their effects; the second part presents the situation in member countries.[49] Later, a Working Party

---

[45] See OECD, Council, Statement by the United States representative in the O.E.C.D. Council on the prospective increase of the German Equalisation tax, Paris, 22 May 1962, C(62)91.

[46] GATT, C/M/46, *supra* n. 42, 8. See also Stewart, Salonen & McDonough, *supra* n. 11, 33–37.

[47] GATT, Working Party on Border Tax Adjustments, Meeting of 30 April to 2 May 1968, Note by the Secretariat, 17 May 1968, L/3009, Annex, 9 (US Statement) (hereafter, 'GATT, L/3009').

[48] See, at the OECD level, OECD, Council, Minutes of the 49th Meeting held at the Château de la Muette, Paris, on Tuesday, 30 July 1963, C/M(63)15 (Prov.), 16 August 1963, item 154, 9; OECD, Working Party No. 4 of the Council on Border Tax Adjustments, The United States Submission on Border Tax Adjustments, Paris, 16 February 1966, C/WP4(66)4; OECD, C(62)91. At the GATT level, see GATT, Border Tax Adjustments. Proposed Terms of References for Working Party, 27 March 1968, C/W/123 (hereafter, 'GATT, C/W/123').

[49] OECD, Council, Fact-finding report on border tax adjustments applied by member countries to exports and imports (note by the Secretariat of the Council), Paris, 12 October 1964, C(64)137 Part I and Part II. See also OECD, Trade Committee, Border Tax Adjustments, Consultation Procedure, Arrangements adopted by the Trade Committee, Paris, 23 June 1967, TC(67)14; OECD, Related Activities Division, Fact-finding report on border tax adjustments applied by member countries to exports and imports, Paris, 13 November 1967.

on BTAs was established both at the OECD level (in 1965) and at the GATT level (in 1968).[50]

At the OECD level, the objective was to give an overview of BTAs and tax structures of OECD member countries as in March 1967.[51] In that sense, the report has mainly an informative value: the report does not reflect the views of the member countries with the exception of the 'country chapters' on which countries have given their agreement.[52]

At the GATT level, the mandate of the Working Party was to examine BTAs in light of the relevant GATT provisions, the practices of contracting parties and their possible effects on international trade.[53] The US hoped-for result was to achieve a common agreed interpretation – if not a modification – of the GATT provisions surrounding BTAs in order to prevent future disagreements between parties.[54] Areas of anticipated difficulties were the following: the use of averaging in respect of certain taxes, the effect of BTAs on international trade and the effect of changes in domestic taxes on international trade, in particular the impact on countries' balance-of-payments positions.[55] Members of the GATT reacted positively to the US request though not all parties agreed with the way the US had presented the issues at stake.[56]

To avoid replicating the work of the OECD on BTAs, the GATT secretariat was authorised to request OECD working papers and documents produced on the topic.[57] Moreover, in order to collect information

---

50 For the OECD, see OECD Report on tax adjustments applied to exports and imports in OECD member countries, 1968, 16, para. 6 (hereafter, 'OECD 1968 Report'); OECD, Ad Hoc Group of the Trade Committee, Consultation on Changes in Border Tax Adjustments in Germany, Date of the next meeting, Paris, 28 November 1967. For the GATT, see GATT, C/W/123, *supra* n. 48.

51 Consequently, only the situation of the original 20 members and Japan is analysed in the report. Where some members have modified their tax structures between March 1967 and March 1968, changes are in principle indicated in footnotes (see OECD 1968 Report, *supra* n. 50, 11 (foreword)).

52 OECD 1968 Report, *supra* n. 50, 11 (foreword).

53 GATT, C/W/123, *supra* n. 48; GATT, Border Tax Adjustments. Proposed Terms of Reference for Working Party, 28 March 1968, C/W/124. See also GATT, C/M/46, *supra* n. 42.

54 GATT, C/M/46, *supra* n. 42, 8–9. See also GATT, L/3009, *supra* n. 47, Annex, 10; GATT, Working Party on Border Tax Adjustments, Meeting of 8 to 11 October 1968, Note by the Secretariat, 23 November 1968, L/3125, Annex, 21.

55 GATT, C/M/46, *supra* n. 42, 8–9. See also the paragraphs concerning the US balance-of-payments difficulties.

56 GATT, C/M/46, *supra* n. 42, 10–11.

57 *Ibid.*, 11.

on BTA practices in non-OECD member countries, a questionnaire based on a simplified version of the OECD questionnaire was prepared and sent by the secretariat to these countries.[58]

1.2.2.3 Highlights

1.2.2.3.1 Definition of BTAs One of the most important contributions of the OECD report is its definition of BTAs. The GATT 1970 report on BTAs confirmed this definition, referring to the OECD 1968 Report.[59] Subsequent WTO reports also define BTAs by reference to the OECD 1968 Report. The OECD 1968 Report defines BTAs – also called 'equalisation taxes' in the report[60] – as follows:

> While border tax adjustments may be defined in various ways, it is most convenient for dealing with the problems which they present to regard them as *any fiscal measures which put into effect, in whole or in part, the destination principle (i.e. which enable exported products to be relieved of some or all of the tax charged in the exporting country in respect of similar domestic products sold to consumers on the home market and which enable imported products sold to consumers to be charged with some or all of the tax charged in the importing country in respect of similar domestic products)* (emphasis added).[61]

This definition calls for three main comments.

First, BTAs are defined as a fiscal mechanism based on the destination principle, which seems to be understood as a principle that allows imposing domestic taxes on imports while relieving exports from those taxes. This (trade-based) understanding of the destination principle does not fully match the one it has been given in other instances. Indeed, in other contexts (e.g. in the tax context), the destination principle has been defined by reference to the fact that taxes on products should be collected

---

[58] GATT, L/3009, *supra* n. 47, 7, para. 26. See also GATT, Border Tax Adjustments, Questionnaire, 6 June 1968, Spec(68)56. Note OECD members were also requested to update the OECD information (L/3009, 7, para. 26).

[59] GATT, Working Party on Border Tax Adjustments, Report, 2 December 1970, L/3464 (hereafter, 'GATT 1970 Report'). See also GATT, Working Party on Border Tax Adjustments, Meeting of 16 and 17 July 1968, Note by the Secretariat, 27 July 1968, L/3048, para. 6. Note that the Fact-Finding Report was distributed in attachment of Spec(68)57 (Spec(68)57/Add.1 and Spec(68)57/Add.2).

[60] OECD 1968 Report, *supra* n. 50, para. 68.

[61] *Ibid.*, 16, para. 6.

in the country of destination, namely where goods are consumed.[62] The destination principle is then opposed to the origin principle, according to which goods are taxed where they are produced.[63]

Second, the OECD definition of BTAs is voluntarily not limited to the 'taxes rebated on the occasion of exportation' and the taxes 'levied on the occasion of importation'.[64] Indeed, such a restrictive definition would exclude taxes with similar effects (such as retail sales taxes or single-stage wholesale taxes) as soon as these taxes are not charged on imports and rebated on exports 'at the time of the crossing of the border'.[65] According to the report, this practical difference is not relevant: it is only a 'technical question relating to what is administratively the most convenient under the particular system of consumption tax in operation'.[66] Moreover, as long as the economic effects of these taxes remain the same, the report indicates that it does not matter whether they are applied at the time when the border is crossed or not.[67] For this reason, the GATT report points out that the concept of BTAs is confusing because it implicitly suggests that the tax should be adjusted 'at the border'.[68] The GATT Working Party therefore recommends speaking about 'tax adjustments applied to goods entering into international trade' instead of BTAs.[69]

Third, the OECD and GATT reports distinguish between BTAs, customs duties and other barriers to trade. The distinction between these measures is, however, not always clear cut. For example, taxes on 'imports of a kind which would be taxable if home-produced, but which are in practice not home-produced' should preferably be considered as customs duties rather than as BTAs due to their potential protective effects.[70] The report, however, assimilates the duties on goods such as 'imported tobacco, alcoholic drinks and hydrocarbon oils' to BTAs for 'methodological' purposes.[71] Two reasons are put forward: first, these duties usually do not aim at protecting domestic industry and second, the

---

[62] OECD, *Taxing Consumption*, 1988, para. 7.4. See also Hufbauer, *supra* n. 11, 23.

[63] See Hufbauer, *supra* n. 11, 23. The two different understandings of the destination principles are analysed in more details in Chapters 3 & 5.

[64] OECD 1968 Report, *supra* n. 50, 68, para. 115.

[65] *Ibid.*

[66] *Ibid.*

[67] *Ibid.*

[68] GATT 1970 Report, *supra* n. 59, para. 5.

[69] *Ibid.*

[70] OECD 1968 Report, *supra* n. 50, para. 38.

[71] *Ibid.*, para. 78 and para. 197.

effects of customs duties and excise duties are difficult to distinguish when so-called 'excise duties' are applied to goods which are not domestically produced (or at least not produced in significant quantities).[72] From a legal viewpoint, however, the qualification of these taxes as BTAs instead of customs duties may have a significant impact. Whereas the rate of customs duties may be strictly limited through WTO members' schedules of concessions (i.e. WTO members' commitments regarding tariffs), BTAs' tax rate may be as high as the rate of taxes imposed on like domestic products. Consequently, in the hypothesis where goods are not produced domestically, the designation of taxes on imports as BTAs would allow countries to freely increase tax rates on imports.[73] In other words, in this case, the methodological choice to assimilate such taxes to BTAs would *a priori* offer member countries a significant margin of appreciation as to the rates imposed on imported goods.

1.2.2.3.2 Taxes eligible for BTAs In the OECD report, taxes that are considered eligible for adjustments under international practice are referred to as 'consumption taxes'.[74] The report distinguishes between two main categories of consumption taxes: general consumption taxes (including 'single-stage taxes', 'multi-stage non-cumulative taxes' and 'multi-stage cumulative taxes') and specific consumption taxes ('traditional excises').[75] Though the OECD report uses the same distinction between general and specific taxes as the one made by Ricardo, the

---

72 *Ibid.*

73 This reasoning, however, does not hold for products that are not subject to substantial tariff commitments. See e.g. Melaku Geboye Desta, 'The GATT/WTO System and International Trade in Petroleum: an Overview' (2003) 21 Journal Energy & Natural Resources Law 393: '… the tariff schedules of GATT contracting parties typically contained hardly any binding tariff commitments in the petroleum sector. Thus, although applied tariffs on petroleum imports are generally low, WTO member countries are free to raise them to any desired levels – provided they remained unbound …'. See also Susan L. Sakmar, 'Bringing Energy Trade into the WTO: The Historical Context, Current Status, and Potential Implications for the Middle East Region' (2008) 18 Indiana International & Comparative Law Review 89, 96–97.

74 OECD 1968 Report, *supra* n. 50, para. 7. Note also that the report mentions – in a footnote p. 16 – few concrete examples of BTAs in respect of other taxes (i.a. the Greek social security charges and payroll taxes, the Spanish property taxes, stamp duties and parafiscal charges and, to some extent, the Turkish payroll and property taxes and the Italian registration and stamp duties).

75 *Ibid.*, para. 9.

report does not use this distinction as a criterion to determine which taxes are eligible for adjustments. The OECD report indeed highlights that countries' practices allow for BTAs in respect of consumption taxes, regardless of their general or specific character.[76]

The report recognises that the concept of 'consumption taxes' may be criticised given that not all goods can be classified as 'consumer goods'.[77] Yet, the report favours the concept of 'consumption tax' over the terms 'indirect tax' (considered too broad) and 'turnover tax' (considered too restrictive). Moreover, the OECD report explains that the distinction between direct and indirect taxes is not appropriate due to the difficulty in classifying taxes as direct or indirect taxes and the 'over-simplification' of assimilating indirect taxes to eligible taxes for adjustments and direct taxes to non-eligible taxes for adjustments.[78] This last argument is rather weak given that the concept of consumption taxes could also be considered an artificial categorisation of the taxes subject to BTAs.

The artificial character of the distinctions used to determine the taxes that should be eligible for BTAs also appears in the GATT report. Indeed, in contrast to the OECD report, the GATT Working Party report distinguishes between direct and indirect taxes (instead of distinguishing between consumption and non-consumption taxes) as a criterion for determining the eligibility of taxes for BTAs, which illustrates the lack of coherence and rational arguments for preferring one distinction over another. Some members of the Working Party rightly criticised the distinction between direct and indirect taxes during the preparatory

---

[76] See OECD, Working Party No. 4 of the Council on Border tax adjustments, remarks by the German Member of the Working Party, at the 3rd Session on 20 September 1965, Paris, 1 October 1965, C/WP4(65)7, 3–4:

> it has been argued that some adjustment at the frontier for an isolated excise tax, not however for a general excise tax, can be justified by economic theory, since a general tax affects the overall price level while the isolated tax alters the relative price relationships among domestic products. This argument is based on the assumption that the general excise is imposed at no more than one standard rate, but that is mostly not the case. As example, I should like to refer to the variety of rates at which the German turnover tax, the U.K. purchase tax and the French TVA are being levied. Apart from that, it is a matter of legislative technique whether a tax is designed as a 'general' or an 'isolated' excise tax. As a theoretical proposition, one could imagine a multi-rate general excise tax being replaced by a multitude of isolated excise taxes.

[77] OECD 1968 Report, *supra* n. 50, para. 8.

[78] *Ibid.*, para. 116.

meetings. For example, the US pointed out the absence of a clear definition of the concepts of direct and indirect taxes:

> The GATT itself does not refer to the distinction, and the report of the Experts Group on this question is ambiguous in many respects. This is not surprising. Even today, economists have difficulty in defining direct and indirect taxes, depending upon the conceptual framework within which they are working and the purpose for which they wish to find definitions.[79]

The concept of *taxe occulte* offers another – more concrete – example of the ineffectiveness of the distinctions mentioned in the reports (both the distinction between direct and indirect taxes and the distinction between consumption and non-consumption taxes). None of the reports reach a clear conclusion as to the eligibility of these taxes, which the OECD report describes as follows:

> In addition to consumption taxes on goods themselves, there may be an element of tax paid in respect of goods or services used in their production or transportation. ... The hidden element of tax in an article, corresponding to the additional tax paid on any of these goods or services, is referred to ... as 'taxe occulte', and the goods or services themselves are referred to as 'producers' goods or services', though they may be used in certain cases by consumers.[80]

Examples of *taxes occultes* include taxes on 'auxiliary materials expended in the transportation or production of goods (e.g. energy, fuel, lubricants, packing, stationery)', taxes on 'durable capital equipment goods', taxes on 'services (e.g. transport, advertising)'.[81] The OECD report notes that countries differ in the amount of *taxes occultes* arising out of consumption taxes.[82] Moreover, the report points out the absence of a uniform practice as to BTAs in respect of *taxes occultes* arising out of consumption taxes.[83] At the time of the OECD and GATT reports, the issue of *taxes occultes* was not considered to be of primary importance as, in practice, 'adjustment was not normally made for "taxes occultes" except in countries having a cascade tax'.[84]

---

79 GATT, L/3009, *supra* n. 47, Annex, 11. See also Leontiades, *supra* n. 33, 173–183.

80 OECD 1968 Report, *supra* n. 50, para. 19.

81 *Ibid.* See also GATT 1970 Report, *supra* n. 59, para. 15.

82 OECD 1968 Report, *supra* n. 50, paras. 20 & 103.

83 *Ibid.*, para. 105.

84 GATT 1970 Report, *supra* n. 59, para. 15. See also Memorandum from Secretary of the Treasury Kennedy, Washington, 30 June 1970, Washington

The classification of eligible or non-eligible taxes for adjustments based on the OECD 1968 Report is summarised in Table 1.1.[85]

Table 1.1 Eligibility of taxes for adjustments in OECD 1968 and GATT 1970 reports

ELIGIBLE TAXES	NON-ELIGIBLE TAXES
Consumption taxes (OECD)/indirect taxes (GATT)	**Other taxes (OECD)/direct taxes (GATT)**
• General o Single-stage taxes (sales taxes) o Multi-stage non-cumulative taxes (TVA) o Multi-stage cumulative taxes (cascade taxes) • Specific o Traditional excises o Duties on tobacco, beer, wines, hydrocarbon oils, etc. o (State monopolies)	o Income taxes o Profits taxes and corporate income taxes o Capital gain taxes and wealth taxes o Estate duty taxes
Exceptions, i.a.: o Social security charges in Greece o Property taxes o Stamp duties in Spain, etc.	**General:** o Social security charges o Property taxes o Payroll taxes o Stamp duties
Taxe occulte Eligibility varies depending on the tax from which the *taxe occulte* arises	

1.2.2.3.3 BTAs' rationales The two reports give an overview of the arguments that have been put forward in favour or against the adoption of BTAs. A first argument in favour of BTAs concerns the objective of neutrality in international trade, as expressed by Ricardo. The reports, however, formulate BTAs' rationale not in terms of trade and tax neutrality but in terms of BTAs' neutrality: BTAs should be trade neutral

National Records Center, Department of the Treasury, Secretary's Memos/Correspondence, FRC 56 74 7, Council of Economic Advisers, Foreign Relations, 1969–1976, Vol. III, Foreign Economic Policy, 1969–1972, International Monetary Policy, 1969–1972, Document 42, available at <http://2001-2009.state.gov/r/pa/ho/frus/nixon/iii/5341.htm> (accessed 17 November 2015).

[85] See OECD 1968 Report, *supra* n. 50, paras. 8–9, 74 & 116–119.

and have no influence on domestic taxation.[86] This new formulation may be explained by the US claim that BTAs were not 'neutral'. The question of the neutrality of BTAs is directly linked to the shifting into prices of taxes eligible for BTAs. Where taxes eligible for BTAs are 'not fully shifted into prices', BTAs could be suspected of benefiting countries relying heavily on consumption/indirect taxes.[87] Both reports mention arguments in favour and against the hypothesis of price shifting (*infra*).[88] A second argument in favour of BTAs is based on practical considerations: 'they would also be justified if it seems likely that any alternative practices would produce a less neutral situation as between different tax systems and/or would be more difficult to apply in practice'.[89] In other words, the reports recognised that the purpose of BTAs was not to achieve 'perfect fiscal neutrality in international trade' – given that this goal is very unlikely to be achieved in practice – but BTAs are considered a step in this direction.[90]

Aside from these two arguments in favour of BTAs, two additional arguments based on historical considerations are mentioned in the OECD and GATT reports to reject BTAs' economic rationale. A first negative view argues that GATT provisions cannot be explained based on strong economic grounds but should rather be considered a mere 'codification of existing practices'.[91] Given the move towards a stronger reliance on indirect taxes in certain countries in the 1960s–1970s, GATT provisions

---

86 *Ibid.*, para. 112. See however OECD, Border tax adjustments applied by member countries to exports and imports, note by the secretariat of the Council, Paris, 27 January 1965, CES/65.08, 3 ('Summary of conclusions of a symposium on border tax adjustments organised by the secretariat on 17–19 September 1964').

87 GATT, L/3009, *supra* n. 47, Annex, 13.

88 For the OECD report, see OECD 1968 Report, *supra* n. 50, paras. 120–127. For the GATT, see GATT 1970 Report, *supra* n. 59, para. 21; GATT, Working Party on Border Tax Adjustments, Meetings of 23 to 25 April and 30 June to 3 July 1969, Note by the Secretariat, L/3272, paras. 31–57 (hereafter, 'GATT, L/3272').

89 OECD 1968 Report, *supra* n. 50, paras. 113 & 150.

90 GATT, L/3272, *supra* n. 88, para. 83. GATT 1970 Report, *supra* n. 59, paras. 9 & 13: 'The point was made that Revenue Departments … had strong reason in the interest of the revenue as well as fiscal justice, to ensure, in the treatment of imports and exports, neutrality with home-produced goods' (para. 9).

91 GATT, L/3009, *supra* n. 47, para. 2. See also Stewart, Salonen & McDonough, *supra* n. 11, 35 quoting John R. Petty, Assistant Secretary of Treasury for International Affairs, Paper prepared for the Twenty-first Annual Conference of the Canadian Tax Foundation (20 November 1968).

no longer reflected the practices of the time and needed to be changed.[92] A second negative argument – not directly touched upon by the reports but mentioned in the literature at that time – considers that BTAs' rationale is related to the introduction of a system of fixed exchange rates that prevailed after the Second World War.[93] According to Baldwin, the purpose of BTAs should be read against this background: it could be argued that BTAs served as an instrument of monetary policy (as countries, in a fixed exchange rate system, could not freely modify their exchange rate) rather than as a tool for compensating for price shifting.[94] On this view, the limitation of the eligibility of BTAs to indirect taxes (excluding direct taxes) could be seen as an arbitrary decision aimed at circumscribing the instruments of monetary policy available for countries. In other words, the distinction between direct and indirect taxes would not be grounded in any logical explanation other than the historical tradition of BTAs being adopted in respect of indirect taxes.

1.2.2.3.4 BTAs' rationale based on the assumption of tax shifting As mentioned above, tax shifting is the principal assumption underlying BTAs' main rationale (i.e. the argument that BTAs are trade neutral). Indirect/consumption taxes are eligible for BTAs because they are shifted into products' prices while direct/other types of taxes are not eligible because they are not shifted into prices. This assumption resembles Ricardo's theory in that a key element of BTAs' rationale is tax shifting.

---

92 GATT, L/3009, *supra* n. 47, Annex, 9–10.

93 The US indirectly mentioned this argument by referring to US balance-of-payments difficulties (GATT, C/M/46, *supra* n. 42, paras. 1–9). See also GATT 1970 Report, *supra* n. 59, para. 26; GATT, L/3272, *supra* n. 88, paras. 31–37 and GATT, L/3009, *supra* n. 47, Annex, 12–13.

94 See Robert E. Baldwin, *Nontariff Distortions of International Trade* (George Allen & Unwin Ltd 1970). See e.g. p. 89:

> Even though they were aware that other countries relied more heavily on indirect taxes and therefore would be able to claim higher border adjustments, they conceived of the rule as a helpful device in overcoming the widespread scarcity of dollars.

See also p. 96:

> Since general and uniform border adjustment changes by themselves are equivalent to a change in the foreign price of a country's currency, an important criterion for judging them is whether the effective alteration in the exchange rate tends to bring about equilibrium in the balance of payments.

See also Roy Blough, 'The Adjustment Process and the International Role of the Dollar' (1969) 24(2) The Journal of Finance 345–359.

It nevertheless differs from Ricardo's theory in that it does not consider whether the tax has a general or specific influence on the relative value of goods. In other words, both reports suggest that, as soon as price shifting can be proven, the tax should be eligible for BTAs. From this perspective, BTAs' economic rationale in the OECD and GATT reports does not match Ricardo's economic claim but better reflects the theory of absolute advantage, BTAs' role being to neutralise the effects of taxes on absolute prices.

This assumption of tax shifting is discussed in both reports, from two different perspectives. First, the reports analyse whether indirect/consumption taxes are effectively fully shifted into products' prices, without reaching any clear-cut conclusion.[95] Second, both reports put into question the measures in respect of which BTAs may be adopted. Indeed, when BTAs' rationale is grounded in the fact that BTAs compensate for tax shifting, the question arises as to whether BTAs may be applied (1) in respect of any tax (including direct taxes), and (2) in respect of non-tax policies as soon as it can be proven that these tax and non-tax policies have been shifted into products' prices.[96]

As to the eligibility of direct/non-consumption taxes for BTAs, the OECD report refers to economic studies carried out in the UK and the US concerning the shifting of profit taxes: 'In general, it seems that studies in the United States usually indicate a greater degree of shifting than studies in the United Kingdom, though it is not clear whether this reflects a difference in actual shifting or in the type of enquiry conducted

---

95 OECD 1968 Report, *supra* n. 50, paras. 129–149 (para 140: 'In the absence of agreement on the degree of shifting of consumption taxes there remains no agreement on the economic rationale of allowing border adjustments in full for consumption taxes'). See also GATT 1970 Report, *supra* n. 59, para. 22.

96 See OECD 1968 Report, *supra* n. 50, para. 153:

> if they [corporation income taxes] are so shifted, it is argued that in the absence of border tax adjustments, commodity flows are distorted by profits tax differentials and that a country with a high rate of profits tax is consequently at a trade disadvantage.

See also, GATT, L/3009, *supra* n. 47, Annex, 11:

> When governments adopt new domestic economic policies which have side effects on trade or payments, domestic action is not necessarily accompanied by offsetting action to neutralize the balance-of-payments effect. Many government actions, for example, affect general price levels. But only in the case of indirect tax measures is there an institutionalized provision for such offsets. What is the characteristic of indirect taxation that makes it uniquely qualified for automatic border adjustments?

in these different countries.'[97] It is noteworthy that the differing results between the US and the UK match the political agenda of these countries at the time.[98] Hence, the question arises as to whether the political debate has been grounded in differing empirical results put forward by researchers in both countries or whether economic research (and the methods favoured) have been influenced by political considerations.

Overall, the reports point out practical difficulties related to the implementation of BTAs in respect of direct/non-consumption taxes.[99] The reports note that it may be difficult to determine the trade effects of such taxes, which means that adjustments will necessarily be based on averaging.[100] This observation could be criticised as it rests on the assumption that consumption taxes are fully shifted forward into products' prices, while this assumption has clearly been questioned.[101] Moreover, BTAs in respect of cascade taxes and *taxes occultes* are also based, in practice, on averaging.[102] In the case of cascade taxes, the tax imposed on imported products has to be determined taking into account the presumed effects of the various taxes that have been applied at each stage of the distribution chain (from the manufacturers to consumers) on the prices of final products. Since not all products are manufactured and sold to consumers following the same distribution chain, similar products may be subject to different tax burdens (the longer the distribution chain, the heavier the tax burden is likely to be). In other words, averaging characterises BTAs imposed on imported products in respect of cascade taxes: the tax rate imposed on imported products is supposed to represent the average tax rate supported by domestic products.[103] Similarly, the effect of *taxes occultes* is necessarily determined by means of averaging since such taxes are supposed to be 'hidden' in domestic products' prices.

---

97 OECD 1968 Report, *supra* n. 50, para. 158.

98 See GATT 1970 Report, *supra* n. 59.

99 GATT, L/3272, *supra* n. 88, paras. 46–47; OECD 1968 Report, *supra* n. 50, para. 171.

100 OECD 1968 Report, *supra* n. 50, para. 171. See also para. 151.

101 In that sense, this passage of the report appears to be in contradiction with the parts that call into question the tax shifting of consumption taxes.

102 OECD 1968 Report, *supra* n. 50, para. 107.

103 *Ibid.*, para. 62:

> It is normal practice among the cascade countries to charge imported goods with a tax at the same rate as that imposed on the sale of similar home-produced goods by a domestic manufacturer to wholesaler, and *on certain products to charge in addition a surcharge to cover tax borne on the home market before goods have reached the manufacturers* (emphasis added).

As to the eligibility of non-fiscal policies, only the OECD report tackles the question, summarising the issue as follows:

> since trade between countries may be affected by various non-fiscal factors such as varying minimum wage laws, social welfare schemes, GNP per capita and even natural resources, there is no reason why distortions arising from fiscal differences should be singled out for neutralisation. Against this it may be argued that the effect of consumption taxes on prices of individual imports and exports is likely to be considerably greater than these other factors. Moreover, *the choice between making and not making border adjustments for taxes is not a choice between doing something and doing nothing, but a choice between applying the destination and the origin principle. On the other hand, the choice between making border adjustments or not making border adjustments for non-fiscal factors is a choice between doing something and doing nothing* (emphasis added).[104]

The OECD report seems to imply that a difference should be made between fiscal and non-fiscal factors for two reasons: on the one hand, the effect of fiscal factors (e.g. consumption taxes) on prices is much greater. On the other hand, taxation must be based on the destination or the origin principle, which is not the case for non-fiscal factors and policies. This last argument is not convincing: the choice between the destination and the origin principle can also be understood as a choice between 'doing something and doing nothing'. When the legislator chooses the destination principle, it can be interpreted as the expression of his choice to 'do something', namely to adopt BTAs. Conversely, when the legislator chooses the origin principle, it can be understood as the expression of his choice to 'do nothing' since he refrains from adopting BTAs.

1.2.2.3.5 Problems in relation to developing countries Only the GATT Working Party report touches upon the issue of developing countries in relation to BTAs, which can be explained by the presence of developing countries in GATT contracting parties.[105] Hence, the GATT report examines BTAs applied to 'products of interest to developing countries'.[106]

---

[104] OECD 1968 Report, *supra* n. 50, para. 127.

[105] See GATT, L/3272, *supra* n. 88, paras. 70–81; GATT, Working Party on Border Tax Adjustments, Meeting of 6–8 July 1970, Note by the Secretariat, 25 August 1970, L/3431, 4–5.

[106] GATT 1970 Report, *supra* n. 59, paras. 28–38.

Three main issues were put forward by developing countries. First, developing countries argued to disallow adjustments in respect of 'products which were not domestically produced by developed countries'.[107] In their opinion, existing adjustment practices were not justified in light of the argument of trade neutrality given that no tax shifting had to be compensated in the absence of domestic products.[108] According to some developed countries, the fact that a good was not produced domestically was not a 'realistic' criterion: revenue considerations should also be taken into account.[109] Moreover, it was argued that GATT provisions could not be understood as prohibiting BTAs in respect of 'products which were not domestically produced' because such an interpretation would be disadvantageous for developing countries, the fiscal revenue of which was for a large part based on non-domestically produced goods.[110] Second, questions arose as to the compatibility of changes in tax structures in developed countries with GATT Article XXXVII, which requires developed contracting parties to 'refrain from introducing new fiscal measures' on imports from less-developed contracting parties.[111] The third issue pertained to specific taxes that were deemed discriminatory by some developing countries (e.g. taxes on tea or on some tropical products).[112] According to some developed countries, these taxes were, however, to be explained by 'special health or revenue reasons'.[113]

1.2.3 National and Regional Views on BTAs

Countries did not only discuss the topic of BTAs at the OECD and GATT levels. BTAs were also discussed at the national and regional levels. National and regional views on BTAs highlight the diversity of political opinions surrounding the topic. Legal proposals and reforms in the US and the EU also illustrate the inconsistencies that exist between states' practices and the political views that they defend in international fora such as the OECD and the GATT.

---

107 GATT, L/3272, *supra* n. 88, para. 72.
108 *Ibid.*
109 GATT 1970 Report, *supra* n. 59, para. 31.
110 GATT, L/3272, *supra* n. 88, para. 76.
111 *Ibid.*, paras. 73 & 78.
112 GATT 1970 Report, *supra* n. 59, paras. 35–37. See also GATT, L/3272, *supra* n. 88, para. 80.
113 GATT 1970 Report, *supra* n. 59, paras. 36–37.

1.2.3.1 US views on BTAs

As already mentioned, the US considers that its economy suffers from the fact that other countries rely heavily on BTAs while it does not make a similar use of the BTA mechanism. The main argument of the US is that its tax system does not contain any taxes that are comparable to the EU VAT system, which is a direct application of the BTA mechanism. In addition to US efforts to adapt GATT/WTO rules on BTAs at the international level, proposals have been made to modify the US tax system.[114]

A first proposal is to adapt the current BTA system by extending it to direct taxes in relation to export-oriented companies.[115] One of the arguments put forward by the US is that 'under the theory used to justify the GATT border tax adjustment rules, direct taxes were not considered to be borne by goods and were held to have no price effect'.[116] In other words, the deferral of direct taxes in relation to exports should have no effect on prices and should consequently not be assimilated to a subsidy.[117] This proposal is however likely to be considered contrary to WTO law, following the reasoning that was held in the case *Domestic International Sales Corporation Statute (DISC)*.[118] In this case, the US tax system allowing the deferral of a part of the profits of export-oriented domestic corporations was considered a tax subsidy prohibited under GATT Article XVI.[119] The US subsequently introduced new measures.

---

[114] Rosendahl, *supra* n. 34, 116–129; Robert F. van Brederode, 'The Metamorphosis of US Corporate Income Tax into a Value Added Income Tax' (2008) 19(4) International VAT Monitor 266. See also US, Hearings before the Committee on Ways and Means, House of Representatives, 'Replacing the Federal Income Tax', Impact on International Competitiveness of Replacing the Federal Income Tax (18 July 1996) & Impact of Replacing the Federal Income Tax on Manufacturing and Energy and Natural Resources (31 July 1996), 104th Congress, 2nd Session, Serial 104-68.

[115] van Brederode, *supra* n. 114, 268.

[116] GATT, Panel Report, United States Tax Legislation (DISC), 12 November 1976, L/4422, BISD 23S/98 (*US – DISC*), para. 58.

[117] *Ibid.*

[118] On the relationship between the DISC legislation and BTAs, see OECD, Fiscal Committee, Note on Discussion of the DISC (Domestic International Sales Corporation). Proposal at the 35th Session of the Fiscal Committee, Paris, 12 June 1970, DAF/EC/70.7, 3, at paras. 5–6. See also Sidney Weintraub, 'Border Tax Adjustments and the GATT' (1964–1965) 17 Tax Executive 304, 312.

[119] GATT, Panel Report, *US – DISC*. See Gary Clyde Hufbauer, 'The Foreign Sales Corporation Drama: Reaching the Last Act?' (2002) International Economics Policy Briefs 1, 3 et al. This case is analysed in more detail in Chapter 5.

They were, however, also rejected on the ground that they were export subsidies contrary to GATT/WTO law.[120]

A second proposal is to adopt VAT in the US. Though the US relies on a system of retail sales taxes at the subnational level, it is one of the only countries not to have introduced any VAT system so far.[121] One of the arguments in favour of the introduction of a federal-wide VAT system is directly related to the favourable trade effects that are expected to derive from VAT systems.[122] Many academics and researchers have discussed the case for the adoption of VAT in the US, without reaching a consensus on whether such change would be trade beneficial or not.[123] In 2005 an Advisory Panel – appointed by George W. Bush in order to propose a reform of the Federal Internal Revenue Code – studied the case for an American VAT and the case for a National Retail Sales Tax.[124] The panel

---

[120] See the FSC and ETI cases (Chapter 5). See Hufbauer, *supra* n. 119; van Brederode, *supra* n. 114, 272–274.

[121] In contrast to most countries, the US does not rely on VAT. In the US, general turnover taxes are retail sales tax (OECD, OECD Consumption Tax Trends 2012, VAT/GST and Excise Rates, Trends and Administration Issues, Annex 2, 216–217). See also Alan Schenk, 'Value Added Tax: Does this Consumption Tax Have a Place in the Federal Tax System?' (1987) 7(2) Virginia Tax Review 207, 209. The US system of sales taxes is further discussed in Chapter 3.

[122] See Joseph J. Thorndike, 'Early Proposals for an American VAT' (2009) Tax Analysts. See also Stewart, Salonen & McDonough, *supra* n. 11, 117 and 127–132; van Brederode, *supra* n. 114, 268–269.

[123] William G. Gale & Benjamin H. Harris, 'Proposal 10: Creating an American Value-Added Tax' (2013) The Hamilton Project, Brookings Institution 1; Gilbert E. Metcalf, 'Life Cycle versus Annual Perspectives on the Incidence of a Value Added Tax', in: James M Poterba (ed.), *Tax Policy and the Economy* (MIT Press 1994, Vol. 8); Rosendahl, *supra* n. 34, 127; Eric Toder, Jim Nunns & Joseph Rosenberg, 'Using a VAT to Reform the Income Tax' (2012) Tax Policy Center, The PEW. See also US Congress, 'Effects of Adopting a Value-Added Tax' (1992) Congressional Budget Office Study.

[124] US, President's Advisory Panel on Federal Tax Reform, Final Report, chapter 8 (Value-added tax) & chapter 9 (National Retail Sales Tax), 1 November 2005. See US, Executive Order 13369, President's Advisory panel on Federal Tax Reform, 7 January 2005. See also James J. Nedumpara, 'Lessons Learned from DISC/FSC/ETI Disputes: Reshaping the Quest Towards a GATT/WTO Friendly Corporate Tax Reform in the United States' (2011) O.P. Jindal Global University, Research Paper No. 10.

came to the conclusion that none of these two options were free of concerns.[125]

A recurrent proposal, introduced in the Congress at every session since 1999, is to adopt a federal sales tax while repealing the income taxes, payroll taxes, estate and gift taxes (the so-called 'Fair Tax Act').[126] One of the objectives, though not clearly mentioned, is to allow the US to benefit from BTAs.[127]

A third proposal is to establish fiscal measures similar to BTAs so as to compensate US producers.[128] The idea is that the US should adopt BTAs on 'imports coming from and exports going to all those countries which themselves now practice a system of border adjustments'.[129] Specific

---

125 US, President's Advisory Panel on Federal Tax Reform, Final Report, chapter 8 (value-added tax) & chapter 9 (National Retail Sales Tax), 1 November 2005.

126 One of the last proposals is the following: US, H.R. 25, FairTax Act of 2017, 115th Congress, 1 March 2017. See also Gary Clyde Hufbauer & Paul L.E. Grieco, 'Reforming the US Corporate Tax' (2005) Peterson Institute for International Economics; Dan R. Mastromarco, 'U.S. International Tax Reform? Define "Reform" for Me' (2006) 43(6) Tax Notes International 481; Robert F. van Brederode, 'Towards a Federal Sales Tax in the United States?' (2008) International VAT Monitor 114.

127 Walter Hellerstein, 'Recent Developments in US Subnational State Taxation with International Implications' (2008) 62(2) IBFD Bulletin 77, 85–86; Mastromarco, *supra* n. 126, 484; N.A, 'State Sales Tax Reform in the United States: The Streamlined Sales Tax Project' (2005) 59(5) IBFD Bulletin for International Taxation 176–181.

128 See e.g., G.N. Carlson, G.C. Hufbauer & M.B. Krauss, 'Destination Principle Border Tax Adjustments for the Corporate Income and Social Security Taxes' OTA Paper 20, November 1976.

129 See US, Minutes of Meeting of the Cabinet Committee on Balance of Payments, 21 December 1967, US Department of State, Foreign Relations, 1964–1968, Vol. VIII, International Monetary and Trade Policy (Document 161); Telegram from the President's Special Assistant (Califano) to president Johnson in Thailand, 22 December 1967, US Department of State, Foreign Relations, 1964–1968, Vol. VIII, International Monetary and Trade Policy (Document 162); Analytical Summary and Issues for Decision Prepared by the National Security Council Staff, NSC Meeting, 9 April 1969, US Department of State, Foreign Relations, 1969–1976, Vol. IV, Foreign Assistance, International Development, Trade Policies, 1969–1972 (Document 192), <http://www.state.goc/r/pa/ho/frus/nixon/iv/15576.htlm> (accessed 8 February 2014), Robert F. van Brederode, *Systems of General Sales Taxation: Theory, Policy and Practice* (Kluwer Law International 2009), 211.

provisions could be introduced in order not to tax imports from less-developed countries or from certain industrial sectors.[130] In recent years, proposals have been brought to the US Congress under the title 'Border Tax Equity Act'.[131] According to Pascrell, who introduced one of these proposals: '[The Border Tax Equity Act] is geared to fight a value-added tax, which would be imposed by foreign nations on American-made products. The Border Tax Equity Act stands up against foreign export subsidies and trade barriers that offshore U.S. jobs.'[132] The proposal in the 2016 Ryan tax reform plan ('A Better Way') to introduce a 'destination-basis tax system' allowing to exempt exports and tax imports goes into the same direction in support of a 'pro-America approach for Global Competitiveness'.[133] So far, such proposals have not been passed into law. In any case, they would likely be considered a violation of WTO law.[134]

1.2.3.2 The EU's views on BTAs

In the EU the discussion focused on very different aspects from the ones under discussion in the US.[135] As soon as in the 1950s, France, Italy, Germany, Belgium, Luxembourg and the Netherlands started to discuss

---

130 See US, Telegram from the President's Special Assistant (Califano) to President Johnson in Thailand, 22 December 1967, US Department of State, Foreign Relations, 1964–1968, Vol. VIII, International Monetary and Trade Policy (Document 162).

131 US, H.R. 6183, Border Tax Equity Act of 2016, 114th Congress, 27 September 2016; US, H.R. 2600, Border Tax Equity Act of 2007, 110th Congress, 6 June 2006; US, H.R. 2927, The Border Tax Equity Act, 111th Congress, 17 June 2009; van Brederode, *supra* n. 129, 213–214.

132 US, H.R. 2927, The Border Tax Equity Act, 111th Congress, 17 June 2009, Floor Speech, Bill Pascrell, Jr., Public Statement, 5 May 2010.

133 Majority Members of House Committee on Ways and Means, A Better Way: Our Vision for a Confident America, 24 June 2016, 27, available at <http://abetterway.speaker.gov/_assets/pdf/ABetterWay-Tax-PolicyPaper.pdf>: 'This Blueprint eliminates the existing self-imposed export penalty and import subsidy by moving to a destination-basis system'.

134 See van Brederode, *supra* n. 114, 270. See also the *Zenith* Case: US. Supreme Court, *Zenith Radio Corporation v. United States*, 437 US 443 (1978); Joseph M. Bracken, 'Zenith Radio Corp. V. United States: Countervailing Duty – Application to Nonexcessive Remission of Indirect Taxes' (1979) 4(2) Maryland Journal of International Law 221; Robert Dziubla, 'Zenith Radio Corp v. United States: The Demise of Congressionally Mandated Countervailing Duties' (1979) 1 Northwestern Journal of International Law & Business 318.

135 For this section, European developments are referred to as developments in the 'European Union' (EU). Though it is true that the EU did not exist before

the effects of BTAs in the case of intra-Community trade (i.e. trade between Member States) and the possibilities of harmonisation in the area of indirect taxes. Against this background, EU reports analysed the differences in tax systems between Member States, including the economic effect of destination-based tax systems. These reports are interesting sources of information as to EU views regarding BTAs applied between Member States. They also allow highlighting the weaknesses and inconsistencies of BTAs' theoretical basis developed at the OECD and GATT levels.

In 1953, the High Authority of the European Coal and Steel Community requested a Committee of Experts to analyse the differences in term of economic effects of destination-based or origin-based turnover taxes.[136] The results reached by the Committee of Experts are summarised in the Tinbergen report, named after the Committee Chairman. The report assesses the economic effects of tax systems based on the origin and destination principles, distinguishing between taxes on specific commodities, general indirect taxes and direct taxes. The report concludes that direct taxes are generally based on the origin principle while indirect taxes usually follow the destination principle.[137] The report nevertheless notes that the opposite could – in theory – also be possible. Direct tax systems could be based on the destination principle – understood here in the sense that imports are taxed and exports are relieved from taxation – while general turnover taxes could follow the origin principle:

> It is, perhaps, of some theoretical interest … to note that, if one particular industry were made to pay a special high income tax, strictly speaking the country ought to give a 'refund' on all products of that industry which were exported to compensate for the specially high tax, and also to impose a compensating duty on imports of such products. The calculation of the amounts would, of course, be extremely difficult.[138]

1993, the term 'EU' is used as a generic term to refer to the former European Economic Community and the EU of today.

[136] European Coal and Steel Community, High Authority, Report on the problems raised by the different turnover tax systems applied within the common market, report prepared by the Committee of experts set up under order No. 1-53 of the High Authority, 5 March 1953, available at <http://aei.pitt.edu/34921/1/A1064.pdf> (accessed 13 November 2015), 7.

[137] *Ibid.*, 37.

[138] *Ibid.* See also p. 24.

This observation of the Tinbergen report highlights that there may be different understandings of the destination principle: the view expressed in the Tinbergen report clearly does not correspond to the one of the OECD 1968 report, where direct taxes are associated with the origin principle.

Some years later, the Commission of the European Economic Community appointed three working groups and a Fiscal and Financial Committee to examine issues in relation to tax harmonisation in the European Economic Community.[139]

The first working group was asked to examine the possibilities for harmonisation of turnover taxes, including the removal of tax frontiers, understood as the 'removal of physical inspection at the internal political frontiers' as well as the 'removal of compensatory regulations on imports and exports between Member States'.[140] The first working group also dealt with the question of fiscal frontiers from an international viewpoint. The report considered BTAs to be necessary in guaranteeing the non-discriminatory application of turnover taxes, meaning that taxes should have 'no influence on the price structure of goods exported' and that imported goods should be 'taxed to the same extent as similar goods which are produced within the country'.[141]

The task of the Fiscal and Financial Committee was to analyse the disparities in tax systems between member countries in an attempt to determine the extent to which differences between tax systems might be eliminated. Against this background, one important part of the Committee report is dedicated to the analysis of the origin and destination principles.[142] First, the report notes that the fact that the destination principle does not characterise 'personal income, company and wealth taxes' does not mean that direct taxes are based on the origin principle.[143] According to the report, the relevant distinctions to be made regarding these taxes are based on the concepts of domicile/establishment, source

---

139 See European Commission, EEC Report on Tax Harmonization, The Report of the Fiscal and Financial Committee (Neumark Report) and the Reports of the Sub-Groups A, B and C, unofficial translation by H. Thurston (IBFD 1963).

140 *Ibid.*, 13.

141 *Ibid.*, 24, 38, 74. See Charles E. McLure, 'EU and US Sales Taxes in the Digital Age: A Comparative Analysis' (2002) 56(4) IBFD Bulletin 135, 145: '... this system is called the "restricted origin system"'.

142 See European Commission, EEC Report on Tax Harmonization, *supra* n. 139, 145.

143 *Ibid.*

and situs.[144] Second, the report explains that the principle of destination (and its application through BTAs between Member States) does not allow eliminating tax frontiers. On the one hand, 'these frontiers exist because of the fact that a good crossing them requires inspection and measures which are necessary because exports are subject to exemptions or refunds, and imports to a compensatory tax'.[145] On the other hand, the report highlights practical problems in relation to BTAs, in particular the difficulty of ensuring that the exemptions on exports and the duties on importations are of the same amounts as domestic taxes. Finally, the report acknowledges the criticisms often used by the US against BTAs, namely the potential discrimination created by BTAs vis-à-vis direct taxes:

> Compensation of disparities of tax burdens does not … , in fact exclude protectionist use of refunds and compensatory taxes, given that in practice this compensation shows often deficiencies. There would occur other disadvantages in the form of disturbances of competition to the extent that it would happen that taxes affecting the formation of income are shifted on, at least partially, that is to say, lead to increase in prices.[146]

Given these difficulties, the report examines the possibility of adopting the origin-based principle for indirect taxes at the EU level. The report concludes that such possibility is not feasible as far as excise duties are concerned due to the important diversity in excise duties between Member States.[147] Regarding turnover taxes, the report concludes that the adoption of origin-based turnover taxes is limited by two conditions: first, differences in tax rates should be 'very small' and second, Member States should have similar systems of exemptions and allowances.[148] In addition to these two conditions, the destination principle should remain applicable in relation to trade with third countries.[149]

Overall, the reports of the working group and the Fiscal and Financial Committee suggest replacing cascade tax systems by VAT.[150] Hence,

---

[144] *Ibid.*, 146. On this point, see Chapter 5, Section 5.2.1.1.1.2.

[145] *Ibid.*, 146 ('except in the case of a tax at the retail trade stage').

[146] See European Commission, EEC Report on Tax Harmonization, *supra* n. 139, 147.

[147] *Ibid.*, 148.

[148] *Ibid.*, 148.

[149] *Ibid.*, 149. Note that the translation of the report is not fully correct at page 149.

[150] Ben J. M. Terra & Peter J. Wattel, *European Tax Law* (Wolters Kluwer 2012), 168.

following these reports, two Directives on VAT were adopted at the EU level, requiring Member States (and future members of the European Economic Community) to introduce VAT into their tax systems in place of their systems based on turnover taxes.[151] Despite the discussions surrounding the possibility of evolving towards an origin-based tax system, the first two Directives maintained the destination principle not only for trade with third countries, but also in the case of trade between EU Member States.[152]

In the 1980s the Commission reopened the debate on the possibility of implementing the origin principle at the EU level. In 1985 the Commission issued a White Paper on the removal of physical, technical and fiscal barriers to complete the internal market. As to the removal of fiscal barriers, the White Paper concluded that limiting differences in tax levels between Member States is essential to achieve the removal of fiscal frontiers.[153] Consequently, proposals were issued by the Commission in

---

[151] Article 1 of the First Council Directive 62/227/EEC of 11 April 1967 on the harmonisation of legislation of Member States concerning turnover taxes, 14 April 1967, OJ 1301/67. See also Third Council Directive 69/463/EEC of 9 December 1969 on the harmonisation of legislation of Member States concerning turnover taxes – introduction of value added tax in Member States, 20 December 1969, OJ L320, 34; Fourth Council Directive 71/401/EEC of 20 December 1971 on the harmonization of the laws of the Member States relating to turnover taxes – Introduction of value added tax in Italy, 24 December 1971, OJ L283; Fifth Council Directive 72/250/EEC of 4 July 1972 on the harmonization of the laws of the Member States relating to turnover taxes – Introduction of value added tax in Italy, 18 July 1972, OJ L167, 18; Sixth Council Directive 77/388/EEC of 17 May 1977 on the harmonization of the laws of the Member States relating to turnover taxes – Common system of value added tax: uniform basis of assessment, 13 June 1977, OJ L145, 1; Council Directive 2006/112/EC of 28 November 2006 on the common system of value added tax, 11 December 2006, OJ L347 (hereafter, 'VAT Directive 2006/112/EC').

[152] See Arts. 2(b), 7 and 10, §1(a) of the Second Council Directive 67/228/EEC of 11 April 1967 on the harmonisation of legislation of Member States concerning turnover taxes, Structure and procedures for application of the common system of value added tax, 11 April 1967, OJ L0228.

[153] See White Paper from the Commission to the European Council, Completing the internal market, 14 June 1985, Brussels, COM(85)310 final, 45, para. 169; Global Communication from the Commission, Completion of the internal market: approximation of indirect tax rates and harmonisation of indirect tax structure, 26 August 1987, Brussels, COM(87)320 final/2, 6: '*The abolition of fiscal frontiers will bring with it the abolition for intra-Community trade of the existing system of relieving goods from tax at export and of imposing tax at import,* as has indeed been envisaged ever since the First VAT Directive was adopted twenty years ago' (emphasis added).

order to approximate VAT and excise duty rates.[154] Moreover, the Commission proposed adopting an origin-based VAT system at the EU level, eliminating the concepts of importation and exportation for trade taking place within the Community.[155] These proposals were, however, rejected by Member States, leading to new proposals from the Commission.[156] In 1991 the Directive on the abolition of fiscal frontiers was adopted, introducing the origin principle for trade by 'private individuals'.[157] Moreover, this Directive replaced the concepts of exportation and importation by the concept of 'intra-Community supplies' and 'intra-Community acquisition'.[158] According to Terra & Wattel, 'the major difference is that from 1 January 1993, fiscal controls at internal frontiers are definitively abolished'.[159] Despite the removal of fiscal controls, the destination principle remained the common practice. BTAs have not been eliminated, only their administration has been changed.[160]

Parallel to the harmonisation of VAT at the EU level, the Commission proposed to harmonise 'consumer taxes other than VAT', in particular excise duties.[161] According to the Commission, the harmonisation of

---

154 See Terra & Wattel, *supra* n. 150, 181, footnote 33.

155 Commission of the European Communities, Completion of the internal market: approximation of indirect tax rates and harmonization of indirect tax structure. Global Communication from the Commission, 26 August 1987, Brussels, COM(87)320 final/2, 4, points 6 & 8.

156 Communication from the Commission to the Council and to the European Parliament, Completion of the Internal market and Approximation of Indirect Taxes, 14 June 1989, Brussels, COM(89)260 final.

157 Terra & Wattel, *supra* n. 150, 185. See also Rita de la Feria, *The EU VAT System and the Internal Market* (IBFD 2009), 70; Council Directive 91/680/EEC of 16 December 1991 supplementing the common system of value added tax and amending Directive 77/388/EEC with a view to the abolition of fiscal frontiers, 31 December 1991, OJ L376, 1.

158 Article 28a, page 5 et al. of Directive 91/680/EEC. See also de la Feria, *supra* n. 157, 71: 'the substitution of concepts appears to be more symbolic than substantive, and thus more of a linguistic change than a conceptual one'.

159 Terra & Wattel, *supra* n. 150, 186 ('The taxable event, *i.e.* the intra-Community acquisition, must be reported on the internal VAT return rather than to customs officials at the borders').

160 de la Feria, *supra* n. 157, 70. See also European Commission, Green Paper, On the future of VAT. Towards a simpler, more robust and efficient VAT system, 1 December 2010, Brussels, COM(2010)695 final, 7.

161 Commission of the European Communities, Proposed Council Directives on excise duties and indirect taxes, other than value added tax, which are levied directly or indirectly on the consumption of products, 23 February 1972, COM(72)225 final.

excise duty rates was 'essential in order to abolish compensatory measures (taxes on imports and tax rebates on exports and related checks and controls) at present being applied at borders'.[162] In other words, the proposal was to abolish tax frontiers in intra-Community trade, not only for VAT, but also for other indirect taxes.[163] The first attempts by the Commission to harmonise excise duties were, however, not successful in the 1970s. The first EU Directives on excise duties were adopted in 1992.[164]

The analysis of the discussions that took place at the EU level against the background of the harmonisation process highlights that different opinions have been expressed on BTAs within the EU. On the one hand, Member States have intended to abolish internal borders, including tax barriers, on products traded within the EU. This project has been supported by expert reports putting forward innovative views on BTAs (such as the idea that direct taxes could also be border adjusted). On the other hand, at the international level, EU Member States – unlike the US – have not called into question the economic relevance of BTAs.

1.3 BTAs' MAIN THEORETICAL FOUNDATIONS

BTAs' economic and political history highlights the diversity of opinion surrounding BTAs, in particular regarding BTAs' economic theoretical foundation and taxes' eligibility for BTAs. BTAs' economic and political history also informs the two main rationales behind BTAs. While Ricardo's foundation for BTAs was the theory of comparative advantage, the OECD and the GATT introduced – based on countries' political views on BTAs – a new theoretical rationale: the theory of absolute advantage.[165]

---

[162] Commission of the European Communities, Proposed Council Directives on excise duties and indirect taxes, other than value added tax, which are levied directly or indirectly on the consumption of products, 23 February 1972, COM(72)225 final, explanatory note, 6.

[163] See Arts. 4 and 6 of the Proposed Council Directive on excise duties and indirect taxes, other than value added tax, which are levied directly or indirectly on the consumption of products, 23 February 1972, COM(72)225 final.

[164] See i.a. Council Directive 92/12/EEC of 25 February 1992 on the general arrangements for products subject to excise duty and the holding, movement and monitoring of such products, 23 March 1992, OJ L76, 1 (later amended and replaced in 2008 by Directive 2008/118/EC).

[165] See e.g. the confusing use of concepts in the dispute *US – FSC:* references were made to the concept of comparative advantage in WTO, Panel

Both the OECD 1968 and GATT 1970 reports provide for arguments in favour of BTAs' economic relevance, which reflects a shift in BTAs' rationale in comparison to the theory of comparative advantage. The two reports base the eligibility of taxes for BTAs on the criterion of tax shifting, regardless of whether the tax affects the relative value of products or not. The need for BTAs is explained by reference to the objective of avoiding the distortion of trade flows because of the impact of domestic consumption taxes on absolute prices. From this perspective, the two reports propose an alternative theoretical foundation for BTAs, which is closer to Smith's theory of absolute advantage than to Ricardo's

BOX 1.1 RICARDIAN THEORETICAL FOUNDATION FOR BTAs

I. Optimal trade takes place when countries' production is based on the theory of comparative advantage, meaning that production takes place where relative production costs are the lowest.

II. Comparative advantages arise out of differences in 'climate, skill, machinery'.

III. The location of production and the specialisation of country should not be distorted by other elements than 'climate, skill, machinery'.

IV. Specific taxes are shifted into price and distort relative production costs. Conversely, general taxes do not distort the relative value of goods.

V. Adjustments are needed to neutralise the potential distortions derived from the adoption of specific taxes. Without BTAs, it is preferable for countries not to adopt specific consumption taxes.

Points III and IV make it clear that the theory relies on the assumption that specific taxes distort the relative value of goods. Moreover, the main assumption of the theory is point I: 'optimal trade is conditioned by the theory of comparative advantage'.

The fact that taxation is aimed at raising public revenue that could be used to give a competitive advantage to enterprises (for example when tax revenue is used to improve transport services) does not put into question the arguments in favour of BTAs. Indeed, competitive advantages deriving from the use of tax revenue benefit to all industries (in contrast to specific taxes that only apply to a limited number of industries). Therefore, no trade distortion takes place.

Report, United States – Tax Treatment for 'Foreign Sales Corporations', 8 October 1999, WT/DS108/R (*US – FSC*), para. 4.1188 and to the concept of competitive advantages in the oral statements of the parties in WTO, Panel Report, United States – Tax Treatment for 'Foreign Sales Corporations', Recourse to Article 21.5 of the DSU by the European Communities, 20 August, WT/DS108/RW (e.g. para. 20 of the US statement in Annex).

theory on the comparative advantage. This alternative political theoretical foundation for BTAs, as well as Ricardo's theory, are summarised in Boxes 1.1 (p. 45) and 1.2.

BOX 1.2 ALTERNATIVE POLITICAL THEORETICAL FOUNDATION FOR BTAs (THE THEORY OF ABSOLUTE ADVANTAGE)

I. Optimal trade takes place when countries' production is defined by the absolute advantage they have in producing certain goods (due to differences in absolute production costs).

II. Indirect taxes affect absolute production costs of goods (economic assumption): they are shifted into products prices.

III. For this reason (II), countries are discouraged from adopting indirect taxes.

IV. Therefore, to neutralise the effect on trade of countries' tax systems, BTAs are needed to preserve countries' possibility to adopt indirect taxes.

V. Against the background of the removal of tariff barriers, GATT provisions on BTAs are necessary in order not to excessively limit member countries' *tax sovereignty* and to allow them to freely adopt indirect taxes.

Points II and IV make it clear that the theory relies on the assumption that *indirect* taxes are shifted into prices. Moreover, the main assumption of the theory is point I: 'optimal trade is conditioned by the theory of absolute advantage'. The fact that point I under this theory differs from Ricardo's main assumption based on the theory of comparative advantage makes it clear that the concept of trade neutrality can be used to refer to different assumptions. According to Ricardo, trade neutrality is guaranteed when trade takes place according to the theory of comparative advantage. Under this alternative theory, trade neutrality means that trade takes place in accordance with the theory of absolute advantage. Finally, an important assumption of this alternative model is that a country is better off when its exports are substantial: the welfare of a country is linked with its production level (if this were not true, the fact that taxes are shifted into price – which consequently would lower the production level – would not be an issue).

If the justification under point III is rejected (because it is not considered a problem that countries are discouraged to adopt indirect taxes), BTAs may still be considered necessary based on another assumption, namely that enterprises should not be disadvantaged by the tax system of the country in which they are located (the so-called 'competitiveness' argument). This assumption – which is based on a certain idea of equality between firms – is weaker than the 'tax sovereignty' assumption, which is a strong attribute of the state (OECD 1968 Report, para. 122).

In comparison to the Ricardian theory, this new theoretical framework seems to allow for BTAs in respect of *any* tax – *and other non-fiscal measures* – so long as it can be proven that the measure has been shifted into products' prices (based on point II).

1.4 INTERIM CONCLUSIONS

The analysis of the economic and political history of traditional BTAs offers a better understanding of the different rationales that justify this fiscal mechanism. BTAs' rationales also play a major role in determining which environmental goals could be achieved through BTAs. As explained later (Part III), WTO law translates – to a certain extent – this definition into legal conditions. For example, it is clear from the theory of comparative advantage and the theory of absolute advantage that BTAs aim at neutralising the effects of domestic taxes on international trade. This aspect also appears in BTAs' legal framework: BTAs need to mirror internal taxes on like products. In other words, environmental BTAs should *a priori* only complement environmental domestic taxes to neutralise their effects on international trade. From this perspective, the main purpose of BTAs would be trade and not environmentally driven.

BTAs have been discussed not only in the context of international trade, but also in the context of national and regional tax policies. At the US level, proposals have been introduced to level the playing field between the US and other states whose tax systems rely heavily on BTAs. At the EU level, the debate has focused on a different question, namely 'how to remove BTAs in the case of intra-Community trade in order to achieve a fully integrated internal market?' The technical reports issued at the EU level to answer this question highlight the inconsistencies in the discourse on BTAs. In particular, inconsistencies appear in the understanding of the distinction between direct and indirect taxes, which is at the heart of BTAs' legal framework. Where, at the OECD and GATT levels, the exclusion of direct taxes for BTAs is partly justified by reference to the origin principle, EU reports seem to indicate that the origin and destination principles are not relevant criteria to distinguish between direct and indirect taxes. These inconsistencies will be used later in the critical analysis of BTAs' legal framework to argue against traditional interpretations of WTO law (Part III).

2. History and theoretical foundations of environmental BTAs

As explained in Chapter 1, the concept of 'traditional BTAs' finds its theoretical underpinning in Ricardo's theory of comparative advantage. The concept was further developed in the 1960s based on the analysis by the OECD of more than 100 years of national practices. The OECD 1968 Report grounds BTAs in a new theoretical foundation: the theory of absolute advantage.

In contrast, the concept of environmental BTAs has been developed out of questions regarding countries' possibilities for using BTAs in favour of environmental protection. One of the first documents where the link was made between traditional BTAs and environmental taxes is an OECD document from 1994 entitled 'Environmental Taxes and Border Tax Adjustments'.[1] The concept of 'environmentally related BTAs' is not used in this document. However, it can be derived from its content that the idea was to study BTAs in respect of environmental taxes, defined by the OECD and other international organisations as taxes 'whose tax base is a physical unit (or a proxy of it) that has a proven specific negative impact on the environment'.[2] The fact that the OECD issued a document on this topic in 1994 may be explained by the increase in environmental consciousness at the beginning of the 1990s; suffice it to recall that the Rio Summit took place in 1992.

This chapter first analyses the economic history of environmental BTAs (Section 2.1). Second, it discusses their political development

[1] OECD, Environment Policy Committee and Committee on Fiscal Affairs. Joint Sessions on Taxation and Environment. 2nd Session. Environmental Taxes and Border Tax Adjustments, COM/ENV/EPOC/DAFFE/CFA(94)31, 27 April 1994, 1 (hereafter, '1994 OECD Note on Environmental BTAs').

[2] United Nations, European Commission, International Monetary Fund, OECD, World Bank, Handbook of National Accounting: Integrated Environmental and Economic Accounting 2003, Studies in Methods (2005) Series F, No. 61, Rev. 1, Glossary, United Nations, New York, paras. 2.102 & 6.26. According to these same organisations, '[f]our subsets of environmental taxes are distinguished: energy taxes, transport taxes, pollution taxes and resources taxes'.

(Section 2.2). Finally, this chapter offers an overview of environmental BTAs' theoretical foundations (Section 2.3).

2.1 ENVIRONMENTAL BTAs' ECONOMIC FOUNDATION

The economic foundation of environmental BTAs is much more recent than that of traditional BTAs. Unlike for traditional BTAs, no single author can be called the 'father' of environmental BTAs as in the case of Ricardo. Besides, there is no common understanding of environmental BTAs in the economic literature. Many economic studies refer to environmental border (tax) adjustments as a generic concept without paying attention to how this concept differs from other models of environmental border taxes, such as import tariffs or countervailing duties.[3] Authors write about 'border carbon adjustments', 'climate-related border tax adjustments' and 'border adjustment measures'.[4]

Most studies focus on tax models where a tax is imposed on imports (with or without tax rebates on exports) in order to compensate for the

---

[3] See Robert F. van Brederode, *Systems of General Sales Taxation: Theory, Policy and Practice* (Kluwer Law International 2009), 210: 'Basically, we deal with parallel worlds [i.e. law & economics] that seem to have no means of effectively communicating with each other, creating Babylonian discussions at best'. See Juan-Carlos Altamirano & Marc Vielle, 'Climate Policies and Competitiveness: Options for Border Adjustment Measures' (2011) NCCR Climate and École Polytechnique Fédérale de Lausanne; Stefan Boeters & Johannes Bollen, 'Fossil Fuel Supply, Leakage and the Effectiveness of Border Measures in Climate Policy' (2012) 215 CPB Netherlands Bureau for Economic Policy Analysis, 13; Justin Caron, 'Estimating Carbon Leakage and the Efficiency of Border Adjustments in General Equilibrium – Does Sectoral Aggregation Matter?' (2012) 34 Energy Economics 111–126; Warwick J. McKibbin & Peter J. Wilcoxen, 'The Economic and Environmental Effects of Border Tax Adjustments for Climate Policy' (2008–2009) Brookings Trade Forum 1–34; Mani S. Muthukumara, 'Environmental Tariffs on Polluting Imports. An Empirical Study' (1996) 7(4) Environmental and Resource Economics 391, 404.

[4] Some authors also refer to the concept of countervailing duties: Mustafa H. Babiker & Thomas F. Rutherford, 'The Economic Effects of Border Measures in Subglobal Climate Agreements' (2005) 26(4) The Energy Journal 99, 101–125; Muthukumara, *supra* n. 3, 404.

emissions' price, which burdens domestic goods in comparison to internationally traded goods.[5] Many economic studies propose to impose border carbon adjustment on products from 'non-regulated countries' or 'non-acting countries', i.e. countries that do not regulate carbon emissions.[6] From this viewpoint, most economic studies do not follow the traditional design of BTAs, which is based on the structure of the taxes imposed on *domestic* products and not on the tax system that applies in third countries. From a legal perspective, these environmental tax models discussed by economists may be better described as environmental tariffs or countervailing measures, which would be subject to different legal provisions than BTAs.[7] References to the BTA concept may therefore be misleading for an audience of non-economists, such as a legal audience. In any case, one should be careful in using economic studies to nourish the political debate on the opportunity to adopt environmental BTAs. Therefore, this section purposely refers to 'environmental border taxes' and not to 'environmental BTAs'.

Four main issues are at the heart of the economic literature surrounding environmental border taxes. The first two issues concern the positive effect of environmental border taxes on the risks related to the unilateral adoption of domestic environmental policies, namely the risk of loss of

---

5 See Birgit Bednar-Friedl, Thomas Schinko & Karl W. Steininger, 'The Relevance of Process Emissions for Carbon Leakage: A Comparison of Unilateral Climate Policy Options With and Without Border Carbon Adjustment' (2012) 34 Energy Economics 168–180; Carolyn Fischer & Alan K. Fox, 'Comparing Policies to Combat Emissions Leakage. Border Carbon Adjustments versus Rebates' (2011) Resources for the Future Discussion Paper 09-02-REV, 11; Madanmohan Ghosh, Luo Deming, Shahid Siddiqui Muhammad & Zhu Yunfa, 'Border Tax Adjustments in the Climate Policy Context: CO_2 versus Broad-Based GHG Emission Targeting' (2012) 34 Energy Economics 154–167; Everett B. Peterson & Joachim Schleich, 'Economic and Environmental Effects of Border Tax Adjustments' (2007) Working paper sustainability and innovation S1, 16.

6 See the references to 'non-regulated countries' in Frédéric Branger & Philippe Quirion, 'Would Border Carbon Adjustments Prevent Carbon Leakage and Heavy Industry Competitiveness Losses? Insight from a Meta-Analysis of Recent Economic Studies' (2013) CIRED Working Paper Series No. 52, 3. See the similar reference ('non-acting countries') in Madison Condon & Ada Ignaciuk, 'Border Carbon Adjustment and International Trade. A Literature Review' (2013) 6 OECD Trade and Environment Working Papers, OECD Publishing, 6–9.

7 Babiker and Rutherford correctly refer to 'countervailing carbon tariffs' rather than to the BTA concept (see Babiker & Rutherford, *supra* n. 4, 110).

competitiveness and the risk of pollution leakage (or carbon leakage).[8] Some economic studies show that environmental border taxes are an efficient tool to support countries in implementing domestic environmental policies.[9] Other studies, however, put forward that such taxes may have no impact or only a limited positive impact, either on competitiveness or on carbon leakage.[10] For example, Burniaux et al. consider that 'carbon-based border tax adjustment' may only have a positive impact on carbon leakage under certain conditions (i.e. when the coalition of countries that establishes the border tax is small) while their impact on competitiveness is uncertain.[11] Kuik and Hofkes, in the specific case of border adjustment for European emissions trading, find that the main justification for such adjustment is to limit the negative economic effects of unilateral climate policies on competitiveness.[12]

A third question that has been analysed by economists relates to the impact of environmental border taxes on the political engagement of third countries in favour of environmental protection ('Would such taxes encourage third countries to enter into multilateral environmental agreements (MEAs)?'). In some studies, authors argue that environmental

---

8 See Zhong Xiang Zhang, 'Competitiveness and Leakage Concerns and Border Carbon Adjustments' (2012) CCEP Working Paper No. 120 (this study provides for a literature review surrounding the topic).

9 Christoph Böhringer, Edward J. Balistreri & Thomas F. Rutherford, 'The Role of Border Carbon Adjustment in Unilateral Climate Policy: Overview of an Energy Modeling Forum Study' (EMF 29) (2012) 34 Energy Economics 97–110; Thomas Eichner & Rüdiger Pethig, 'Unilateral Consumption-Based Carbon Taxes and Negative Leakage' (2015) 40 Resource and Energy Economics 127–142; Joshua Elliott, Ian Foster, Samuel Kortum, Todd Munson, Fernando Pérez Cervantes & David Weisbach, 'Trade and Carbon Taxes' (2010) 100 American Economic Review: Papers & Proceedings 465–469. See also Branger & Quirion, *supra* n. 6; Fischer & Fox, *supra* n. 5.

10 See McKibbin & Wilcoxen, *supra* n. 3, 1–34; Muthukumara, *supra* n. 3, 391.

11 Jean-Marc Burniaux, Jean Chateau & Romain Duval, 'Is There a Case for Carbon-Based Border Tax Adjustment? An Applied General Equilibrium Analysis' (2010) OECD Economics Department Working Papers No. 794. See also Stéphanie Monjon & Philippe Quirion, 'A Border Adjustment for the EU ETS: Reconciling WTO Rules and Capacity to Tackle Carbon Leakage' (2011) 11(5) Climate Policy, 1212–1225; Niven Winchester, Sergey Paltsev & John Reilly, 'Will Border Carbon Adjustments Work?' (2010) 184 MIT Joint Program on the Science and Policy of Global Change.

12 Onno Kuik & Marjan Hofkes, 'Border Adjustment for European Emissions Trading: Competitiveness and Carbon Leakage' (2010) 38 Energy Policy 1741–1748.

border taxes may indeed be useful in countering free riding and encouraging third countries to join MEAs.[13]

Finally, a fourth issue concerns the potential negative impacts of environmental border taxes on the economy, such as their effect on welfare. Some studies find positive results while others consider that such taxes significantly reduce welfare in the implementing countries.[14] These results add up to the usual discussions surrounding environmental border taxes in political debates as well as in legal literature.[15] Usually, analyses of the welfare factor are based on a mainstream approach of international economics that favours undistorted trade and does not always consider externality costs.[16] Aside orthodox economics, other approaches, which

---

[13] See Zeynep Burcu Irfanoglu, Juna P. Sesmero & Alla Golub, 'Potential of Border Tax Adjustments to Deter Free Riding in International Climate Agreements' (2015) 10 Environmental Research Letters; Charles F. Mason, Edward B. Barbier & Victoria I. Umanskaya, 'On the Strategic Use of Border Tax Adjustments as a Second-Best Climate Policy Measure' (2015) 20(4) Environment and Development Economics 539, 558. See also Dieter Helm, Cameron Hepburn & Giovanni Ruta, 'Trade, Climate Change, and the Political Game Theory of Border Carbon Adjustments' (2012) 28(2) Oxford Review of Economic Policy 368–394; Matthias Weitzel, Michael Hübler & Sonja Peterson, 'Fair, Optimal or Detrimental? Environmental vs. Strategic Use of Border Carbon Adjustment' (2012) 34 Energy Economics 198–207.

[14] E.g. Gros & Egenhofer find positive results on global welfare (see Daniel Gros & Christian Egenhofer, 'The Case for Taxing Carbon at the Border' (2011) 11 Climate Policy 1262–1268) while Winchester et al. find a significant reduction of welfare (Winchester, Paltsev & Reilly, *supra* n. 11). See also Alessandro Antimiani, Valeria Costantini, Chiara Martini, Luca Salvatici & Maria Cristina Tommasino, 'Carbon Leakage and Trade Adjustment Policies', in: Valeria Costantini & Massimiliano Mazzanti (eds.), *The Dynamics of Environmental and Economic Systems. Innovation, Environmental Policy and Competitiveness* (2013 Springer), 25; Branger & Quirion, *supra* n. 6; Aaditya Mattoo, Arvind Subramanian, Dominique van de Mensbrugghe & Jianwu He, 'Trade Effects of Alternative Carbon Border-Tax Schemes' (2013) 149 Review of World Economics 587–60.

[15] See also the comment of Nils Axel Braathen to McKibbin & Wilcoxen, *supra* n. 3, 25.

[16] See Branger & Quirion, *supra* n. 6, 4: 'The welfare (or in some studies GDP) variation of the abating coalition ranges from –1.58% to 0.02% without BCA and from 0.9% to 0.40% with BCA (the environmental impact is never taken into account in the welfare estimation)'. See, however, Gros & Egenhofer, *supra* n. 14, 36.

see the 'human economy as part – or subsystem – of the greater whole that is nature', should nevertheless also be considered.[17]

In the same way as for traditional BTAs, a lack of unity characterises economic scholarship surrounding environmental border taxes. This lack of coherence may be explained by the fact that economic literature is characterised by a great diversity of methods and assumptions. Economic literature is indeed mostly based on projections, economic models based on assumptions and not much on empirical studies, even though some authors have analysed concrete legislative proposals (e.g. economic studies on how border taxes could complement the EU emission trading system (ETS) or other American proposals).[18] Only few environmental border taxes have been put into effect, which does not permit conclusions to be drawn based on practical examples. Moreover, even when examples exist, it is extremely difficult to determine the economic effects of such taxes: 'How to distinguish the effects derived from the adjustment policy from those derived from other factors (such as, for example, the slowdown of the economy due to an economic crisis)?'[19]

---

[17] Clóvis Calvacanti, 'Conceptions of Ecological Economics: Its Relationship with Mainstream and Environmental Economics' (2010) 24(68) Estudos Avançados 53–54. See also Roberto Bermejo, *Handbook for a Sustainable Economy* (Springer 2014), 15–17. On the economic theory of law and its influence on environmental law, see e.g. Michael Faure, *L'analyse économique du droit de l'environnement* (Bruylant 2007).

[18] See Branger & Quirion, *supra* n. 6. Regarding the EU ETS, see Kuik & Hofkes, *supra* n. 12; Tom Manders & Paul Veenendaal, 'Border Tax Adjustments and the EU-ETS. A Quantitative Assessment' (2008) 171 Centre Planning Bureau (CPB) Document; Monjon & Quirion, *supra* n. 11; Marco Springmann, 'A Look Inwards: Carbon Tariffs versus Internal Improvements in Emissions-Trading Systems' (2012) 34 Energy Economics 228–239. Regarding American proposals, see Muthukumara, *supra* n. 3, 391; Winchester, Paltsev & Reilly, *supra* n. 11 (they discuss the case of H.R. 2454).

[19] See, on the effects of the EU ETS on carbon leakage: Julia Reinaud, 'Issues Behind Competitiveness and Carbon Leakage. Focus on Heavy Industry' (2008) OECD/IEA, 7. See Robert Gale, Stephan Barg & Alexander Gillies, *Green Budget Reform: An International Casebook of Leading Practices* (1995 Earthscan), 191–192; Janet Stone McGuigan, 'The Potential Economic Impact of Environmental Liability: The American and European Contexts' (2000) Study for the European Commission; Peter Wooders & Aaron Cosbey, 'Climate-linked Tariffs and Subsidies: Economic Aspects (Competitiveness & Leakage)', background paper written for the conference 'Climate Change, Trade and Competitiveness: Issues for the WTO', 16–18 June 2000, 6. *Contra:* World Bank, 'Five Years after Rio. Innovations in Environmental Policy' (1997) Environmentally Sustainable Development Studies and Monographs Series No. 18, 31.

2.2 POLITICAL HISTORY OF ENVIRONMENTAL BTAs

As mentioned above, environmental BTAs are to be understood against the background of the environmental awareness that arose in the second half of the 20th century. Both the OECD and WTO have issued reports on the topic of environmental BTAs (Section 2.2.1). In addition, countries have expressed their views on the integration of environmental considerations at the national and regional levels (Section 2.2.2).

2.2.1 International Fora on Environmental BTAs: The OECD and the GATT/WTO

2.2.1.1 Role of the OECD and the GATT/WTO in environmental tax matters

The role of the OECD and the GATT/WTO in environmental tax matters has been reinforced over the years.

At the OECD level, the Environment Committee has from early on dealt with environmental matters.[20] In the 1990s the growing interest in environmental taxes led to the creation of the 'Task Force on Taxation and Environment' – later called the Joint Session on Taxation and Environment – supervised by the Committee on Fiscal Affairs and the Environment Policy Committee.[21] In parallel, a Joint Session of National Experts on Trade and Environment – which later became the Joint Working Party on Trade and Environment – was established in 1991 in order to analyse the relationships and potential areas of tension between trade and environmental issues.[22] The Joint Meetings of Tax and Environment Experts were created in 1999. Their mandate is to analyse current environmental taxes while providing expertise on the effectiveness of environmental taxes and their practical implementation.[23]

---

[20] Bill L. Long, 'International Environmental Issues and the OECD 1950–2000: An Historical Perspective' (2000) OECD Publishing, 27–116.

[21] See OECD, Group on Economic and Environment Policy Integration, 'Taxation and Environment. Draft Programme', 1998, ENV/EPOC/GEEI(98)8.

[22] Long, *supra* n. 20, 89. See also OECD, Trade and Environment, June 1993, OECD/GD(93)99, Annex 3 (description of items for analysis in the further work programme).

[23] OECD, Directory of Bodies of the OECD (2012) OECD Publishing, 48. Note that the mandate of the joint meetings of tax and environment experts was planned to end in December 2013. From an exchange of emails (dated 19 November 2015) with the OECD archive service, it seems nevertheless that the joint meeting is still effective.

Regarding the GATT, despite the limited reference to environmental issues in the text of the GATT, growing environmental awareness in the 1970s led the GATT Secretariat to prepare reports on trade and environment.[24] The report 'Industrial Pollution Control and International Trade' was issued for the UN 1972 Stockholm Conference on Human Environment, the first international gathering on environmental matters.[25] This GATT report contains a reference to BTAs as a legal instrument to tackle pollution, considering that GATT provisions surrounding BTAs would permit 'penalty taxes on the sale or use of particular [pollutant] products'.[26] Around the same time, a Group on Environmental Measures and International Trade was created 'to examine, upon request any specific matters relevant to the trade policy aspects of measures to control pollution and protect human environment'.[27] The Group met for the first time in 1991, one year before the 1992 Rio Earth Summit.[28] In 1994, the Marrakesh Agreement Establishing the World Trade Organization was adopted. Its preamble highlights the need to reconcile the objectives of economic development with the protection of the environment.[29] Moreover, Ministers decided to establish a Committee on Trade and Environment with its main objective to make 'international trade and environmental policies mutually supportive'.[30]

---

[24] Long, *supra* n. 20, 11–12.

[25] GATT, Industrial Pollution Control and International Trade, Note by the GATT Secretariat, 9 June 1971, L/3538, 13 (hereafter, 'GATT, L/3538'); WTO, 'History: Early years: Emerging environment debate in GATT/WTO', available at <http://www.wto.org/english/tratop_e/envir_e/hist1_e.htm> (accessed 27 October 2015).

[26] GATT, L/3538, *supra* n. 25, 17.

[27] GATT, Group on Environmental Measures and International Trade, 16 November 1971, L/3622. See also GATT, Council (9–10 November 1971), Industrial Pollution Control (draft terms of reference for standing working party), 3 November 1971, C/W/194.

[28] See GATT, Airgram, 'Group on Environmental Measures and International Trade', 19 November 1991, GATT/AIR/3264. See also, GATT, Group on Environmental Measures and International Trade, Report of the Meeting of the Group on Environmental Measures and International Trade of 27 November 1991, 17 December 1991, TRE/1.

[29] Final Act embodying the results of the Uruguay Round of Multilateral Trade Negotiations, Marrakesh, 15 April 1994.

[30] Multilateral Trade Negotiations (The Uruguay Round), Trade Negotiations Committee, Meeting at Ministerial Level, Palais des Congrès, Marrakesh (Morocco), 12–15 April 1994, Annex II (Trade and Environment, Decision of 14 April 1994), 6 May 1994, MTN.TNC/45(MIN), 16. See WTO, General Council, Decision on the WTO Committee on Trade and Environment, WT/L/42, 23

2.2.1.2 Background – environmental BTAs

At the OECD level, the topic of environmental BTAs gained importance in the 1990s and the first references to BTAs in respect of environmental taxes date back to 1993.[31] In 1994, the Environment Policy Committee and Committee on Fiscal Affairs issued a first note on the relationship between 'environmental taxes and border tax adjustments', based on a report written by Demaret and Stewardson on the topic (the '1994 OECD Note').[32] This note is to be understood against the background of the growing interest in environmental tax reforms and the related questions surrounding countries' possibilities to rely on BTAs in respect of environmental taxes. The note is also to be understood against the background of the controversial decisions on the interactions between environmental policies and international trade issued by GATT Panels at the end of the 1980s and at the beginning of the 1990s (e.g. the *Tuna/Dolphin* cases, the *Superfund* case).[33]

At the GATT and WTO levels, a first reference to environmental BTAs appears in the GATT 1971 report on 'Industrial Pollution Control and International Trade', as mentioned earlier.[34] Other references to the issue of BTAs in respect of environmental taxes appear in a note of the Secretariat from June 1993 on 'the trade effects of environmental measures'.[35] Some months later, in a meeting of the Group on Environmental Measures and International Trade, Sweden requested a note, referring directly to BTAs as an economic instrument to 'achieve environmental policy goals'.[36] During the same meeting, the representative of Canada also indirectly referred to the mechanism of BTAs, using

---

February 1995. See also James K.R. Watson, *The WTO and the Environment. Development of Competence Beyond Trade* (Routledge 2013), 153–180.

[31] See OECD, Summary Report of the Workshop on Environmental Policies and Industrial Competitiveness, 28–29 January 1993, OECD/GD(93)83, 8–9.

[32] 1994 OECD Note on Environmental BTAs, *supra* n. 1, 1. Paul Demaret & Raoul Stewardson, 'Border Tax Adjustments under GATT and EC Law and General Implications for Environmental Taxes' (1994) 28(4) Journal of World Trade 5–66.

[33] The 1994 OECD Note on Environmental BTAs (*supra* n. 1) analyses these decisions in point IV ('border tax adjustments and GATT panel decisions').

[34] GATT, L/3538, *supra* n. 25, in particular 8–9.

[35] GATT, Group on Environmental Measures and International Trade, The Trade Effects of Environmental Measures: Note by the Secretariat, 29 June 1993, TRE/W/13 (hereafter, 'GATT, TRE/W/13').

[36] GATT, Group on Environmental Measures and International Trade, Report of the Meeting held on 5–6 October 1993, 21 October 1993, TRE/13, para. 154 (hereafter, 'GATT, TRE/13').

the example of disposal fees 'applied to both domestic and imported goods' in order to illustrate the various trade effects of economic instruments.[37] Later, in 1994 and 1997, two notes touched upon the topic of environmental BTAs (Section 2.2.1.3).

2.2.1.3 General overview: the 1994 OECD Note and the 1994 and 1997 GATT/WTO Notes

The 1994 OECD Note is structured in four main parts.[38] The first part returns to the distinction between direct and indirect taxes. The second part discusses the case of BTAs on taxes on inputs. The third part briefly describes GATT Panel decisions in relation to BTAs.[39] Finally, in the fourth part, the report reviews the European legal framework regarding BTAs, highlighting the main differences with the GATT provisions. Only the first two parts are analysed below. The contents of the last two parts of the report are discussed in Part III of this book. In each part, the report emphasises the specificities – or the absence of specificities – of BTAs in respect of environmental BTAs in comparison to BTAs made in respect of 'traditional' taxes, namely taxes that are primarily aimed at raising revenue.

At the GATT and WTO levels, various documents also touched upon the issue of 'BTA to environmental taxes or charges'. One of the first documents that directly relates to the topic is a note of 1994 entitled 'Border Tax Adjustment' and prepared at the request of the Group on Environmental Measures and International Trade, in particular, at the request of the Swedish representative.[40] This note returns to the findings of the GATT 1970 Working Party report, filling the conclusions of the report with the recent case law. The report makes very few references to environmental taxes. At the very end, however, the report analyses the case of taxes on inputs and concludes that the new developments of the Uruguay Round may 'allow for exemption, remission or deferral of taxes levied on the energy, fuel, and/or oil inputs "consumed in the production

---

[37] GATT, TRE/13, *supra* n. 36, 25–26, para. 136.

[38] See 1994 OECD Note on Environmental BTAs, *supra* n. 1.

[39] GATT, *US – Tuna (Mexico)*; GATT, *US – Tuna (EEC)*; GATT, *US – Tuna II (Mexico)*; GATT, *Japan – Alcoholic Beverages I*; WTO, *Japan – Alcoholic Beverages II*; GATT, *US – Malt Beverages*.

[40] See GATT, Group on Environmental Measures and International Trade, Border Tax Adjustment, 11 January 1994, TRE/W/20 (hereafter, 'GATT, TRE/W/20'); GATT, TRE/13, *supra* n. 36, 30, para. 156.

of" an exported product'.[41] Some years later, in 1997, a second note was issued by the Secretariat under the title 'Taxes and Charges for Environmental Purposes – Border Tax Adjustment' (hereafter, the 'WTO 1997 Note').[42] The title of the note may be misleading since the note does not directly address the topic of BTAs in respect of environmental taxes. Rather, it discusses – in three separate parts – the use of economic instruments to tackle environmental issues (from eco-taxes to subsidies and tradable emissions schemes), the trade effects of environmental taxes and charges and, finally, the issue of BTAs as examined by the Committee on Trade and Environment.[43]

2.2.1.4 Highlights

2.2.1.4.1 Definition of environmental BTAs The concept of 'environmental BTAs' is not mentioned in the OECD, GATT and WTO reports. As it discusses the relationship between BTAs and environmental taxes, the OECD report, however, provides for a definition of 'BTAs of environmental taxes'.[44] Demaret and Stewardson used this concept to describe the legal issues arising out of the use of BTAs in respect of environmental taxes.[45] Similarly, the 1994 OECD Note points out the peculiarities that would derive from BTAs made in respect of environmental taxes.[46]

2.2.1.4.2 Rationale of environmental BTAs In its introduction, the OECD report explains that environmental taxes – 'levied on a product or process' – 'can affect the competitiveness of the product which enters into international trade relative to competing products'.[47] The report explains that it is the reason why 'governments may wish to impose

---

[41] GATT, TRE/W/20, *supra* n. 40, 16, para. 34. See the same reference in 1994 OECD Note on Environmental BTAs, *supra* n. 1.

[42] WTO, Committee on Trade and Environment, Taxes and Charges for Environmental Purposes: Border Tax Adjustment, Note by the Secretariat, 2 May 1997, WT/CTE/W/47 (hereafter, '1997 WTO Note').

[43] WTO, Committee on Trade and Environment, Report (1996) of the Committee on Trade and Environment, 12 November 1996, WT/CTE/1 (hereafter, 'WTO, WT/CTE/1').

[44] See also WTO, WT/CTE/1, *supra* n. 43, paras. 49–54, referring to the concept of 'BTA to environmental taxes or charges'.

[45] Demaret & Stewardson, *supra* n. 32, 58.

[46] 1994 OECD Note on Environmental BTAs, *supra* n. 1, 3, para. 4 and 23, para. 88.

[47] *Ibid.*, 4, para. 6.

corresponding environmental taxes on imported products and also to remit environmental taxes on exported products'.[48] A similar idea is expressed in the 1997 WTO Note: BTAs in respect of environmental product taxes are considered to allow for trade neutrality between domestic and imported products. According to the WTO Secretariat, BTAs in respect of product taxes '... will ensure that exports do not fall below their pre-tax levels'.[49] The 1997 WTO Note also quotes an extract from the *Superfund* case where the Panel stated that GATT Article III:2, first sentence '... protects expectations on the competitive relationship between imported and domestic products'.[50]

In other words, the OECD and WTO reports seem to suggest that the rationale for BTAs in respect of environmental taxes is to neutralise the effects of environmental taxes on competitiveness. This rationale is based on the assumption that environmental taxes – either on products or on production processes – are shifted into products' prices and therefore have an impact on competitiveness. This rationale corresponds to the theory of absolute advantage described in Chapter 1.

In addition to this 'economic' rationale, the OECD report further elaborates on the rationale of traditional BTAs without any coherence, summing up a variety of objectives without explaining how these objectives relate to each other:

> In brief, border tax adjustments are intended to give effect to the destination principle, first stated by *Ricardo in 1824*. According to the destination principle, goods should be taxed only in the country of consumption. Under the opposite principle, the origin principle, goods would be taxed only in the country of production and there would be no border tax adjustments. BTAs made in accordance with the destination principle mean that: *while each country is able to implement its own domestic taxation regime*, products from all countries are able to compete in international trade on the same competitive terms. These products do not suffer from double taxation nor derive *an advantage from a more favourable domestic tax regime* (emphasis added).[51]

Three different theoretical foundations are mentioned in this short extract: (1) the reference to Ricardo can be linked to the theory of comparative advantage; (2) the possibility for each country to remain 'able to implement its own domestic taxation' refers to the argument related to 'countries' environmental and tax regulatory freedom'; and

---

48 *Ibid.*

49 GATT, TRE/W/13, *supra* n. 35, para. 19.

50 1997 WTO Note, *supra* n. 42, para. 42.

51 1994 OECD Note on Environmental BTAs, *supra* n. 1, 5, para. 9.

(3) the last argument (namely to avoid the situation whereby products do 'derive an advantage from a more favourable domestic tax regime') refers to a theory of free trade that distinguishes between legitimate and illegitimate absolute advantages (Section 2.3.3).

Finally, at the WTO level, within the Group on Environmental Measures and International Trade, some countries – especially Sweden – portrayed environmental BTAs as an efficient and transparent tool, which may eventually encourage third countries to adopt MEAs.[52]

2.2.1.4.3 Taxes eligible for adjustment: BTAs in respect of direct/indirect taxes and production/product taxes The 1994 OECD Note returns to the distinction between direct and indirect taxes and elaborates on the reasons behind this distinction, the related criticisms and the potential implications for environmental taxes, mainly summarising the findings of the OECD 1968 and GATT 1970 reports. Like the 1968 and 1970 reports, it also calls into question the 'theoretical assumption underlying the different treatment of direct and indirect taxes' and recalls the practical arguments that may have played a role in making the distinction. According to the report, '[i]n the context of international trade, it may be more feasible administratively to adjust taxes imposed on the consumer than to adjust those imposed on the producer'.[53]

The 1994 OECD Note makes an analogy between (1) direct taxes and 'environmental process taxes', and (2) indirect taxes and 'environmental product taxes'. The first are 'levied on production processes and facilities which pollute or degrade the environment, and include taxes on air emissions, waste disposal and water effluent' and the others are 'levied on products which may pollute or degrade the environment when they are used or consumed'.[54] Only 'environmental product taxes' would *a priori* be eligible for adjustment. The 1994 OECD Note points out that this limitation could be detrimental to the efficiency of environmental policies by encouraging countries to favour these taxes over 'environmental process taxes':

> In the environmental case, taxes on the sources of pollution (i.e. production or process taxes) are far more effective in discouraging the activity than taxes on the resulting products. It is far better to address the environmental problem at

---

[52] GATT, TRE/13, *supra* n. 36, 8, para. 43, 8. See also GATT, TRE/W/13, *supra* n. 35, 2, para. 8.

[53] 1994 OECD Note on Environmental BTAs, *supra* n. 1, 7, para. 21.

[54] *Ibid.*, 8, para. 22.

> the source, namely the plant or facility which is producing the pollution or the company which is harvesting resources in an unsustainable manner.[55]

The note nevertheless explains that the distinction may be justified based on practical considerations: '... the distinction between product and process is made partly for practical considerations. It is difficult, if not impossible to ascertain how an imported product has been produced or what share of production taxes it bears'.[56]

At the GATT/WTO level, a similar distinction is drawn between product and process taxes. A first indication of the assumption that only product taxes are eligible for adjustments appears in the 1971 note on 'Industrial Pollution Control and International Trade'.[57] The note suggests that a distinction should be made between (1) taxes on 'products considered to be pollutants', and (2) taxes 'for pollution control with regard to processes'.[58] This second category is divided into two other sub-categories: (2.1) process taxes designed to control how domestic and foreign products are 'actually produced by sub-standard processes' and (2.2) process taxes designed to control 'all goods the product of industries whose processes sometimes pollute, irrespective of how actually produced'.[59] The note disregards the first sub-category of process taxes (2.1) as an eligible option for BTAs: 'Differentiating between goods alike in their physical characteristics and use only on grounds of different costs of production would almost certainly contravene the most-favoured-nation principle, and would in addition offer insurmountable practical difficulties ...'.[60] In contrast, the second sub-category of process taxes (2.2) is deemed to '... be possible, and consistent with GATT'.[61]

In 1993 a note entitled 'Trade Effects of Environmental Measures' proposed a three-fold distinction between (1) 'product taxes and charges' (which are considered not to create border restrictions), (2) 'taxes and charges on components (including packaging and waste handling services)' – with varying trade effects – and (3) 'taxes and charges levied on

---

[55] 1994 OECD Note on Environmental BTAs, *supra* n. 1, 8, para. 25. The note seems to suggest that environmental production taxes are 'better' than environmental product taxes but does not explain why. This assumption is clearly questionable: are they 'better' or merely 'easier' to implement?

[56] 1994 OECD Note on Environmental BTAs, *supra* n. 1, 9, para. 27.

[57] GATT, L/3538, *supra* n. 25, 17.

[58] *Ibid.*

[59] *Ibid.*

[60] *Ibid.*

[61] *Ibid.*

the production process in order to reduce production pollution'.[62] According to the note, this last category (3) could lead to 'significant trade effects' if production taxes are levied on 'imported products as surrogate process tax'.[63] Similar trade effects would result from export rebates in respect of process taxes.[64] In 1997 the WTO Secretariat confirmed the distinction between product and production/process taxes, pointing out that 'article III:2 has been interpreted as regulating the treatment of products as opposed to regulating the behaviour of producers'.[65]

Even though many references in OECD and GATT/WTO documents support the assumption that BTAs should be limited to 'product taxes' (in contrast to 'process taxes'), the distinction between product and process taxes does not rely on a clear analytical basis (Part III).[66] First, as in the case of traditional BTAs where the economic assumptions surrounding the distinction between direct and indirect taxes have been called into question, the same questions arise as to the economic assumptions on the effects of process and product taxes. Second, the relevance of the categorisation of environmental taxes in process and product taxes can be questioned in light of the difficulty to clearly distinguish these two categories. One example – put forward by the representative of Brazil in a meeting of the Sub-Committee on Trade and Environment in September 1994 – is the case of a 'tax related to the recycled content of paper products'.[67] The Brazilian representative explains that this tax is an environmental *tax on a product*, related to the disposal of the product but which concerns the 'production behaviour (recycling paper)', which highlights that the distinction between process and product taxes may not be clear cut.[68] Third, GATT/WTO members have expressed contradictory views on the distinction between process and product taxes (as well as their economic impact). For example, in 1994, Malaysia – speaking on behalf of the Association of Southeast Asian Nations (ASEAN) group –

---

62 GATT, TRE/W/13, *supra* n. 35, 3–4, paras. 12–19.

63 *Ibid.*, 3, para. 18.

64 *Ibid.*, 4, para. 19.

65 1997 WTO Note, *supra* n. 42, para. 41.

66 See for example in WTO, Preparatory Committee, Preparatory Committee for the Sub-Committee on Trade and Environment, Report of the Meeting held on 15–16 September 1994, Note by the Secretariat, 10 October 1994, PC/SCTE/M/3, para. 50 (hereafter, 'WTO, PC/SCTE/M/3').

67 *Ibid.*, para. 29.

68 *Ibid.*

acknowledged that 'environmental taxes, whether imposed on the products or processes, had the potential to change the competitiveness of the product' but considered that 'BTA should be imposed only on products and not on production or process conditions'.[69]

2.2.1.4.4 Taxes eligible for adjustments: taxes on inputs The significant role of BTAs in respect of *taxes occultes* is explained by the absence of a clear-cut distinction between production and product taxes in the case of environmental taxes.[70] For example, a tax on highly polluting industries could also be framed as a tax on the products of these highly polluting industries (instead of imposing tax on steel industries, the tax could be imposed on steel). Many types of pollution can be framed either as a consequence of a production process or as a by-product of consumption. Production and consumption are two sides of the same coin. This is particularly true for environmental taxes on intermediate products.[71] These taxes on intermediate products can be analysed either as production taxes (considering that intermediate products are those needed by producers to produce final goods) or as product taxes (considering that these taxes are imposed on products).[72] Alternatively, these taxes may also be compared to taxes on 'auxiliary materials used in the production of other taxable goods' and therefore to *taxes occultes*. In other words, under the hypothesis that *taxes occultes* are deemed eligible for BTAs, a broad range of domestic environmental taxes would *de facto* be deemed eligible for BTAs. Consequently, *taxes occultes* play an extremely important role in the case of the environmental excise duty models as well as in the case of environmental taxes on producers (Chapter 4).

Both the 1994 OECD and 1997 WTO notes analysed the case of BTAs in respect of *taxes occultes*. The 1994 OECD Note analyses the case of taxes on inputs – which corresponds to the concept of *taxes occultes* – distinguishing between 'taxes on inputs physically incorporated in the product', 'taxes on energy inputs' and 'taxes on other process inputs or non-physically incorporated inputs'. The two first categories should be

---

69 *Ibid.*, para. 47.

70 On this topic see Demaret & Stewardson, *supra* n. 32, 58. See also Jennifer Hillman, 'Changing Climate for Carbon Taxes, Who's Afraid of the WTO?' (2013) German Marshall Fund of the United States, 6.

71 Demaret & Stewardson, *supra* n. 32, 18.

72 See, for example, OECD, The Political Economy of Environmentally Related Taxes (2006), 103.

eligible for adjustments while 'taxes on other process inputs or non-physically incorporated inputs' should not be eligible. The 1994 OECD Note also discusses the case of carbon taxes, which it defines as 'a special kind of environmental product tax normally applied on the carbon content of fuels'.[73] Hence, the note assimilates carbon taxes to 'product taxes'. This definition of carbon taxes as 'product taxes' seems to contradict the report finding that 'carbon taxes would most likely be considered taxes on inputs which are not "physically incorporated" as they would fall primarily on energy used as fuel'.[74] According to the report, 'Many countries have refrained from levying high levels of carbon taxes partly because of their inability to adjust these taxes at the border'.[75] In other words, the note indirectly supports the assumption that countries lose their free choice to adopt carbon taxes due to the impossibility of adjusting these taxes. Finally, the note recalls the practical arguments that may explain the distinction behind taxes on inputs 'physically incorporated' and taxes on other inputs: 'In the case of a tax on an input which is no longer present in the product … , it can be difficult to assess how much of the tax on the input is incorporated in each particular product'.[76]

The 1997 WTO Note also elaborates on the case of taxes on inputs incorporated or exhausted in the production process of imported or exported products based on the recent case law.[77] No consensus is, however, reached as to the specific case of BTAs in respect of these taxes on inputs and other process-related taxes. Three main positions may be distinguished. The first position argues that these taxes simply fall under the category of non-product taxes and are therefore ineligible for adjustments.[78] The second view considers that these taxes can be assimilated to *taxes occultes*, for which it remains unclear whether adjustments are possible or not.[79] The last and third opinion argues that

---

73 1994 OECD Note on Environmental BTAs, *supra* n. 1, 12, para. 39.

74 *Ibid.*, para. 40. Felicity Deane has also raised this question in Felicity Deane, *Emissions Trading and WTO Law. A Global Analysis* (Edward Elgar Publishing 2015), 188–190.

75 1994 OECD Note on Environmental BTAs, *supra* n. 1, 12, para. 40.

76 *Ibid.*, 12–13, para. 42. The report nuances this criticism ('However, in many instances it can be extremely difficult or impossible to trace a tax even on a physically-incorporated input (raw material or semi-finished product) into any particular final product').

77 1997 WTO Note, *supra* n. 42, paras. 66–76.

78 WTO, WT/CTE/1, *supra* n. 43, para. 52.

79 *Ibid.*

WTO rules related to traditional BTAs are unsuitable for dealing with environmental BTAs given the specificity of environmental taxes.[80]

2.2.1.4.5 Reception of the OECD and GATT reports At the OECD level, three main issues were considered to need further analysis: the exact impact on BTAs' provisions on environmental taxes; the economic rationale of BTAs; and the provisions on taxes on inputs, the case of carbon taxes and taxes on electricity.[81]

At the WTO level, some representatives raised the question as to whether BTAs provisions should be changed considering the new developments regarding environmental taxation. For example, the representative of Sweden stated as follows:

> BTA was generally allowed for indirect taxes or charges on products but not for environmental charges and taxes that had been levied on the production process. Since countries should be free to use a mixture of measures, the present system of BTA might unduly influence the formulation of environmental policies … . In the further process, the Sub-Committee should look at economic instruments that were not considered eligible for adjustment under present rules and see if and what changes to the GATT provisions were called for.[82]

The questions concerning the need to modify GATT/WTO law provisions often reflect arguments related to the need to preserve countries' (environmental) regulatory freedom. These arguments can be linked with one of the traditional rationales behind BTAs, according to which BTAs are necessary to preserve countries' tax sovereignty. From this perspective, it could be argued that GATT provisions do not need to be modified but simply need to be reinterpreted in light of the evolution of the (economic) assumptions underlying BTAs' provisions, allowing for the adoption of

---

80 *Ibid.*

81 OECD, Environmental Policy Committee and Committee on Fiscal Affairs. Joint session on taxation and environment, Summary Record of the Second Session 16–17 May 1994, 3 June 1994, COM/ENV/EPOC/DAFFE/CFA/M(94)66. See also OECD, Joint Session of Trade and Environment Experts. Summary Record of the meeting held on 23 and 24 June 1994, 29 September 1994, COM/ENV/TD/M(94)84.

82 WTO, PC/SCTE/M/3, *supra* n. 66, para. 68 (Swedish representative). See also para. 85 of the same document (Austrian representative).

BTAs in respect of environmental taxes, regardless of the nature of such taxes (product or production taxes).[83]

2.2.1.5 Further international developments

The topic of environmental BTAs has remained on the OECD and WTO agendas until now. At the OECD level, various reports have analysed the topic in further detail. In 1996 the OECD issued a report providing for 'implementation strategies for environmental taxes', where the issue of BTAs was considered under the chapter on the 'international implications of environmental taxes'.[84] Overall, the report considers that BTAs are only effective in case of 'an environmental tax aimed at reducing emissions that arise out of consumption patterns, but not emissions that arise out of domestic production processes'.[85] A similar report was issued in 2006 entitled 'The Political Economy of Environmentally Related Taxes'.[86] Moreover, various OECD documents have discussed the case of BTAs in the framework of the climate debate, either from a legal perspective or from an economic perspective.[87] Economic studies usually focus on one specific sector and aim at determining whether the adoption of border measures can help to reduce loss of competitiveness related to the unilateral implementation of environmental policies as well as the risk of carbon leakage.[88] Finally, many OECD documents include references to BTAs, describing them as complementary measures to national

---

83 See also Charnovitz's views on the initial interpretation of GATT provisions surrounding BTAs (Steve Charnovitz, 'GATT and the Environment: Examining the Issues' (1992) 4(3) International Environmental Affairs 203–223).

84 OECD, Implementation Strategies for Environmental Taxes (1996).

85 *Ibid.*, 39, box 3.1.

86 OECD, The Political Economy of Environmentally Related Taxes (2006).

87 OECD, Economic/fiscal instruments: taxation (i.e. carbon/energy), Annex I Expert Group on the UNFCCC (1997) Working Paper No. 4, OCDE/GD(97)188, 83; OECD, Economic/Fiscal Instruments: Competitiveness Issues related to carbon/energy taxation, Annex I Expert Group on the United Nations Framework Convention on Climate Change (1997) Working Paper No. 14, OCDE/GD(97)190; OECD, Working Party on Global and Structural Policies, Linkages between Environmental Policy and Competitiveness, 13 August 2009, ENV/EPOC/GSP(2008)14/FINAL (hereafter, 'OECD, ENV/EPOC/GSP(2008)14/FINAL'); OECD, Directorate for Financial and Enterprise Affairs, Competition Committee, Emission Permits and Competition, DAF/COM(2010)35; OECD, Working Party on Global and Structural Policies, Update on recent Modelling Work in the Context of Green Growth, 18–20 May 2010, ENV/EPOC/GST(2010)7.

88 OECD, Directorate for Science, Technology and Industry, Steel Committee, Steel and the Environment, 29 September 1997, DSTI/SI/SC(97)45; OECD,

environmental taxes. Overall, the assessment of BTAs lacks coherence: while some OECD documents suggest that countries should consider BTAs as effective policy options, some other documents suggest the opposite, based on the negative economic impact that BTAs may have.[89]

Joint Meetings of Tax and Environmental Experts, Draft terms-of-Reference for a Case Study of Potential Impacts for the Steel Sector of Increased Use of Environmentally Related Taxes in OECD Member Countries, Paris, 16 November 2001, COM/ENV/EPOC/DAFFE/CFA(2001)93; OECD, 8th Joint Meeting of Tax and Environment Experts, The Competitiveness Impact of CO_2 Emissions Reduction in the Cement Sector, 19 November 2004, COM/ENV/EPOC/CTPA/CFA(2004)68/FINAL; Peter Wooders, 'Border Carbon Adjustments and Free Allowances in the Steel Sector', OECD Steel Committee meeting, 6–7 May 2010, DSTI/SU/SC(2010)8; John Newman, 'Climate Change Policy and Iron and Steel Industry', OECD Steel Committee (2010) DSTI/SU(2010)17.

[89] See OECD, Environmental Directorate, Directorate for Financial, Fiscal and Enterprise Affairs, Greening Tax Mixes in OECD Countries: A Preliminary Assessment, COM/ENV/EPOC/DAFFE/CFA(99)112/final, 1999, 14–15; OECD, National Climate Policies and the Kyoto Protocol (1999) OECD Publishing, 50; OECD, Environmental Directorate, Directorate for Financial, Fiscal and Enterprises Affairs, Implementing Environmental Fiscal Reform: Income Distribution and Sectoral Competitiveness Issues, Proceedings of a Conference held in Berlin, Germany, 27 June 2002, COM/ENV/EPOC/DAFFE/CFA(2002)76/FINAL; OECD, Joint Working Party on Trade and Environment, OECD Activities relating to subsidies and the environment, Paris, 1–2 July 2002, COM/ENV/TD(2002)58; OECD, Draft Synthesis of recent work of joint meetings of tax and environment experts, by the Secretariat, 31 November 2003, COM/ENV/EPOC/DAFFE/CFA(2003)74; OECD, Council, Sustainable Development – defining the way forward, Note by the Secretary-General, 12 February 2004, C(2004)13; OECD, OECD's Gurria welcomes Stern Review into consequences of climate change, Paris, 3 November 2006, PAC/COM/NEWS(2006)19; Michel Poitier & Cristina Tébar Less, Joint Working Party on Trade and Environment, 'Trade and Environment at the OECD: Key Issues since 1991', Working Paper on Trade and Environment, No. 2008-01, COM/TAD/ENV/JWPTE(2007)38/FINAL, 17. *Contra:* OECD, General Secretariat, Round Table on Sustainable Development, Chair's Summary, 23rd meeting of the Round Table on Sustainable Development, Competitiveness, Leakage, and Border Adjustment: Climate Policy Distractions?, 22–23 July 2009, Singapore, SG/SD/RT(2009)4; John Stephenson & Simon Upton, 'Competitiveness, Leakage, and Border Adjustment: Climate Policy Distractions?', Round Table on Sustainable Development, 23–23 July 2009, SG/SD/RT(2009)3; OECD, Meeting of the Council at Ministerial Level, 24–25 June 2009, Progress Report on Climate Change, C/MIN(2009)10; OECD, Environment Working Paper No. 17, Differentiated Intellectual Property Regimes for Environmental and Climate Technologies, ENV/WKP(2010)3; OECD, Meeting of the Council at Ministerial Level, 24–25 June 2009, Progress Report on OECD's Work on Policy Coherence for Development, C/MIN(2009)1615;

At the WTO level, the most important development is a report issued in 2009 by the WTO Secretariat in collaboration with the United Nations Environment Programme (UNEP).[90] The report discusses the interactions between trade and climate change. Border measures are analysed as one of the possible national policy options based on a price and market mechanism used to internalise the environmental costs of greenhouse gas (GHG) emissions.[91] The report first recalls the rationale for border measures, considering that they are aimed at reducing the double risk related to the unilateral implementation of carbon policies (i.e. the risk of competitiveness as well as the risk of carbon leakage).[92] Second, the report sums up the main characteristics of border measures, distinguishing between 'border tax adjustments to carbon taxes or energy taxes', 'border adjustments in relation to an emission trading scheme', and 'other border measures' (such as countervailing duties and anti-dumping subsidies).[93] Finally, the report analyses the legal and practical challenges faced by border measures.[94] The report illustrates that the idea of environmental BTAs is clearly considered as a policy option in the framework of the climate debate. Two years later, in 2011, a Communication by Singapore brought the issue of BTAs in relation to climate change to the floor one more time, requiring the WTO Secretariat to provide for a note on 'carbon-related BTAs'.[95] The reactions of other WTO members have been diverse, some countries supporting Singapore's suggestion, others considering the request unnecessary since the UNEP/WTO had already provided sufficient analysis on the topic.[96]

OECD, Taxation, Innovation and the Environment (2010); OECD, Southeast Asian Economic Outlook (2011).

[90] WTO/UNEP Report, Trade and Climate Change (2009).

[91] *Ibid.*, 87 et al.

[92] *Ibid.*, 98–100.

[93] *Ibid.*, 100–101.

[94] *Ibid.*, 101–110.

[95] WTO, Committee on Trade and Environment, Communication from Singapore. Promoting Mutual, Supportiveness Between Trade and Climate Change Mitigation Actions: Carbon-Related Border Tax Adjustments, 30 March 2011, WT/CTE/W/248.

[96] WTO, Report of the Committee on Trade and Environment, 21 November 2011, WT/CTE/18; WTO, Committee on Trade and Environment, Report of the Meeting held on 6 July 2011, Note by the Secretariat, 6 September 2011, WT/CTE/M/52. The main countries in favour of the proposal were New Zealand, Australia, Canada, Barbados, Switzerland, European Union, Malaysia. The countries against the proposal were China, Kingdom of Saudi Arabia, India, Argentina, Brazil, South Africa, Indonesia.

In addition to the OECD and the WTO, other international organisations have touched upon the issue of environmental BTAs. For example, carbon-related BTAs have also been discussed during United Nations Climate Conferences. Some members of the Group of developing countries indeed proposed to adopt a decision to forbid developed countries from adopting BTAs against developing countries.[97] Similarly, the United Nations Conference on Trade and Development (UNCTAD) has analysed – though not in detail – the issue of environmental BTAs. In UNCTAD documents BTAs are usually described as 'protectionist measures', which may affect trade with developing countries.[98]

---

[97] UNFCCC, Submission by the Bolivarian Republic of Venezuela for a decision of the COP on item 3.2.6 on Economic and Social Consequences of Response Measures, Decision to further implement Chapter III. E of Decision 1. CP/16. See also UNFCCC, Ad Hoc Working Group on Long-term Cooperative Action under the Convention, Submission from India on behalf of Argentina, China, African Group, Organization of Petroleum Exporting Countries (OPEC), Arab Group, Thailand, Malaysia, Uruguay and Philippines on economic and social consequences of response measures, 1 October 2011, FCCC/AWGLCA/2011/CRP.14; UNFCCC, Ad Hoc Working Group on Long-term Cooperative Action under the Convention, Fourteenth session, part three, Panama City, 1–7 October 2011, Agenda item 3.2.6 'Economic and social consequences of response measures', Submission by India, Argentina, China, Iran, The Arab Group and OPEC Member States on Economic and Social Consequences of Response Measures, Decision to further implement paragraphs 88, 89, 90 and 93 of 1/CP.16, FCCC/AWGLCA/2011/CRP.29; UNFCCC, Written input by Saudi Arabia on behalf of India, China, Iran, Venezuela, Argentina and The Arab Group under LCA agenda item 3.2.6, submitted on 7 December 2011.

[98] See, for example, UNCTAD, Report of the Topical Seminar on Environment, Competitiveness and Trade: a development perspective, Helsinki, 9th session of the UNCTAD, January 1996, paras. 41–42; UNCTAD, Trade and Development Board, Draft report of the Trade and Development Board on its fifty-fifth session, Geneva, 15–26 September 2008, TD/B/55/L2/Add2, 2; UNCTAD, Trade and Development Board, Evolution of the international trading system and of international trade from a development perspective: The impact of the crisis-mitigation measures and prospects for recovery, Note by the UNCTAD Secretariat, Geneva, 57th Session, 15–28 September 2010, TDB/57/3, 20; UNCTAD, The interface between trade and climate change policies and the role of UNCTAD, Note by the UNCTAD Secretariat, Accra, 12th session, 20–25 April 2008, TD(XII)/BP/2, 3; UNCTAD, Report of the Ad Hoc Expert Meeting on the Green Economy: Trade and Sustainable Development Implications, Geneva, 8–10 November 2011, UNCTAD/DITC/TED/2011/8, 8.

2.2.2 National and Regional Views on Environmental BTAs

The US and the EU as well as other countries or regions have been proactive in proposing to adopt environmental BTAs. This section provides an overview of the main political initiatives and proposals in relation to environmental BTAs.[99]

2.2.2.1 US views on environmental BTAs

In the framework of GATT and WTO negotiations, the US has not clearly expressed its opinion on the case of environmental BTAs.[100] However, the US has – on at least two occasions – taken a favourable position in relation to environmentally related BTAs.[101]

A first example is the adoption of excise taxes on certain chemicals and certain imported substances.[102] These taxes – very often mentioned in studies on environmental BTAs – were adopted in 1986 in order to finance a federal trust fund (called the 'Superfund') aimed at cleaning hazardous waste sites.[103] The tax was designed with adjustments for imported and exported chemicals.[104] Moreover, BTAs were made not only in respect of imported (or exported) chemicals identical to those which were taxed domestically, but also in respect of certain imported substances for which the chemicals taxed at the domestic level had been

---

[99] This section focuses on the EU and the US, though other countries have discussed and proposed environmental BTAs (see OECD, Environmentally Related Taxes in OECD Countries. Issues and Strategies (2001), 107).

[100] See WTO, PC/SCTE/M/3, *supra* n. 66, paras. 101–105.

[101] These two examples are referred to in OECD, Joint Meeting of tax and environmental experts, The Political Economy of Environmentally Related Taxes, 18 November 2005, COM/ENV/EPOC/CTPA/CFA(2005)42 as 'case studies of process-based BTA mechanisms in environmental excise legislation'. See also OECD, The Political Economy of Environmentally Related Taxes (2006), 100–104.

[102] The legal framework of these two taxes is to be found in Title 26 (internal revenue code of United States Code), Subtitle D (miscellaneous excise taxes), chapter 38 (environmental taxes), subchapters B & C, sections 4661–4662 and 4671–4672: 26 US CODE §§4661–4662 (tax on certain chemicals) and §§4671–4672 (tax on certain imported substances). See Anuschka Bakker, *Tax and the Environment: A World of Possibilities* (IBFD 2009), 483.

[103] US Superfund Amendments and Reauthorization Act of 1986. See also 26 US CODE §9507. The taxes expired in 1995: 26 US CODE §4611(e)(1) and §4661(c).

[104] For imports, see 26 US CODE §4661(a). For exports, see §4662(e).

used in the manufacturing or production process.[105] In a draft OECD report of 2005, and later in a 2006 OECD Report on 'The Political Economy of Environmentally Related Taxes', the process-based character of BTAs' Superfund tax on certain imported substances was put forward:

> The significance of the BTA mechanism in the Superfund Tax was that the tax was calculated by reference to the amount of chemicals *used in the manufacturing process*; it was not necessary for all of the atoms contained in the taxable chemical to be physically incorporated into the final substance, and the tax rate was not adjusted if only a portion of the original chemicals were actually present at the end. Thus it was a true process-based BTA.[106]

After its adoption, the EU, Mexico and Canada rapidly challenged the tax, considering it contrary to the GATT. The GATT Panel, however, did not find the tax incompatible with GATT Article III:2, first sentence (see Part III).[107]

A second example is the excise tax on ozone-depleting chemicals (ODC tax), which was enacted in 1989.[108] The tax has a dual purpose. On the one hand, the tax is aimed at reducing ODC to protect the ozone layer in accordance with the provisions of the Montreal Protocol.[109] On the other hand, the objective is simply to raise revenue.[110] The tax is imposed on ODC sold or used by manufacturers and producers as well as on importers of any ODC listed in the Internal Revenue Code, which can be assimilated to a BTA on imports.[111] Moreover, the tax is imposed on

---

105 For imports, see 26 US CODE §4671(a) and (b)(1). For BTAs on exports, see 26 US CODE §4662(e)(2)(A)(i), (ii).

106 OECD, Joint Meeting of tax and environmental experts, The Political Economy of Environmentally Related Taxes, 18 November 2005, COM/ENV/EPOC/CTPA/CFA(2005)42, para. 315. OECD, The Political Economy of Environmentally Related Taxes (2006), 101.

107 GATT, Panel Report, United States – Taxes on Petroleum and Certain Imported Substances, 5 June 1987, L/6175, 34S/136 (*US – Superfund*).

108 US Congress, Omnibus Budget Reconciliation Act of 1989, P.L. 101-239, 19 December 1989.

109 See Montreal Protocol on Substances that Deplete the Ozone Layer, 16 September 1987.

110 J. Andrew Hoerner, 'Taxing Pollution', in: Elizabeth Cook & Reynaldo Forte (eds.), *Ozone Protection in the United States: Elements of Success* (World Resources Institute 1996), 42.

111 For imports, see 26 US Code §4681(a)(1); §4682(a)(2) & Tres. Reg. §52.4681-1; Tres. Reg. §52.4682-1. See also 26 US Code §4682(h): 'floor stock taxes' imposed on 'any person (other than the manufacturer, producer, or importer thereof) for sale or for use in further manufacture').

'any imported taxable product sold or used by the importer thereof'.[112] Finally, exports of such chemicals may be exempted under strict conditions and in limited quantity (considering the amount of ODC that was exported in 1986).[113]

In addition to these examples, various proposals have been put forward in the US to adopt climate- or energy-related policies including provisions for BTAs. One of the first of these proposals was the British thermal unit (BTU) energy tax proposed by former President Clinton in 1993.[114] The main idea was to adopt an excise tax on fossil fuels, the tax rate of which would be based on the amount of BTU of each fuel, with an additional tax on oil.[115] The proposal also intended to taxing 'hydro- and nuclear-generated electricity'.[116] The proposal included BTAs on

---

[112] 26 US CODE §4681(a)(2); 26 US CODE §4682(c)(1). See also the 'imported products table' in Tres. Reg. 524682-3 ('imported taxable products). See also the Tax Audit Techniques Guide of the IRS, published in 2007, on the Ozone Depleting Chemicals (ODC) Excise, available at <https://www.irs.gov/Businesses/Small-Businesses-&-Self-Employed/Ozone-Depleting-Chemicals-ODC-Excise-Tax-Audit-Techniques-Guide#Chapter_03> (accessed 20 November 2015). In this guide, the tax on imported taxable substances is justified to tackle 'imported items, especially items imported from developing countries, [which] have a high potential of having ODCs used in their manufacturing process'.

[113] For exports, see 26 US CODE §4682(d)(3) & Tres. Reg. §52.4682-5. No refund is provided in the hypothesis where ODC chemicals have been used 'as a material in the manufacture or production' of the exported goods (see 26 US CODE §4682(d)(3)(A), which refers to §4662(e) (excluding §4662(e)(2)(A)(ii)(II)). See also Duncan Brack, Michael Grubb & Windram Craig, *International Trade and Climate Change Policies* (Earthscan 2000), 79.

[114] See US Joint Committee on Taxation, Summary of the President's Revenue Proposals, Washington, 8 March 1993, 61. See US, H.R. 2141, To provide for budget reconciliation with respect to revenue and spending matters within the jurisdiction of the Committee on Ways and Means for fiscal year 1994 and subsequent fiscal years, 103rd Congress, 18 May 1993 (subtitle B, Part IV). See also US, H.R. 4805, To amend the Internal Revenue Code of 1986 to reduce emissions of carbon dioxide by imposing a tax on certain fuels based on their carbon content, 101st Congress, 10 May 1990; US, H.R. 1086, To amend the Internal Revenue Code of 1986 to reduce emissions of carbon dioxide by imposing a tax on certain fuels based on their carbon content, 102nd Congress, 21 February 1991. See Amy C. Christian, 'Designing a Carbon Tax: The Introduction of the Carbon-Burned Tax (CBT)' (1991–1992) 10 UCLA Journal of Environmental Law and Policy 221, 276.

[115] US Joint Committee on Taxation, Summary of the President's Revenue Proposals, Washington, 8 March 1993, 61. US, H.R. 2141, subtitle B, Part IV.

[116] *Ibid.* US, H.R. 2141, subtitle B, Part IV, §4446.

imported fuels and on imported electricity.[117] The tax on imported fuels was to be calculated 'at a rate equal to the average tax imposed on equivalent domestic products' while the tax on imported electricity was to be imposed 'at a rate equal to the national average of tax embedded in electricity generated from fossil fuel'.[118] Additional adjustments on imported manufactured goods, which were considered to be 'energy intensive' (because at least 2 per cent of their value was made of direct energy input), were also considered.[119] The 'tax on high-energy products' was aimed at mitigating the potential loss of competitiveness for US manufacturers resulting from the 'increased energy cost embedded in manufactured goods'.[120] The tax was to be based on the presumed energy consumption, by reference to the 'predominant method used in the United States for like products, and assuming the same direct energy inputs as for such domestically produced like products'.[121] The BTU tax was finally not adopted for various – mainly economic and political – reasons.[122]

Following the BTU proposals, many other proposals have been introduced, usually in the framework of the climate debate, for example the

---

[117] US Joint Committee on Taxation, Summary of the President's Revenue Proposals, Washington, 8 March 1993, 61.

[118] *Ibid.* See however US, H.R. 2141, subtitle B, Part IV, §4446 (d), (3) (C).

[119] US Joint Committee on Taxation, Summary of the President's Revenue Proposals, Washington, 8 March 1993, 61; Janet E. Milne, 'Carbon Taxes in the United States: The Context for the Future' (2008–2009) 10 Vermont Journal of Environmental Law 1, 12. See also US, Hearings before the Committee on Finance, 'Administration's Energy Tax Proposals', 103rd Congress, 1st Session, 20 & 22 April 1993, Serial 103-215; US, Committee on the Budget, House of Representatives, Report to accompany recommendations from the Committee on Ways and Means, D. Energy and Motor Fuels Tax Provisions, 103rd Congress, 1st Session Serial 103-111, 729; OECD, Trade and Environment: Processes and Production Methods (1994) OECD Documents, 94; OECD, OCDE/GD(97)18, *supra* n. 87, 84.

[120] See US, Testimony of Victor G. Beghini, American Petroleum Institute, in Hearings before the Committee on Ways and Means, House of Representatives, 103rd Congress, 1993, para. 754, available at <http://archive.org/stream/presidentclinton02unit/presidentclinton02unit_djvu.txt> (accessed 20 November 2015).

[121] US, Committee on the Budget, House of Representatives, Report to accompany recommendations from the Committee on Ways and Means, D. Energy and Motor Fuels Tax Provisions, 103rd Congress, 1st Session, Serial 103-111, 747. See also OECD, Trade and Environment: Processes and Production Methods (1994), 94; US, H.R. 2141, subtitle B, Part V, § 4457.

[122] Milne, *supra* n. 119, 11.

famous Lieberman-Warner Climate Security Act introduced in 2008 (110th Congress) and the Waxman-Markey Bill introduced in the 111th Congress (2009–2010).[123] In their book on *Global Warming and the World Trading System*, Hufbauer, Charnovitz and Kim present a clear overview of the main Bills related to climate action that were introduced in the 110th Congress (2007–2009), highlighting which of these Bills contain competitiveness provisions.[124] Some of the listed Bills clearly include a mechanism that can be assimilated to BTAs. The two most obvious examples are the Bills entitled Save Our Climate Act of 2007 (H.R. 2069) and America's Energy Security Trust Fund Act (H.R. 3416), which both propose to amend the Internal Revenue Code of 1986 to impose a tax on the carbon content of certain fuels.[125] These taxes were supposed to be designed in accordance with the destination principle: imports of fuels being taxed while exports being exempted. In contrast to the BTU proposal, the two Bills did not, however, include any adjustments for energy-intensive products.

Other examples include Bills that propose to amend the Internal Revenue Code to create a federal emission permit system, including an adjustment mechanism requiring importers of carbon-intensive goods to pay a 'greenhouse gas emission permit equivalency fee'.[126]

2.2.2.2 The EU's views on environmental BTAs

In the framework of WTO negotiations, the EU's position on environmental BTAs has been primarily negative. The EU seems to have

---

[123] US, S. 3036, Lieberman-Warner Climate Security Act of 2008, 110th Congress, 20 May 2008, spec. title VI; US, H.R. 2454, American Clean Energy and Security Act of 2009, 111th Congress, 26 June 2009, spec. section 767 & section 768.

[124] Gary Clyde Hufbauer, Steve Charnovitz & Jisun Kim, *Global Warming and the World Trading System* (Peterson Institute for International Economics 2009), 11–29.

[125] US, H.R. 2069, Save Our Climate Act of 2007, 110th Congress, 26 April 2007; US, H.R. 3416, America's Energy Security Trust Fund Act of 2007, 110th Congress, 3 August 2007. See also, in the 111th and 112th Congress, US, H.R. 594, Save our Climate Act of 2009, 111th Congress, 15 January 2009; US, H.R. 1337, America's Energy Security Trust Fund Act of 2009, 111th Congress, 5 March 2009; US, H.R. 3242, Save Our Climate Act, 112th Congress, 24 October 2011. See also US, H.R. 2202, Tax Pollution, Not Profits Act of 2015, 114th Congress, 1 May 2015.

[126] US, H.R. 6338, Managed Carbon Price Act of 2012, 112th Congress, 2 August 2012. See also, US, S. 332, Climate Protection Act of 2013, 113th Congress, 14 February 2013.

considered that BTAs in respect of environmental taxes are to be distinguished from 'traditional' BTAs. The EU's attitude to environmentally related BTAs suggests that environmental BTAs could be subject to additional conditions in comparison to traditional BTAs.

Basically, the EU seems to divide environmental BTAs into two categories: BTAs made in respect of environmental taxes aimed at combating 'global' environmental issues and BTAs made in respect of environmental taxes aimed at combating 'local' environmental damage. The EU seems to consider that only the first BTAs are eligible for adjustments. This reasoning appears in the arguments of the EU in the *Superfund* case. The EU indeed claimed that the US tax on certain imported chemicals violated the polluter-pays principle since the tax revenue was aimed at mitigating local environmental damage through the establishment of a National Fund.[127]

In contrast to the US, the EU has not adopted any tax schemes including environmental BTAs at the EU level. The issue of environmental BTAs has, however, been widely discussed in relation to EU climate mitigation measures. In its first proposal for a Council Directive introducing a tax on carbon dioxide emissions and energy, the European Commission recognised that the use of tax instruments may lead to competitiveness problems but considered that BTAs may not be adopted in respect of taxes applied at extraction or manufacture.[128] In other words, the EU seemed to reject the legal option of BTAs to solve the competitiveness problems that European enterprises may face due to the adoption of a carbon/energy tax. Instead, the EU Commission proposed

---

[127] WTO, PC/SCTE/M/3, *supra* n. 66, para. 98. See the arguments of the EU in the GATT *Superfund* case: GATT, Panel Report, *US – Superfund.* See also WTO, Group on Environmental Measures and International Trade, Report of the Meeting held on 19 November 1992, Note by the Secretariat, January 1993, TRE/8, para. 7.

[128] Commission of the European Communities, Proposal for a Council Directive Introducing a Tax on Carbon Dioxide Emissions and Energy, 30 June 1992, Brussels, COM(92)226 final, 4. See also the amendments proposed in Commission of the European Communities, Amended proposal for a Council Directive introducing a tax on carbon dioxide emissions and energy, 10 May 1995, Brussels, COM(95)172 final. See also Kurt Deketelaere, 'European Environmental Tax Law and Policy: Greenspeak!' (2000) 123 Water, Air, and Soil Pollution 361, 372–373; Christian Pitschas, 'GATT/WTO Rules for Border Tax Adjustment and the Proposed European Directive Introducing a Tax on Carbon Dioxide Emissions and Energy' (1995) 24 Georgia Journal of International and Comparative Law 479–500, 479.

to protect the competitiveness of energy-intensive enterprises through the granting of graduated tax reductions and conditional exemptions.[129]

The proposal for a carbon/energy tax was never adopted at the EU level. In 2001 the Commission proposed another type of economic instrument to tackle climate change: a greenhouse gas emission-trading system.[130] The emission-trading scheme is *a priori* to be distinguished from a tax.[131] Questions arose, however, as to whether adjustments should be made to the scheme to protect EU energy-intensive industries. Though no proposals were initially made to adopt adjustment mechanisms, amendments in 2009 introduced new language into the Directive, which could allow for future adjustments. The 25th recital of the 2009 Directive states as follows:

> an effective carbon equalisation system could be introduced with a view to putting installations from the Community which are at significant risk of carbon leakage and those from third countries on a comparable footing. Such a system could apply requirements to importers that would be no less favourable than those applicable to installations within the Community, for example by requiring the surrender of allowances.[132]

---

[129] Commission of the European Communities, Proposal for a Council Directive Introducing a Tax on Carbon Dioxide Emissions and Energy, 30 June 1992, Brussels, COM(92)226 final, 5–6, 13–16 and Art. 10 of the proposal. The same proposals were made in Commission of the European Communities, Proposal for a Council Directive restructuring the Community framework for the taxation of energy products, 12 March 1997, Brussels, COM(97)30 final, 97/0111(CNS) (see ‘Measures to assist firms’, 7).

[130] Commission of the European Communities, Proposal for a Directive of the European Parliament and of the Council establishing a scheme for greenhouse gas emission allowance trading within the Community and amending Council Directive 96/61/EC, 26 March 2002, Brussels, COM(2001)581 final. See also Directive 2003/87/EC of the European Parliament and of the Council of 13 October 2003 establishing a scheme for greenhouse gas emission allowance trading within the Community and amending Council Directive 96/61/EC (text with EEA relevance), 25 October 2003, OJ L275.

[131] See ECJ, *The Air Transport Association of America and Others*, 21 December 2011, Case C-366/10, Opinion of Advocate General Kokott, 6 October 2011, paras. 213–235. See also Felicity Deane, ‘The Border Adjustments of the Australian Clean Energy Package’ (2014) 17 International Trade and Business Law Review 66, 98–99.

[132] Directive 2009/29/EC of the European Parliament and of the Council of 23 April 2009 amending Directive 2003/87/EC so as to improve and extend the greenhouse gas emission allowance trading scheme of the Community, 5 June 2009, OJ L140. The possibility for including importers in the scheme is further repeated in the new Art. 10b, paragraph 1(b) of the 2009 Directive. A similar

In addition to the idea that importers should surrender allowances, the carbon equalisation system could also be designed as a tax. According to Louise van Schaik, 'a carbon equalisation mechanism would mean import charges on products of industry sectors covered within the EU by the ETS'.[133] Similarly, Dhar and Das consider that a tax could be imposed on importers to compensate for the cost of the ETS borne by EU installations.[134] Proposals in France also indicate that the carbon equalisation system could take the form of BTAs, though the adoption of taxes in respect of a quota system such as the EU ETS is deemed complex.[135] In 2009 the Belgian High Council of Finance advocated in favour of EU environmental tax measures, eventually accompanied by BTAs.[136]

The EU's call for the introduction of a carbon equalisation system may be understood as a threat to other countries. Indeed, the EU clearly links the potential introduction of equalisation measures to the 'outcome of the

---

position was also expressed earlier by the European Parliament on 17 December 2008 in the framework of the Climate and Energy package (see European Parliament, Position adopted at first reading on 17 December 2008 with a view to the adoption of Directive 2009/.../EC of the European Parliament and of the Council amending Directive 2003/87/EC so as to improve and extend the greenhouse gas emission allowance trading system of the Community).

[133] Louise G. van Schaik, *EU Effectiveness and Unity in Multilateral Negotiations. More Than the Sum of Its Parts?* (Palgrave Macmillan 2013), 131. See also WTO/UNEP Report, Trade and Climate Change (2009), 100–101.

[134] Biswajit Dhar & Kasturi Das, 'The European Union's Proposed Carbon Equalization System: Can It Be WTO Compatible?' (2009), 156. Research and Information System for Developing Countries, 12. See also Biswajit Dhar, 'The European Union's Proposed Carbon Equalisation System: Some Implications for India's Exports' (2014) 191 Research and Information System for Developing Countries, 17–18.

[135] France, Sénat, Rapport d'information fait au nom de la commission des finances (1) par le groupe de travail (2) sur la fiscalité environnementale, sur l'instauration d'une contribution 'climat-énergie', le fonctionnement et la régulation des marchés de quotas de CO_2, session extraordinaire de 2008–2009, n°543, spéc. page 121; France, Sénat, Rapport fait au nom de la commission de l'économie, du développement durable et de l'aménagement du territoire (1), comportant le texte de la commission, sur la proposition de résolution européenne de Mme Fabienne Keller, présentée au nom de la commission des affaires européennes en application de l'article 73 quater du Règlement sur le marché des quotas de CO_2 et le mécanisme d'inclusion carbone aux frontières, par M. Jean Bizet, session ordinaire de 2009–2010, N°129, 28.

[136] Belgium, Conseil Supérieur des Finances, Section Fiscalité et Parafiscalité, La Politique Fiscale et l'environnement, September 2009, 31.

international negotiations'.[137] In other words, equalisation measures, including BTAs, are considered a second-best option in light of the absence of action of the international community. Here, again, this approach shows that the EU distinguishes environmental border measures from traditional BTAs: in contrast to the EU's approach on environmental border measures, traditional BTAs are not a 'second best option'. Traditional BTAs are required – as such – to guarantee that trade takes place following Ricardo's theory of comparative advantage or the theory of absolute advantage. Traditional BTAs are not implemented based on how third countries' tax systems are designed. In contrast, at the EU level, environmental border measures would not only be aimed at guaranteeing that free trade takes place in accordance with the theory of comparative or absolute advantage but also at encouraging other countries to pursue environmental goals.[138] This attitude of the EU towards environmental border measures seems at odds with the opinion that the EU expressed on the topic in the framework of WTO negotiations. For example, in 1992, the EU rejected the use of trade measures 'based on the need to force countries to sign an agreement or to punish "free-rider" behaviour' in the framework of GATT discussions on trade provisions in multilateral agreements.[139]

In recent years the EU has nevertheless made clear that it could adopt measures in order to curtail the effects of free-riders, such as, for example, with the inclusion of the aviation sector in the EU ETS. In 2009, in light of the absence of action at the level of the International Civil Aviation Organisation (ICAO), the EU decided to include the aviation sector in the EU ETS without limiting this inclusion to flights taking place within the EU but incorporating all 'flights which depart from or arrive in an aerodrome situated in the territory of a Member State to which the Treaty applies'.[140] The broad scope of the Directive

[137] See recitals 24 and 25 of Directive 2009/29/EC. See, however, Opinion of the European Economic and Social Committee on the Market-based instruments towards a resource efficient and low carbon economy in the EU (own-initiative opinion), 16 July 2014, OJ C226/1, point 3.5.

[138] See also EU, Second Report of the High Level Group on Competitiveness, Energy and the Environment, Contributing to an Integrated approach on competitiveness, energy and environment policies, 30 October 2006.

[139] GATT, Group on Environmental Measures and International Trade, The GATT and the Trade Provisions of Multilateral Environmental Agreements, Submission from the European Community, 17 November 1992, TRE/W/5, 4, point II para. 3.

[140] Directive 2008/101/EC of the European Parliament and of the Council of 19 November 2008 amending Directive 2003/87/EC so as to include aviation

was clearly aimed at tackling the environmental impact of the aviation sector in the broadest way possible. In the hypothesis in which other countries would have joined the EU in mitigating the climate impact of the aviation sector, the Aviation Directive required the Commission to find options to manage the interaction between the EU ETS and other countries' environmental measures. For example, the Commission could have decided to exclude flights arriving or departing from the third countries that had adopted environmental regulations on emissions from aviation.[141]

The inclusion of non-EU flights in the EU ETS has sometimes been compared to a first EU environmental adjustment measure.[142] The negative reaction of the international community – considering the EU's measure as extraterritorial – has led the EU to reconsider its decision,

---

activities in the scheme for greenhouse gas emission allowance trading within the Community, 13 January 2009, OJ L8, 3–21 (Annex I). See also recital 16.

[141] See Art. 25a, introduced by Directive 2008/101/EC.

[142] Regardless of whether the EU ETS is to be compared to a tax or not, the design of the provisions of Directive 2008/101/EC (amending Directive 2003/87/EC so as to include aviation activities in the scheme for greenhouse gas emission allowance trading within the Community, 19 November 2008) aimed at including the aviation sector into the EU ETS presents similarities with the design of BTAs. See, e.g., the considerations of Advocate General Kokott on the differences between the EU ETS and customs duties (para. 235 of her opinion in C-366/10). On this topic, see Lorand Bartels, 'The Inclusion of Aviation in the EU ETS. WTO Law Considerations' (2012) 6 Trade and Sustainable Energy Series, International Centre for Trade and Sustainable Development; Aaron Cosbey, Susanne Droege, Carolyn Fischer, Julia Reinaud, John Stephenson, Lutz Weischer & Peter Wooders, 'A Guide for the Concerned: Guidance on the Elaboration and Implementation of Border Carbon Adjustment' (2012) 3 Entwined Policy Report, 9, §21; Brian F. Havel & John Q. Mulligan, 'The Triumph of Politics: Reflections on the Judgment of the Court of Justice of the European Union Validating the Inclusion of Non-EU Airlines in the Emissions Trading Scheme' (2012) 37(1) Air & Space Law 3, 27; Kati Kulovesi, 'Addressing Sectoral Emissions outside the United Nations Framework Convention on Climate Change: What Roles for Multilateralism, Minilateralism and Unilateralism?' (2012) 21(3) Review of European Community & International Environmental Law 193; Jon Truby, 'Extraterritoriality or an Illegal Tax? A Challenge to the Inclusion of Aviation in the EU Emissions Trading Scheme' (2012) 14(4) Environmental Law Review 301.

suspending the implementation of the Directive for 'flights to and from aerodromes located in countries outside the European Economic Area (EEA)'.[143]

In addition to the considerations expressed at the EU level, the topic of environmental BTAs has also been addressed at the national level within the EU. One of the most important cases is known as the *Outokumpu Oy* case, by reference to the name of a Finnish company, which questioned the compatibility of a Finnish electricity duty with EU law. According to the Finnish company, the Finnish electricity duty was discriminatory under Article 95 of the Treaty (now Article 110 Treaty on the Functioning of the European Union (TFEU)) because its application differentiated between domestically produced and imported electricity, which could lead to a heavier tax burden being imposed on imported electricity. Indeed, the duty on electricity produced in Finland was calculated based on environmental considerations related to the method of production. Conversely, imported electricity was subject to a flat rate, which was deemed to 'correspond to the average rate levied on electricity produced in Finland'.[144] Finland explained this difference in the calculation of the rate by practical reasons related to the difficulty in determining the origin of imported electricity.[145] From the perspective of the BTA's mechanism, the Finnish excise tax on electricity was based on the destination principle, in the sense that both domestic and imported products were

---

143 See Art. 28a of Coordinated Directive 2003/87/EC introduced by Regulation No 421/2014 of the European Parliament and of the Council of 16 April 2014 amending Directive 2003/87/EC establishing a scheme for greenhouse gas emission allowance trading within the Community, in view of the implementation by 2020 of an international agreement applying a single global market-based measure to international aviation emissions, 30 April 2014, OJ L129, 1–4. See also – as for the year 2012 – Decision No. 337/2013/EU of the European Parliament and of the Council of 24 April 2013 derogating temporarily from Directive 2003/87/EC establishing a scheme for greenhouse gas emission allowance trading within the Community, 25 April 2013, OJ L113, 1–4. See European Commission, Proposal for a Regulation of the European Parliament and of the Council amending Directive 2003/87/EC to continue current limitations of scope for aviation activities and to prepare to implement a global market-based measure from 2021, 3 February 2017, Brussels, COM(2017)54 final.

144 ECJ, *Outokumpu Oy*, 2 April 1998, C-213/96, para. 11. On the *Outokumpu Oy* case, see Geert Van Calster, 'Topsy-turvy: the European Court of Justice and Border (Energy) Tax Adjustments – Should the WTO Follow Suit?', in: Janet Milne, Kurt Deketelaere, Larry Kreiser & Hope Ashiabor (eds.), *Critical Issues in Environmental Taxation: International and Comparative Perspectives* (OUP 2003), 311–341.

145 ECJ, *Outokumpu Oy*, 2 April 1998, C-213/96, para. 37.

subject to the tax. However, the tax rate applied to domestic and imported products was different. The ECJ considered that EU law did not preclude Finland from differentiating between products based on 'the nature of the raw materials used or the production process employed'.[146] The Court nevertheless considered that the difference in the rates applied to domestic and imported electricity was contrary to EU law as it could lead, 'if only in certain cases, to higher taxation being imposed on imported electricity'.[147]

In 2003 a Directive restricting the Community framework for the taxation of energy products and electricity was adopted.[148] The Directive expressly provides for a minimum level of taxation while allowing Member States to differentiate and to use exemptions or reductions.[149] Direct reference is made to the risk of loss of competitiveness for European enterprises.[150] Despite this new Directive, questions remain as to the design of a tax system including differentiated tax rates on electricity based on the production method used.[151] A study issued in April 2014 under the scientific coordination of Cottier illustrates the absence of a clear European legal framework as to the differential taxation of electricity by the Member States as well as countries that are part of a free trade agreement with the European Union, such as Switzerland.[152] The study describes the tax (and certificate) systems applied to imported electricity in various Member States. It appears that imported electricity does not always benefit from a similar treatment as

---

[146] *Ibid.*, para. 30.

[147] *Ibid.*, para. 41.

[148] Council Directive 2003/96/EC of 27 October 2003 restructuring the Community framework for the taxation of energy products and electricity, 31 October 2003, OJ L283, 51–70.

[149] *Ibid.*, Arts. 5 & 15.

[150] *Ibid.*, recitals 8 & 23.

[151] On this topic, see Michael Rodi, 'Ecological Tax Reform in Germany' (2000) 54(8) IBFD Bulletin 486.

[152] Thomas Cottier, Ilaria Espa, Simon Hirsbrunner, Kateryna Holzer & Tetyana Payosova, 'Differential Taxation of Electricity. Assessing the Compatibility with WTO Law, EU Law and the Swiss-EEC Free Trade Agreement', legal opinion established for the Federal Finance Administration, the Swiss Federal Office of Energy and the State Secretariat for Economic Affairs, 18 April 2014, available at <http://www.wti.org/research/publications/735/differential-taxation-of-electricity-assessing-the-compatibility-with-wto-law-eu-law-and-the-swiss-eec-free-trade-agreement/> (accessed 31 January 2017).

domestically generated electricity, which may be contrary to EU and WTO law provisions on BTAs.[153]

2.2.2.3 Other actors: Japan, Switzerland and Australia

In 1996 the Japanese Research Panel on Economic Instruments of the Environment released a report on the 'Utilization of Economic Instruments in Environmental Policies – Taxes and Charges'. This report is a clear call for the adoption of economic instruments to foster environmental goals.[154] The report also points out the potential negative impact of economic instruments on trade and presents BTAs as a means for mitigating this impact. The report makes a somewhat artificial distinction between pollution caused by products in the country of production and pollution taking place in the country of consumption.[155] According to the report, BTAs will only be effective in the last case through the reduction of domestic consumption.[156] In 2010 a Research Group on Environment and Tariff Policies was also established.[157] This group recognised that 'tariff policies and customs administrations have been deeply related to environmental policies for years'.[158] Their report sums up the main elements to be taken into consideration for the implementation of instruments used to avoid carbon leakage, including BTAs. In the annex, various schemes summarise the legal rules surrounding the case of BTAs, their rationale, and the measures that have been so far proposed in the US and in Europe.

In Switzerland proposals for environmental BTAs in respect of carbon or energy taxes have also been considered. In 2007 a Green deputy proposed to apply the CO_2 tax to 'grey emissions', meaning 'emissions released during the production, the transportation and the processing of

---

[153] *Ibid.*, e.g. p. 12 (regarding the Italian system), p. 19 (regarding the Swedish system).

[154] Japan, Ministry of the Environment, First Report of the Research Panel on Economic Instruments such as Taxation and Charges in Environmental Policies, 1996, available at <http://www.env.go.jp/en/policy/tax/econo/et2e.html> (accessed 20 November 2015).

[155] *Ibid.* (see the last part on 'International Impact and Mitigation Measures').

[156] *Ibid.*

[157] Japan, Summary of Discussions by the Research Group on Environment and Tariff Policies, June 2010, available on the Japan Customs website <http://www.customs.go.jp/english/news/report/report.htm> (accessed 27 October 2015).

[158] *Ibid.*

imported products'.[159] According to the proposal, taxing 'grey emissions' would allow better account to be taken of the real total emissions of Switzerland, such emissions per capita being very high.[160] The proposal was rejected in November 2011.[161] Moreover, in a 2014 report of the Federal Finance Administration aimed at assessing the viewpoints of political parties as well as economic, energy-related and environmental organisations on the case for an energy tax, various references were made to BTAs as a useful complementary tool to the energy tax.[162]

In Australia, similar taxes to the US ODC tax have existed since 1995. As in the US, Australia adopted specific measures in order to comply with the requirements of the Montreal Protocol on Substances that Deplete the Ozone Layer.[163] A tax was established in 1995 in addition to the licensing, quotas and control measures applied to manufacturers, importers and exporters of substances that deplete the ozone layer.[164] The initial duty on manufacture and importation of certain chemicals was an exemplary application of BTAs on imports, with identical levies applied on domestic and imported chemicals. The duty did not provide for BTAs on exports. In 2003 synthetic greenhouse gases (SGG) were added to the list of taxed substances in the legislation to allow Australia to comply with its obligations under the UNFCCC and later the Kyoto Protocol.[165] In 2011 new amendments under the Clean Energy Future Package modified the design of the manufacture and import levy on SGG.[166] In particular, the 2011 amendments added an import levy on equipment

---

159 Switzerland, Conseil National, postulat déposé par le Groupe des Verts au Conseil national, Extension de la taxe sur le CO_2 aux émissions grises, 21 November 2007, available at <http://www.parlament.ch/F/Suche/Pages/geschaefte.aspx?gesch_id=20073564> (accessed 27 October 2015).

160 *Ibid.*

161 *Ibid.*

162 Switzerland, Administration fédérale des finances, Rapport sur les résultats de la consultation préliminaire. Variantes d'un système d'incitation en matière climatique et énergétique, avril 2014.

163 Australia, Ozone Protection and Synthetic Greenhouse Gas Management Act 1989 (Cth), sub s. 3(a).

164 Australia, Ozone Protection and Synthetic Greenhouse Gas (Manufacture Levy) Act 1995 – C2012C00926 (Cth).

165 Australia, Ozone Protection (Licence Fees—Imports) Amendment Act 2003 (Cth); Australia, Ozone Protection and Synthetic Greenhouse Gas Legislation Amendment Act 2003 (Cth); Australia, Ozone Protection (Licence Fees – Manufacture) Amendment Act 2003 (Cth).

166 See new objectives of the Ozone Protection and Synthetic Greenhouse Gas Management Act 1989 (Cth) (Part I, 3 (objectives)). See also Parliament of the Commonwealth of Australia, House of Representatives, Ozone Protection and

containing ozone-depleting substances (ODS) – i.e. air-conditioning equipment, refrigeration equipment that contains a substance that is (or would be) hydrochlorofluorocarbons (HCFCs) – as well as an import levy on 'SGG equipment'.[167] These levies can be compared to the US ODC BTA on imported products containing ODC chemicals or to the double adjustment of the US Superfund tax.[168] Moreover, the amendments modified the tax rate of the levy on SGG equipment to take account of the carbon dioxide equivalence of the SGG in the calculation of the tax, so that importers of SGG equipment would be subject to 'a carbon charge which equates with the liability that the importer would have incurred if the importer was a liable entity and had been responsible for an equivalent quantity of greenhouse gas emissions under the *Clean Energy Act 2011*'.[169] Finally, the amendments provided for BTAs on exports in respect of duties paid on SGG or ODS/SGG equipment, allowing 'remission or refund of the carbon price component' in case of

---

Synthetic Greenhouse Gas (import levy) amendment Bill 2011 (Cth), Explanatory Memorandum, 2011.

[167] Australia, Act No. 164 of 2011 (An Act to amend the Ozone Protection and Synthetic Greenhouse Gas (Import Levy) Act 1995, and for related purposes) 8 Section 4, inserting 4A and 4B in 1995 Act (Cth). For the definition of ODS and SGG equipment, see 8C and D of the Ozone Protection and Synthetic Greenhouse Gas Management Act 1989 (Cth). See also Australia, FAQ on the 'Ozone Depleting Substance/Synthetic Greenhouse Gas Equipment Licences', especially the indicative list of 'common types of products imported as ODS/SGG equipment', available at <http://www.environment.gov.au/topics/environment-protection/ozone/licences/equipment-licences-eqpl-and-lvil/frequently-asked> (accessed 27 October 2015).

[168] Felicity Deane compares the tax to the Superfund tax (Deane, *supra* n. 131, 83–85).

[169] See 3A(7) of Australia, Ozone Protection and Synthetic Greenhouse Gas (Import Levy) Act 1995 as amended in 2011 (Cth). See also 4A(5) & 4A(6) of Australia, Ozone Protection and Synthetic Greenhouse Gas (Import Levy) Act 1995 as amended in 2011 (Cth). Parliament of the Commonwealth of Australia, House of Representatives, Ozone Protection and Synthetic Greenhouse Gas (import levy) amendment Bill 2011 (Cth), Explanatory Memorandum, 2011, para. 32, available at <http://www.comlaw.gov.au/Details/C2011B00170/Explanatory%20Memorandum/Text> (accessed 27 October 2015). See also Australia, 'Equivalent carbon price for synthetic greenhouse gases calculator', available at <http://www.environment.gov.au/node/13623> (accessed 27 October 2015). Note that in 2014 these amendments were modified one more time to cancel the reference to the amount of carbon dioxide equivalence (Australia, Amendment (Carbon Tax Repeal) Act no. 88 2014 (Cth), sections 9 & 13).

export of SGG or ODS/SGG equipment.[170] Aside from these levies, Australia adopted a carbon pricing mechanism that required allowances to be submitted not only in respect of domestic products, but also in respect of imported products.[171] While the Abbott Government in 2014 repealed the carbon pricing system and associated amendments, the 2011 amendments certainly highlight that environmentally related BTAs are more than a hypothetical policy option for countries when they adopt market-based instruments to pursue environmental goals.[172]

2.3 ENVIRONMENTAL BTAs' MAIN THEORETICAL FOUNDATIONS

While Ricardo is considered the theoretical father of traditional BTAs, environmental BTAs do not rely on a clear theoretical foundation. If environmental BTAs are assimilated to traditional BTAs, the two main theoretical foundations that have been mentioned in relation to traditional BTAs could also serve as the rationale for environmental BTAs. However, when environmental BTAs are distinguished from traditional BTAs, other theoretical grounds could be used. Three theories may serve as the theoretical basis of environmental BTAs in the case where environmental BTAs are not fully assimilated to traditional BTAs: the revised theory of comparative advantage (Section 2.3.1), the revised theory of absolute advantage (Section 2.3.2) and the theory of the legitimate absolute

[170] Australia, Commentary on provisions, Clean Energy (consequential Amendments) Bill 2011, 28 July 2011 (Cth), Chapter 5, para. 5.15, available at <http://210.193.178.189/government/submissions/closed-consultations/clean-energy-legislative-package/clean-energy-consequential-amendments-bill-2011/commentary.aspx> (accessed 27 October 2015). See also Sections 68 AA, 68 AB, 69 AC of Australia, Ozone Protection and Synthetic Greenhouse Gas Management Act 1989 (Cth). No rebate/refund is provided for non-SGG substances (see email exchanged with Felicity Deane, 30 June and 1 July 2014).

[171] Parliament of the Commonwealth of Australia, House of Representatives, Explanatory Memorandum, Clean Energy Legislation Amendment Bill 2012, Clean Energy (excise tariff legislation amendment) Bill 2012, Clean Energy (Customs Tariff Amendment) Bill 2012, 36–38.

[172] Australia, Carbon Tax Repeal Act (No. 88) 2014 (Cth). See also Australia, Omnibus Repeal Day (Autumn 2014) Bill 2014, A Bill for an Act to repeal certain Acts and provisions of Acts and to make various amendments of the statute law of the Commonwealth, and for related purposes (Cth), schedule 5, part 3.

advantage (Section 2.3.3).[173] They explain why adjustments are necessary to compensate for national environmental policies. Though different, these three theories are directly related to the theoretical grounds developed for traditional BTAs: the theory of comparative advantage and the alternative political theory of absolute advantage (Chapter 1).

The three theories explained in this section have been developed based on the economic and legal scholarship on environmentally related BTAs. The objective is to give an overview of the potential links between traditional and environmental BTAs, taking into account the rationale behind these measures. Moreover, the analysis aims to highlight that some economic and political rationales linked to environmental BTAs have no connection with traditional BTAs' rationale, which calls into question the relevance of using BTAs to pursue these economic and political goals.[174]

2.3.1 Ricardo's Theory Revised: The Revised Theory of Comparative Advantage

Under Ricardo's theory of comparative advantage, traditional BTAs are necessary to ensure 'fair competition'. As far as taxation is concerned, the normative message of the comparative advantage theory is that compensating measures are necessary to prevent specific domestic taxes from affecting the relative costs of goods.

A similar argument is used to explain the normative requirement for the adoption of environmental BTAs (in respect of specific environmental taxes, or even in respect of any specific environmental regulations). The argument relies on the assumption that domestic environmental policies (including environmental taxes) are shifted into products' prices. Consequently, the theory of comparative advantage requires the adoption of environmental BTAs in respect of these taxes and regulations when they affect the relative cost of products. This approach assumes that, without

---

[173] See GATT, Group on Environmental Measures and International Trade, GATT and International Environmental Agreements, Submission by Austria, 1 October 1993, TRE/W/19, 2 para. 4 on the 'internationalization of environmental issues' (hereafter, 'GATT, TRE/W/19').

[174] In an article, Lockwood & Whalley argue that environmental-related BTAs present the exact same issue as the traditional concept of BTAs (Ben Lockwood & John Whalley, 'Carbon Motivated Border Tax Adjustments: Old Wine in Green Bottles?' (2008) NBER Working Paper Series No. 14025). This section aims to provide a framework to compare both measures and highlight the extent to which they differ from each other.

BTAs, countries would be strongly discouraged from adopting environmental taxes which have – in the same way as non-environmental taxes – an impact on products' prices. In other words, they would lose some part of their (environmental) regulatory power.[175] In the literature, this approach may be linked to the arguments that BTAs allow the phenomenon of pollution havens to be limited. In contrast, the adoption of environmental measures without BTAs may lead to a global increase in pollution due to the relocation of production to countries with lower environmental standards.[176] Alternatively, in the case where the argument related to the protection of countries' environmental regulatory power is rejected, the adoption of BTAs may be justified on the basis of the need for maintaining the competitiveness of national enterprises: enterprises should not be disadvantaged by the tax system of the country where they are located. This competitiveness argument has often been mentioned in the debate on environmentally related BTAs.[177] As Howse and Trebilcock explain, this assumption is, however, 'largely incoherent' and not based on a precise benchmark: 'How to determine and then ensure that firms are equal?'[178]

---

175 Note that the questions of sovereignty and regulatory freedom are only relevant against the legal background of the WTO. Where no international agreement limits countries' possibility to adopt taxes on 'internationally traded goods', the arguments in favour of the adoption of BTAs do not relate to the need to preserve countries' (tax) sovereignty but to the idea that BTAs are necessary to guarantee optimal trade (taking place following the theory of comparative advantage).

176 See e.g. OECD, Joint Meetings of Tax and Environmental Experts, Environmental Policy in the Steel Industry: Using Economic Instruments, 8 January 2003, COM/ENV/EPOC/DAFFE/CFA(2002)68/FINAL, para. 122.

177 Benjamin M. Eichenberg, 'Greenhouse Gas Regulation and Border Tax Adjustments: The Carrot and the Stick' (2008) 3(2) Golden Gate University Environmental Law Journal 283, 288. See also OECD, ENV/EPOC/GSP(2008)14/FINAL, *supra* n. 87, 34–35 (summary of the 'pros and cons' of the adoption of environmental measures in order to address competitiveness issues); Elisa Lanzi, Damian Mullaly, Jean Chateau & Rob Dellink, 'Addressing Competitiveness and Carbon Leakage Impacts Arising from Multiple Carbon Markets: A Modelling Assessment' (2013) OECD Environment Working Paper No. 58, ENV/WKP(2013)5.

178 Robert Howse & Michael J. Trebilcock, 'The Fair Trade–Free Trade Debate: Trade, Labor, and the Environment' (1996) 16(1) International Review of Law and Economics 61, 74–75. See also GATT, L/3538, *supra* n. 25, 13. See also WTO, Preparatory Committee, Sub-Committee on Trade and Environment, Report of the Meeting held on 26–27 October 1994, Note by the Secretariat, 14 November 1994, PC/SCTE/M/4, para. 21 (hereafter, 'WTO, PC/SCTE/M/4').

Under this theory, any specific policy – not only environmental policies – should be adjusted as soon as it modifies the relationship between products' prices (the so-called 'relative value of goods'). In other words, labour policies should also be considered for adjustments as soon as evidence exists of their effect on the relative value of goods.[179] Under Ricardo's assumptions, such policies would, however, likely affect the absolute value of goods rather than their relative value since they are general in their implementation.

Various reasons may explain why environmentally related BTAs are given a similar theoretical foundation to traditional BTAs. A first reason is based on the idea that differences between environmental taxes and non-environmental specific taxes are not significant enough. Under this hypothesis, no attention should be paid to the – non-existent or, at least, irrelevant – environmental character of BTAs. For example, in the *Superfund* case (a GATT case often cited in studies on environmental BTAs), the US argued that 'the Superfund Act's primary function was to raise revenue, not to alter consumer or product behaviour to take into account the cost of environmental resources'.[180] A second reason pertains to the belief that potential differences between environmental and non-environmental specific taxes do not (or should not) influence the design and effects of BTAs in respect of these taxes.

2.3.2 Revised Theory of the Absolute Advantage

An alternative theoretical ground for BTAs is the theory of the absolute advantage. As explained above, absolute advantage arises out of differences in absolute production costs. These differences may be influenced by national policies, such as tax policies, environmental policies, social policies, etc. Based on the traditional understanding of GATT provisions, only differences in absolute production costs influenced by the adoption of indirect taxes could be subject to adjustment.

In the same way as indirect taxes are assumed to be shifted into products' prices under the theory of absolute advantage, this theory could further assume that environmental policies are shifted into prices, hence

179 See OECD, Trade and Environment: Processes and Production Methods (1994) OECD Documents, 98 ('In economic terms, labour is an input to production of a good in the same sense that raw materials are, and a tax on labour affects the price of the good, why then should a tax on labour (a payroll tax, which is a direct tax) not be seen as being a tax indirectly on a product?').

180 GATT, Panel Report, *US – Superfund*, para. 3.2.9.

influencing trade flows between countries.[181] Consequently, countries may be discouraged from adopting strict environmental policies.[182] As under the revised theory of comparative advantage, adjustments would be needed to ensure that countries maintain the possibility of freely adopting environmental policies.[183] In the case where this justification is rejected, the adoption of environmentally related BTAs may still be justified by the need to support national enterprises' competitiveness.[184]

The main difference between this theory and the one of the revised comparative advantage concerns the economic assumption on which they rely. Under this theory, all measures shifted into products' prices, regardless of the effect on the relative value of goods, should be eligible for adjustments. The question therefore arises as to the reasons why countries' environmental regulatory freedom should be protected and whether other legal areas should benefit from the same kind of protection. For example, 'Should adjustments also neutralise the impact of labour standards on products' prices?'[185] In contrast to the theory of the revised comparative advantage, no distinction can be made between specific and general policy measures to limit the possibility of adopting border adjustments. Consequently, more policies could meet the economic requirements to fall into the category of the eligible measures for adjustments.

2.3.3 Theory of the Legitimate Absolute Advantage

Under the theory of the legitimate absolute advantage, the adjustments in respect of environmental policies are not explained by the need to maintain countries' environmental regulatory freedom or national enterprises' competitiveness but by reference to the illegitimate character of the absolute advantage deriving from the absence of internalisation of

---

181 See John A. Barrett, 'The Global Environment and Free Trade: A Vexing Problem and a Taxing Solution' (2001) 76(4) Indiana Law Journal 829, 831.

182 This assumption is explained in GATT, 'Expanding trade can help solve environmental problems', Trade and The Environment Report (advance copy), 3 February 1992, GATT/1529, 17 (hereafter, 'GATT, GATT/1529').

183 Arguments related to countries' environmental sovereignty are to be found in the following document: WTO, PC/SCTE/M/3, *supra* n. 66, para. 54, para. 68 & para. 91. See also GATT, TRE/13, *supra* n. 36, para. 41.

184 This idea was expressed as early as 1971 in a GATT report (GATT, Industrial Pollution Control and International Trade, 19 July 1971, GATT/1083, 2).

185 See Howse & Trebilcock, *supra* n. 178, 74 on 'competitiveness-based arguments for environmental or labor-rights-based trade measures'.

environmental costs in relation to production in third countries.[186] Hence, a distinction is made between trade taking place according to absolute production costs, including externality costs, and trade taking place according to 'illegitimate' absolute advantages, disregarding externality costs.[187]

To achieve fairness in international trade, the theory of the legitimate absolute advantage requires neutralising the effect of domestic policies aimed at internalising externalities on absolute production costs. Under this theory, the internalisation of externality costs is supposed to concern the whole international community. Consequently, in the case of environmental policies, the competitive (dis)advantage arising out of the adoption of environmental policies should be neutralised by integrating externality costs into imports' prices.

Many scholars have expressed their support for a 'fair international trade', where account is taken of externality costs. For example, Gillespie considers as follows:

> A conflict arises between internalising environmental externalities and comparative advantage when one nation chooses to internalise environmental costs, through for example the creation of taxes, whereas another does not, and, in contrast, actively externalises environmental costs in an attempt to obtain comparative advantage. In such settings, the externalising nation will be actively exploiting a malfunctioning market place, as it is in effect claiming an environmental subsidy by not insisting that the correct price, that takes into account the externality considerations, be paid.[188]

Donald H. Regan also seems to distinguish between 'legitimate' and 'illegitimate' absolute advantage, even though he uses different terms to name the distinction he makes, namely 'normative' and 'positive' comparative advantage. Regan defines the concept of 'normative comparative advantage' as follows: '... "normative comparative advantage" reflects *real costs of production, including externalities*, and it is this concept that

[186] See Kateryna Holzer, *Carbon-Related Border Adjustment and WTO Law* (Edward Elgar Publishing 2014), 56.

[187] This distinction is inspired by Donald H. Regan, see below (Donald H. Regan, 'How to Think about PPMs (and Climate Change)', in: Thomas Cottier et al. (eds.), *International Trade Regulation and the Mitigation of Climate Change. World Trade Forum* (CUP 2009), 97–123. *Contra:* Jagdish Bhagwati, 'Trade Liberalisation and 'Fair Trade' Demands: Addressing the Environmental and Labour Standards Issues' (1995) 18(6) The World Economy 745, 748–749).

[188] Alexander Gillespie, 'The Contradiction between Comparative Advantage in International Trade and Environmental Protection' (1995) 3 Waikato Law Review 127, 131–132 (footnote omitted).

tells us where production should be located for global efficiency' (emphasis added).[189]

Regan's concept of 'normative comparative advantage' resembles Smith's absolute advantage (with the reference to 'real production costs'), to which Regan adds the externality factor as defined by Pigou. In comparison to the Ricardian theory of comparative advantage and Smith's theory of absolute advantage, Regan does not start with the assumption that free trade (resulting from the theory of comparative or absolute advantage) always makes the world better off. According to Regan, free trade only makes the world better off when production is located according to 'real production costs, including externalities'.[190] Regan defines the concept of 'externalities' in a very broad way, including, for example, the 'cost to American sensibilities', which he illustrates with the example of the unhappiness suffered by Americans due to the killing of dolphins.[191]

Similarly, Howse distinguishes between 'real' and 'illegitimate' comparative advantage. In contrast to illegitimate comparative advantage, real comparative advantage (which Howse also calls 'comparative advantage in the efficiency-relevant sense') is independent from legal facts and only 'depends on the facts about production functions and preferences'.[192] Howse considers that 'removing trade barriers between economies, one of which requires its producers to internalise some externality and the other of which does not, is likely to be inefficient, for standard "second-best" reasons'.[193] This reflects the idea that the internalisation of externalities by domestic law should not give countries absolute advantage and influence trade flows.

The distinction between 'real' and 'unreal' absolute advantage (even though some authors call it *comparative* advantage) is also used in a detailed analysis by Metcalf and Weisbach concerning the design of a

---

189 Regan, *supra* n. 187, 106–107.

190 *Ibid.*

191 *Ibid.*, 112. See also Robert Howse & Donald Regan, 'The Product/Process Distinction – An Illusory Basis for Disciplining "Unilateralism" in Trade Policy' (2000) 11(2) European Journal of International Law 249, 381–382. *Contra*: Gilbert E. Metcalf & David Weisbach, 'The Design of a Carbon Tax' (2009) 33 Harvard Environmental Law Review 499, 545.

192 Robert Howse, *The WTO System: Law, Politics & Legitimacy* (Cameron May 2007), 115.

193 *Ibid.*, 115, footnote 44. The idea of 'efficiency' is also used by Krugman (Paul Krugman, 'Climate, Trade and Obama' (2009), *The New York Times*, The Opinion Pages, available at <http://krugman.blogs.nytimes.com/2009/06/29/climate-trade-obama/comment-page-3/?_r=0> (accessed 3 November 2015).

carbon tax. They indeed consider that '[a] country without a carbon price does not have a true comparative advantage in producing carbon-intensive goods relative to a country with a carbon price; it produces at what looks like a lower cost only because the nominal price of the good does not include the full costs of production'.[194] Here again, the ordinary assumption that free trade makes everyone better off is nuanced. Metcalf and Weisbach suggest that free trade only makes the world better off when production is located based on full production costs.

2.3.3.1 The definition of externalities

Under Gillepsie, Regan, Howse, Metcalf and Weisbach's theoretical foundations, a question arises as to the definition of the externalities that should be taken into account in order to determine full production costs. 'Should only general environmental externalities – meaning those externalities which put a cost on the international community by affecting the global environmental commons – be considered?';[195] 'Or should other types of externalities also be taken into consideration?'; 'What about social standards?';[196] 'Should social standards also be seen as a way to internalise externalities?'

In fact, externality costs (Pigou's concept of 'negative externalities' by contrast to the concept of 'positive externalities') can be divided into three groups:

(1) externalities that put a cost on the international community because they affect the 'global commons';[197]
(2) externalities that are limited to one country;
(3) externalities that take place within one country but may have spillover effects in other countries (externalities with cross-border effects).

The category of externalities with cross-border effects can be subdivided into two categories:

(3.1) the externalities resulting from the production process, the effects of which are directly suffered by a third country (e.g. the smell

[194] Metcalf & Weisbach, *supra* n. 191, 540.

[195] See Howse & Trebilcock, *supra* n. 178, 63 & 66 (on the 'global welfare effects').

[196] *Ibid.* See WTO, PC/SCTE/M/4, *supra* n. 178, para. 23.

[197] On the concept of 'global commons', see OECD, Environmental Principles and Concepts, 1995, OCDE/GD(95)124, 10.

from factories located at the border of a country, which is a cost for the inhabitants of the neighbouring country);

(3.2) the indirect externalities resulting from the importation of products, either (3.2.1) due to the inherent characteristics of the products (e.g. the product is dangerous, unhealthy, creates pollution when it is used) or (3.2.2) due to the political sensitivity of the importing country to the production process of the product (e.g. importation of products made by children could affect the sensibility of the citizens of country X).[198]

Environmental externalities may fall into category (1), (2) or (3) depending on the prevailing philosophical approach to the protection of the environment.[199]

When environmental protection is seen as a purely local/national matter, BTAs – under the theory of the legitimate absolute advantage – should never be considered at the cross-border level (in accordance with the idea of category (2)).[200] In contrast, when the protection of the environment is considered a global responsibility, *any* negative externality affecting the environment (e.g. the killing of any animal Y in country X) could be defined as an externality that puts a cost on the international community as a whole.[201] This approach – which reflects category (1) described above – was indirectly introduced by the US in the GATT *Superfund* case. It argued as follows:

> the EEC was in any case basing its objections on the erroneous assumption that environmental resources were consumed only in the *production* of goods. In fact certain substances could *cause pollution throughout their life-cycle, from production to disposal.* That meant that they could cause pollution not only before but also after importation. If the objective of the Polluter-Pays Principle was to *internalize all negative externalities caused by polluting*

---

[198] See OCDE, Process and Production Methods (PPMs): Conceptual framework and considerations on use of PPM-based trade measures, OCDE/GD(97)137, 10–11 (see the distinction made between 'production' and 'consumption externalities').

[199] The concepts of 'nature', 'natural environment' or 'ecosystems' reflect – as such – a certain conception of the relationship between human beings and nature. The concept of 'nature' is used here in the most neutral sense possible.

[200] GATT, GATT/1529, *supra* n. 182, 16 (the report analyses the case of 'purely domestic environmental problems', which it defines has 'those which do not involve physical transborder spillovers'); GATT, TRE/W/19, *supra* n. 173, point I, para. 3.

[201] See e.g. Kulovesi, *supra* n. 141, 199.

activities, environmental taxes had to take into account not only the pollution caused in the production process but also the costs of disposal (emphasis added).[202]

By referring to a life-cycle approach, the US opened the door – at least indirectly – to a broad approach to environmental externalities. A sort of 'environmental footprint' is associated with products to consider all types of pollution released during their lifetime.[203]

A more political approach to the environment would, however, limit category (1) to those issues that have openly been recognised by the international community as 'global issues' (e.g. the recognition of the issue of climate change through the UNFCCC).[204] According to Metcalf and Weisbach, the internalisation of externalities through border adjustments should be limited to this first category of externality (i.e. the environmental standards that are recognised by the international community).[205] In contrast, labour standards should not be considered.

Under a political approach to global environmental issues, other types of environmental externalities may also be recognised. Categories (3.1) and (3.2.1) are largely recognised by the international community.[206] Category (3.2.2) is, however, the subject of controversy (Chapter 6).

---

[202] GATT, Panel Report, *US – Superfund*, para. 3.2.10.

[203] On the concept of 'life-cycle assessment', see OECD, Environmental Principles and concepts, 1995, OCDE/GD(95)124, 19. On the concept of environmental footprint, see Javier Godar, U. Martin Persson, E. Jorge Tizado & Patrick Meyfroidt, 'Towards More Accurate and Policy Relevant Footprint Analyses: Tracing Fine-Scale Socio-Environmental Impacts of Production to Consumption' (2015) 112 Ecological Economics 25–35.

[204] This view is to be found, for example, in the GATT report of 1992 on 'trade and the Environment' which states: 'pollution may be spilling over borders and harming either the regional environment (acid rain) or the global commons (ozone depletion)' (see GATT, GATT/1529, *supra* n. 182, 8). See also OECD, Annex I Expert Group on the United Nations Framework Convention on Climate Change, Full Cost Pricing (1997) Working Paper No. 3, OCDE/GD(97)71, 12.

[205] Metcalf & Weisbach, *supra* n. 191, 545. See also Howse, *supra* n. 192, 118–119 ('… laws regarding labour conditions tend to be different in important respects that make them significantly less eligible for incorporation into import restrictions. Many labour laws are primarily redistributive in nature; few labour laws are justified on the ground that they compel the internalization of externalities').

[206] As far as category (3.1) is concerned, see e.g. UN, *Trail Smelter* arbitration, 16 April 1938 & 11 March 1941, Reports of International Arbitral Awards (vol. 3), 1905–1982. As far as category (3.2.1) is concerned, see e.g. the WTO case *EC – Asbestos.*

2.3.3.2 The definition of the externalities to be internalised

According to Pigou – one of the famous economists who contributed to the development of environmental taxes – state intervention may serve to encourage activities that lead to positive externalities and to discourage activities leading to negative externalities.[207] One form of state intervention recommended by Pigou is taxation.

This theory – called the Pigouvian theory – has been relied upon to adopt domestic policies to internalise negative externalities at the national level.[208] In the case of cross-border externalities (categories (1) and (3)), Pigou's theory, however, is not enough to justify the internalisation of global and cross-border externalities.[209] Against the background of international law, the definition of externalities to be internalised is intrinsically linked to how international trade law is interpreted and to the role it is deemed to pursue. In other words, the possibility for a country to internalise cross-border externalities mainly depends on the extent to which WTO law is interpreted as limiting countries' regulatory freedom.

In the case where a country decides to internalise global and/or cross-border externalities (categories (1) and (3)) based on the theory of the legitimate absolute advantage, the question arises as to the obligation for this country to consider how other countries (and foreign private actors) internalise externalities.[210] In the literature on environmentally related BTAs, arguments have often been made for limiting BTAs in respect of imported products from countries that are assumed to have lower levels of internalisation of environmental costs. In other words,

---

[207] Arthur C. Pigou, *The Economics of Welfare* (Macmillan 1930), available at <http://www.econlib.org/library/NPDBooks/Pigou/pgEW.html> (accessed 10 November 2015), II.IX.16. Interestingly, the vocabulary used by Regan, Weisbach & Metcalf, and Howse echoes Pigou's vocabulary. For example, Pigou also used the word 'compensation'.

[208] In Pigou's work, references can also be found to the 'disservices' (Pigou's word for 'negative externalities') in the international context, e.g. disservices deriving from foreign investment (Pigou, *supra* n. 207, II.IX.12, II.IX.17).

[209] See i.a. Hans-Werner Sinn, *The New Systems Competition* (Blackwell 2003), 162.

[210] A related question concerns the interaction between the internalisation of environmental costs and the principle of common but differentiated responsibility (see WTO, Preparatory Committee, Preparatory Committee for the Sub-Committee on Trade and Environment, Report of the Meeting held on 15–16 September 1994, Note by the Secretariat, Addendum, 20 October 1994, PC/SCTE/M/3/Rev.1/Add.1, para. 172).

BTAs would be adopted as a reaction against the absence (or low level) of internalisation policies in third countries.

Nevertheless, since internalisation may not only take place through national policies, but also through the action of private actors (e.g. an enterprise could compensate the pollution released during the production process by financing environmental projects), countries that intend to adopt BTAs on the basis of the theory of the legitimate absolute advantage should design their BTA system so as to take into account how environmental costs are internalised in third countries either through the environmental policies in place in these countries or through a voluntary decision of the enterprises located there. In other words, the implementation of BTAs should not be 'country focused' but rather 'product focused'. In this sense, the design of BTAs should take into account the case where an enterprise – even when located in a country without internalisation policies – internalises the environmental costs related to its production. No BTAs should be adopted in respect of imported products for which environmental costs have already been internalised. Moreover, the theory of the legitimate absolute advantage does not support the adoption of BTAs, meaning the release of domestic environmental taxes, in respect of exported products.

2.3.4 Interactions between Traditional and Environmental BTAs' Theoretical Foundations: Legal Impact

The preference given to one theory over another is likely to have an impact on the design and the legal analysis of environmental BTAs. Environmental BTAs based on a rationale close to the *ratio legis* of traditional BTAs are more likely to be found compatible with WTO law. Indeed, when the rationale of environment-related BTAs differs to a significant extent from BTAs' traditional rationale, the legal consequence could be that these models of environmental BTAs will necessarily violate WTO law, such as, for example, in the case of the theory of the legitimate absolute advantage (Chapters 4 and 6).

When environmental BTAs are assimilated with traditional BTAs, reference is simply made to BTAs' traditional theoretical foundation. Under this hypothesis, environmental BTAs are likely to be analysed in the exact same way as traditional BTAs under WTO law provisions.

In contrast, in the hypothesis where environmental BTAs are not fully assimilated to traditional BTAs, non-traditional theoretical grounds will be preferred (the three theoretical grounds mentioned above: the revised theories of the comparative/absolute advantage and the theory of the legitimate absolute advantage). Consequently, questions arise as to whether current WTO law provisions surrounding traditional BTAs also apply in the case of environmental BTAs. As for the two first non-traditional theoretical grounds (i.e. the revised comparative and absolute advantage theories), WTO law provisions could be applied by analogy to environmental BTAs. These two theoretical grounds are indeed comparable to the theoretical grounds of traditional BTAs. The third non-traditional theoretical ground – the theory of the legitimate absolute advantage – differs the most from the theoretical grounds that have been put forward in support of the adoption of traditional BTAs. It redefines the assumption on which international trade has been based so far by adding the idea of 'fair trade'.

From a legal viewpoint, BTAs under the theory of the legitimate absolute advantage and the related objective of internalising (environmental) externalities present substantial differences from the case of traditional BTAs. BTAs should in principle be applied to compensate for the effects of national tax policies and not for the effects of (the absence of) third countries' policies on international trade.[211] Consequently, differences related to how countries internalise externalities should not serve as a basis for the adoption of BTAs *against* countries that are assumed to have 'lower' levels of internalisation of environmental costs. Proposals in favour of internalisation measures usually do not respect the design and features of the traditional concept of BTAs and rather relate to other trade-related measures such as anti-dumping, countervailing measures or even customs duties.

Finally, each type of theoretical foundation is likely to raise specific questions of tax design. One example relates to the adoption of BTAs on imports. If the tax is implemented based on the theory of the legitimate absolute advantage, exports should preferably not be rebated. Conversely, when the tax is implemented based on the revised theory of comparative or absolute advantage, the exemption of exports is justified, either on competitiveness grounds or even on environmental grounds (by reference to the objective of avoiding the creation of pollution havens).[212] Another

---

211 See WTO, PC/SCTE/M/3, *supra* n. 66, para. 53. Indeed, under GATT and WTO law, BTAs are not an instrument used to compensate for differences between countries' policies. BTAs serve to compensate for the impact related to a country's *own policies* on products' prices, regardless of the policy framework implemented in third countries.

212 See Geert Van Calster, 'Climate Change Taxes, Emissions Trading, and International Trade Law', in: Marjan Peeters & Kurt Deketelaere (eds.), *EU Climate Change Policy. The Challenge of New Regulatory Initiatives* (Edward Elgar Publishing 2006), 213. See also Olivier De Schutter, *Trade in the Service*

example concerns the revenue arising from the adjustments. If the theoretical foundation behind the adjustment is to preserve global commons (as under the theory of the legitimate absolute advantage), the revenue of the tax should not go to the country that would adopt the adjustment but rather to international projects, such as, for example, projects in favour of environmental protection (Chapter 4).[213]

2.4 INTERIM CONCLUSIONS

Environmental BTAs' economic and political history highlights that there is no single definition of environmental BTAs. In certain cases, environmental BTAs seem to be primarily defined by reference to the traditional concept of BTAs. In other cases, however, BTAs are clearly not a replication of traditional BTAs, to which an environmental dimension has been added.

The theoretical foundations that have been suggested in the literature for environmental BTAs do not always match the theoretical grounds that are the basis for traditional BTAs. To a certain extent, when differences in the rationale of traditional and environmental BTAs are too significant, one could wonder whether it is adequate to refer to the concept of 'BTAs' to call environmental trade measures that resemble rather customs duties, anti-dumping or countervailing measures. This is particularly the case for the theory of the legitimate absolute advantage. The revised theories of the comparative and absolute advantage seem closer to the grounds on which traditional BTAs rely.

The topic of BTAs in respect of environmental taxes has been discussed by the same international organisations as those that have analysed the case of traditional BTAs (namely the OECD and the GATT/WTO). Moreover, at the national level, some countries – such as the US – have already implemented measures that are described as environmental BTAs. The EU and other countries have started to think about the adoption of similar measures.

The next chapters analyse in more detail the design of traditional (Chapter 3) and environmental (Chapter 4) BTAs.

---

of Sustainable Development. Linking Trade to Labour Rights and Environmental Standards (Hart Publishing 2015), 86–87.

[213] See WTO, PC/SCTE/M/3, *supra* n. 66, para. 43 (Nigeria's representative).

PART II

From traditional consumption taxes to innovative environmental BTAs: an analysis of their tax design

Analysis of the rationale underlying traditional BTAs allows us to determine whether and how BTAs may serve to pursue environmental objectives (Part I). This second part discusses the tax design of traditional BTAs to assess how such taxes may integrate environmental considerations. Therefore, the analysis first explains how traditional BTAs are implemented into practice, by means of illustrative examples such as the EU VAT and excise duties systems or the US sales tax (Chapter 3). Then, based on the traditional models of BTAs, the analysis highlights how new models that integrate environmental considerations could be developed (Chapter 4).

3. Tax design of traditional BTAs

This chapter highlights BTAs' distinguishing features in comparison to other trade-related measures. As their name indicates, BTAs are border measures, tax measures and adjustment measures. Each concept ('border'; 'tax'; 'adjustment') informs the essence of BTAs (Section 3.1). Aside from this conceptual definition, countries' practices also permit BTAs to be understood in term of tax design, which is crucial for the development of environmental BTAs. Traditional models of BTAs include EU VAT and excise duties systems as well as US sales taxes (Section 3.2).

3.1 GENERAL CHARACTERISTICS

3.1.1 BTAs and the Concept of 'Border'

As already mentioned, the OECD 1968 Report and the GATT 1970 Report do not limit the definition of BTAs to tax adjustments taking place 'at the border'. The GATT 1970 Report states as follows:

> In fact, under certain tax systems exports never become liable to tax and so no adjustment actually takes places at the border; in addition, under certain tax systems imports are usually taxed, as is home production, by the importing country at the time they are sold by registered traders to other traders or consumers, and so the adjustment takes place after the goods cross the border.[1]

In other words, the reference to 'border' in the concept of BTAs does not refer to the place and time where the adjustments take place but to the fact that the goods on which the tax is applied are 'internationally traded goods', namely imported and/or exported goods.[2] This explains the

[1] GATT, Working Party on Border Tax Adjustments, Report, 2 December 1970, L/3464 (hereafter, 'GATT 1970 Report'), para. 5.

[2] This can be clearly derived from the OECD, Border Tax Adjustments and Tax Structures in OECD Member Countries, 1968 (hereafter, 'OECD 1968 Report'), at para. 115.

suggestion of the GATT 1970 Report to refer to 'tax adjustments applied to goods entering into international trade' instead of to BTAs.[3]

3.1.2 BTAs and the Concept of 'Tax'

BTAs are in principle only allowed in respect of 'taxes'. As such, WTO law does not provide for a specific definition of tax measures.[4] In the framework of WTO law – such as under GATT Article III – taxes are understood as a different category from the one of 'regulatory measures'. Consequently, adjustments in respect of non-fiscal policies would in principle fall outside the scope of BTAs.[5] Non-fiscal market-based measures could nevertheless fall into GATT/WTO provisions surrounding BTAs (Chapter 6).[6]

3.1.3 BTAs and the Concept of 'Adjustment'

BTAs differ from customs duties as they can only be applied to complement domestic taxes. In principle, BTAs should not be applied on internationally traded goods where corresponding domestic goods are not taxed. The same reasoning could be held for the case where no domestic product exists.[7] This interpretation is consistent with the etymology of the word 'adjustment', which means 'to make conform; to make just'.[8] In contrast to customs duties, which usually have a trade-protectionist purpose, BTAs are supposed to compensate for the effect of domestic

---

[3] GATT 1970 Report, *supra* n. 1, para. 5.

[4] See Felicity Deane, *Emissions Trading and WTO Law. A Global Analysis* (Edward Elgar Publishing 2015), 191, 182 & 196. See however, Richard A. Westin, *Environmental Tax Initiatives and Multilateral Trade Agreements: dangerous collisions* (Kluwer Law International 1997), 23, referring to GATT, Panel Report, United States – Taxes on Automobiles, 11 October 1994, DS31/R, unadopted (*Taxes on Automobiles*), para. 5.42–4.43 (on the distinction between taxes and penalties).

[5] In chapters 4 & 6, the distinction between tax and regulatory adjustments will, however, be nuanced. See Kateryna Holzer, *Carbon-Related Border Adjustment and WTO Law* (Edward Elgar Publishing 2014), 72.

[6] See *ibid.*, 72–78 (regarding BTAs on exports, Holzer also considers that regulatory adjustments would be possible).

[7] See OECD 1968 Report, *supra* n. 2, para. 38.

[8] Le Littré, Dictionnaire de la langue française, available at <http://www.littre.org> (accessed 5 February 2014). See also online etymology dictionary, available at <http://www.etymonline.com/index.php?term=adjust> (accessed 13 November 2015).

consumption taxes on prices and ensure fair competition between international and domestic products (Chapter 1).[9]

In practice, the design of BTAs may lead to overcompensation for the effect of domestic taxes on prices. According to Rosendhal, BTAs are sometimes applied on the duty-paid value of imported goods, including insurance and freight costs.[10] Consequently, the amount of BTAs may be higher than the levy imposed on domestic goods.

3.1.4 BTAs and Goods

In contrast to the broad analysis of BTAs' provisions in respect of goods, the issue of BTAs *in respect of trade in services* has been barely analysed.[11] This may be explained by two main reasons.

First, the Ricardian economic rationale of BTAs calls for BTAs in respect of specific taxes which have an impact on goods' relative value. The absence of BTAs in respect of taxes on services under Ricardo's theoretical framework may be explained by the fact that these taxes are usually general taxes. Second, from an historical perspective, very few services were traded internationally at the time the first international trade agreements were adopted.[12] This observation is consistent with the general definition of the concept of BTAs, which only refers to goods and not to services.[13] Today, it remains true that international trade in services

---

[9] Ben J.M. Terra, 'Chapter 8, Excises', in: Victor Thuronyi (ed.), *Tax Law Design and Drafting* (IMF 1996), 2. See Harry Johnson & Mel Krauss, 'Border Taxes, Border Tax Adjustments, Comparative Advantage, and the Balance of Payments' (1970) 3(4) The Canadian Journal of Economics 595–596. See also Tracey Epps & Andrew James Green, *Reconciling Trade and Climate: How the WTO Can Help Address Climate Change* (Edward Elgar Publishing 2010), 128.

[10] Roger W. Rosendahl, 'Border Tax Adjustments: Problems and Proposals' (1970) 2 Law and Policy in International Business 85, 108–109, note 85; Sidney Weintraub, 'Border Tax Adjustments and the GATT' (1964–1965) 17 Tax Executive 304, footnote 73.

[11] Note that the concepts of 'goods' and 'products' are used interchangeably though, in tax literature, the concept of product may be considered to be broader than the concept of goods. See Charles E. McLure, 'Could VAT Techniques be Used to Implement Border Carbon Adjustments?' (2012) 66(8) Bulletin for International Taxation 436, n. 17.

[12] Charles E. McLure, 'Globalization, Tax Rules and National Sovereignty' (2001) 55(8) Bulletin for International Taxation 328, 334.

[13] The GATT 1970 Report (*supra* n. 1) defines BTAs by reference to 'fiscal measures … which enable *exported products* to be relieved'.

is less important than international trade in goods.[14] Moreover, international trade agreements did not establish strict rules on trade in services comparable to those that apply to trade in goods (such as, for example, the strict rules concerning tariffs). In that sense, trade in services did not face the same need for specific provisions such as BTAs to maintain the ability of countries to tax 'internationally traded services'. Besides, no provision in the GATS gives a clear indication of their legal framework.

Yet, taxes on goods and services present similarities in how they are applied in cross-border situations. Both types of taxes usually follow the destination principle, understood by reference to the fact that taxes are charged by the jurisdiction in which the goods and services are consumed.[15] The GATT 1970 Report openly considers certain services in the framework of the discussion on BTAs, although BTAs are still defined by reference to 'fiscal measures … applied to *products*'. This illustrates that the frontier between goods and services is not clear cut, certainly not in the case of services directly related to goods. For example, in *Canada – Periodicals*, the Appellate Body was asked to determine whether an excise tax applied to split-run editions of periodicals was 'a measure affecting trade in goods to which Article III:2 of the GATT 1994 applies, or whether it is a measure affecting trade in services to which the GATS applies'.[16] The concept of *taxes occultes* also reflects the idea that taxes on services may be assimilated to taxes on products. The rationale for BTAs based on the theory of absolute advantage presented in the OECD and GATT reports seems to allow for BTAs in respect of any tax that is shifted into price, which could include taxes on services.

Hufbauer, one of the few authors who has studied the case of BTAs on the 'imports' and 'exports' of services, considers that the legal framework of BTAs in respect of trade in services may be constructed based on the general provision on national treatment (Article XVII GATS) by analogy

---

14 Robert E. Lipsey, 'Measuring International Trade in Services', in: Marshall B. Reinsdorf & Matthew J. Slaughter (eds.), *International Trade in Services and Intangibles in the Era of Globalization* (University of Chicago Press 2009), 27–70. See also OECD Data on international trade available at <https://data.oecd.org/trade/trade-in-goods-and-services.htm#indicator-chart>.

15 See Rebecca Millar, 'Echoes of Source and Residence in VAT Jurisdictional Rules' (2009) 09/44 Legal Studies Research Paper 1, 8–10.

16 WTO, Appellate Body Report, Canada – Certain Measures Concerning Periodicals, 30 June 1997, WT/DS31/AB/R (*Canada – Periodicals*). See also WTO, Appellate Body Report, European Communities – Regime for the Importation, Sale and Distribution of Bananas, 9 September 1997, WT/DS27/AB/R (*EC – Bananas III*).

with the GATT provisions.[17] In his opinion, the GATS allows for the adoption of BTAs for indirect as well as direct taxes on services.[18] Though this assumption seems to flow from the text of the GATS, questions arise as to the practical consequences of this conclusion as far as direct taxes are concerned: 'What are direct taxes on services?'; 'How to apply BTAs in respect of direct taxes on services?'; 'Does the distinction between goods and services really make sense in the case of direct taxes?'; 'How can BTAs be defined in respect of taxes on services?'. Indirect (and direct) taxes on goods and services are to be distinguished in many aspects. Goods literally cross borders, which is not *a priori* the case for services.[19] The GATS defines four modes of trade in services (i.e. cross-border trade, consumption abroad, commercial presence and presence of natural persons), which may not be easily compared with the import and export goods.[20] Although it may be difficult to define the supply of services in terms of import and export, the supply of cross-border services under the EU VAT system is in certain cases taxed in the country which is deemed to be the country of 'consumption'.[21] The

---

[17] Gary Clyde Hufbauer, 'Tax Discipline in the WTO' (2010) 44(4) Journal of World Trade 763, 773. See also Gary Clyde Hufbauer, *Fundamental Tax Reform and Border Tax Adjustments* (Institute for International Economics 1996), 57.

[18] Note, however, that Hufbauer's article dates back to 1996.

[19] See Howell H. Zee, 'Inter-Jurisdictional Sharing of the VAT', in: Richard Krever (ed.), *VAT in Africa* (Pretoria University Law Press 2008), available at <http://www.pulp.up.ac.za/pdf/2008_04/2008_04.pdf> (accessed 13 November 2015), 163, footnote 9. The case of 'online services' could, however, call into question the fact that services do not cross borders, as is the case with goods.

[20] See Art. I:2 of the GATS.

[21] See Art. 44 and the specific rules provided in Articles 46 onwards of VAT Directive 2006/112/EC. See Rita de la Feria, *The EU VAT System and the Internal Market* (IBFD 2009), 107–108 (referring to the Proposal for a Council Directive amending Directive 77/388/EEC as regards the place of supply of services, 23 December 2003, Brussels, COM(2003)822 final, 2); Ben J.M. Terra & Peter J. Wattel, *European Tax Law* (Wolters Kluwer 2012), 183; David Williams, 'Chapter 6, Value-Added Tax', in: Victor Thuronyi (ed.), *Tax Law Design and Drafting* (IMF 1996), 10. See also European Commission, Consultation Paper, VAT – The Place of Supply of Services to Non-Taxable Persons, Brussels, D (2005). This consultation paper gives a good overview of the different options regarding the determination of the place of the supply of services to non-taxable persons.

same questions do not arise to the same extent as far as excise duties are concerned since excises generally only apply to products.[22]

Though BTAs may theoretically be designed in respect of taxes on services, the relatively low practical impact of such BTAs justifies that the subsequent analysis will focus on BTAs in respect of taxes on goods. Where relevant, reference will, however, be made to BTAs in respect of taxes on services.

3.2 ILLUSTRATION: TRADITIONAL BTAs IN PRACTICE

3.2.1 Practices in the 1960s: Findings of the OECD and GATT Reports

The OECD 1968 Report provides a clear analysis of how BTAs were applied at the time.[23] The report contains two tables summarising the various BTA mechanisms used in case of exports and imports and their differences, depending on the tax concerned (VAT, sales tax, cascade tax). The tables are reproduced in one single table in Table 3.1.[24] At the level of the GATT, the Working Party also reviewed country practices in relation to BTAs. The results were similarly summarised in a consolidated document issued in May 1970.[25]

---

[22] Terra, *supra* n. 9, 2. The same can be said about the sales taxes in the US (see Robert F. van Brederode, 'Introduction to the US State Sales and Use Taxes' (2007) 18(4) International VAT Monitor 270, 271 & 273: 'sales tax is primarily levied on sales of goods to final consumers and, to a considerable extent, to business').

[23] OECD 1968 Report, *supra* n. 2, para. 94 et al.

[24] *Ibid.*, tables 10 & 11, 54–55. The table reproduced here is directly inspired by the tables of the OECD 1968 Report.

[25] GATT, Consolidated Document on the Examination of Practices of Contracting Parties in Relation to Border Tax Adjustments, 6 May 1970, L/3389.

Table 3.1 BTA practices in the 1960s

	Adjustment method for exports	Adjustment method for imports	Amount
Sales tax (production stage) or excise	In principle, no tax paid at export stage by manufacturing exporters. For other exporters, refund is possible.	In principle, tax paid at time of importation (but subsequently for imports by registered manufacturers).	When applicable, equal to total tax paid on product (actual amount).
Sales tax (wholesale stage)	No tax paid at export stage. Refund for any tax paid.	In principle, tax paid after importation. At time of importation for imports by unregistered traders or consumers.	When applicable, equal to total tax paid on product (actual amount).
Sales tax (retail stage)	No tax paid at export stage.	In principle, tax paid after importation. At time of importation for imports by unregistered traders or consumers.	When applicable, equal to total tax paid on product (actual amount).
VAT	No tax paid at export stage; in principle, tax refunds in respect of tax paid at earlier stages.	Tax paid at time of importation (but could 'be paid at subsequent stage').	When applicable, likely to be a large proportion of total tax paid on product (actual amount).
Cascade tax	No tax paid at export stage; tax refunds in respect of tax paid to suppliers at earlier stages.	Tax paid at time of importation.	Likely to be a relatively small proportion of total tax paid on product (estimated amount).

Source: Based on OECD (1968), 'Report on tax adjustments applied to exports and imports in OECD member countries'.

3.2.2 Current Practices: The Examples of EU VAT and Excise Duty Systems and of US Retail Sales Taxes

Since the end of the 1960s, new developments have modified countries' tax structures. The examples of the EU VAT and excise duty systems as well as the US retail sales taxes illustrate current BTA practices.[26] Examples from the EU and the US tax systems highlight the difficulties in translating BTAs' OECD definition into practice.

In practice, the destination principle needs to be defined with proxies. Indeed, the implementation of the destination principle relies on proxies used by the legislator to determine when a product is to be considered a 'domestic', 'imported' or 'exported' product. Moreover, the notion of 'home market' and the distinction between 'domestic', 'imported' and 'exported products' also imply that countries need to clearly determine what they consider to be part of their territory. From this perspective, the concept of frontier plays a great role in the practical implementation of BTAs.

3.2.2.1 General consumption taxes: the example of EU VAT

The VAT Directive defines the common system of VAT as 'a general tax on consumption exactly proportional to the price of the goods and services …'.[27] The tax is imposed on each transaction of the production and distribution process and is 'chargeable after deduction of the amount of VAT borne directly by the various cost components'.[28] In other words, the logic behind the EU VAT system is to tax the 'value added' at each stage of the production and distribution process. The final consumer should, in principle, be the only one supporting the VAT tax burden.[29] The VAT Directive subjects four types of transactions to VAT: the supply

---

[26] This section is aimed at illustrating some countries' practices and not at explaining the theoretical basis of VAT, excise duties or sale taxes. For more information of the various design options regarding VAT, see Sijbren Cnossen, 'A VAT Primer for Lawyers, Economists, and Accountants' (2011) Tax Analysts 23; Sijbren Cnossen, 'Three VAT Studies' (2010) 90 CPB Netherlands Bureau for Economic Policy Analysis; Charles E. McLure, 'The Carbon-Added Tax: An Idea Whose Time Should Never Come' (2010) 3 Carbon & Climate Law Review 250–259; Charles E. McLure, 'Panel Discussion: Alternative Tax Policies for the Future in Light of the Current Economic and Budget Outlook' (1989) 4(3) Journal of Accounting, Auditing & Finance 388. Note also that there are countries where VAT is applied based on the origin principle. See Williams, *supra* n. 21, footnote 32.

[27] Art. 1, para. 2 of VAT Directive 2006/112/EC.

[28] *Ibid.*

[29] However, when VAT is not deductible because the intermediary operator is not a registered person allowed to deduct the VAT previously paid, VAT also burdens intermediary operators. Michael Keen, 'VAT, Tariffs, and Withholding: Border Taxes and Informality in Developing Countries' (2008) 92(10) Journal of Public Economics 1892–1906, in particular p. 1895.

of goods; the intra-Community acquisition of goods; the supply of services; the importation of goods.

In the EU, VAT provisions apply to two types of cross-border transactions involving goods: transactions taking place between EU Member States (i.e. in the case of intra-Community trade) and transactions taking place between EU Member States and third countries or third territories.[30] The definition of the EU's borders plays a major role in distinguishing between these two types of transactions. Under the VAT Directive, the EU's borders do not have the exact same meaning as under the European Treaties.[31] In the VAT Directive, the territory of the Community is to be understood as the 'territory of each member State of the Community to which the Treaty establishing the European Community is applicable, in accordance with Article 299 of the Treaty [i.e. Article 355 of the TFEU]', with the exception of the 'third territories'.[32] The expression 'third territories' refers to territories that are part or not of the customs territory of the Community and to which the VAT Directive does not apply. It includes Mount Athos, the Canary Islands, some French territories, the Aland Islands, the Channel Islands, the Island of Heligoland, the territory of Büsingen, Ceuta, Melilla, Livigno, Campione d'Italia, and the Italian waters of Lake Lugano.[33] As regards the Principality of Monaco, the Isle of Man, and the UK Sovereign Base Areas of Akrotiri and Dhekelia, these territories are considered as part of France, the UK and Cyprus respectively.[34]

Among EU Member States, VAT provisions do not reflect the mechanism of BTAs as understood under international trade law. The main reason is that, within the EU, Member States are not categorised in terms of importing and exporting countries. The destination principle is therefore not defined by reference to the fact that imported products are taxed and exported products are not taxed. The destination principle is rather understood as a feature of tax systems where taxes are imposed in the country of consumption (or rather in the country where consumption is supposed to take place as there is no guarantee that the product will indeed be consumed there) by comparison to an origin-based tax system where taxes are imposed in the country of production. Moreover, the objective of VAT provisions surrounding transactions between Member

---

[30] Arts. 5 & 6 of VAT Directive 2006/112/EC.

[31] See Art. 52 of the Treaty on the European Union (TEU) and Art. 355 of the Treaty on the Functioning of the European Union (TFEU).

[32] Art. 5 of VAT Directive 2006/112/EC.

[33] Arts. 5 & 6 of VAT Directive 2006/112/EC.

[34] Art. 7 of VAT Directive 2006/112/EC.

States is not to neutralise the effects of domestic taxes in the context of EU trade but rather to allocate taxing powers within the EU, avoiding both double taxation and non-taxation.[35]

In the case of goods traded between Member States and territories outside the EU (including third territories), the VAT Directive distinguishes between two types of taxable transactions: importation and exportation.

The entry of goods into the Community is in principle subject to VAT as an 'importation of goods'.[36] Under the VAT Directive, the place of importation is deemed to be the 'Member State within whose territory the goods are located when they enter the Community'.[37] In general, VAT becomes chargeable as soon as the goods are imported, following the rules applied to customs duties.[38] The taxable amount should be defined according to the same rules: 'in respect of the importation of goods, the taxable amount shall be the value for customs purposes, determined in accordance with the Community provisions in force'.[39] Williams notes, therefore, that 'the normal practice of states is to use their customs laws as a vehicle for imposing the VAT on goods that are imported, subject to necessary modifications'.[40] In principle, the tax rate on the importation of goods is the same as the one 'applied to the supply of like goods within the territory of the Member State'.[41] These provisions follow the logic of BTAs: imports are subject to taxes that are similar to the taxes imposed on domestic goods. Following the same logic, exemption should apply for the importation of goods, which are also exempted at the national level.[42] Some additional exemptions are nevertheless granted based on other justifications. This is the case for the exemptions for the import of goods in travellers' personal luggage with no commercial character, under certain quantitative and value-related conditions.[43] These exemptions are justified by the objective of

---

[35] See for example Art. 138, para. 1 of VAT Directive 2006/112/EC.

[36] Art. 2, para. 1(d) of VAT Directive 2006/112/EC. See also Art. 30 of VAT Directive 2006/112/EC, which defines the importation of goods.

[37] Arts. 60 and 61 of VAT Directive 2006/112/EC.

[38] See Arts. 70 and 71 of VAT Directive 2006/112/EC.

[39] Art. 85 of VAT Directive 2006/112/EC. The taxable amount should include all taxes, duties, levies and charges, except for the VAT to be levied itself (Art. 86).

[40] Williams, *supra* n. 21, 10. See also Arts. 274 et al. of the Directive.

[41] Art. 94 of VAT Directive 2006/112/EC.

[42] Art. 143, para. 1(a) of VAT Directive 2006/112/EC.

[43] See Art. 143, para. 1(b) of VAT Directive 2006/112/EC and Council Directive 69/169/EEC of 28 May 1969 on the harmonisation of provisions laid

avoiding double taxation.[44] This justification differs from the reasons that are put forward to justify BTAs. Other examples of exemptions are linked to the fact that the imported goods concerned are exempted from customs duties.[45]

The VAT Directive does not provide a definition of exportation. As a rule, the supply of goods dispatched or transported to a destination outside the Community by or on behalf of the vendor should be exempted.[46] Similarly, the supply of goods dispatched or transported by or on behalf of a customer not established within Member States' territory should in principle be exempted.[47] In two cases, however, no exemption will apply to this type of exports. First, the supply of goods transported by the customer himself for the equipping, fuelling and provisioning of pleasure boats and private aircraft or any other means of transport for private use is subject to VAT.[48] Second, in the case of goods carried in the personal luggage of travellers, the exemption only applies under three conditions, related to the residence of the traveller, the value of the goods and the lapse of time between the transportation of the goods and the supply.[49] Other types of transactions are exempted as 'exports': for example, the supply of goods related to humanitarian and teaching activities or the 'supply of services consisting in work on movable property acquired or imported for the purpose of undergoing

down by law, regulation or administrative action relating to exemption from turnover tax and excise duty on imports in international travel (69/169/EEC), replaced by Council Directive 2007/74/EC of 20 December 2007 on the exemption from value added tax and excise duty of goods imported by persons travelling from third countries, 29 December 2007, OJ L346, 6–12. See also Council Directive 83/181/EEC of 28 March 1983 determining the scope of Art. 14(1)(d) of Directive 77/388/EEC as regards exemption from value added tax on the final importation of certain goods, 23 April 1983, OJ L105, 38; Council Directive 2006/79/EC of 5 October 2006 on the exemption from taxes of imports of small consignments of goods of a non-commercial character from third countries, 17 October 2006, OJ L2286, 14.

44 Preamble of the Council Directive of 28 May 1969, 69/169/EEC.

45 Art. 143, para. 1(e), (f) of VAT Directive 2006/112/EC. See also Council Directive 83/181/EEC.

46 Art. 146, para. 1(a) of VAT Directive 2006/112/EC. See also Art. 147 of VAT Directive 2006/112/EC.

47 Art. 146, para. 1(b) of VAT Directive 2006/112/EC.

48 *Ibid.*

49 Art. 147 of VAT Directive 2006/112/EC.

such work within the Community, and dispatched or transported out of the Community'.[50]

In principle, exemption means that no VAT is due on exports. The Directive nevertheless provides for the possibility of refund of the VAT in the case of the supply of goods related to humanitarian and teaching activities.[51]

3.2.2.2 Specific consumption taxes: the example of the EU's excise duty system[52]

Excise taxes are taxes levied on the consumption of certain goods, including energy products, alcohol and tobacco. As in the case of the EU VAT system, internationally traded goods are subject to different fiscal treatment, depending on whether the goods concerned are traded between Member States or with countries outside the EU and third territories.[53] The definition of EU territory therefore plays an important role, as is the case with the EU VAT system. In the framework of the Excise Directives, the territory of the Community has also a specific meaning. For example, the Canary Islands, some French territories and the Channel Islands do not fall under the scope of the Directive, though they are part of the 'customs territory of the Community'.[54]

In general, excise duties are defined as specific consumption taxes. Accordingly, in the EU Excise Directive, excise duties are 'chargeable at the time, and in the Member State, of release of consumption'.[55] Article 7, §2 defines the 'release of consumption' through the following proxies:

> For the purposes of this Directive, 'release for consumption' shall mean any of the following: (a) the departure of excise goods, including irregular departure, from a duty suspension arrangement; (b) the holding of excise goods outside a duty suspension arrangement where excise duty has not been levied pursuant to the applicable provisions of Community law and national

---

50 Art. 146, para. 1(c) and (d) of VAT Directive 2006/112/EC.

51 Art. 146, para. 2 of VAT Directive 2006/112/EC.

52 In the EU the general legal framework for excise duties is defined by Directive 2008/118/EC (which has replaced Directive 92/12/EEC): Council Directive 2008/118/EC of 16 December 2008 concerning the general arrangements for excise duty and repealing Directive 92/112/EEC, 14 January 2009, OJ L9, 12.

53 The territorial scope of application of Excise Directive 2008/118/EC is comparable to the territorial scope of application of VAT Directive 2006/112/EC (see Arts. 5 and 6 of Directive 2008/118/EC).

54 Art. 5, para. 2 of Excise Directive 2008/118/EC. See also Art. 6.

55 Art. 7 of Excise Directive 2008/118/EC.

> legislation; (c) the *production* of excise goods, including irregular production, outside a duty suspension arrangement; (d) the *importation* of excise goods, including irregular importation, unless the excise goods are placed, immediately upon importation, under a duty suspension arrangement (emphasis added).[56]

As a side note, subparagraph (c) of Article 7.2. may be pointed out.[57] Indeed, the reference to 'the production of excise goods' raises questions as to the nature of excise duties: 'Are excise duties taxes on consumption or taxes on production, when consumption is defined through proxies clearly referring to the production of the excise goods?'[58] This question highlights the artificial character of the distinction between consumption and production taxes (Chapters 5 and 6).[59] In fact, the traditional definition of excise duties as consumption taxes seems to relate to the fact that importations are subject to tax, which again illustrates the frequent confusion as between consumption taxes and the destination principle. Nevertheless, though production may be used as a proxy to define consumption, the intent of the legislator may be to tax the use of excise products (i.e. their consumption) and not the production of the excise products.

As in the case of EU VAT, excise duties imposed on goods traded between Member States do not fully reflect BTAs' general logic. Member States are not defined in terms of importing/exporting countries and excise duties are sometimes applied following the destination principle, sometimes following the origin principle.[60] In contrast, BTAs fully apply on goods traded from and to countries outside the EU to compensate for excise duties applied on domestic goods: while importations of goods in the EU are subject to excises, exportations are not.[61] The Excise Directive defines the 'importation of excise goods' as 'the entry into the territory of the Community of excise goods unless the goods upon their

---

[56] Art. 7, para. 2 of Excise Directive 2008/118/EC.

[57] See also Art. 2 of Excise Directive 2008/118 EC.

[58] Art. 7, para. 2(c) of Excise Directive 2008/118/EC. See also Art. 2 of the Excise Directive.

[59] Art. 7, para. 2(c) of Excise Directive 2008/118/EC.

[60] See Matthias Bongartz, 'Trade in Goods Subject to Excise Duties which Have Been Released for Consumption in other Member States. Analysis with Reference to Directive 2008/118/EC and German Excise Law' (2012) 6(2) World Customs Journal 19.

[61] According to John H. Due, however: 'historically … excises apply only to domestically produced goods' (John H. Due, 'Excise Taxes' (1994) World Bank Policy Research Working Paper No. 1251, 1, 26).

entry into the Community are placed under a customs suspensive procedure or arrangement, as well as their release from a customs suspensive procedure or arrangement'.[62]

According to Article 7 of the Excise Directive, excise duties are 'chargeable at the time, and in the Member State, of release of consumption', which – in the case of importation – means the time and place of the importation of the excise goods.[63] As with VAT, in the case of goods imported by persons travelling from third countries, exemptions may be granted under certain conditions related to the quantity, the value and the non-commercial character of the import.[64] The person liable for paying the tax is the person 'who declares the excise goods or on whose behalf they are declared upon importation and, in the case of irregular importation, any other person involved in the importation'.[65] Regarding the rates, no distinction is made between the rate of excise duties on imported and domestic goods.[66]

Exportations are not specifically dealt with in the Excise Directive. The Directive rather provides for the suspension of excise duties when excise goods are moved from a tax warehouse to a 'place where the excise goods leave the territory of the Community'.[67] In these cases, the competent authorities of the Member State of export should fill in a report of export to certify that 'the excise goods have left the territory of the Community'.[68]

3.2.2.3 BTAs in the US: the case of retail sales taxes

Though they are used in a much lower proportion than in the EU, BTAs also apply in the US in respect of retail sales taxes and excise duties.[69] In

---

62 Art. 4, point 8 of Excise Directive 2008/118/EC.

63 Art. 7, para. 1 and para. 2(d) of Excise Directive 2008/118/EC.

64 Council Directive 2007/74/EC.

65 Art. 8, para. 1(d) of Excise Directive 2008/118/EC.

66 See, nevertheless, Due, *supra* n. 61, 26:

> For both political and economic considerations, excises should apply equally to imported and domestic goods. This rule is simple with specific rate levies. It is more complicated with ad valorem levies, because of problems of ensuring that the taxable price is the same for imported and domestic goods, the problem that also arises with sales taxes at the manufacturing level.

67 Art. 17, para. 1(a) iii of Excise Directive 2008/118/EC.

68 Art. 25 of Excise Directive 2008/118/EC.

69 This section focuses on the case of retail sales taxes. See John C. Healy & Michael S. Schadewald, *2012 Multistate Corporate Tax Guide Vol. II (Sales/Use Tax)* (CCH Wolters Kluwer Business 2012), 14,001; Robert F. van Brederode,

the US, sales taxes are collected at the subnational level, by the states and local governments.[70] In general, subnational tax systems follow the destination principle in the sense that exports are tax exempt and imports are taxed. From that viewpoint, the EU VAT and US subnational retail sales taxes may be compared.[71] As within the EU, a distinction should be made between the taxes imposed on goods imported from third countries and taxes applied on the interstate trade of goods.

The interstate trade of goods is subject to use taxes, the tax rate of which is in principle equal to the tax rate of sales taxes imposed on the intrastate trade of goods.[72] A credit is usually granted for the taxes (sales tax or use tax) paid in other states.[73] The use tax on interstate sales is in principle collected by the vendor. Remote vendors may, however, not be asked to collect use taxes when they have 'no physical presence (nexus) in the taxing state'.[74] According to McLure, this goes against the destination principle as private persons will rarely remit the use tax in this last case.[75]

Regarding taxes on goods imported from a third country to the US, two main hypotheses may be distinguished: the case of foreign goods that are brought into the US and that are not intended to be resold; and the case of products imported for resale into the US.[76] In the first

---

Systems of General Sales Taxation: Theory, Policy and Practice (Kluwer Law International 2009).

[70] van Brederode, *supra* n. 22, 270.

[71] Robert F. van Brederode, 'The Metamorphosis of US Corporate Income Tax into a Value Added Income Tax' (2008) 19(4) International VAT Monitor 266, 270. See also Richard M. Bird & Pierre-Pascal Gendron, 'Sales Taxes in Canada: the GST-HST-QST-RST "System"' (2009–2010) 63 Tax Law Review 517; William F. Fox & Leann Luna, 'Subnational Taxing Options: Which Is Preferred, a Retail Sales Tax or a VAT?' (2002–2003) 21(1) Journal of State Taxation 875–884; Charles E. McLure, 'EU and US Sales Taxes in the Digital Age: A Comparative Analysis' (2002) 56(4) IBFD Bulletin 135, 136–137; McLure, *supra* n. 11, 438; Charles E. McLure, 'Rethinking State and Local Reliance on the Retail Sales Tax: Should We Fix the Sales Tax or Discard It?' (2000) Brigham Young University Law Review 77, 88–92.

[72] Walter Hellerstein, 'State Sales Tax Reform in the United States: The Streamlined Sales Tax Project' (2005) (59)5 IBFD Bulletin 170, 172; van Brederode, *supra* n. 69, 79–80.

[73] Hellerstein, *supra* n. 72, 172; van Brederode, *supra* n. 22, 274; van Brederode, *supra* n. 69, 74.

[74] Hellerstein, *supra* n. 72, 172–173; McLure, *supra* n. 71, 138; van Brederode, *supra* n. 69, 80.

[75] McLure, *supra* n. 71, 138; van Brederode, *supra* n. 22, 274.

[76] See van Brederode, *supra* n. 69, 73–75.

hypothesis, a use tax is in principle due. A duty declaration should be filled in and reported to US Customs when the goods are brought into the US.[77] The implementation of use taxes mimics the way sales taxes are implemented: similar tax rates, exemptions, etc. From this perspective, use taxes may be described as BTAs in respect of sales taxes. According to van Brederode, 'They serve the dual purpose of filling in the interstate gap in sales tax coverage and of preventing a competitive disadvantage for "domestic" as compared to out-of-state sellers'.[78] In the second hypothesis, products imported for resale are only subject to tax at the retail stage, meaning that these products are not subject to the sales tax on business inputs.[79] Hence, the mechanism of BTA only allows imported products to be partially subjected to the taxes charged on domestic products. Indeed, in contrast to imported products, domestic products may also bear sales taxes on business inputs as not all business-to-business transactions are exempted.[80] Hence, BTAs do not fully compensate for taxes paid by intrastate producers.

Exported goods are exempted but taxes paid on business inputs are not rebated, meaning that BTAs on exports similarly do not fully compensate for taxes paid by intrastate producers.[81]

3.3 INTERIM CONCLUSIONS

The analysis of EU VAT, excise duty and US retail sales tax systems explains how BTAs' theoretical definition is translated into practice, following or not the destination principle, which is at the heart of the OECD definition of BTAs. The US and EU tax systems illustrate that the destination principle is rarely fully put into practice: VAT, excise duties and sales taxes are not imposed on all imported goods and not all exported goods are relieved from taxation. Essential concepts of BTAs' practical definition include the terms of 'importation' and 'exportation'.

---

[77] See e.g. the webpage of the California State Board of Equalization, California Use Tax Information, <http://www.boe.ca.gov/taxprograms/usetax/foreign_purchase.html>. See also Revenue and Taxation Code Section 7054.

[78] van Brederode, *supra* n. 22, 274.

[79] McLure, *supra* n. 71, 137.

[80] See van Brederode, *supra* n. 22, 271. See also William F. Fox and Leann Luna, 'How Broad Should State Sales Tax Bases Be? A Review of the Empirical Literature' (2013) Tax Analysts ('Economic effects of taxing business-to-business transactions'); Alan D. Viard, 'Use Tax Collection on Interstate Sales: The Need for Federal Legislation' (2012) 66(9) Tax Analysis State Tax Notes 657.

[81] McLure, *supra* n. 71, 145.

The EU's dual regime, which distinguishes between taxes imposed on trade taking place between Member States and trade taking place with third countries, also highlights that the destination principle may be given different meanings, although it is often merely understood as a principle that characterises consumption taxes (in the sense that taxation should take place in the country of consumption). In the OECD definition of BTAs ('[BTAs] as any fiscal measures which put into effect ... the destination principle'), however, the destination principle refers rather to the ability of countries to tax imports and relieve exports from taxation. From that perspective, the destination principle functions as a rule that limit countries' taxing powers. At the EU level, the destination (and origin) principles function as rules to allocate tax jurisdiction between Member States (so that double taxation should be avoided).[82] This EU understanding of the destination principle does not match the historical development of BTAs. Indeed, as explained above, the original reason for adopting BTAs was to neutralise the impact of domestic taxes on international trade (and not to neutralise the differences between tax systems in different countries or to allocate taxing powers between countries). With the adoption of the GATT, the role of BTAs – and the destination principle – has evolved towards a legal framework defining the limits for countries to adopt taxes on imports and exemptions (or refunds) on exports. Although this understanding of the destination principle may resemble a rule that allocates taxing powers between jurisdictions, WTO law provisions surrounding BTAs do not aim at avoiding double taxation in contrast to EU provisions on VAT and excise duties concerning goods traded between Member States.[83] Indeed, WTO law does not, as such, allocate tax jurisdiction given that it does not require countries to establish a tax system where indirect taxes are imposed in the country of consumption. WTO law merely puts limits on the extent to which countries may tax or not imports and exports (Chapter 5).

Finally, BTAs' implementation highlights that EU and US practices do not fully match their political statement in international fora. For example, though the US has criticised BTAs' legal framework both at the

---

[82] The destination principle has indeed been described as a principle 'designed to allocate tax jurisdiction'. See Alan Schenk & Olivier Oldman, *Value Added Tax: A Comparative Approach* (CUP 2006), 184–186.

[83] See also Paul Demaret & Raoul Stewardson, 'Border Tax Adjustments under GATT and EC Law and General Implications for Environmental Taxes' (1994) 28(4) Journal of World Trade 5–66, 31; Wolfgang Schön, 'World Trade Organization Law and Tax Law' (2004) 58(7) IBFD Bulletin 283, 291.

OECD and GATT levels, it nevertheless relies on BTAs in the implementation of sales and use taxes. The mismatches in the EU and US political views also illustrate that countries do not hesitate to support different interpretations of BTAs' legal framework based on their personal interest.

4. Tax design of environmental BTAs

In contrast to traditional BTAs, there is no commonly agreed definition of environmental BTAs. Environmental BTAs are here defined by reference, and in comparison, to the essential features of traditional BTAs (Section 4.1). Moreover, environmental BTAs may be described by means of their tax design. Some models of environmental BTAs copy the structure of excise duties and VAT. Other models are inspired by policy measures that have been implemented or proposed in the US, the EU and Australia (Section 4.2). Finally, all models of environmental BTAs are characterised by similar tax design issues as far as the valuation of the imported products, the risks of abuse and the allocation of the revenue derived from the tax are concerned (Section 4.3).

4.1 GENERAL CHARACTERISTICS

4.1.1 Environmental BTAs and the Concept of 'Border'

For traditional BTAs, the concept of 'border' indicates that the goods on which the tax is applied are 'internationally traded goods', namely 'imported' and 'exported' products.[1]

Environmentally related BTAs on imports allow for imposing domestic environmental taxes on imported products. This mechanism is sometimes considered to offer countries the possibility of having an environmental impact beyond their territory, which is in principle impossible by means of merely national environmental policies. Indeed, environmental BTAs would allow countries to extend the effects and territorial scope of application of their environmental tax policies through the goods they import.[2]

[1] See OECD, Border Tax Adjustments and Tax Structures in OECD Member Countries, 1968, 16, para. 115 (hereafter, 'OECD 1968 Report').

[2] See Congress of the United States, Office of Technology Assessment, Trade and Environment. Conflicts and Opportunities, Washington DC. Government Printing Office, May 1992, OTA-BP-ITE-94, 6–7.

Here, a distinction should be made between (1) the situation where a country imposes domestic environmental taxes on foreign products (i.e. products that have been produced outside its national territory) in the same way as it imposes these taxes on domestic products, and (2) the situation where a country imposes environmental taxes on imported products because the level of environmental policies in the country (or countries) where the products have been manufactured/processed is not as strict as that of domestic environmental policies. Of these two situations, only the first follows the design of traditional BTAs. The reason is that the concept of BTAs – in contrast to customs duties, countervailing subsidies and anti-dumping measures – is directly linked to the internal tax system, which is central to the application of BTAs. Indeed, BTAs should be designed by taking into account the effect of national taxes on domestic products' prices and not the differences between national policies and third countries' policies.

The distinction between the two situations described above can also be explained by reference to the definition of the concept of 'border'. In the case of BTAs, internationally traded goods are not differentiated based on the borders they have crossed. In principle, it should not matter that a product is imported from China, Brazil or anywhere else, though it is true that products from countries where production processes are highly polluting will likely be subject to high tax burdens in case of environmental taxes the tax rate of which is proportionate to the pollution released during production. However, high tax rates are not automatically linked to the country of production/exportation. In the case of countervailing duties, anti-dumping measures and – to a certain extent – customs duties, the concept of 'border' has a far greater impact: these trade measures are indeed imposed on products imported from well-defined countries. As mentioned in Chapter 1, the distinction between BTAs and customs duties is nevertheless sometimes unclear (Section 1.2.2.3.1).

4.1.2 Environmental BTAs and the Concept of 'Tax'

Traditionally, only indirect taxes are supposed to be eligible for BTAs (Chapter 1). The debate and the literature surrounding environmental BTAs call into question this assumption as well as the definition of 'indirect taxes' (Chapter 2, Section 2.2.1.4.3).[3] An important feature of environmentally related taxes is that they normally do not primarily aim

---

[3] See Felicity Deane, *Emissions Trading and WTO Law. A Global Analysis* (Edward Elgar Publishing 2015), 191–192.

at raising revenue – as is the case with traditional taxes – but rather at protecting the environment.[4] This feature distinguishes environmentally related taxes from the taxes that have traditionally been eligible for BTAs. The environmental objective of environmentally related taxes may make it difficult to draw a clear line between environmental taxes and (market-based) regulatory instruments. Consequently, a first question raised by environmental BTAs concerns the distinction between tax and (market-based) regulatory measures.

4.1.2.1 Distinction between taxes and other market-based instruments

The distinction between tax and regulatory adjustments at the border is not clear cut. In the literature, the distinction has sometimes been blurred, including in the framework of the climate debate. For example, the concept of 'border carbon adjustment' is often used in the literature to refer to a broad category of adjustments including BTAs in respect of carbon taxes and adjustments in respect of regulatory measures, such as the EU emissions trading system.[5] Hufbauer et al., however, suggest that adjustments should be limited to taxes and not be extended to regulations.[6] Under their approach, the concept of tax becomes a central element in the definition of BTAs. Indeed, as soon as a regulatory measure is designed in a similar way as a levy or as soon as a measure imposes a financial burden on products or producers, questions are likely

---

[4] Alain Steichen, *Manuel de droit fiscal. Droit fiscal général* (Saint Paul 2006), 46, 53–54. In my opinion, taxes always pursue regulatory objectives, even when their primary objective is to raise revenue. The legislator always makes a political choice when it chooses to tax. See Amy C. Christian, 'Designing a Carbon Tax: The Introduction of the Carbon-Burned Tax (CBT)' (1991–1992) 10 UCLA Journal of Environmental Law and Policy 221, 225. See also Louis Eisenstein, *The Ideologies of Taxation* (Harvard University Press 2000; first published by Roland Press Co. 1961).

[5] See i.a. Madison Condon & Ada Ignaciuk, 'Border Carbon Adjustment and International Trade. A Literature Review' (2013) 6 OECD Trade and Environment Working Papers, OECD Publishing; Aaron Cosbey, Susanne Droege, Carolyn Fischer, Julia Reinaud, John Stephenson, Lutz Weischer & Peter Wooders, 'A Guide for the Concerned: Guidance on the Elaboration and Implementation of Border Carbon Adjustment' (2012) 3 Entwined Policy Report. See also OECD, Directorate for Financial and Enterprise Affairs Competition Committee, Emission Permits and Competition, 2010, DAF/COMP(2010)35, 49.

[6] Gary Clyde Hufbauer, Steve Charnovitz & Jisun Kim, *Global Warming and the World Trading System* (Peterson Institute for International Economics 2009), 66.

to arise as to whether the measure can be assimilated to a tax or not (Chapter 6).[7] For example, one may wonder whether the obligation to surrender emission permits (or units, allowances, credits) could be assimilated to a tax measure.[8]

4.1.2.2 Fiscal nature of environmental taxes

In addition to the question concerning the nature of market-based regulatory instruments, the question arises as to whether the regulatory character of environmental taxes may impact on their qualification as a 'tax measure'. In other words, 'Could a measure, which is called an environmental tax by the legislator, lose its fiscal nature and be considered a regulatory measure under WTO law, in light of its regulatory objective?'

It has been derived from the *Superfund* case that the environmental character of a tax has no impact on its legal treatment under WTO law.[9] However, it could be argued that the environmental character of a tax is unimportant as long as it is not so strong as to modify the legal nature of the measure, transforming the tax into a purely regulatory measure.[10] This reading likely translates the logic of the Panel in the *Superfund* case, which seemed to have started its analysis from the assumption that the *Superfund* tax is a tax, without questioning its tax nature.

The relevance of the distinction between BTAs and regulatory adjustments is discussed in more detailed in Chapter 6.

4.1.3 Environmental BTAs and the Concept of 'Adjustment'

The concept of 'environmental BTAs' refers to fiscal measures used to complement domestic (environmental) taxes. Environmental BTAs should be distinguished from other fiscal measures applied without corresponding environmental taxes (or regulations) on domestic goods. Indeed,

---

[7] Felicity Deane, 'The Border Adjustments of the Australian Clean Energy Package' (2014) 17 International Trade and Business Law Review 66–107, 96–103.

[8] *Ibid.* See also Jon Truby, 'Extraterritoriality or an Illegal Tax? A Challenge to the Inclusion of Aviation in the EU Emissions Trading Scheme' (2012) 14(4) Environmental Law Review 301–306.

[9] See WTO, Preparatory Committee, Preparatory Committee for the Sub-Committee on Trade and Environment, Report of the Meeting held on 15–16 September 1994, Note by the Secretariat, 10 October 2004, PC/SCTE/M/3, paras. 70 & 98.

[10] *Ibid.*, para. 84: 'because a country decided to call a tax an internal tax did not automatically make it one'.

an important characteristic of BTAs is that the burden imposed by the implementing country on imported goods reflects the burden imposed on domestic goods. The comparison between imported and domestic goods is only based on a comparison of the tax burden imposed by the implementing country. In principle, the comparison is not an 'absolute' comparison between all the costs imposed on domestic products in the implementing country and all the costs in the country (or countries) of production of the imported products.[11] Though BTAs may permit avoidance of double taxation, it is not BTAs' main purpose. BTAs' objective is rather to neutralise the effect of domestic taxes on international trade.

Environmental BTAs are nevertheless very often confused with compensating fiscal measures aimed at offsetting the differences in the level of environmental policies between countries.[12] In contrast to BTAs, these fiscal measures aim at compensating the difference between the (allegedly) high costs of domestic environmental policy borne by domestic goods and the (allegedly) lower costs of foreign environmental policies borne by imported products. Hence, these 'compensating' measures are designed by taking into account the supposed level of foreign environmental policies, this level being determined by the country applying the compensating measures. These measures differ from the traditional conception of BTAs (aimed at compensating for domestic indirect taxes adopted in the implementing country) and should preferably not be called BTAs. As mentioned above, under WTO law, these measures should rather be analysed under the categories of customs duties and countervailing duties, which are applied in reaction to another country's trade practice.[13]

---

[11] On this distinction, see Donald Feaver & Benedict Sheehy, 'Climate Policy and Border Adjustment Regulation: Designing a Coherent Response' (2012) 13 Melbourne Journal of International Law 792–817, 814.

[12] See WTO, Committee on Trade and Environment, Report of the Meeting held on 6 July 2011, Note by the Secretariat, 6 September 2011 WT/CTE/M/52, 68–69; WTO, PC/SCTE/M/3, *supra* n. 9, paras. 34 & 53; Stephen Smith, 'Environmental Taxes and Competitiveness: An Overview of Issues, Policy Options, and Research Needs', OECD paper, 11 June 2003, COM/ENV/EPOC/DAFFE/CFA(2001)90/REV1, paras. 62 & 67. See also Jon M. Truby, 'Towards Overcoming the Conflict Between Environmental Tax Leakage and Border Tax Adjustment Concessions for Developing Countries' (2010–2011) 12(1) Vermont Journal of Environmental Law 149–183, 154–155.

[13] The concepts of BTAs, tariffs and countervailing duties are very often confused or used inadequately: see, e.g., Jean-Marc Burniaux, Jean Chateau, Romain Duval & Stéphanie Jamet, 'The Economics of Climate Change Mitigation: Policies and Options for the Future', OECD Economics Department

Given their role as compensating measures in respect of domestic taxes, environmental BTAs should be distinguished from customs duties. Confusion sometimes arises when the legislator uses the concept of 'customs duties' to refer to BTAs in respect of excise duties. For example, in the Australian system of excise duties, the BTAs in respect of certain domestic excises seem to be established through 'customs duties' as defined in the 1995 Customs Tariff Act.[14]

4.1.4 Environmental BTAs and Goods

Environmental BTAs have usually been assimilated to taxes imposed on goods. As mentioned earlier (Chapter 3), for traditional BTAs, taxes on services – directly connected to products – may sometimes be assimilated to taxes on products (under the concept of *taxes occultes*). Environmental taxes on services could therefore also be considered for adjustments, for example in the case of environmental BTAs in respect of (environmental) taxes on transportation.[15] Moreover, some cross-border services are highly polluting, such as the GHG emissions released by the aviation

---

Working Paper No. 658, 17 December 2008, ECO/WKP(2008)66, 24, para. 37; OECD, Meeting of the Council at Ministerial Level, Preparation of the 4–5 June 2008, The Economics of Climate Change, 14 May 2008, C/Min(2008)3, para. 22; OECD, The Economics of Climate Change Mitigation: Policies and Options for Global Action beyond 2012, 18 September 2009, 89; UN GA, International trade and development, Report of the Secretary-General, 26 July 2013, A/68/205, 26–27 (para. 61 and Box 3). See also Julien Bueb, Lilian Richieri Hanania & Alison Le Clézio, 'Border Adjustments Mechanisms. Elements for Economic, Legal, and Political Analysis (2016) 20 WIDER Working Paper.

[14] Australia, Customs Tariff Act 1995, Act No. 147, An Act to impose duties of customs, to repeal the Customs Tariff Act 1987, and for related purposes, as amended, taking into account amendments up to the Customs Tariff Amendment Act 2012 (Cth), in particular Section 19A (Changes of rates of duty), which refers to Sections 6FA and 6FB of the Excise Tariff Act 1921. See also Parliament of the Commonwealth of Australia, House of Representatives, Clean Energy (Customs Tariff Amendment) Bill 2011, Explanatory Memorandum, 2010–2011, para. 3.21; Deane, *supra* n. 7, 85–87.

[15] Lorand Bartels, 'The Inclusion of Aviation in the EU ETS. WTO Law Considerations' (2012) 6 Trade and Sustainable Energy Series, International Centre for Trade and Sustainable Development, 22–25. See also, Kommers-kollegium (Swedish National Board of Trade), 'Climate and Trade Rules – Harmony or Conflict?' (2004) available at <http://www.kommers.se/Documents/dokumentarkiv/publikationer/2004/rapporter/report-climate-and-trade-rules.pdf> (accessed 3 November 2015), 63–64.

sector or the pollution associated with data centres.[16] The inclusion of the aviation sector in the EU ETS in 2009 illustrates that cross-border measures may be relevant in the case of services.

4.2 ILLUSTRATION: ENVIRONMENTAL BTAs IN PRACTICE

A variety of environmental tax models, including environmental BTAs, have been implemented or proposed so far. Their tax design copies the fiscal mechanism of traditional taxes that include BTAs: excise duties, VAT and sales taxes.

4.2.1 Excise Duty-based Models

4.2.1.1 Traditional (environmental) excise duty model

Some traditional excise taxes are nowadays assimilated to environmentally related taxes although their original purpose was purely to raise revenue. The best example is the case of excise taxes on energy products (e.g. fossil fuels) usually described as 'environmentally related taxes', even though, from an historical viewpoint, these excise taxes were not adopted for environmental reasons.[17]

BTAs in respect of traditional (environmental) energy taxes are imposed on imported polluting products in a similar way in which domestic polluting products are taxed (Figure 4.1). No adjustments are made to compensate for the potential impact of 'hidden' excise taxes on other products. For example, when an excise duty is applied on oil, no adjustments are made in respect of imported products for which a significant amount of oil has been used in the production process.[18] This model is the traditional model of excise duties: in general, no adjustments

---

[16] See Janet Milne, 'Mining the Air and Minding the Consequences: A Dark Cloud Tax', presentation at the 16th Global Conference on Environmental Taxation, 23–26 September 2015, University of Technology Sydney.

[17] For statistical purposes, energy excise taxes are usually classified as 'environmentally related taxes'. See OECD, Taxation, Innovation and the Environment (2010), 34–36; OECD, The Political Economy of Environmentally Related Taxes (2006); Eurostat, Environmental tax statistics, available at <http://ec.europa.eu/eurostat/statistics-explained/index.php/Environmental_tax_statistics> (accessed 28 October 2015).

[18] Rosanne Altshuler, 'The GATT-Legality of Border Adjustments for Carbon Taxes and the Cost of Emissions Permits', Prepared for the ATPI Conference on US Energy Taxes, 15–16 October 2009.

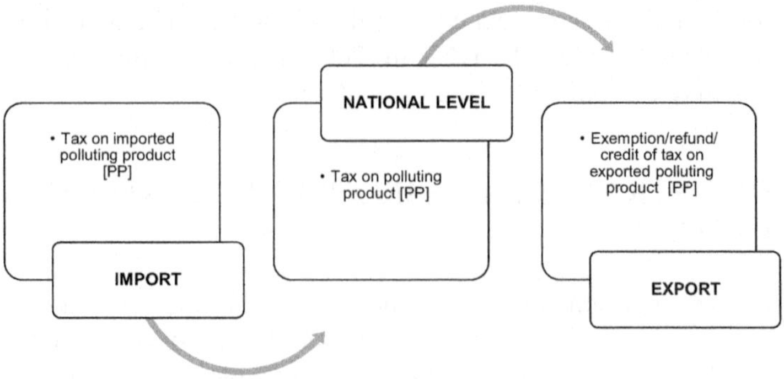

Figure 4.1 Traditional (environmental) excise tax model

are made to compensate for the 'hidden' taxes borne by domestic products due to the excise duties imposed on raw materials, energy sources, etc.

The excise tax is specific (meaning that it is calculated as a fixed amount per quantity of energy source/raw material). Sometimes, the tax rate differentiates between products based on their polluting impact.[19] For example, fuel products could be differentiated based on their CO_2-to-energy content, which would imply that coal – which has a higher CO_2 content – is subject to a higher tax than gas for the same amount of energy.[20]

---

[19] At the EU level, see Art. 18(1) and Annex II of Council Directive 2003/96/EC. See also Communication from the Commission to the European Parliament, the Council and the European Economic and Social Committee, Smarter energy taxation for the EU: proposal for a revision of the Energy Taxation Directive, COM(2011)168/3. This proposal has now been withdrawn given the unsuccessful character of the negotiations (Annex to the Communication from the Commission to the European Parliament, the Council, the European Economic and Social Committee and the Committee of the Regions, Commission Work Programme 2015, A New Start, 16 December 2014, COM(2014)910 final, at p. 6). See also Mikael Skou Andersen, 'Denmark/Sweden – Reflections on the Scandinavian Model: Some Insights into Energy-Related Taxes in Denmark and Sweden' (2015) 55(6) European Taxation 235–244.

[20] See US, Energy Information Administration, Frequently asked questions, *How much carbon dioxide is produced when different fuels are burned?*, available at <http://www.eia.gov/tools/faqs/faq.cfm?id=73&t=11> (accessed 22 June 2015).

Avi-Yonah and Uhlman support this model in their proposal to establish a carbon tax in the US.[21] They consider that a carbon tax should take the form of an 'upstream carbon tax' imposed on 'only three industries: coal, oil, and natural gas producers and importers'.[22] Proposals for 'upstream carbon taxes' were introduced in the US House of Representatives.[23] The Bills usually propose to add a subchapter E to chapter 38 of the Internal Revenue Code, which is the chapter in which the Superfund and ODC taxes were also included. The idea is to add a tax on the carbon dioxide content of primary fossil fuels, defined as coal (including lignite and peat), petroleum and any petroleum product and natural gas.[24]

Various countries have implemented traditional (environmentally related) excises in the EU.[25] In Denmark, for example, an energy tax and a CO_2 tax apply on fossil fuels and electricity.[26] The tax is paid by the producer or importer, as in the case of traditional excises.[27] No BTAs are made in respect of the 'hidden' energy and CO_2 tax paid in respect of

---

21 Reuven S. Avi-Yonah & David M. Uhlmann, 'Combating Global Climate Change: Why a Carbon Tax is a Better Response to Global Warming than Cap and Trade' (2009) 28(1) Stanford Environmental Law Journal 3–50.

22 *Ibid.*, 48.

23 US, H.R. 2069, Save Our Climate Act of 2007, 110th Congress, 26 April 2007; US, H.R. 3416, A Bill to amend the Internal Revenue Code of 1986 to reduce carbon dioxide emissions in the United States domestic energy supply, 110th Congress, 1st Session, 3 August 2007; US, H.R. 594, Save Our Climate Act, 111th Congress, 15 January 2009; US, H.R. 5796, State's Choice Act of 2014, 113th Congress, 4 December 2014; US, H.R. 5873, Gas Tax Replacement Act of 2014, 113th Congress, 11 December 2014; US, H.R. 309, Gas Tax Replacement Act of 2015, 114th Congress, 13 January 2015.

24 *Ibid.*

25 See also European Commission, Proposal for a Council Directive amending Directive 2003/96/EC restructuring the Community framework for the taxation of energy products and electricity, Brussels, COM(2011)169/3, 2011/xxxx(CNS), SEC(2011)409, SEC(2011)410. See also ECJ, *Outokumpu Oy*, 2 April 1998, C-213/96.

26 See OECD, Environmental Performance Reviews Denmark (2007) 125–131. See also Denmark, Act on energy tax on mineral oil products (Lov om afgift af stenkul, brunkul og koks m.v.); Act concerning tax on coal, lignite and coke (Lov om afgift af stenkul, brunkul og koks m.v.).

27 Danish Environmental Protection Agency, Economic Instruments in Environmental Protection in Denmark, available at <http://www.statensnet.dk/pligtarkiv/fremvis.pl?vaerkid=4973&reprid=0&filid=40&iarkiv=1#11.5.2> (accessed 27 October 2015), see 'Structure and levels of taxation on energy', point 5.1.3. See also, UCD Dublin, Economic Instruments – Charges and Taxes. Energy Taxation (including CO_2 -and SO_2-taxation) Denmark.

products for which a significant amount of fuel or electricity has been used in the production process. However, in order to mitigate the effect of the energy and CO_2 taxes on business competitiveness, enterprises may apply for partial or total reimbursement of the tax, which varies according to the activity of the enterprise and the presence of an energy efficiency agreement between the enterprise and the Danish authorities.[28] In the Belgian system, the rate of excise duties on energy products and electricity varies according to the quantity (expressed in litres, kilograms or MWh) of the product concerned as well as its use.[29] In the Canadian province of British Columbia, this traditional model has also served for the adoption of a carbon tax on the combustion of fossil fuels.[30]

An alternative to this traditional excise tax model is to impose differentiated excise duties based on the production process of a limited number of goods the polluting process of which is highly polluting.[31] Where the rate of the excise duties usually varies based on the polluting potential of the taxable goods, this alternative model proposes to tax products based on the polluting impact of their production process. For example, a country could decide to tax certain energy-intensive (manufactured) products (e.g. steel), taking into account the amount of pollution that has been generated to produce steel.[32] This alternative model differs from the case of 'CO_2 taxes' adopted in many countries, such as the Danish tax, in that they would be directly proportional to the pollution emitted during the production process of intermediate products. In other words, the products concerned would not be divided into

[28] Danish Environmental Protection Agency, *supra* n. 27, point 5.1.3. See also, UCD Dublin, Economic Instruments – Charges and Taxes. Energy Taxation (including CO_2 and SO_2 taxation) Denmark.

[29] Belgium, Art. 419 de la Loi-programme du 27 décembre 2004, Chapitre XVIII ('la taxation des produits énergétiques et de l'électricité'). See also Art. 429 (which lists the uses of fuels that benefit from an exemption).

[30] David G. Duff, 'Carbon Taxation in British Columbia' (2008–2009) 10 Vermont Journal of Environmental Law 87.

[31] This distinction is inspired by Paul Demaret & Raoul Stewardson, 'Border Tax Adjustments under GATT and EC Law and General Implications for Environmental Taxes' (1994) 28(4) Journal of World Trade Law 5–65, 58. This alternative model should be aimed at integrating the pollution related to production of a limited number of goods. When all goods are taxed in accordance with pollution released during production, the tax is no longer designed after the structure of excise taxes but resembles VAT (*infra*).

[32] In this alternative model, the products concerned should be products that have been manufactured/processed since the tax rate would be proportionate to the pollution released during production.

categories related to specific tax rates as is the case with the traditional environmental excise taxes described above. The tax would rather be calculated based on an equation including the amount of pollution released during production.[33] Although this model provides for an instrument that allows better differentiation between products based on the pollution emitted, it is likely to be practically infeasible in the near future. For now, instruments do not exist to easily determine the pollution resulting from production processes (Section 4.3).

4.2.1.2 Environmental excise duty model based on the US Superfund and ODC taxes

Under this model, an excise tax is imposed on certain polluting substances. The tax is applied on domestic products as well as imported products while exported products may be relieved from the tax.[34] The tax is specific and is based on the quantity of the polluting substances. The tax rate usually varies depending on the polluting nature of the substance or products: the more polluting a substance is, the higher the tax rate should be.[35] For example, in the case of the ODC tax, the amount of the tax varies based on the 'ozone-depleting factor' of the chemical.[36] In the Australian model, the amount of the SGG levy was calculated based on the 'global warming potential' of the substances subject to the levy.[37]

In addition to the tax on domestically produced and imported polluting substances, an additional tax is imposed on imported products containing the polluting substances (or intermediate products) and/or on products for which such substances or intermediate products have been used in the production process (Figure 4.2). Following this logic, the ODC tax is imposed on 'imported taxable products', defined as 'any product (other than an ozone-depleting chemical) entered into the United States for consumption, use or warehousing if any ozone-depleting chemical was used as a material in the manufacture or production of such product'.

---

[33] For example: [Tax = 'pollution released during production' multiplied by 'rate'] or [Tax = 'price' multiplied by 'rate'], where 'rate' is equal to [X multiplied by 'pollution released during production'].

[34] For the ODC and Superfund taxes, see 26 US CODE §§4661 & 4681.

[35] See however, on the objective of the Superfund Tax, Don Fullerton, 'Why Have Separate Environmental Taxes?', in: James M. Poterba (ed.), *Tax Policy and the Economy* (MIT Press 1996, Vol. 10), 47.

[36] 26 US CODE §4681, (b)(1)(A) & §4682(b).

[37] Australia, Ozone Protection and Synthetic Greenhouse Gas (Manufacture Levy) Regulations 2004, Statutory Rules 2004 No. 18 as amended (Cth), Section 5.

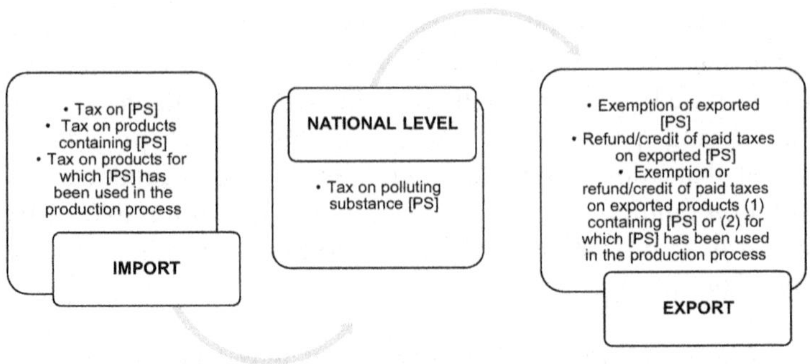

Figure 4.2 Environmental excise model based on the US Superfund and ODC taxes

Similarly, the Superfund tax is imposed on 'listed substances', which contain or result from the use of taxable chemicals.[38] For practical reasons, the tax is not imposed on all imported products that have been produced/manufactured with the polluting substances (or intermediate products) that are taxed domestically. The tax is limited to the products that contain a significant amount of polluting substances or intermediate products and to the products for which a significant amount of substances or intermediate products has been used in the production process. In the case of the ODC tax, a US Treasury Regulation lists all products that fall into the category of imported taxable products, provided that the ODC tax on the product is not 'less than one/tenth of one percent of the importer's cost of acquiring such product' (the so-called *de minimis* exception).[39] Similarly, a list determines the taxable substances subject to the Superfund tax. Any addition of a new substance to the list is limited to substances for which 'taxable chemicals constitute more than 50 percent of the weight (or more than 50 percent of the value) of the materials used to produce such substances (determined based on the predominant method of production)'.[40]

---

[38] For the ODC tax, see 26 US CODE §4682(c). For the Superfund tax, see 26 US CODE §4672(a). See also GATT, Industrial Pollution Control and International Trade, Note by the GATT Secretariat, 9 June 1971, L/3538, 15 where the specific tax design of 'double BTAs', as in the case of the ODC/Superfund tax, had already been thought of: '... the importing country might consider a border tax adjustment in an amount equivalent to the tax content of the second-stage product'.

[39] US, Treasury Regulation, section 52.4682-3(b)(2)(B), Imported Taxable Products.

[40] 26 US CODE §4672(a)(2)(B).

From a theoretical viewpoint, the examples of the ODC and Superfund taxes on imported products – either products incorporating polluting substances or products for which such polluting substances have been used but not incorporated in the production process[41] – could be compared to BTAs in respect of a *taxe occulte*, namely the 'hidden' tax on polluting substances and intermediate products paid on domestically produced goods. These examples provide a practical argument in favour of process-related BTAs.[42] Since the BTAs on imported products as described above are aimed at compensating for the taxes paid on polluting substances and intermediate products, the amount of the tax on imported products should be the same as the hidden tax borne by domestically produced goods.[43] Therefore, the amount of the polluting substances and intermediate products related to the imported products should be determined. In other words, additional information is needed about either the content of the imported products or their production method. In contrast to traditional excise duties, it does not suffice to know the quantity or the value of the imported products since the tax is not imposed on the product as such but on its components or on substances used in its production process. In the cases of both the ODC and the Superfund taxes, the importer is supposed to provide sufficient information to determine the amount of the tax.[44] When no or insufficient information is provided, alternative methods are applied. Regarding the ODC tax, when the importer cannot determine the weight of ODC related to the imported products (i.e. the 'exact method'), the ODC weight

---

[41] In the literature, controversies exist as to whether the ODC and Superfund taxes only apply to products incorporating polluting substances or also to products for which polluting substances have been used but not incorporated. However, I discussed the topic with biologists and they seemed to indicate that the ODC and Superfund taxes did not exclude products on the basis that the polluting substances were not incorporated.

[42] OECD, Joint Meeting of tax and environmental experts, The Political Economy of Environmentally Related Taxes, 18 November 2005, COM/ENV/EPOC/CTPA/CFA(2005)42, 93, para. 327. The question of process-related BTAs does not only concern the type of taxes that may be eligible for adjustments (such as *taxes occultes*) but also the differentiation of products based on their production process.

[43] See, for the Superfund tax, 26 US CODE §4671(b)(1). The language in the provisions related to the ODC tax is very similar (26 US CODE §4681(a)(2)(A)).

[44] 26 US CODE §4671(b). See §4681(b)(2)(B) for the ODC tax. See also Treasury Regulation §52.4682-3(e).

should be determined based on the 'table method', in the light of the products and related ODC weight listed in the US regulation on the ODC tax.[45] When this method also fails because the 'table ODC weight of the product is not specified', the tax should amount to 'one percent of the entry value of the product'.[46] As for the Superfund tax, two methods have been proposed. First, the tax could be calculated as '5 percent of the appraised value of such substance [i.e. the imported product] as of the time such substance was entered into the United States for consumption, use, or warehousing'.[47] Second, the tax could be calculated on the presumed polluting substances or intermediate products related to the imported products, determined as if the imported product had been produced 'using the predominant method of production of such substance [i.e. product]'.[48] According to the Panel in the *Superfund* case, the '5 per cent rate' method would not allow for complying with the equivalence requirement of the GATT 'because the tax rate would in that case no longer be imposed in relation to the amount of taxable chemicals used in their production but the value of the imported substance'.[49] The Panel, however, concluded that the tax 'was in principle consistent with Article III:2, first sentence', disregarding the issue of the '5 per cent rate' considering that 'the tax authorities had regulatory power to eliminate the need for the imposition of the penalty rate'.[50]

On the export side, exported polluting substances or intermediate products are in principle not subject to the tax. The same treatment may also be applied to exported products for which the polluting substances have been used during the production process. For example, in the case of the Superfund tax, limited BTAs on exports allowed for the credit or refund of the tax 'paid with respect to any taxable chemical' when 'such chemical was exported by any person' or when 'such chemical was used as a material in the manufacture or production of a substance which was exported by any person and which, at the time of export, was a taxable substance'.[51] From an environmental viewpoint, BTAs on exported products are less easily justified. The main rationale for BTAs on

---

[45] US, Treasury Regulation, §52.4682-3(e)(3).

[46] US, Treasury Regulation, §52.4682-3(e)(4).

[47] 26 US CODE §4671(b)(2).

[48] 26 US CODE §4761(b)(3).

[49] GATT, Panel Report, United States – Taxes on Petroleum and Certain Imported Substances, 5 June 1987, L/6175, BISD 34S/136 (*US – Superfund*), para. 5.2.9.

[50] GATT, Panel Report, *US – Superfund*, para. 5.2.10.

[51] See 26 US Code §4662(e)(2)(A)(i) & (ii)(I) & (II).

exported products indeed relates to the need for avoiding the risk of loss of competitiveness caused by the adoption of environmental taxes at the national level. The only environmental reason to adopt BTAs on exported products is to avoid the creation of 'pollution havens'. The argument goes as follows: without BTAs on exported products, domestic enterprises could be encouraged to relocate in countries with less stringent environmental policies, which would lead to a global increase of pollution, from a worldwide perspective.

4.2.1.3 CO_2 tax model inspired by the environmental excise model

Based on the environmental excise model, a CO_2 tax model has been proposed at both the academic and political levels.[52] The idea is to impose an upstream tax on energy products, the rate of which would be based on the CO_2 emissions potential of the energy product concerned. In addition to this traditional environmental excise tax, a BTA is applied to compensate the hidden tax related to this traditional excise and borne by energy-intensive domestic products. The idea is comparable to the Belgian or Danish examples of energy and CO_2 taxes described above, except that a BTA mechanism would be added to energy-intensive

---

[52] E.g. Christian, *supra* n. 4, 266; Harry Clarke, 'Some Basic Economics of Carbon Taxes' (2011) 44(2) The Australian Economic Review 123, 129; Harry Clarke, 'Carbon Leakages, Consumption Tax Bases and International Climate Change Agreements' (2010) 29(2) Economic Papers: A Journal of Applied Economics and Policy 156–68; Duff, *supra* n. 30, 106; J. Andrew Hoerner & Frank Muller, 'Carbon Taxes for Climate Protection in a Competitive World', paper prepared for the Swiss Federal Office for Foreign Economic Affairs, June 1996; Sam Kortum & David Weisbach, 'Border Adjustments for Carbon Emissions: Basic Concepts and Design' (2016) Resources for the Future; Gilbert E. Metcalf & David Weisbach, 'The Design of a Carbon Tax' (2009) 33 Harvard Environmental Law Review 499–556. See, at the US level, the following legislative proposals (some of them relative to a CO_2 tax, some others on emissions permits): US, S. 332, Climate Protection Act of 2013, 113th Congress, 14 February 2013; H.R. 4754, Managed Carbon Price Act of 2014, 113th Congress, 28 May 2014; US, H.R. 5271, Healthy Climate and Family Security Act of 2014, 113th Congress, 30 July 2014; US, H.R. 5307, America's Energy Security Trust Fund Act of 2014, 113th Congress, 31 July 2014; US, H.R. 972, Managed Carbon Price Act of 2015, 114th Congress, 13 February 2015; US, H.R. 1027, Healthy Climate and Family Security Act of 2015, 114th Congress, 24 February 2015; US, H.R. 2202, Tax Pollution, Not Profits Act, 114th Congress, 1 May 2015; US, US, S. 2399, Climate Protection and Justice Act of 2015, 114th Congress, 10 December 2015, US, H.R. 2014, Tax Pollution, Not Profits Act, 115th Congress, 4 June 2017.

imported (and possibly exported) products. In other words, energy-intensive imported products would be taxed and, if needed for competitiveness reasons, energy-intensive exported products could be relieved from taxation through reimbursement (in order not to support the domestic energy taxes that have been imposed on the energy products used in the production process). This mechanism would replace the specific (exemption) provisions that currently apply to national energy-intensive industries in the Belgian and Danish systems.

The proposal copies the logic of the ODC or the Superfund tax. Indeed, as regards the ODC tax, a tax is applied on imported products for which the polluting substances (here energy products) have been used in the production process. Moreover, exported products for which the polluting substances have been used in the production process should not bear the domestic tax on energy products. Where the ODC tax is applied to chemicals based on their ozone-depleting potential, the CO_2 tax could be imposed on energy products based on their global warming potential.

Despite their similarities, CO_2 tax models nevertheless differ from the ODC and Superfund taxes, at least in three main aspects. A first difference is a practical one: where ODC chemicals are used in the production process of a limited number of products, energy products are used in the production process of a very large number of products. Hence, the assumed impact on competitiveness is more difficult to neutralise. As in the case of the ODC tax on imported products, the CO_2 tax could, however, be applied on a well-defined and limited number of energy-intensive imported products. For example, carbon-intensive goods could include primary products (such as iron, steel, aluminium, cement, glass, pulp, paper, chemicals) and other manufactured products generating comparable GHG emissions as those generated by primary products.[53] As for the ODC and Superfund taxes, the question arises as to the determination of the exact content of polluting substances in imported energy-intensive products. Various approximation methods have been proposed. As in the case of the ODC and Superfund taxes, importers and exporters should have the possibility of providing evidence of the

[53] See US, H.R. 1337, America's Energy Security Trust Fund Act of 2009, 111th Congress, 5 March 2009, proposed Internal Revenue Code Sec. 4694(a)(5) & (6). See also US, H.R. 2380, A Bill to amend the Internal Revenue Code of 1986 to reduce social security payroll taxes and to reduce the reliance of the United States economy on carbon-based energy sources, 111th Congress, 13 May 2009, proposed Internal Revenue Code Sec. 4696.

presumed energy content of the products.[54] Alternatively, authors have proposed calculating the average energy content based on the 'predominant method of production' or the 'best available technique' in producing the goods concerned, either in the country where the CO_2 tax has been adopted or in the exporting country.[55]

A second difference relates to the nature of energy products and CO_2 emissions compared to ODC. Energy products are rarely incorporated into the final imported products and, consequently, CO_2 emissions are not easily traceable. In contrast, ODC and other chemicals may either be physically incorporated into the final imported products (e.g. in the cooling circuit of a refrigerator) or not physically present but easily traceable (e.g. ODC chemicals used to make insulating foam).[56] This difference may play a role in the legal analysis of the eligibility of *taxes occultes* on energy products for adjustments. As for inputs (physically) incorporated in other products, the BTAs can indeed be analysed as a traditional BTA in respect of a tax imposed on a product. The tax could indeed be formulated as follows: 'a tax is imposed on chemicals sold by producers, manufacturers as well as any chemicals imported in the United States; no tax is imposed with respect to chemicals if the person liable for the tax establishes that a prior tax has already been imposed on such chemicals at the US level'.[57] In this case, domestic chemicals would primarily be taxed when producers sell them in their 'raw form'.

---

54 E.g. US, H.R. 2380, A Bill to amend the Internal Revenue Code of 1986 to reduce social security payroll taxes and to reduce the reliance of the United States economy on carbon-based energy sources, 111th Congress, 13 May 2009, proposed Internal Revenue Code Sec. 4695(c). See also Hoerner & Muller, *supra* n. 52, 21.

55 See e.g. Metcalf & Weisbach, *supra* n. 52, 549. See also Benjamin M. Eichenberg, 'Greenhouse Gas Regulation and Border Tax Adjustments: The Carrot and the Stick' (2008) 3(2) Golden Gate University Environmental Law Journal 283, 348–349. See also Charles E. McLure, 'The Carbon-Added Tax: An Idea Whose Time Should Never Come' (2010) 3 Carbon & Climate Law Review 250, 251; Truby, *supra* n. 12, 156.

56 Frank Biermann & Rainer Brohm, 'Implementing the Kyoto Protocol without the USA: The Strategic Role of Energy Tax Adjustments at the Border' (2005) 4(3) Climate Policy 289–302, 294; Duncan Brack, Michael Grubb & Windram Craig, *International Trade and Climate Change Policies* (Earthscan 2000), 77 (p. 84 seems, however, to contradict p. 77). Joost Pauwelyn, 'Carbon Leakage Measures and Border Tax Adjustments under WTO Law', in: Geert Van Calster & Denise Prévost (eds.), *Research Handbook on Environment, Health and the WTO* (Edward Elgar Publishing 2013), footnote 82; Demaret & Stewardson, *supra* n. 31, 26.

57 The second part of the sentence is inspired by 26 US CODE §4612(b).

'Domestic' chemicals incorporated in other products would also be taxable but would in principle be relieved from taxation as a 'prior tax' has already been imposed on the chemicals. Imported chemicals in their raw form would be taxed as well as imported chemicals incorporated in other products since these chemicals would not have been subject to a 'prior tax' (understood as a domestic US tax, regardless of taxes previously paid in the country where the goods have been produced). Briefly, in the case of a tax on physically incorporated inputs, the tax could be analysed as a mere product tax, a category traditionally recognised to be eligible for BTAs. In contrast, in the case of a tax on non-physically incorporated inputs (like the CO_2 tax model) the tax should be analysed as belonging to the category of *taxes occultes*, a category for which the adoption of BTAs is controversial.

Finally, a third distinction is related to the nature of energy products: energy products are found in specific geographical areas, which makes them politically sensitive products. In contrast to ODC, which are used in a limited number of products in the economy, energy products are a crucial element for the whole economy. Moreover, where affordable substitutes exist to replace ODC, this is not (yet) the case for energy products. From this perspective, energy policy is very much a question of national security. Governments may be afraid that the rise of taxes on energy products will lead to retaliation measures from energy-producing countries.

Alternatives to this model have been proposed at both the academic and political levels. For example, Metcalf and Weisbach propose adopting BTAs limited to countries without a carbon pricing system.[58] Concrete political proposals for CO_2 taxes in the US usually follow a similar logic by limiting the implementation of BTAs to imports from countries that have not (yet) adopted equivalent carbon measures (either a tax or a regulatory measure imposing a similar carbon price on manufacturers of carbon-intensive goods operating outside the US).[59] As mentioned earlier, such approach contradicts the idea that BTAs permit the

---

[58] Metcalf & Weisbach, *supra* n. 52, 522.

[59] US, H.R. 1337, America's Energy Security Trust Fund Act of 2009, 111th Congress, 5 March 2009, proposed Internal Revenue Code Sec 4693(c)(B) and Sec. 4694(a)(7). See also US, H.R. 3242, Save Our Climate Act, 112th Congress, 24 October 2011, proposed Internal Revenue Code Sec. 4691(i). This Bill proposes not only limiting BTAs to countries without equivalent carbon prices, but also allowing a refund when higher carbon prices are imposed by a foreign country on the imported products. See also US, H.R. 2380, A Bill to amend the Internal Revenue Code of 1986 to reduce social security payroll taxes and to

neutralisation of the impact of domestic taxes, not the impact of differences between domestic policies and policies of third countries. From this perspective, the proposal of Metcalf and Weisbach should be described as a special tariff rather than as a BTA.

4.2.2 VAT-based Models

The various models explained below are either partially based on the VAT system (the so-called 'carbon-added tax', inspired by the design of the VAT) or fully based on the VAT system, proposing to provide exemptions or rate differentials for certain categories of goods at the final consumption stage (the so-called 'environmental VAT model'). The comparison with VAT has sometimes been criticised.[60] This section, however, takes the viewpoint that the comparison with VAT is relevant since the various models all copy the mechanism and tax design of VAT.

4.2.2.1 Carbon-added tax (CAT)

In the literature on environmentally related BTAs, reference is often made to CAT.[61] However, few authors have truly argued in favour of the

---

reduce the reliance of the United States economy on carbon-based energy sources, 111th Congress, 13 May 2009, proposed Internal Revenue Code Sec. 4695.

[60] The reference to VAT has been very much criticised by McLure (Charles E. McLure, 'Could VAT Techniques Be Used to Implement Border Carbon Adjustments?' (2012) 66(8) IBFD Bulletin 436–446, 436). See also OECD, Creating Market Incentives for Greener Products, Policy Manual for Eastern Partnership Countries, 18 March 2014, ENV/EPOC/EAP(2013)4, 43.

[61] See, among others, Joseph E. Aldy, Eduardo Ley & Ian Parry, 'A Tax-Based Approach to Slowing Global Climate Change' (2008) 26 Resources for the Future 3; Thomas J. Courchene, 'Climate Change, Competitiveness and Environmental Federalism: The Case for a Carbon Tax' (2008) Background document for an Address to the Canada 2020 Speakers' Series; Thomas J. Courchene & John R. Allan, 'Climate Change: The Case for a Carbon Tariff/Tax' (March 2008) 29(3) Policy Options 59; David G. Duff & Margaret MacDonald, 'Towards a Destination-Based Carbon Tax', 14th Global Conference on Environmental Taxation, Kyoto, 17–19 October 2013; Salman Farmanfarmaian, 'The Case for CATS (Carbon Added Taxes) – Tackling Environmental Externalities in a Global Economy' (2008) Salman's blog, available at <https://docs.google.com/document/d/1rejuqJLf3OsswX5JIxy944ULPPV4tKpcIoEOLQtgDQU/edit)> (accessed 27 October 2015); Feaver & Sheehy, *supra* n. 11, 26; Hoerner & Muller, *supra* n. 52, 21; Eloi Laurent & Jacques Le Cacheux, 'An Ever Less Carbonated Union? Towards a Better European Taxation against Climate Change' (2009) 74 Notre Europe, Studies & Research, 33–34, 51–52; Eloi Laurent & Jacques Le

implementation of a CAT.[62] The European Parliament nevertheless discussed the idea in 2011, though its members finally opposed the proposal to request the Commission to 'research the feasibility of a European carbon-added tax along the lines of VAT, imposed on every product within the internal market'.[63]

Cacheux, 'Taxe carbone: TCA contre CO_2' (2009) 311 Lettre de l'OFCE 1, 3; Eloi Laurent & Jacques Le Cacheux, 'Réforme de la Fiscalité du Carbone dans l'Union européenne. Les options en présence' (2011) 16(1) Revue de l'OFCE 393, 405; Carol McAusland & Nouri Najjar, 'The WTO Consistency of Carbon Footprint Taxes' (2013) available at <http://people.landfood.ubc.ca/carol.mcausland/The%20WTO%20Consistency%20of%20Carbon%20Footprint%20Taxes.pdf> (accessed 27 October 2015); Carol McAusland & Nouri Najjar, 'Carbon Footprint Taxes' (2014) 61(1) Environmental and Resource Economics 37–70; Christian Pitschas, 'GATT/WTO Rules for Border Tax Adjustment and the Proposed European Directive Introducing a Tax on Carbon Dioxide Emissions and Energy' (1995) 24 Georgia Journal of International and Comparative Law 479–500; Charles Sampford, 'Global Transparency: Fighting Corruption for a Sustainable Future: From National Integrity Systems to Global Integrity Systems' commissioned conference discussion paper for 13 IACC, Athens, November 2008; Charles Sampford, 'Reconceiving the Good Life – The Key to Sustainable Globalisation' (2009), Good Life Conference, 12 February 2009, Griffith University, Brisbane, available at <http://eprints.qut.edu.au/43380/1/Sampford-Reconceiving-the-Good-Life-HL.pdf> (accessed 27 October 2015); Joseph E. Stiglitz, 'Sharing the Burden of Saving the Planet: Global Social Justice for Sustainable Development. Lessons from the Theory of Public Finance', Paper presented at the International Economic Association meetings, Istanbul, June 2009, available at <http://academiccommons.columbia.edu/catalog/ac%3A126988> (accessed 27 October 2015). For the published version: Joseph Stiglitz, 'Sharing the Burden of Saving the Planet: Global Social Justice for Sustainable Development: Lessons from the Theory of Public Finance', in: Joseph Stiglitz & Mary Kaldor (eds.), *The Quest for Security: Protection without Protectionism and the Challenge of Global Governance* (Columbia University Press 2013), 161.

[62] Authors who have expressed favourable opinions on the CAT are, among others, John R. Allan, Thomas J. Courchene, Joseph Stiglitz and Charles Sampford.

[63] European Parliament, Report on innovative financing at global and European level (2010/2105(INI)) Committee on Economic and Monetary Affairs, Rapporteur Anni Podimata, A/-0036/2011, 12 (para. 42) & 20. See also Oral explanation of vote (Vilja Savisaar-Toomast (ALDE)) of European Parliament Resolution of 8 March 2011 on innovative financing at global and European level (2010/2015(INI)), 8 March 2011, Strasbourg, P7_TA(2011)0080. See also Algirdas Šemeta, 'Key Options for Innovative Financing in the EU', ECON Committee in the European Parliament, 10 January 2011, Brussels, SPEECH/11/5.

4.2.2.1.1 Similarities with the VAT system The CAT model is based on the idea that the design of the VAT (such as the European VAT system) could be used to mitigate climate change.[64] Instead of taxing the value-added of products, the CAT imposes a tax on the 'carbon embedded' in products.[65] In other words, a tax is imposed on 'added' carbon at each stage of the production chain. The consequence of such model is that products would be taxed where they are consumed on the basis of their carbon footprint.[66] All emissions related to imported products would be taxed (the emissions related to inputs such as fuels and raw material, the emissions related to transport, etc.) and exported products would be exempted.[67] Applied on a global scale, this model could completely change the current accounting system for emissions, which focuses on the emissions released during production and not on the emissions related to consumption.[68] The objective is indeed – at least in theory – that the tax burden is finally borne by consumers, in the consumption country.[69]

4.2.2.1.2 Differences from the VAT system (the carbon value vs. the purchase price) The main difference from the VAT system is that the tax is applied based on the 'carbon value' of the product and not based on its 'purchase price' or 'customs value' (in the case of imports). Indeed, the specificity of the CAT model in comparison with the VAT system

---

[64] McLure has also discussed the case of the subtraction and addition VAT method, concluding that neither of these methods could help to implement border carbon adjustments (McLure, *supra* n. 60, 436). See also Christian, *supra* n. 4, 240. Amy C. Christian proposes imposing a 'Carbon-Burned Tax (CBT)', which is based on 'a method analogous to the VAT subtraction method'.

[65] The expression of 'embedded carbon' is a metaphor given that the carbon is largely released during the production process.

[66] Courchene, *supra* n. 61, 5.

[67] *Ibid.*, 7.

[68] See e.g. how emissions are reported under the UNFCCC reporting guidelines on annual inventories (UN, Updated UNFCCC reporting guidelines on annual inventories following incorporation of the provisions of decision 14/CP/11, Note by the secretariat, 18 August 2006, FCCC/SBSTA/2006/9). Emissions are reported by sectors (agriculture, land use, waste, energy, industrial process, solvent and other product use), which reflect production – rather than consumption – activities.

[69] See Charles E. McLure, 'The Carbon-Added Tax: A CAT That Won't Hunt' (2010) Policy Options 62, 66; McLure, *supra* n. 55, 257.

relies on the fact that the CAT is directly related to the amount of carbon 'embedded' in the product.[70]

The carbon value could be assessed in two different ways: (1) either on the basis of the carbon that is embedded in the products, regardless of the fact that the enterprise that has manufactured the products has already internalised the carbon costs, or (2) on the basis of the environmental cost of the embedded carbon that has not yet been internalised (i.e. taking into account the fact that an enterprise may already have internalised carbon costs so as to meet its environmental obligations derived from environmental laws of the country where it is located or from its internal rules). In the first case, the CAT could be based on the theory of comparative advantage or the theory of absolute advantage: the objective is to impose the same tax on domestic products and on imports. In the second case, the CAT could also be based on the theory of the legitimate absolute advantage: imports would be taxed based on their carbon content, taking into account the fact that the exporting country has already adopted carbon taxes so as to internalise carbon costs or the fact that the enterprise that has manufactured the product already has internalised its carbon costs for internal policy reasons (e.g. by sponsoring environmental projects so as to compensate for the carbon cost). In both cases, the carbon associated with products may be assessed in different ways. For example, the carbon value could be limited to the carbon released during the production process. It could, however, also include the carbon embedded in inputs (which has not yet been released) or the carbon related to the transportation of the products.[71]

The CAT could, for example, be defined by means of the following formula: [CAT = Rate (percentage) multiplied by the 'embedded carbon']. Another example of a formula – in order to make the rate less dependent on the embedded carbon – could be expressed as follows: [CAT on product X = (Fixed rate (percentage) multiplied by 'price') + (Rate (percentage) multiplied by the 'embedded carbon')]. The fact that the CAT is based on a 'carbon value' breaks the relationship that exists

---

70 See McLure, *supra* n. 55, 253–254; McAusland & Najjar, *supra* n. 61. See also, on the computation of carbon values, Xin Zhou, 'Chapter 14: Environmentally Extended Multi-Region Input-Output Model: Sharing Responsibility Across the Globe', in: Joy Murray & Richard Wood (eds.), *The Sustainability Practitioner's Guide to Input-Output Analysis* (Common Ground Publishing 2010), 165–176.

71 Authors rarely define with precision what they mean by 'carbon embedded into products', with the exception of McAusland & Najjar (*supra* n. 61) who clearly explain which emissions should be taken into consideration.

between VAT and the 'purchase price' of products. Under the first formula, the amount of the CAT would be in no way related to the value of products. This means that the amount of the CAT can be much higher on products of a relatively low purchase value than on products of high purchase value, as soon as the carbon value of the products of low purchase value is higher than the products of high purchase value. Such measure may lead to legal issues: such taxes could be considered contrary to the ability-to-pay principle.[72]

This difference may also lead to implementation issues, as the carbon value is much more difficult to determine than the purchase price or the customs value of products (Section 4.3.1).[73] First, the legislator should define the 'carbon value' to make clear which carbon is considered associated with a product and which is not.[74] Second, the legislator should provide for a clear method to determine the embedded carbon in products. According to Stiglitz, firms should provide information on the carbon value of products at each production stage.[75] Similarly, Laurent and Le Cacheux propose that the implementation of the CAT is based on 'carbon reports' made by companies.[76] McAusland and Najjar have developed a full economic model in order to calculate 'default' carbon

---

72 See Michael Rodi & Hope Ashiabor, 'Legal Authority to Enact Environmental Taxes', in: Janet E. Milne & Mikael Skou Andersen (eds.), *Handbook of Research on Environmental Taxation* (Edward Elgar Publishing 2012), 71.

73 McLure, *supra* n. 60, 443. According to McLure, this is the 'Achilles' Heel' of the CAT: 'Markets do not reveal the carbon content of sales, as they do their value'.

74 In the Kyoto Protocol, carbon accounting is based on the carbon emissions related to countries (and not to consumption of products): UNFCCC, Kyoto Protocol Reference Manual on Accounting of Emissions and Assigned Amount (2008) available at <http://unfccc.int/resource/docs/publications/08_unfccc_kp_ref_manual.pdf> (accessed 27 October 2015). A specific methodology has been developed by the Intergovernmental Panel on Climate Change (IPCC). McLure makes a distinction between carbon and CO_2 (McLure, *supra* n. 69, 64). See also Astrid Kander, Magnus Jiborn, Daniel D. Moran & Thomas O. Wiedmann, 'National Greenhouse-Gas Accounting for Effective Climate Policy on International Trade' (2015) 5 Nature Climate Change 431–435.

75 Stiglitz also proposes that, in case of lack of or insufficient information, inputs should be considered to have been made 'in the least carbon efficient way' (Stiglitz, *supra* n. 61, 169).

76 Laurent and Le Cacheux speak about 'a carbon bookkeeping' (Laurent & Le Cacheux, *supra* n. 61, 52). See also Hufbauer, Charnovitz & Jisun, *supra* n. 6, 68–69. They refer to the following report: Ademe, Guide des Facteurs d'émissions Version 5.0, Calcul des facteurs d'émissions et sources bibliographiques utilisées, 2007. See also McAusland & Najjar (*supra* n. 61).

footprint, which would be used when firms do not have the means to calculate their 'real' carbon footprint.[77] This last approach based on products' carbon footprint is larger than an approach limited to carbon released during production. Indeed, products' carbon footprint is a larger concept that includes the carbon released during the production process, the transport and the distribution of the products.

4.2.2.1.3 From the CAT to a green-added tax based on global environmental impacts The idea to tax consumption based on the carbon value of products could be extended to incorporate not only the carbon-related climate impact of products, but also the impact linked to other GHG emissions.[78] Similarly, the CAT model could be enlarged to incorporate not only the climate impact of products, but also their 'general' environmental impact. In other words, the tax would not be imposed on the carbon value of products at each production stage but on their 'global environmental impact' at each production stage. Here again, this possibility is inherently conditioned by the availability of data to measure the 'global environmental impact' of products. Some methods have been developed, for example the 'life cycle assessment' (LCA).[79] However, the determination of the global environmental impact of products necessarily requires ranking environmental issues and giving a (subjective) value to the various impacts that a product may have on the environment.[80] However, this subjective assessment is also present in the CAT, at least

---

77 McAusland & Najjar, *supra* n. 61.

78 *Ibid.*

79 The possibility of using LCA methods has been tackled by Farmanfarmaian, *supra* n. 61. See also Frans Oosterhuis et al., 'The use of differential VAT rates to promote changes in consumption and innovation', Final Report commissioned by the European Commission, DG Environment, 25 June 2008, available at <http://ec.europa.eu/environment/enveco/taxation/pdf/vat_final.pdf> (accessed 27 October 2015), 4. See also the reference to LCA in Monica De Oliveira Rodrigues, 'Case Study: Most-Favoured-Nation Treatment and National Treatment in the GATT and the GATS and the Differentiated Tax Treatment as National Policy on Climate Change in Brazil' (2013) Revista Con-texto 39, available at <http://papers.ssrn.com/sol3/papers.cfm?abstract_id=2307330> (accessed 2 May 2015).

80 On the subjectivity of indicators, see Camillo De Camillis & Malgorzata Goralczyk, 'Towards Stronger Measures for Sustainable Consumption and Production Policies: Proposal of a New Fiscal Framework Based on a Life Cycle Approach' (2013) 18(1) International Journal of Life Cycle Assessment 263, 266. See also Walter Klöpffer & Birgit Grahl, *Life Cycle Assessment (LCA): A Guide to Best Practice* (Wiley 2014).

indirectly. As the objective of such tax is to discourage the consumption of products with a 'high' carbon value, the tax also relies on the subjective assessment made by the legislator on the need to prioritise the mitigation of climate change in comparison to other environmental issues.

4.2.2.2 Environmental VAT

In addition to the CAT model, other VAT-based models may allow the pursuit of the regulatory objective of encouraging low-carbon consumption patterns, for example by providing lower rates for 'eco-friendly products' or by adopting higher rates for polluting products.

The traditional VAT model may indeed be used to pursue regulatory objectives (including the objective of protecting the environment) by distinguishing between products through the application of differentiated tax rates.[81] Examples of environmental VAT have been proposed by authors and considered by the European Commission.[82] Albrecht makes the case for differentiated VAT rates based on a 'pragmatic sustainability classification of selected product categories'.[83] De Camillis and Goralczyk argue in favour of a 'green VAT', where the tax rate on products would be determined by reference to the environmental performance of products.[84] They propose a 'modulated' VAT rate, taking into account the 'environmental efficiency' of goods consumed based on the environmental efficiency of 'reference goods'. The logic behind their proposal is to make VAT rates dependent on the environmental performance of products concerned in comparison to the environmental performance of a

---

81 On the issue of the 'optimal design of commodity tax rates', see Ian Crawford, Michael Keen & Stephen Smith, 'Value Added Tax and Excises', in: Institute of Fiscal Studies (ed.), *Dimensions of Tax Design. The Mirrlees Review* (OUP 2010), 284 et al. See, for example, Johan Albrecht, 'The Use of Consumption Taxes to Re-Launch Green Tax Reforms' (2006) 26(1) International Review of Law and Economics 88–103; Oosterhuis et al., *supra* n. 79; Copenhagen Economics, Reduced VAT for Environmentally Friendly Products (2008) DG Taxud, Final Report; Stefan Wirsenius, Frederik Hedenus & Kristina Mohlin, 'Greenhouse Gas Taxes on Animal Food Products: Rationale, Tax Scheme and Climate Mitigation Effects' (2011) 108(1–2) Climate Change 159–184.

82 See Commission of the European Communities, Green Paper on Integrated Product Policy, 7 February 2001, Brussels, COM(2011)68 final, 1.

83 Albrecht, *supra* n. 81, 96. See also Oosterhuis et al, *supra* n. 79, 4 and 105–110.

84 De Camillis & Goralczyk, *supra* n. 80, 263–272. De Camillis is part of the Joint Research Centre of the European Commission.

reference product.[85] In other words, De Camillis and Goralczyk's proposal divides goods in different categories to which a specific rate is attached. Differences in rates between products aim at encouraging the consumption of the least environmentally damaging products of the same category. The amount of the tax is not directly related to the amount of embedded carbon in a product but the tax is calculated by multiplying the price of the product by the related tax rate, which depends on the amount of embedded carbon in the product in comparison to the carbon embedded in a 'reference product'.

4.2.2.3 Assessment of VAT-based models

The CAT and the environmental VAT models present similarities but also differences. In comparison to the CAT, the carbon-related VAT includes environmental considerations only at the final consumption stage, as is the case with specific rates in traditional VAT systems. Moreover, in comparison to the CAT, the carbon-related VAT is not directly defined by the embedded carbon in a product. These 'technical' distinctions between the carbon-related VAT and the CAT reflect how these two VAT-based models may be used to pursue different policy objectives. Though both taxes aim at reducing the emissions of CO_2, the carbon-related VAT proposed by De Camillis and Goralczyk attempts to achieve this objective by encouraging the consumption of the 'environmentally friendly' version of products. In contrast, the CAT pursues this objective by increasing the price of all goods according to their carbon value, thus encouraging a general reduction of consumption.

Both the CAT and carbon-related VAT present advantages and disadvantages to pursuing environmental goals.

4.2.2.3.1 CAT The main argument against the CAT concerns its cost-ineffectiveness. According to McLure, the CAT is not cost-effective in light of its 'expensive process of calculating embodied carbon'.[86] This viewpoint is only valid when the objective of the CAT is – as McLure argues – to 'prevent emission of CO_2'.[87] Under such hypothesis, other 'simpler alternatives' exist to prevent the release of CO_2 emissions: for example, the taxation of carbon at the upstream level by levying a carbon tax on fossil fuels.[88] Indeed, upstream taxes are *a priori* easier to implement given they do not require determining the carbon value of all

---

85 *Ibid.*, 266.
86 McLure, *supra* n. 55, 254.
87 *Ibid.*, 258.
88 *Ibid.*, 255.

products as is the case with the CAT. The CAT's advocates, however, consider that the role of the CAT is not merely to prevent the release of CO_2 emissions but to prevent the release of CO_2 emissions by taxing products at the place where they are consumed.[89]

The consideration that emissions should be taxed in the country of consumption relies on three main arguments.[90] A first argument relates to the 'efficiency' of the tax as it appears more efficient to impose emissions at the place of consumption since this allows the tackling of emissions released in (developing) countries that are not required, under the UN climate regime, to reduce their emissions.[91] Moreover, according to Stiglitz, the tax should be imposed on the use of carbon at each stage of production because a tax on fuels could be rapidly included into market prices, neutralising the effect of the tax on prices.[92] Finally, in contrast to a VAT-based tax, a tax on producers leads to the risk of carbon leakage as it may encourage enterprises to relocate abroad in order not to face the carbon tax on carbon-intensive products.[93] A second argument concerns the 'fair' character of the tax. Based on this 'fairness' argument, it is argued that the liability for reducing carbon emissions should be borne by consumers and not by (developing) countries from where most products and natural resources are imported into (developed/industrialised) countries.[94] This argument is not fully convincing in the case of the CAT. Indeed, the CAT does not fully hold the consumers of developed/industrialised countries responsible for CO_2 emissions related to the products that they have consumed since the CAT revenue is in principle allocated to the national revenue of the implementing country and not to an international fund. In principle, the CAT is not an international instrument and therefore it cannot be used to distribute responsibility to reduce CO_2 emissions, as does the Kyoto Protocol. Yet, a third political argument could be added in favour of taxing emissions in consumption countries. Indeed, the adoption of a CAT expresses a strong political message to consumers, namely that 'consumerism significantly contributes to climate change'. Such tax measures could be part of

---

89 See e.g. Stiglitz, *supra* n. 61, 169.

90 *Ibid.*, 168.

91 See Farmanfarmaian, *supra* n. 61 about the 'Structural Problems with the Producer Responsibility Paradigm'.

92 Stiglitz, *supra* n. 61, 170.

93 *Ibid.*, 168.

94 Thomas J. Courchene & John R. Allan, 'Missing the Bigger Picture: A Response to McLure's View of the Carbon-Added Tax' (2011) Policy Options 75, 77. See also Farmanfarmaian, *supra* n. 61; Sampford, *supra* n. 61.

policies in favour of a decrease in consumption. Needless to say, the current trend in favour of growth policies – whether green or not – does not follow this path.

A CAT, imposed on all products at each production stage towards consumption, allows the 'ideal' taxation of carbon emissions in consumption countries to be achieved.[95] In other words, the broad base of the CAT is praised not for maximising revenue as under traditional VAT systems but for guaranteeing that emissions are imposed where products are consumed.[96] In light of the objective of taxing emissions where consumption is located, the cost-effectiveness of the CAT should depend on the existence of alternative measures to fulfil this objective. Given the 'ideal conceptual character' of the CAT, Courchene and Allan nuance the challenges related to the 'quantification of carbon footprints' in the light of existing carbon footprint projects and the likely progress to be made.[97] Overall, a tax based on the 'new excise tax model' could nevertheless be more cost-effective in achieving the goal of taxing emissions where consumption takes place as soon as it is assumed that the tax is passed through to consumers. The CAT could still be preferred over the 'new excise tax model' on the basis that it sends a clear political message (namely that its objective is to tax consumers), which may not be the case for an excise tax, which – to a certain extent – resembles a tax on producers.[98]

4.2.2.3.2 Environmental VAT The main argument in favour of the adoption of an environmental VAT is based on economic considerations. By differentiating between goods based on their environmental impact, the higher prices of environmentally friendly products could be neutralised through lower taxes, allowing them to compete with non-environmentally friendly products in a fair way, integrating the externality costs of polluting products.[99]

---

95 Courchene & Allan, *supra* n. 94, 75. According to the two authors, the CAT offers an 'ideal conceptual yardstick or standard against which all approaches to carbon pricing may be assessed'.

96 See McLure, *supra* n. 55, 258. See also Thomas Cottier & Nashina Shariff, 'International Trade and Climate Change', in: Geert Van Calster & Denise Prévost (eds.), *Research Handbook on Environment, Health and the WTO* (Edward Elgar Publishing 2013), 436.

97 Courchene & Allan, *supra* n. 94, 76.

98 McAusland & Najjar, *supra* n. 61, 3–4.

99 De Camillis & Goralczyk, *supra* n. 80, 265.

Practical difficulties related to the design of VAT systems, however, temper the advantages deriving from the adoption of differentiated tax rates based on environmental criteria (e.g. products' environmental performance). According to de la Feria and Krever, differentiated tax rates are a 'serious deviation from the theoretically ideal VAT'.[100] They consider that the adoption of multiple rates leads to higher administration costs due to the complexity of distinguishing between products that sometimes look similar, if not identical.[101] Given that the basic condition for the adoption of an environmental VAT system is the possibility of distinguishing between products based on their environmental impact, this criticism only recalls that such system necessarily involves high administrative costs.[102] Aside from this criticism, the categorisation of products according to environmental criteria could also be questioned under WTO law (Chapter 6).

4.2.3 Models Based on the Retail Sales Tax

This model is comparable to the proposals in favour of a CAT or in favour of a system of environmental VAT. The basic idea is to integrate environmental criteria in the sales tax, which is – like VAT – a tax on consumption. As in the case of the CAT, a retail carbon tax (RCT) could be imposed on the carbon value of all products sold in the market.[103] Alternatively, a RCT could also be designed in the same way as the environmental VAT described above. In this case, the RCT would impose differentiated rates on products based on their climate impact. The main problems of an RCT are – again – related to the difficulty of determining the carbon value of the taxable products (i.e. all products sold to households) and the administrative complexity associated with the

---

[100] Rita de la Feria & Richard Krever, 'Ending VAT Exemptions: Towards a Post-Modern VAT' (2012) Oxford University Centre for Business Taxation, WP 12/28 (footnote 6, 1). See also Crawford, Keen & Smith, *supra* n. 81, 290–291; Sijbren Cnossen, 'Commentary on "Value Added Tax and Excises"', in: Institute of Fiscal Studies (ed.), *Dimensions of Tax Design. The Mirrlees Review* (OUP 2010), 370; Coen Teulings, preface to Sijbren Cnossen, 'Three VAT Studies' (2010) 90 CPB Netherlands Bureau for Economic Policy Analysis, 7.

[101] Sijbren Cnossen, 'Key Questions in Considering a Value-Added Tax for Central and Eastern European Countries' (1991) 91/69 IMF Working Paper 1, 13–14.

[102] Don Fullerton, Andrew Leicester & Stephen Smith, 'Environmental Taxes' (2008) 14197 National Bureau of Economic Research 440.

[103] McLure, *supra* n. 60, 440.

implementation of such a tax.[104] Briefly, McLure considers that the RCT model is 'totally impractical'.[105]

4.2.4 Other Models – Environmental Tax on Producers

In principle, proposals to tax CO_2 emissions on producers based on the CO_2 emissions emitted during the production process should be distinguished from proposals aimed at taxing products based on their emission potential. The possibility of adopting BTAs in respect of CO_2 taxes imposed on producers could, however, be considered from the perspective of *taxes occultes*. Indeed, a tax imposed on producers in respect of the CO_2 emissions released during production could be assimilated to a 'hidden tax' borne by certain products and eligible for adjustment. Moreover, under unorthodox views, BTAs could arguably be made in respect of production taxes as soon as their effect on products prices has been proven (Chapter 5).

The proposals for a carbon equalisation system at the EU level in the framework of the EU ETS may be compared to BTAs in respect of taxes on producers. Under the assumption that the EU ETS is assimilated to a tax, the EU ETS is indeed easier to compare to a production tax rather than to a tax on a product.[106] In contrast to CO_2 taxes imposed on energy products, cap-and-trade systems are usually imposed on CO_2 emissions from certain producers.[107] Consequently, even though proposals to adopt BTAs in respect of carbon-intensive products resemble BTAs applied in respect of *taxes occultes* in the new CO_2 excise model taxes, such proposals differ from this model in that the domestic tax that constitutes the 'hidden tax' is not a tax imposed on domestic products (e.g. the domestic tax applied to energy products in the new excise model) but a tax imposed on producers.

---

[104] McLure, *supra* n. 60, 440–441. McLure notes that 'the carbon content of millions of products sold at retail' should be determined and 'millions of retailers would be involved in collecting the tax'.

[105] *Ibid.*, 441.

[106] See Deane, *supra* n. 3, 185–188.

[107] Janet E. Milne, 'Carbon Taxes in the United States: The Context for the Future' (2008–2009) 10 Vermont Journal of Environmental Law 1–30, 22, figure 3. See also Kasturi Das, 'Can Border Carbon Adjustments Be WTO-Legal?' (2011) 8(3) Manchester Journal of International Economic Law 65, 69–71. *Contra:* Mark L. Belleville, 'The Key Stone in the Carbon Tariff Wall: The Alberta Oil Sands and the Legality of Taxing Imports Based on Their Carbon Footprint' (2013) 43 Environmental Law 365, 375.

4.3 COMMON ISSUES OF TAX DESIGN

All models of environmental BTAs will face similar tax design issues. The adoption of environmental BTAs requires the determination of the environmental value of the products concerned (Section 4.3.1). Moreover, the design of such tax should consider the risks of abuse (Section 4.3.2) and define how to allocate the revenue derived from the tax (Section 4.3.3).

4.3.1 Valuation – Environmental Proxies

One issue common to all models of environmental BTAs is the practical question of how to determine the 'environmental value' of products on which the tax is based. In all models described above, the environmental character of products is assessed by means of proxies. As mentioned above, the 'environmental value' of products may be defined in different ways, depending on the objective of the environmental tax on domestic products.

Where the objective is to encourage consumption of products with the least polluting production process possible, BTAs will apply on imported products based on their 'environmental value' to be defined regardless of whether pollution released during the production process has (already) been internalised or not. In other words, the environmental value is defined based on the pollution that has been released during production, without taking account of whether internalisation has taken place in the country of production. In this case, BTAs may be justified either by means of the revised theory of comparative advantage or by means of the revised theory of absolute advantage. In the hypothesis where the environmental value of an imported product cannot be defined based on an assessment of the product itself, two main methods have been proposed in the literature to determine products' environmental impact, taking account of their process and production methods (PPMs): the 'predominant method of production' and 'the best available technique'.[108] In the case of the 'predominant method of production', the environmental character of imported products is determined based on the environmental impact of the predominant method of production of the products concerned. In general, the proposal is to take as a proxy the predominant

[108] Other methods mentioned in the literature are based on averaging. For example, Condon & Ignaciuk refer to an 'industry-wide average emission baseline from the origin country' (Condon & Ignaciuk, *supra* n. 5, 13).

method of production in the importing country.[109] However, the country could also make use of the predominant method of production in the world or in the exporting country. In the case of the 'best available technique', imported products are supposed to be made by means of the production technique with the least negative environmental impact. Aside from the 'predominant method of production' and 'the best available technique', the environmental value of imported products could also be assessed by reference to products' own features, which could be based, in the case of environmental BTAs, on products' PPM. The methods that have been proposed in the literature to determine the environmental value of products include: carbon footprint analyses based on the embedded carbon in products, analyses based on the standard ISO 14067[110] and life cycle assessments. These methods are usually based on a certification process. The environmental value of products is indeed often linked to PPMs, which are not directly related to final products' physical properties.

In contrast, where the objective of the domestic tax is to internalise the environmental cost of products, BTAs should only serve to tax the environmental cost of imported products that has not yet been internalised. In other words, the internalisation of environmental costs that has taken place abroad, either by the foreign enterprises themselves or through the regulatory framework in place in the exporting country, should be considered.[111] Under this hypothesis, BTAs can be justified by

---

[109] See Pauwelyn, *supra* n. 56, 493, footnote 117 (referring to the US ODC tax and the BTU tax proposal). See also the Superfund tax.

[110] See the many references in Daniel Gros & Christian Egenhofer, 'Climate Change and Trade. Taxing Carbon at the Border?' (2010) Centre for European Policy Studies.

[111] Under this hypothesis, the risk exists that an exporting country would adopt an 'export tax' to internalise the environmental costs of exported products. WTO members should, however, apply export duties in accordance with GATT Art. I, which reduces the risks that members would make use of export duties to counter the adoption of environmental cross-border taxes based on products' level of internalisation of environmental costs. See WTO, Working Party on the Accession of the Russian Federation, Report of the Working Party on the Accession of the Russian Federation to the World Trade Organization, 17 November 2011, WT/ACC/RUS/70; WT/MIN(11)/2, paras. 635–638. See also Kateryna Holzer, *Carbon-Related Border Adjustment and WTO Law* (Edward Elgar Publishing 2014), 170 & 214–218; Tom Hu Tao, Comments on the article of McKibbin & Wilcoxen: Warwick J. McKibbin & Peter J. Wilcoxen, 'The Economic and Environmental Effects of Border Tax Adjustments for Climate Policy' (2008–2009) Brookings Trade Forum 1, 27.

means of any of the three theories that have been developed in Chapter 2. From a practical perspective, the main challenge is to define the concept of 'internalisation' in an objective way. Under an environmental tax aimed at internalising environmental costs, internalisation takes place through monetisation of the environment. Internalisation of environmental costs that has taken place in other countries should also be considered in the calculation of the environmental BTAs imposed on imported products. It is, however, difficult to compare internalisation policies as there is no international standard as far as the internalisation of environmental costs is concerned. Moreover, internalisation in non-monetisation forms should also be considered, such as, for example, where an enterprise decides to internalise the environmental costs related to products on a voluntary basis by using compensation methods, for example in financing nature conversation projects, etc.[112] From a practical viewpoint, it is likely to be extremely difficult to distinguish products on the basis of their associated environmental costs, even more to differentiate between the associated environmental costs that have been internalised and those which have not.

The question of the valuation of products subject to BTAs is nevertheless not limited to environmental BTAs. Valuation issues also take place in the case of 'traditional border taxes', which explains that WTO members have adopted specific rules to help them determine the 'customs value' of imported goods.[113]

4.3.2 Risk of Abuse

The implementation of new taxes usually triggers tax evasion practices. For example, in the case of the ODC tax, some authors argue that one part of the projected tax revenue has been lost due to tax evasion.[114] In the case of the Superfund tax, Hoerner believes that evasion was only a 'minor problem'.[115] However, regarding the tax on imported substances, only 51 per cent of the projected tax revenue has been collected from

---

[112] See the topic of the systems of compensation for ecosystem services.

[113] WTO, Agreement on Implementation of Article VII of the General Agreement on Tariffs and Trade 1994 (Customs Valuation Agreement).

[114] Brack, Grubb & Windram, *supra* n. 56, 80; J. Andrew Hoerner, 'The Role of Border Tax Adjustments in Environmental Taxation: Theory and US Experience', Working Paper presented at the International Workshop on Market Based Instruments and International Trade of the Institute for Environmental Studies, Amsterdam, the Netherlands, 19 March 1998, 12.

[115] Hoerner, *supra* n. 114, 16.

1989 to 1991.[116] In the light of the different models of environmental BTAs and the distinguishing criteria that could trigger the application of higher tax rates, two types of abusive behaviours are likely to take place in addition to the usual abusive behaviours that characterise taxation.[117]

4.3.2.1 Types of abuse

A first risk is that the 'environmental value' of a product is labelled as 'green' with the aim of being subject to lower tax rates. As already mentioned, it may be difficult – if not impossible – to assess whether a product has been produced in an environmentally friendly way by only looking at the final product. The PPMs of final products are often 'invisible', which makes it possible to pretend that polluting products have been produced in a 'green way', even though this is not the case. As far as imported products are concerned, the national authorities of the importing country also lack direct control on production processes taking place abroad, which contributes to the possibility for fraudulent behaviour. This risk of abuse is, however, not limited to environmental BTAs.[118] Another example is the case of tariffs as the transaction value of imported products cannot always easily be determined. The Customs Valuation Agreement therefore provides for guidelines to facilitate the determination of products' value for customs purposes.[119] Similar solutions should be found to limit the risks of abuse in the implementation of environmental BTAs.

---

[116] Industrial Economics, Incorporated, 'Economic Impacts of Superfund Taxes', report prepared for the Office of Policy Analysis, the Office of Policy, Planning and Evaluation and the US Environmental Protection Agency, February 1994, section 3-7.

[117] Other types of abuse mentioned by Hoerner (*supra* n. 114, 14) include the case of 'false exports', 'daisy-chaining', 'classic smuggling'.

[118] Robert Ireland, 'Implications for Customs of Climate Change Mitigation and Adaptation Policy Options: a Preliminary Examination (2010) 4(2) World Customs Journal 21–36, 28. See also the examples given by de la Feria to explain the complexity of specific VAT rates (the UK *Marks & Spencer* case and the *Pringles* case): Rita de la Feria, 'EU VAT Rate Structure: Towards Unilateral Convergence?', WP 13/05 Oxford University Centre for Business Taxation, Saïd Business School, available at <http://www.sbs.ox.ac.uk/sites/default/files/Business_Taxation/Docs/Publications/Working_Papers/Series_13/WP1305.pdf> (accessed 1 December 2015).

[119] WTO Agreement on Implementation of Article VII of the General Agreement on Tariffs and Trade 1994. See also GATT Art. VII.

A second risk characterises models of environmental BTAs that distinguish between product categories, such as the model of the carbon-related VAT. 'Non-environmentally friendly products' could be classified under the category of 'environmentally friendly products'. This risk of abuse is comparable to the risks that exist under traditional tariffs that certain products be taxed under more favourable product categories.[120]

4.3.2.2 Anti-abuse measures

WTO law provisions contain measures to avoid abusive practices in relation to countervailing and anti-dumping duties, regional trade agreements (RTAs), preferential trade arrangements (PTAs) and customs duties.[121] Similar provisions could apply to models of environmental BTAs to limit the risks of abuse described above.

Abusive behaviour in relation to the 'greening' of imported products may be counteracted by means of a well-defined certification system. Though specific difficulties arise from environmental BTAs, traditional border taxes, such as customs duties, also raise difficulties in relation to the classification of products. Robert Ireland – head of the Research Unit Staff at the World Customs Organization – believes that the administration of environmental BTAs is not an impossible task.[122] Ireland considers that, in order to facilitate certification procedures, a simplified certification programme could be established following a similar logic as that of the 'Authorized Economic Operator Programmes' set up by the

---

[120] See Daniel C.K. Chow & Thomas J. Schoenbaum, *International Trade Law: Problems, Cases and Materials* (Wolters Kluwer Law & Business 2013), 195, referring to WTO, Appellate Body Report, *EC – Chicken Cuts*; GATT, Panel Report, *Spain – Unroasted Coffee.*

[121] See for example the measures put in place to define the origin of products. See WTO Agreement on Rules of origin. See also, at the EU level: Art. 23, para. 3 of Council Regulation (EC) No 597/2009 of 11 June 2009 on protection against subsidised imports from countries not members of the European Community, 18 July 2009, OJ L188/93. Art. 13, para. 1 of Council Regulation (EC) No. 1225/2009 of 30 November 2009 on protection against dumped imports from countries not members of the European Community, 22 December 2009, OJ L343/51. At the US level, see 19 US CODE 1677(j). See Chow & Schoenbaum, *supra* n. 120, 408; Ralph Folsom, *Principles of International Trade* (West Academic Publishing 2014), 161.

[122] Ireland, *supra* n. 118, 27. See also Thomas Cottier, Ilaria Espa & Kateryna Holzer, 'Renewable Electricity Tax Exemptions and Trade Remedies under International Law. An Assessment of Policy Space under WTO Law, the Swiss-EU FTA and EU Law', Confédération Suisse, 8 March 2015.

World Customs Organization in order to simplify customs procedures for economic trade operators.[123]

The issue of certification based on features that are not directly related to products' physical properties also appeared in the framework of the Kimberley Process. In 2002 the Kimberley Process Certification Scheme was created in order to stop the trade of 'conflict diamonds', namely trade in diamonds that served to finance conflicts involving rebel movements.[124] The certification scheme requires participating countries to adopt certification and control measures so as to prevent the trade of 'conflict diamonds'.[125] As in the case of products that have been produced in an environmentally friendly way, 'conflict-free diamonds' are not easy to recognise based on their physical properties.[126] Consequently, problems of fraudulent certificates also occurred under the Kimberley Process, which illustrates that the risk of abusive behaviour and fraudulent certificates should not prevent the development of environmental BTAs. It should, however, be noted that environmental BTAs would be unlikely to be based on WTO law waiver provisions as is the case with the Kimberley Process.[127] Consequently, the establishment of an obligatory certification system could raise legal issues. For example, environmental BTAs implemented based on such an obligatory certification system could be found contrary to GATT Article III:2 (Chapter 6).

Finally, a special tax force could be created, following the example of the 'Interagency Task Force on Enforcement of Ozone-Depleting Substance Laws and Regulation', which was established in order to better react to tax evasion practices in respect of the ODC tax.[128] This task force has undertaken a range of activities in order to improve the

---

[123] Ireland, *supra* n. 118, 27.

[124] Kimberley Process, available at <www.kimberleyprocess.com> (accessed 30 October 2015). The Kimberley Process Certification Scheme defines 'conflict diamonds' as follows: 'rough diamonds used by rebel movements or their allies aimed at undermining legitimate governments, as described in relevant United Nations Security Council (UNSC) resolutions insofar as they remain in effect, or in other similar UNSC resolutions which may be adopted in the future, and as understood and recognised in United Nations General Assembly (UN GA) Resolution 55/56 (29 January 2001), or in other similar UN GA resolutions which may be adopted in the future' (section 1).

[125] See Section 2 of the Kimberley Process Certification Scheme.

[126] See Commission Staff Working Document, Trade and Worst Forms of Child Labour, 30 April 2013, Brussels, SWD(2013) 173 final, 16.

[127] WTO, Waiver concerning Kimberley Process Certification Scheme for Rough Diamonds, Decision of 15 May 2003, 27 May 2003, WT/L/518.

[128] Hoerner, *supra* n. 114, 13.

implementation of the tax, including training activities for customs officials to better recognise mislabelled products and information sharing between agencies.[129] Similar mechanisms could be used to reinforce the implementation of environmental BTAs.

4.3.3 Allocation of Revenue

Unlike most traditional taxes, environmental taxes usually raise specific questions regarding the allocation of tax revenue. Aside from the traditional objective of contributing to the state revenue, the scholarship often suggests that the revenue derived from environmental taxes could either be used to reduce other taxes (such as taxes on labour) or to finance environmentally related policies and projects (Section 4.3.3.1).[130] Environmental BTAs do not differ much from pure domestic environmental taxes as far as revenue allocation is concerned. However, unlike domestic environmental taxes, environmental BTAs question the legitimacy of allocating tax revenues to purely domestic purposes when these taxes are based on a rationale related to the internalisation of environmental costs across borders (Section 4.3.3.2).

4.3.3.1 Allocation of revenue of environmental taxes

The literature on environmental taxation usually suggests that the revenue derived from environmental taxes could be used either to pursue 'environmental tax reform' by reducing other taxes or to finance projects in favour of a higher level of environmental protection. A third proposal is to allocate the revenue to the taxpayers that suffer the most from the introduction of the environmental tax.

The case for environmental tax reform is based on the idea that the adoption of environmental taxes opens the door for making the tax system more efficient.[131] The reform should permit reducing inefficient

---

[129] *Ibid.* See also UNEP, INECE, 'Enforcement Strategies for Combating the Illegal Trade in HCFCs and Methyl Bromide' (2013), available at <http://www.unep.org/ozonaction/Portals/105/documents/7622-e-Enforcement_strategies_illegal_trade_HCFCs.pdf> (accessed 1 December 2015), 25.

[130] See Jennifer Hillman, 'Changing Climate for Carbon Taxes, Who's Afraid of the WTO?' (2013) German Marshall Fund of the United States 14; Holzer, *supra* n. 111, 23; Michael Rodi, Kai Schlegelmich & Michael Mehling, 'Designing Environmental Taxes in Countries in Transition: A Case Study of Vietnam', in: Janet E. Milne & Mikael Skou Andersen (eds.), *Handbook of Research on Environmental Taxation* (Edward Elgar Publishing 2012), 133.

[131] European Environment Agency, 'Environmental Tax Reform in Europe: Opportunities for Eco-Innovation' (2011) EEA Technical report; Dirk Heine,

taxes, with no effect on states' budgets, thanks to the revenue derived from the introduction of environmental taxes. In other words, environmental tax reform would be 'revenue neutral' from a budgetary viewpoint and, at the same time, have a positive impact on society, both on the environment and on the economy (the so-called 'double dividend' hypothesis).[132] Against this background, environmental taxes would not affect the competitiveness of the implementing country given that the reduction of labour taxes compensates for the higher tax burden resulting from the adoption of environmental taxes. Consequently, it could be argued that the lack of impact of environmental taxes on competitiveness should prevent countries from adopting environmental BTAs when their objective is based on economic grounds.[133]

In contrast to environmental tax reforms, proposals to earmark the revenue derived from environmental taxes for investing in environmentally related projects do not require a complete rethinking of the tax system.[134] The provisions introducing the new environmental tax should merely indicate that the revenue is to be dedicated to a specific fund to support environmental purposes, following the 'polluter-pays' principle. For example, in the US, the Superfund tax with other environmental

---

John Norregaard & Ian W.H. Parry, 'Environmental Tax Reform: Principles from Theory and Practice to Date' (2012) IMF, WP/12/180; Wallace E. Oates, 'Green Taxes: Can We Protect the Environment and Improve the Tax System at the Same Time?' (1995) 61(4) Southern Economic Journal 915; Stefan Speck, Philip Summerton, Daniel Lee & Kirsten Wiebe, 'Chapter 5. Environmental Taxes and ETRs in Europe: The Current Situation and a Review of the Modelling Literature', in: Stefan Speck & Paul Ekins (eds.), *Environmental Tax Reform (ETR): A Policy for Green Growth* (Oxford Scholarship Online 2011), 99–130. See also Gilbert E. Metcalf, 'Tax Reform and Environmental Taxation' (2005) NBER Working Paper No. 11665.

[132] On the double dividend hypothesis, see i.a. Lawrence H. Goulder, 'Environmental Taxation and the Double Dividend: A Reader's Guide' (1995) 2 International Tax and Public Finance 157–183; William K. Jaeger, 'Environmental Taxation and the Double Dividend', paper prepared for the Internet Encyclopedia of Ecological Economics.

[133] See OECD, Programme of Dialogue and Co-operation with China, Workshop on Environmental Taxes in China and OECD Member Countries, Background Paper No. 1, Environmental Taxes in OECD Countries: An Overview, Paris, 5th and 6th October 1998, CCNM/CHINA/EPOC(98)4, document prepared by Jean-Philippe Barde, 27. OECD, Taxation and the Environment. Complementary Policies, 1993.

[134] See Claudia Dias Soares, 'Earmarking Revenues from Environmentally Related Taxes', in: Janet E. Milne & Mikael Skou Andersen (eds.), *Handbook of Research on Environmental Taxation* (Edward Elgar Publishing 2012), 102.

taxes contributed to funding the Superfund Trust Fund, which was used to clean up hazardous substances from contaminated sites.[135] Similarly, many legislative proposals in favour of the adoption of carbon taxes suggest that the revenue from such taxes could be used for projects aimed at mitigating climate change.[136] Though earmarking of revenue does not require a full reform of the tax system, it raises the question as to whether the constitution allows the tax legislator to dedicate some taxes for specific purposes, subtracting them from the general budget. Indeed, in some countries, the constitutional principle of non-affectation prohibits certain taxes from being dedicated to specific purposes.[137] Moreover, earmarking could, to a certain extent, possibly be compared to an (indirect) subsidy in favour of domestic production.[138]

---

[135] See 26 US CODE §9507 ('Hazardous Substance Superfund'). Note that the Fund is now financed by other revenue sources as the taxes expired in 1995 (Martha L. Judy & Katherine N. Probst, 'Superfund at 30' (2009–2010) 11 Vermont Journal of Environmental Law 191, 216–218). See also 42 US CODE §§9601–9675.

[136] See e.g. US, S. 984, International Pollution Deterrence Act of 1991, 102nd Congress, 25 April 1991, (proposing to establish a 'pollution control export fund' and a 'pollution control research & development fund'); US, S. 3036, Lieberman-Warner Climate Security Act of 2008, 110th Congress, 20 May 2008, in particular Title IV, Sec. 4101. See also Belgium, Sénat, Proposition de résolution demandant l'instauration au niveau européen de droits sociaux et environnementaux dans le Code des douanes communautaire, déposée par M. Jacky Morael et consorts, Session de 2012–2013, 11 October 2012, n° 5-1807/1, proposing to use the revenue from the green customs to reinforce the funding of EU funds. See also Benito Müller, 'To Earmark or Not to Earmark? A Far-reaching Debate on the Use of Auction Revenue from (EU) Emissions Trading' (November 2008) Oxford Institute for Energy Studies, EV 43.

[137] J. Wilner Sundelson, 'Budgetary Principles' (1935) 50(2) Political Science Quarterly 236, 261–263. See also Holger Bonin, *Generational Accounting. Theory and Application* (Springer 2001), 213–214; Viktor J. Vanberg, 'Competition among Governments: The State's Two Roles in a Globalized World', in: Young Back Choi (ed.), *Institutional Economics and National Competitiveness* (Routledge 2012), 30.

[138] See the analysis by Prof. Thomas Cottier et al.: Thomas Cottier, Ilaria Espa, Simon Hirsbrunner, Kateryna Holzer & Tetyana Payosova, 'Differential Taxation of Electricity. Assessing the Compatibility with WTO Law, EU Law and the Swiss-EEC Free Trade Agreement', legal opinion established for the Federal Finance Administration, the Swiss Federal Office of Energy and the State Secretariat for Economic Affairs, 18 April 2014, available at <http://www.wti.org/research/publications/735/differential-taxation-of-electricity-assessing-the-compatibility-with-wto-law-eu-law-and-the-swiss-eec-free-trade-agreement/> (accessed 31 January 2017), 73; see also Wolfgang Schön, 'World Trade

Finally, the revenue from environmental tax could be used to limit the potential negative impact of the environmental tax on the most affected taxpayers such as low-income families or energy-intensive companies. As far as economic actors are concerned, one of the main issues related to the introduction of environmental taxes is the risk that domestic enterprises lose competitiveness at the international level. To reduce this risk, one option is to subsidise the most affected enterprises to neutralise the effect of the environmental tax while allowing them to become more energy efficient. Countries that decide to follow this path should, however, make sure that they respect WTO law provisions surrounding subsidies. In the case of environmental BTAs, this last option is less relevant. As mentioned above, one of the common objectives of environmental BTAs is to provide a level playing field between enterprises, therefore limiting the risk of loss of competitiveness for national enterprises.

4.3.3.2 Allocation of revenue of environmental BTAs

Unlike purely domestic environmental taxes, environmental BTAs call into question the legitimacy of allocating the revenue to domestic objectives. Indeed, if the theoretical foundation behind the adjustment is to preserve global commons (as under the theory of the legitimate absolute advantage), it would appear incoherent to use the revenue stemming from the tax to finance policy objectives that are purely national. Moreover, when the objective of environmental BTAs is to internalise environmental costs, a strong case exists for devoting the revenue of the taxes to environmental projects aimed at compensating for the environmental damage caused by the polluting activity that is subject to the tax. Given that the application of the tax on imported products is based on the idea that environmental issues cross national borders, it seems appropriate not to limit the use of the revenue derived from those taxes to purely domestic environmental purposes.

One proposal is to invest the revenue derived from taxes on imported products to projects located in those countries from where the products have been imported.[139] In other words, taxes on foreign products would

---

Organization Law and Tax Law' (2004) 58(7) IBFD Bulletin 283–296, 292. In EU law, see the following cases: ECJ, *Compagnie commerciale de l'Ouest and Others and Receveur principal des douanes de la Pallice Port*, 11 March 1992, Joined Cases C-78/90 to C-83/90; ECJ, *Essent Netwerk Noord and Others*, 24 January 2008, C-206/06.

139 See WTO, PC/SCTE/M/3, *supra* n. 9, para. 43. See also Stephen Sewalk, who distinguishes between domestic and foreign reinvestment: Stephen Sewalk,

be invested abroad to foster environmental protection in third countries. Such an idea, however, faces the same criticism as the ones against proposals to allocate revenue to environmental projects at the national level: 'How to justify that tax revenue is invested based on territorial criteria when environmental BTAs are based on a holistic approach to the environment, which suggests that environmental degradation is never limited to one specific territory but may always have a global impact?'[140]

When environmental BTAs are based on the idea that all environmental costs should be internalised, the tax revenue should preferably be allocated to an international environmental fund to invest in environmental projects based on environmental needs rather than on a territorial basis based on the location where the products are from. In other words, the idea is to dedicate the revenue from environmental BTAs to foster environmental protection on a global scale, recognising the global nature and interconnectedness of environmental issues. Even though environmental action pursued through the fund could still target one specific country or territory (e.g. because it is easier to implement a project in one specific region), the proposal to allocate the revenue of environmental BTAs to an international fund reinforces the global environmental character of the tax over its monetary objective. Indeed, by allocating tax revenue to an international fund, the legislator makes clear that the genuine objective is to foster environmental protection rather than to raise tax revenue at the national level. Aside from the political coherence of allocating tax revenue to an international environmental fund, this environmentally related allocation of the tax revenue could also serve to support the claim that the tax is not protectionist in nature and could, in any case, be justified under GATT Article XX (Chapter 6).[141] Moreover, environmental BTAs serving the common good would be less likely to attract criticism from third countries. Concurrently, the allocation of the tax revenue to an international fund could, however, reduce the potential leverage of environmental BTAs to encourage third countries to adopt

'A Carbon Tax with Reinvestment Is WTO Compatible' (2013–2014) 25(2) Fordham Environmental Law Review 338, 387.

[140] See the call of Matthew J. Kotchen, Gilbert E. Metcalf & William A. Pizer in favour of the Green Climate Fund: 'The Case for the Green Climate Fund', The Hill, 6 March 2015, available at <http://thehill.com/opinion/op-ed/243974-the-case-for-the-green-climate-fund> (accessed 30 October 2015).

[141] See Gros & Egenhofer, *supra* n. 110, 62; Hillman, *supra* n. 130, 14. Note, however, that in the *Superfund* case, the Panel did not consider that the environmental purpose of the tax was relevant to assess its compatibility with WTO law.

similar environmental taxes, as the tax revenue would in any case benefit the international community.[142]

Various international environmental funds already exist and countries could simply decide to allocate tax revenue from environmental BTAs to one of these funds.[143] For example, the Global Environment Facility permits the financing of environmental projects in developing countries.[144] Other examples are the UNEP environment fund,[145] the Green Climate Fund[146] and the Multilateral Fund for the Implementation of the Montreal Protocol.[147] Since most of these funds are related to specific environmental issues, they would not be appropriate for collecting the money from all types of environmental BTAs. One alternative could be to allocate part of the revenue to each of these funds to tackle a broad range of environmental challenges.[148] A more ambitious option would be to create a new international environmental fund with a broad mandate. Although the creation of such a new 'umbrella organization for sustainable development' or a 'specialized agency' (as a 'world environmental

---

142 See Rodi & Ashiabor, *supra* n. 72, 80.

143 See Christiane Gerstetter, Benjamin Görlach, Susanah Stoessel, Maria Ivanoca, Sandra Cavalieri, Elizabeth Tedsen & Haran Bar-On, 'Rio+20: Financial Resources for Improved International Environmental Governance' (May 2012) Project No. (FKZ) 3711 19 104 on behalf of the federal environment agency, 56–127.

144 See Global Environment Facility, 'Investing in Our Planet', available at <https://www.thegef.org/gef/whatisgef> (accessed 30 October 2015).

145 See UNEP, 'About Our Funding', available at <http://www.unep.org/about/funding/SourcesofFunding/EnvironmentFundandVISC/tabid/131364/Default.aspx> (accessed 30 October 2015).

146 See Green Climate Fund, 'Behind the Fund, Credentials', available at <http://www.gcfund.org/about/the-fund.html> (accessed 30 October 2015); UNFCCC, 'Green Climate Fund', available at <http://unfccc.int/cooperation_and_support/financial_mechanism/green_climate_fund/items/5869.php> (accessed 30 October 2015).

147 See Multilateral Fund for the Implementation of the Montreal Protocol, available at <http://www.multilateralfund.org/default.aspx> (accessed 30 October 2015).

148 See, for example, the approach taken in the Belgian proposal to allocate the tax revenue to EU funds, including funds with an international reach such as Global Monitoring for Environment and Security, the Global Environment Facility, the EU development funds, etc. (Belgium, Sénat, Proposition de résolution demandant l'instauration au niveau européen de droits sociaux et environnementaux dans le Code des douanes communautaire, déposée par M. Jacky Morael et consorts, Session de 2012–2013, 11 October 2012, n° 5-1807/1).

organization') had been proposed in the framework of the Rio Summit, such an international institution has not yet been established.[149]

4.4 INTERIM CONCLUSIONS

The tax design of environmental BTAs may be based on traditional taxes that include BTAs: VAT, excise duties and sales taxes. The integration of environmental considerations into these tax models, however, implies certain modifications to 'green' these traditional taxes. Important tax design issues should be considered, including the definition of methods to assess the environmental value of imported products, the prevention of abusive behaviours that could render the tax system ineffective and the allocation of the tax revenue. These issues make the adoption of environmental BTAs more difficult, though not impossible. Legislators should be aware that solutions exist. Well-defined valuation methods could help solve valuation issues. The adoption of anti-abusive measures could permit facing the risks of abuse. Questions concerning the allocation of tax revenue should be analysed beforehand by legislators but should not be considered as a serious brake on the adoption of environmental BTAs.

Each model has its own peculiarity. Models based on excise duties are generally closer to traditional BTA models. VAT-based models, in contrast, may be more innovative. For example, a CAT could permit to fully internalise environmental costs. In practice, these models may be more difficult to implement. From the perspective of WTO law, excise-based models also seem easier to justify than VAT-based models, as one may rely on the examples of the US Superfund and ODC tax to argue in favour of other environmental BTAs copying their design. The analysis of the legal compatibility of environmental BTAs with WTO law shows that this hypothesis may be true (Part III).

---

[149] See UN, Rio+20, United Nations Conference on Sustainable Development, Institutional framework for sustainable development, available at <http://www.uncsd2012.org/index.php?page=view&type=12&nr=228&menu=63> (accessed 30 October 2015). See also UN GA, The future we want, Resolution adopted on 27 July 2012, 66th session, A/RES/66/288, paras. 262 and 265.

PART III

From old legal debates to brand new legal issues: an assessment of the compatibility of traditional and environmental BTAs under WTO law (and beyond)

This third part aims to evaluate the legal limits deriving from superior international norms, with a focus on WTO law, to the adoption of traditional and environmental BTAs. The main goal is to assess the scope of the limits that individual countries – or groups of countries – will face under international trade law if they decide to develop the environmental dimension of cross-border taxation. This part demonstrates that – even though WTO law's mainstream interpretations may significantly limit the possibility of adopting environmental BTAs – WTO law provisions surrounding BTAs may be interpreted in such a way as to permit their development. In other words, this part argues that WTO law does not necessarily need to be modified, pointing out that non-traditional interpretations of WTO law could suffice to allow for the adoption of environmental BTAs.

This part first focuses on the legal framework of traditional BTAs (Chapter 5). Second, this part analyses in more detail the legal framework surrounding environmental BTAs, under WTO law and beyond (Chapter 6).

5. Legal framework of traditional BTAs

As explained in Chapter 1, the legal framework surrounding BTAs was developed in the 18th and 19th centuries when some countries concluded bilateral trade agreements including provisions aimed to subject the adoption of BTAs to certain conditions.[1] In 1947 the GATT codified this practice at the multilateral level as part of the general commitment to reduce tariffs and other barriers to trade and eliminate discriminatory treatment in international commerce.[2] The legal framework surrounding BTAs is primarily derived from various provisions of this General Agreement. The relevant provisions are Articles II and III (regarding BTAs on imports), Articles VI and XVI (regarding BTAs on exports) and Articles I and VII. Moreover, BTAs on exports are regulated by the Agreement on Subsidies and Countervailing Measures (ASCM).

This chapter first focuses on BTAs' main legal grounds, from the general GATT provisions that form part of BTAs' legal framework to WTO legal provisions that are specific to BTAs on imports and BTAs on exports (Section 5.1). The objective is to analyse the main legal provisions surrounding the adoption of BTAs on imports and exports, drawing attention to their interactions and procedural consequences. Second, these provisions are discussed from a substantive viewpoint, analysing the conditions and limits set up by WTO law on the adoption of BTAs (Section 5.2).

---

[1] See OECD, The Political Economy of Environmentally Related Taxes (2006), 92. See also OECD, Environment Policy Committee and Committee on Fiscal Affairs. Joint Sessions on Taxation and Environment. 2nd Session. Environmental Taxes and Border Tax Adjustments (hereafter, 'OECD 1994 note on Environmental BTAs, COM/ENV/EPOC/DAFFE/CFA(94)31'), 4, para. 7; Roger W. Rosendahl, 'Border Tax Adjustments: Problems and Proposals' (1970) 2 Law & Policy in International Business 85, 144–145, Appendix A (the agreements mentioned by Rosendahl are available online on the website of the Hathi Trust Digital Library, <http://www.hathitrust.org>).

[2] See GATT Preamble.

5.1 BTAs' MAIN LEGAL GROUNDS

5.1.1 General GATT Provisions and BTAs

Some GATT rules – GATT Articles I and VII – apply generally to any measure on internationally traded goods, including BTAs.

5.1.1.1 GATT Article I: The Most-favoured Nation (MFN) principle

GATT Article I:1 is a general article that prohibits *de facto* as well as *de jure* discrimination.[3] It also applies – as a general provision – to the case of BTAs and aims at guaranteeing non-discrimination between products of WTO members: 'like products' should be treated the same way regardless of the country from where they are imported or to which they are exported. In other words, the MFN principle forbids BTAs from being implemented in such a way as to favour certain WTO members in comparison to other members. As to BTAs, this principle is also intrinsically linked with the 'national treatment' (NT) principle, which requires countries not to discriminate against foreign products in comparison with domestic products.[4]

5.1.1.2 GATT Article VII: valuations rule

Article VII is usually not considered by authors discussing BTAs. One of the reasons may be that this article only gives some indirect indication on BTAs' conditions of implementation. Article VII concerns the valuation rules for customs purposes. These rules include the obligation to use the actual value of the imported merchandise as a basis for customs purposes. The valuation rules mentioned in GATT Article VII are not applicable for the valuation of imported products on which BTAs are imposed. The Ad Note to Article VII makes clear that Article VII does not apply to 'internal taxes or equivalent charges imposed on or in connection with imported products' (i.e. BTAs on imports).[5] The reason behind this interpretative note is linked to BTAs' national practice in

---

[3] See i.a. GATT, Panel Report, European Economic Community – Imports of Beef from Canada, 10 March 1981, L/5099, BISD 28S/92 (*Imports of beef*); GATT, Panel Report, Spain – Tariff treatment of unroasted coffee, 11 June 1981, L/5135, BISD 28S/102 (*Spain – Unroasted Coffee*); GATT, Panel Report, Canada/Japan – Tariff on Imports of Spruce-Pine-Fir (SPF) Dimension Lumber, 19 July 1989, L/6470, BISD 36S/167 (*Japan – SPF Dimension Lumber*).

[4] See Section 2.

[5] Ad Note to Art. VII, para. 1.

respect of imports. Countries do not always apply BTAs on the customs value of the imported goods; the value may include previously paid duties or be established according to different rules.[6] Rosendahl correctly points out that this practice of levying BTAs on the duty-paid value may be criticised in the light of the objective of BTAs.[7] Indeed, the traditionally agreed purpose of BTAs is to compensate domestic taxes on 'like products', not to put a heavier burden on imported than domestic products by charging imported products on a value including the duties paid on these products.[8] GATT Article VII:3 also indirectly touches upon BTAs on exports, specifying that, for customs purposes, the value of imported products should not include the amount of the potential internal taxes that have been rebated through the mechanism of BTAs.[9]

5.1.2 WTO Law: Specific Rules Surrounding BTAs

Aside from GATT general provisions that apply to BTAs, BTAs are regulated by specific provisions that clearly define the limits of countries in implementing these tax measures.

5.1.2.1 BTAs on imports

GATT Articles II and III regulate BTAs on imports. In other words, these two articles define the general obligations of WTO members in relation to the taxes that they apply on imported goods. GATT Article II sets up the main obligations for WTO member states in relation to the use of 'customs duties, duties and charges of any kind imposed on or in connection with importation'. GATT Article III establishes the NT principle on internal taxation and regulation, which – roughly speaking – prohibits measures that discriminate between domestic and imported products.

Within GATT Articles II and III, Articles II:2(a) and III:2 regulate BTAs on imports. Article II:2(a) provides that countries should not be prevented from imposing – at any time – on the importation of any product 'a charge equivalent to an internal tax imposed consistently with the provisions of paragraph 2 of Article III in respect of the like domestic product or in respect of an article from which the imported product has

---

[6] See GATT, Review Working Party II on Tariffs Schedules and Customs Administration, Report to the Contracting Parties, Ninth Session, 24 February 1955, L/329, para. 13.

[7] Rosendahl, *supra* n. 1, 93 (footnote 26) & 108–109 (footnote 85).

[8] *Ibid.*

[9] GATT Art. VII:3.

been manufactured or produced in whole or in part'. Article III:2 also sets up limits to the application of internal taxes and charges on imported products. Roughly speaking, BTAs should not exceed the internal taxes and charges applied to like domestic products.[10]

5.1.2.1.1 Interaction between GATT Articles II:2(a) and III:2 Though Article II:2(a) and Article III:2 of the GATT both seem to express a similar idea – namely that BTAs on imports may be established under certain conditions – the question arises as to how these provisions should be articulated with the general rules established by GATT Articles II and III as well as in relation to each other. So far, the articulation between these provisions has never been clearly defined, notwithstanding the legal consequences that may derive from the interpretation of the relations between GATT Articles II:2(a) and III:2. In the OECD 1968 Report, only GATT Article III is mentioned in the list of GATT provisions on BTAs.[11] The GATT Working Party on BTAs analysed both GATT Articles II and III, without clearly stating how these two articles relate to each other, although more attention seemed to be paid to Article III: 'The principal GATT article dealing with border tax adjustments which may be made on the import side is Article III'.[12] In light of the absence of formal explanations on the articulation of GATT Articles II:2(a) and III:2, one may rely on Panel and Appellate Body reports. The reports, however, rarely allow for one single interpretation. Three main hypotheses may be distinguished as to the relationship between GATT Articles II:2(a) and III:2.

A first hypothesis amounts to considering that GATT Article II:2(a) and Article III:2 are overlapping provisions.[13] This position has been supported by the EU as a third participant in the case *India – Additional Import Duties*, pointing out that the Panel may have been unable to 'take into account the possibility that Articles II and III may to some extent

---

[10] GATT Art. III:2. Note that Art. III:4 expresses a similar idea.

[11] OECD, Border Tax Adjustments and Tax Structures in OECD Member Countries, 1968 (hereafter, 'OECD 1968 Report'), Annex 2, 187–190.

[12] GATT, Working Party on Border Tax Adjustments, Note by the Secretariat, The GATT rules on Border Tax Adjustments, 31 May 1968, Spec(68)55, para. 2 (hereafter, 'GATT, Spec(68)55').

[13] Many authors do not distinguish between GATT Art. II:2(a) and Art. III:2 in their analysis of the legal framework of BTAs. See, for example, Jennifer Hillman, 'Changing Climate for Carbon Taxes, Who's Afraid of the WTO?' (2013) German Marshall Fund of the United States 1, 5.

overlap'.[14] In the case *EEC – Animal Feed Proteins*, the Panel report also seems to support this idea.[15]

A second hypothesis argues that the 'true' legal basis for BTAs on imports is GATT Article III:2 while Article II:2(a) only serves to clarify the scope of Article II.[16] In other words, the objective of GATT Article II:2(a) is only to exclude 'charges equivalent to internal taxes' from the scope of application of Article II:1(b), which prohibits the imposition of 'ordinary customs duties' and 'all other duties or charges of any kind' in excess of those agreed in the Schedule by each contracting party.[17] The Panel in *India – Additional Import Duties* supported this hypothesis. According to the Panel, 'a border charge on the importation of a product which fulfils the same function as an internal tax on the like domestic product should be, and is, subject to the provisions of Article III:2'.[18]

---

[14] WTO, Appellate Body Report, India – Additional and Extra-Additional Duties on Imports from the United States, Third participant written submission, European Communities, 26 August 2008, WT/DS360/AB/R, para. 11.

[15] GATT, Panel Report, EEC – Measures on Animal Feed Proteins, 14 March 1978, L/4599, BISD 25S/49 (*EEC – Animal Feed Proteins*), para. 4.16(c).

[16] See Adrian Emch, 'Same Same But Different? Fiscal Discrimination in WTO Law and EU Law: What Are "Like" Products?' (2005) 32(4) Legal Issues of Economic Integration 369, 370; Ernst-Ulrich Petersmann, 'International Trade Law and International Environmental Law: Environmental Taxes and Border Tax Adjustment in WTO Law and EC Law', in: Richard L. Revesz, Phillipe Sands & Richard B. Stewart (eds.), *Environmental Law, the Economy, and Sustainable Development* (CUP 2000), 142–143; Michael Trebilcock, Robert Howse & Antonia Eliason, *The Regulation of International Trade* (4th edn. Routledge 2013), 687–689; Peter Van den Bossche & Werner Zdouc, *The Law and Policy of the World Trade Organization* (CUP 2013), 354–355. *Contra:* De Schutter seems to imply the opposite in an article, where he puts the emphasis on GATT Art. II:2(a): Olivier De Schutter, 'Trade in the Service of Climate Change Mitigation: The Question of Leakage' (2014) 5 Journal of Human Rights and the Environment 65, 88–89.

[17] Paola Conconi & Jan Wouters, 'Appellate Body Report, India – Additional and Extra-Additional Duties on Imports from the United States (WT/DS360/AB/R, adopted on 17 November 2008)' (2010) 9(1) World Trade Review 239. They quote (p. 246, footnote 22) the Panel Report in *India – Additional Import Duties*, footnote 202. See also WTO, Appellate Body Report, India – Additional and Extra-additional Duties on Imports from the United States, 30 October 2008, WT/DS360/AB/R (*India – Additional Import Duties*), para. 153; WTO, Appellate Body Report, United States – Measures Relating to Zeroing and Sunset Reviews, Recourse to Art. 21.5 of the DSU by Japan, 18 August 2009, WT/DS322/AB/RW, (*US – Zeroing (Japan)*), para. 209.

[18] See Conconi & Wouters, *supra* n. 17, referring to the Panel and Appellate Body Reports in India – Additional Import Duties, 247: WTO, Panel Report,

A third way of looking at the relationship between GATT Article II:2(a) and Article III:2 is to consider that Articles II:2(a) and III:2 regulate two different types of BTAs, respectively BTAs in the form of 'border charges' and BTAs in the form of 'internal charges'.[19] This distinction was touched upon in *EEC – Animal Feed Proteins*, where the Panel considered 'the question of whether the EEC measures should be examined both as internal measures under Article III and border measures under Article II'.[20] As mentioned above, the Panel also noted, however, that, as far as Articles II:2(a) and III:2 were concerned, the scope of these articles 'should be the same as to the kind of measures being covered'.[21] The reasoning of the Panel in the *Superfund* case could support the hypothesis that GATT Articles II:2(a) and III:2 serve as two different legal grounds.[22] In the *Superfund* case, the Panel was asked to

---

India – Additional Import Duties, paras. 7.196, 7.206–7.215. The Appellate Body seems to have rejected this view (para. 180). See also the Appellant Submission of the United States, 8 August 2008, India – Additional Import Duties, available at <http://www.ustr.gov/trade-topics/enforcement/dispute-settlement-proceedings/wto-dispute-settlement/additional-and-extra-> (accessed 30 October 2015), para. 8. See also GATT, Panel Report, United States – Taxes on Petroleum and Certain Imported Substances, 5 June 1987, L/6175, 34S/136 (*US – Superfund*), para. 5.2.7.

[19] See the position of Conconi & Wouters, *supra* n. 17; Paul Demaret & Raoul Stewardson, 'Border Tax Adjustments under GATT and EC Law and General Implications for Environmental Taxes' (1994) 28(4) Journal of World Trade Law 5, 19; Joost Pauwelyn, 'Carbon Leakage Measures and Border Tax Adjustments under WTO Law', in: G. Van Calster & D. Prévost (eds.), *Research Handbook on Environment, Health and the WTO* (Edward Elgar Publishing 2013), 475. See also Trebilcock, Howse & Eliason, *supra* n. 16, 688–689. *Contra:* Henrik Horn & Petros C. Mavroidis, 'Border Carbon Adjustments and the WTO', study part of the ENTWINDED – Environment and Trade in a World of Interdependence – project, 14 March 2010; Henrik Horn & Petros C. Mavroidis, 'To B(TA) or Not to B(TA)? On the Legality and Desirability of Border Tax Adjustments from a Trade Perspective' (2011) 34(11) The World Economy 1911, 1913. See also Kateryna Holzer, *Carbon-Related Border Adjustment and WTO Law* (Edward Elgar Publishing 2014), 73, table on p. 85.

[20] GATT, Panel Report, *EEC – Animal Feed Proteins*, para. 4.15.

[21] *Ibid.*, para. 4.16.

[22] GATT, Panel Report, *US – Superfund*, paras. 3.2.5. & 5.3.7. See also GATT, Panel Report, United States – Measures Affecting Alcoholic and Malt Beverages, 19 June 1992, DS23/R, BISD 39S/206 (*US – Malt Beverages*), para. 5.3 ('The Panel considered that excise taxes levied on imported and domestic products *are internal taxes* subject to the national treatment provision of Article III:2, first sentence …'); WTO, Panel Report, Thailand – Customs and Fiscal Measures on Cigarettes from the Philippines, 15 November 2010, WT/DS371/R

analyse two types of tax: a 'tax on certain imported substances' (which appears to be a tax triggered by the act of importation) and a 'tax on certain chemicals' (which seems to be an internal tax). For the analysis of the 'tax on certain imported substances', the Panel referred to GATT Article II:2(a). Conversely, for the analysis of the 'tax on certain chemicals', the Panel only mentioned GATT Article III:2. Though the Panel did not explain the distinction between GATT Articles II:2(a) and III:2, the Panel Report in *Superfund* could be used in support of the hypothesis that these two provisions regulate different types of BTAs.

References to this distinction were also made in the Appellate Body Reports in *India – Additional Import Duties* and *China – Auto Parts*.[23] In *China – Auto Parts*, the Appellate Body pointed out that a distinguishing feature between border and internal charges could be based on the different legal meaning of the material act of importation for each of these charges.[24] According to the Appellate Body, a charge cannot be classified as an 'ordinary customs duty' under Article II when the taxable event takes place 'after the importation of the product'.[25] In other words, a necessary component of ordinary customs duties – and border charges in general – is that they apply 'at the moment and by virtue of importation'.[26] Such component is, however, not exclusive to border charges: the interpretative note on Article III specifies that Article III is also to be applied to internal taxes or other internal charges collected or enforced 'at the time or point of importation'.[27] A distinction could nevertheless be drawn between border charges and 'internal charges' based on the legal consequences deriving from the material act of importation. In the case of 'internal charges', the 'obligation to pay internal charges … accrues because of an internal factor and is merely

(*Thailand – Cigarettes (Philippines)*, in which VAT is analysed as an internal tax covered by GATT Art. III:2.

23 See Joel P. Trachtman, 'WTO Law Constraints on Border Tax Adjustments and Tax Credit Mechanisms to Reduce the Competitive Effects of Carbon Taxes' (2016) Resources for the Future, 6–7.

24 WTO, Appellate Body Report, China – Measures Affecting Imports of Automobile Parts, 15 December 2008, WT/DS339/AB/R; WT/DS340/AB/R; WT/DS342/AB/R (*China – Auto Parts*), para. 165.

25 *Ibid.*

26 *Ibid.*, para. 165. See also GATT, Panel Report, EEC – Regulation on Imports of Parts and Components, 16 May 1990, L/6657, BISD 37S/132 (*EEC – Parts and Components*), paras. 5.4–5.8.

27 Ad Note Art. III.

collected for imported products at the border'.[28] By contrast, importation *triggers* border charges.[29]

Hence, as soon as the material act of importation triggers the payment of BTAs on imports, GATT Article II:2(a) – and not Article III:2 – should serve as the 'true' legal basis for BTAs on imports.[30] In other words, what matters is that the act of importation is defined as the taxable event. In principle, GATT Article II:2(a) should not apply when the material act of importation is only the 'chargeable event' as in the case of VAT and excise duties, where the taxable event is the act of consumption.[31]

---

[28] Conconi & Wouters, *supra* n. 17, 251–252. See also Frieder Roessler, 'Comment. India – Additional and Extra-Additional Duties on Imports from the United States' (2010) 9(1) World Trade Review 265, 267–268. See WTO, Appellate Body Report, *China – Auto Parts*, paras. 161 & 163.

[29] Conconi & Wouters, *supra* n. 17, 251. See WTO, Appellate Body Report, *China – Auto Parts*, paras. 161 & 163.

[30] Conconi & Wouters, *supra* n. 17, 247–248; Donald Feaver & Benedict Sheehy, 'Climate Policy and Border Adjustment Regulation: Designing a Coherent Response' (2012) 13 Melbourne Journal of International Law 792; Patrick Low, Gabrielle Marceau & Julia Reinaud, 'The Interface between the Trade and Climate Change Regimes: Scoping the Issue' (2012) 46(3) Journal of World Trade 485, 489; Zhu Zhu, Lee Eun-sup & Kim Sun-ok, 'A Discussion on the Legitimacy of Carbon Tariffs under the WTO' (2011) 10 International Conference on Sociality and Economics Development IPEDR 221, 222.

[31] In the case of VAT, various proxies (such as, for example, the supply of goods, the importation, etc.) are used to subject consumption to tax. The EU VAT Directive defines the concept of 'chargeable event' as 'the occurrence by virtue of which the legal conditions necessary for VAT to become chargeable are fulfilled' (Art. 62(1)). The concept of 'chargeable event' is arguably artificial as the act of importation could always be said to serve as a proxy for consumption. However, for taxes to fall under Art. III:2 – and the act of importation to be considered as a proxy for consumption – the act of importation should be one of various proxies used to tax consumption. It is certainly the case for VAT where consumption is taxed not only through importation, but also through the supply of goods, etc. In the case *India – Additional import duties*, the excise tax was considered to fall under Art. II:2(a), most probably because it was not part of a larger internal tax system on consumption. Note also that the concepts of taxable and chargeable event do not have unique definitions in the literature. See Ben J.M Terra, 'Chapter 8, Excises', in: Victor Thuronyi (ed), *Tax Law Design and Drafting* (IMF 1996), 7–8; IBFD, *Glossary* (Online Tax Research Platform); VAT Directive. Here, the concept of taxable event is understood by reference to the 'rationale' of the tax, the event for which the legislator provides proxies (in the sense employed by Millar: Rebecca Millar, 'Echoes of Source and Residence in VAT Jurisdictional Rules' (2009) 09/44 Legal Studies Research Paper 1; Rebecca

In addition to the distinction based on the legal meaning of the material act of importation, a second distinguishing feature between internal and border charges applied to imports could be based on the extent to which these charges are 'equal' or merely 'equivalent' to the internal charges applied to 'like domestic products'.[32] The concept of 'internal charges' (GATT Article III:2) is supposed to refer to taxes which are 'identical' to the charges applied to 'like domestic products'. The concept of 'border taxes' (GATT Article II:2(a)) is supposed to refer to taxes that are not 'identical' but merely 'economically equivalent' to the charges applied to 'like domestic products'.[33] This understanding of the concept of 'equivalence' (including a quantitative component) is supported by the legislative history of the General Agreement. As recalled in the Appellate Body report in the case *India – Additional Import Duties* as well as in the *Superfund* case, the drafters of the GATT 'had clearly contemplated the possibility for making border tax adjustments in respect of imported products that contained substances subject to an internal tax':

> Thus they had agreed with respect to the word 'equivalent' in Article II:2(a) that it meant: 'For example, if a [charge] is imposed on perfume because it contains alcohol, the [charge] to be imposed must take into consideration the value of the alcohol and not the value of the perfume, that is to say the value of the content and not the value of the whole'.[34]

Millar, 'Jurisdictional Reach of VAT' in: Richard Krever (ed.), *VAT in Africa* (Pretoria University Law Press 2008) 182–185).

[32] WTO, Panel Report, *India – Additional Import Duties*, paras. 7.173–7.198; WTO, Appellate Body Report, *India – Additional Import Duties*, paras. 165–182.

[33] See Roessler, *supra* n. 28, 268; Conconi & Wouters, *supra* n. 17, 248, referring to Appellate Body Report, *India – Additional Import Duties*, footnote 304.

[34] WTO, Appellate Body Report, *India – Additional Import Duties*, paras. 172–173; GATT, Panel Report, *US – Superfund*, para. 3.2.6. Note that the same extract has been used in *India – Additional Import Duties* in support of a different interpretation of the concept of 'equivalence' (Panel Report, para. 7.187). The concept of BTA is explicitly used by the EU in its Oral Statement before the Appellate Body, para. 10: 'These border tax adjustments can well present features which are those typically found in customs duties. For instance, in the present dispute the measures at issue are levied on the basis of India's customs legislation, by the customs authorities, when the goods are imported into India' (WTO, Appellate Body, Oral Statement by the European Union, *India – Additional Import Duties*, 4 September 2008, AB-2008-7).

The concept of equivalence was further discussed in the case *Argentina – Hides and Leather*, where the Panel analysed the compatibility of the advance payment of a turnover tax with GATT Article III. The Panel considered this tax to be an internal measure that falls under GATT Article III:2, recalling that 'Article III:2 does not prescribe the use of any specific method or system of taxation'.[35] Hence, GATT Article III does not seem to require that internal taxes on imported products and 'like' domestic products be perfectly identical. The meaning of the term 'equivalent' in GATT Article II:2(a) is not to be understood by reference to the design of the tax.[36] In *India – Additional Import Duties*, the Appellate Body indicated '... that the term "equivalent" calls for a comparative assessment that is both qualitative and quantitative in nature'.[37] On the one hand, the qualitative assessments relates to the relative function of the internal tax and the border tax.[38] On the other hand, the quantitative assessment includes an evaluation as to the effect and value of the tax.[39]

5.1.2.1.2 Legal consequences derived from these different hypotheses
Under the first and second hypotheses, there is no legal difference between BTAs on imports and internal charges mentioned in GATT

---

[35] WTO, Panel Report, Argentina – Measures Affecting the Export of Bovine Hides and the Import of Finished Leather, 19 December 2000, WT/DS155/R (*Argentina – Hides and Leather*), para. 11.149, quoting Panel in *Japan – Alcoholic Beverages I*. See also WTO, Panel Report, *Argentina – Hides and Leather*, para. 11.150; GATT, Panel Report, *Superfund*, para. 5.2.9. See, however, GATT, Panel Report, Belgian Family Allowances, 7 November 1952, G/32, BISD 1S/59 (*Belgium – Family Allowances (allocations familiales)*), para. 2.

[36] As far as we know, the concept of 'equivalence' has usually been positively interpreted by Panel and Appellate Body by reference to the requirements that need to be met for a tax to be considered 'equivalent' to an internal tax (see, e.g. the *Superfund* case: GATT, Panel Report, *US – Superfund*, para. 181). References to a negative definition may be found in the Panel Report in *India – Additional Import Duties*: see paras. 7.179–7.198, especially paras. 7.179–7.180, where the Panel draws a distinction between the adjectives 'equivalent' and 'equal'. See also para. 7.189, para. 7.196 and especially para. 7.197. Though the Appellate Body Report does not explicitly reject the 'negative definition' of the concept, the Appellate Body overturned most of the reasoning of the Panel as far as the concept of 'equivalence' is concerned.

[37] WTO, Appellate Body Report, *India – Additional Import Duties*, para. 175.

[38] *Ibid.*

[39] *Ibid.*

Articles II:2(a) and III:2. Both measures are subject to the same conditions, namely the conditions mentioned in GATT Article III:2. As soon as the conditions mentioned in GATT Article III:2 are met, BTAs on imports are considered compatible with the GATT.

In contrast to these two first hypotheses, the third hypothesis assumes that different legal regimes should be applied to the category of 'charges equivalent to an internal tax' (those falling under GATT Article II:2(a)) and the category of 'internal taxes and charges' (those falling under GATT Article III:2), both at procedural and substantive levels.[40]

At the procedural level, the legal grounds on which a complainant bases its claim potentially influence the weight and the distribution of the burden of proof between the complaining and defending parties. In her book *Evidence, Proof, and Fact-Finding in WTO Dispute Settlement*, Grando points out that the 'pleading criterion', according to which a '… party who raises a certain provision must bear the burden of proof with respect to the element of that provision' could explain that certain parties prefer to base their claims on certain provisions rather than on others.[41] With regard to GATT Article III:2 and II:2(a), the weight of the burden of proof could be heavier on the complaining party for claims under GATT Article III:2 than under Article II:2(a).[42] Under both provisions, the complaining party should establish a '*prima facie* case of violation'.[43] However, under Article II:2(a) of the GATT, the Appellate Body in *India – Additional Import Duties* seems to imply that the burden of proof may be shared between the complaining and responding parties, depending on the circumstances of the case.[44] Under the hypothesis

40 Conconi & Wouters, *supra* n. 17, 248.

41 Michelle T. Grando, *Evidence, Proof, and Fact-Finding in WTO Dispute Settlement* (OUP 2009), 179–180. See also Japan's views on this issue in WTO, Appellate Body Report, *India – Additional Import Duties*, para. 109.

42 See Conconi & Wouters, *supra* n. 17, 251–254. *Contra:* WTO, India Additional Third participant written submission European Communities, Geneva, 26 August 2008, para. 9. According to the EU, 'an alternative would [perhaps] be to read the relevant provisions constantly together and to apply some robust common sense when it comes to burden of proof'.

43 Conconi & Wouters, *supra* n. 17, 251–252.

44 WTO, Appellate Body Report, *India – Additional Import Duties*, para. 193. Note that Australia (Appellate Body Report, para. 100) supported an interpretation which went far beyond the one supported by the Panel: as Art. II:2(a) had to be considered an exception to Art. II:1, the burden of proof should be on the responding parties. As Japan explained (Appellate Body Report, para. 109), such an interpretation would have led to a 'reversal of the burden of proof' under Art. III:2. In other words, according to Australia, the burden of proof under

where BTAs can either be grounded on GATT Article II:2(a) or GATT Article III:2, the case for a less heavy burden of proof under Article II:2(a) could be explained by reference to the measures that fall under this article. Indeed, where GATT Articles II:2(a) and III:2 are considered as two different legal grounds for BTAs, GATT Article II:2(a) would regulate measures for which the link with corresponding domestic measures is much looser. Consequently, it could be deemed too difficult for the complaining party to prove on its own that the disputed measure is 'not equivalent to internal taxes'.

At the substantive level, the third hypothesis offers a clear legal ground for the case of *taxes occultes*. As this type of BTA is in principle not part of an internal tax system, the adjustments would be made in respect of 'hidden' taxes.[45] In other words, the third hypothesis would imply a certain recognition of the case of *taxes occultes*, which is rather controversial. This substantive effect is probably the most critical consequence that would follow from an interpretation of GATT Articles II:2(a) and III:2 as two separate legal grounds. A second – less significant – effect derived from such an interpretation concerns the possibility of invoking GATT Article II:1(b) in the case where the border charge is not considered eligible for adjustment under GATT Article II:2(a). Where a charge falls under the category of 'charges equivalent to internal taxes' and does not meet the conditions mentioned therein, the charge should consequently fall under GATT Article II:1(b), which could lead to the charge finally being deemed compatible with the GATT.[46] In the hypothesis where a charge is deemed to be an 'internal charge' under GATT Article III:2, this second test would not take place.[47] This substantial difference is, however, to be nuanced: an internal tax prohibited under GATT Article III:2 could easily be redesigned as a customs duty in the (unlikely) event where GATT Article II:1(b) is considered more permissible.

Art. II:2(a) would be primarily on the responding party, where, under Art. III:2, the *prima facie* case of violation should be established by the complaining party.

[45] It could nevertheless be argued that BTAs in respect of *taxes occultes* are part of a 'fictive' internal tax system. See also Trebilcock, Howse & Eliason, *supra* n. 16, 688–689. See also Demaret & Stewardson, *supra* n. 19, 19.

[46] Conconi & Wouters, *supra* n. 17, 248–250.

[47] See the Appellant submission of the US (mentioned in para. 177 of the Appellate Body Report, *India – Additional Import Duties*). See also GATT, Panel Report, *EEC – Parts and Components*, para. 5.4.

Under the three hypotheses, the main conditions for BTAs on imports are laid down in GATT Article III:2 (Section 5.2).[48] As mentioned above, in the case where a distinction is made between 'internal' and 'border charges' (i.e. the third hypothesis), it could be argued that the condition that the tax on imports must be part of an internal tax system is to be replaced by an 'equivalence test' to assess the equivalence between the border charge and the internal charge that should serve as a basis for the adjustment.

5.1.2.2 BTAs on exports

The main legal grounds for BTAs on exports have evolved over time.[49]

GATT Articles VI (concerning anti-dumping and countervailing duties), XVI (concerning subsidies) and the interpretative note on Article XVI regulate BTAs on exports. In addition to these provisions, the contracting parties agreed in 1960 on an illustrative list of measures to be considered as 'prohibited export subsidies'.[50] In 1979 the Tokyo Round led to an agreement on the interpretation and application of GATT Articles VI, XVI and XXIII.[51] This agreement, which was known as the Subsidies Code and which was only binding on its signatories, includes a list of export subsidies similar to the 1960 illustrative list.[52] In the Uruguay Round, a new legal framework for subsidies was designed. The ASCM is binding upon all WTO contracting parties. As in the Tokyo Subsidies Code, an illustrative list of export subsidies is to be found in Annex I of the ASCM.

GATT Article XVI regulates the use of certain forms of subsidies by contracting parties. The first paragraph establishes a notification procedure for contracting parties granting or maintaining 'any form of subsidy which operates directly or indirectly to increase exports of any product

---

[48] See WTO, Panel Report, *Argentina – Hides and Leather*, para. 11.131 (where these conditions are summarised).

[49] For more details on the first provisions surrounding BTAs on exports, see Rosendahl, *supra* n. 1, 85–146.

[50] GATT, Report of the Working Party on Subsidies, Contracting Parties, Seventh Session, 19 November 1960, L/1381, para. 5 (hereafter, 'GATT, L/1381'): 'the Working Party agreed that this list should not be considered exhaustive …'.

[51] See GATT, Multilateral Trade Negotiations, Group 'Non-Tariff Measures', Sub-Group 'Subsidies and Countervailing Duties', Subsidies/Countervailing Measures, Note by the Chairman, MTN/NTM/W/236, 5 April 1979.

[52] *Ibid.*, Annex 'Illustrative List of Export Subsidies', 37–39.

from, or to reduce imports of any product into, its territory'.[53] The third and fourth paragraphs provide for more detailed rules on export subsidies on primary and non-primary products. The interpretative note to GATT Article XVI provides for the conditions guaranteeing that BTAs on exports are not assimilated to subsidies: 'The exemption of an exported product from duties or taxes borne by the like product when destined for domestic consumption, or the remission of such duties or taxes in amounts not in excess of those which have accrued, shall not be deemed to be a subsidy.'[54]

GATT Article VI is structured in a similar way to GATT Article XVI. On the one hand, the article condemns dumping practices, defined as practices 'by which products of one country are introduced into the commerce of another country at less than the normal value of the products' under certain conditions.[55] On the other hand, GATT Article VI:4 recognises that the establishment of BTAs on exports should not be assimilated to a dumping or subsidy practice, consequently prohibiting member states from levying anti-dumping measures or countervailing duties on the products subject to BTAs. The role of GATT Article VI may be explained in the light of the relationship between GATT Articles XVI and VI. GATT Article VI:4 would permit a distinction to be made between BTAs on exports and 'authorized subsidies' under GATT Article XVI. While 'authorized subsidies' may trigger third countries to adopt countervailing duties, GATT Article VI:4 prohibits such duties vis-à-vis BTAs on exports.[56]

Against the background of the WTO, the ASCM clarifies the legal framework surrounding subsidies, distinguishing between prohibited subsidies and actionable subsidies (i.e. non-prohibited subsidies that may nonetheless be challenged and subject to countervailing action under certain conditions).[57] Relevant articles of the ASCM help define the conditions for the adoption of BTAs on exports. Relevant provisions are Article 1.1., especially Article 1.1(a)(1)(ii), Article 3.1(a), Annex I (which contains the illustrative list of export subsidies), Annex II and some

---

[53] GATT Art. XVI, para. 1.

[54] Notes Ad GATT Art. XVI. See also footnote 1 of the ASCM.

[55] GATT Art. VI:1.

[56] See GATT, Second Report of the Group of Experts on Anti-dumping and Countervailing Duties, 29 January 1960, L/1141.

[57] See also Art. 31 of the ASCM, which provides for the category of 'non-actionable subsidies' (which applied for only five years from 1995 to 31 December 1999).

footnotes to the Agreement. These provisions express a similar idea as the one mentioned in GATT Article XVI.

Article 1.1. of the ASCM defines the concept of subsidy, referring to two elements: (1) 'a financial contribution by a government or any public body within the territory of a Member (referred to in this Agreement as "government")' or 'any form of income or price support in the sense of Article XVI of GATT 1994'; *and* (2) 'a benefit thereby conferred'. According to Article 1.1(a)(1)(ii) of the ASCM, 'a government revenue that is otherwise due [that] is foregone or not collected (e.g. fiscal incentives such as tax credits)' should be considered 'a financial contribution ...'. Article 3.1. of the ASCM defines the subsidies which should be prohibited, referring *inter alia* to 'subsidies contingent in law or in fact, whether solely or as one of several other conditions, upon export performance, including those illustrated in Annex I'.

Annex I of the ASCM contains an illustrative list of export subsidies, which is used to indirectly determine the conditions for BTAs on exports. Points (e) and (g) of Annex I seem to help define these conditions. First, it is usually derived from point (e) of Annex I that direct taxes are not eligible for BTAs on exports. Second, it is derived from point (g) of Annex I that BTAs on exports are permissible so far as they take place through the exemption or remission of indirect taxes *not in excess of* those levied in respect of the production and distribution of like products sold for domestic consumption. Third, point (h) of Annex I has raised controversial questions regarding the eligibility of taxes on inputs for BTAs on exports. Footnote 58 of the ASCM gives some indication as to the distinction between 'direct' and 'indirect taxes' by means of an exemplary definition of these taxes:

> The term 'direct taxes' shall mean taxes on wages, profits, interests, rents, royalties, and all other forms of income, and taxes on the ownership of real property ... The term 'indirect taxes' shall mean sales, excise, turnover, value added, franchise, stamp, transfer, inventory and equipment taxes, border taxes and all taxes other than direct taxes and import charges.[58]

The provisions related to BTAs on exports may be distinguished from the GATT articles that regulate BTAs on imports.[59] Since the GATT, one of the main objectives of GATT/WTO law has been to strictly limit taxes contingent on imports. In contrast, the approach with regard to subsidies

---

[58] Footnote 58 of the ASCM.

[59] Against the background of the GATT, see GATT, Spec(68)55, *supra* n. 12, para. 22. See also Rosendahl, *supra* n. 1, 95, footnote 35.

(and taxes related to exportation) has been slightly different. Only certain categories of subsidies are prohibited under the GATT and the ASCM. Consequently, GATT provisions surrounding BTAs on imports are usually perceived as conditions for the adoption of such BTAs. In contrast, the GATT and ASCM provisions surrounding BTAs on exports provide rather for the conditions for complaining parties to initiate measures against the disputed subsidies. In other words, BTAs on imports are prohibited unless they meet the conditions mentioned in GATT Article III:2 (in addition to the conditions mentioned in GATT Article II:2(a) in the hypothesis where these two dispositions are read separately as explained above). In contrast, the conditions mentioned in the ASCM (and GATT Articles VI and XVI) define the conditions under which BTAs on exports may be prohibited and/or trigger the adoption of countervailing duties by other parties.[60]

5.2 CONDITIONS FOR THE ADOPTION OF BTAs ON IMPORTS AND EXPORTS

The conditions for the adoption of BTAs on imports and exports can be summarised under three main issues. A first issue pertains to how BTAs are conceptually framed under WTO law: 'Which types of taxes may be used as BTAs?' 'Will BTAs always take the form of "indirect taxes" or are there other possibilities for adjustments?' This first issue has rarely been discussed in the literature so far. A second issue concerns the taxes that may be eligible for adjustments: 'Does WTO law prohibit the adoption of BTAs in respect of direct taxes and *taxes occultes*?' Finally, a third issue relates to the products on which BTAs may be imposed as well as the acceptable tax burden that may be imposed on imports through BTAs: 'What does the concept of "like products" mean?' 'When is the tax burden imposed by BTAs considered to exceed the burden imposed on like products at the domestic level?'

[60] The use of subsidies is not, as such, prohibited. In the case of BTAs on exports which do not meet the GATT/ASCM conditions, it is likely that the measures will nevertheless fall under the category of prohibited subsidies as such measures are in principle contingent on export performance (see Art. 3.1(a) of the ASCM).

5.2.1 Taxes Concerned – Conceptual Framing of BTAs

The traditional view on BTAs calls for a definition of BTAs in the form of indirect taxes. Indeed, based on the definition mentioned in the OECD 1968 Report, BTAs are limited to fiscal measures that put into effect the destination principle. In tax law, this principle is usually linked to consumption taxes, which are designed as indirect taxes.[61] This traditional model of BTAs can be described as follows:

- indirect taxes are imposed on imported products while equivalent indirect taxes are imposed on like domestic products;
- indirect taxes are remitted/refunded/not imposed in respect of the production and distribution of (like) exported products.

The assumption that BTAs always take the form of indirect taxes and are always imposed in respect of indirect taxes may, however, be called into question. This formal definition could indeed be considered contradictory to the original objective of BTAs to guarantee fair competition between countries by allowing for the adjustment of (all) taxes, which are passed forward into products' prices. Such consideration is grounded in an economic – in contrast to a legal – understanding of BTAs. Where a legal understanding of the destination principle puts the emphasis on the direct or indirect character of the tax, the economic understanding of BTAs gives importance to the economic effect of the taxes subject to adjustment. As soon as it is proven that a tax is passed into the price of a product, the tax – either indirect or direct – should be eligible for BTAs.

Other models of BTA based on an economic rationale of the concept could be designed regardless of the direct or indirect character of the tax.[62] For example, BTAs on imports could be imposed in the form of *indirect* taxes on imported products to adjust for the economic burden imposed by *direct* taxes on like domestic products.[63] Another model of

---

[61] As explained in the first section, the OECD 1968 report (*supra*, n. 11) refers to 'consumption taxes' and the GATT 1970 report (GATT, Border Tax Adjustments. Report of the Working Party adopted on 2 December 1970, L/3464 (hereafter, 'GATT, L/3464')) refers to 'indirect taxes'.

[62] In support of such a broad interpretation based on economic considerations, see WTO, Panel Report, *Argentina – Hides and Leather*, paras. 11.182–11.183.

[63] See GATT, Panel Report, *Belgium – Family Allowances (allocations familiales)*: this case concerned a sort of indirect tax on imported goods imposed by the Belgian authorities to 'compensate' for a tax on wages which was supposed to affect the competitiveness of Belgian producers (See Wolfgang

'economic' BTAs on imports could take the form of *direct* taxes imposed on imported products where equivalent *direct* taxes are (economically) imposed on like domestic products. Though it is less self-evident to design *direct* taxes on products, some concrete examples of 'destination-based direct taxes' have been proposed in the literature.[64] For example, Bradford examines what he calls a 'destination-based X tax', which he describes as a model where a business tax is imposed on all businesses on the difference between their sales and purchases and a compensation tax is imposed on individuals on the 'payments for labor services'.[65] Bradford proposes to apply the 'X tax' (which may be described as falling into the category of direct taxes) following the destination

Schön, 'World Trade Organization Law and Tax Law' (2004) 58(7) IBFD Bulletin 283, 287). The GATT Panel did not analyse the measure from the perspective of GATT provisions surrounding BTAs as the measure was clearly contrary to GATT Art. I (the MFN principle).

[64] James J. Nedumpara, 'Lessons Learned from DISC/FSC/ETI Disputes: Reshaping the Quest Towards a GATT/WTO Friendly Corporate Tax Reform in the United States' (2011) O.P. Jindal Global University, Research Paper No. 10, 12. See also Jon M. Truby, 'Towards Overcoming the Conflict Between Environmental Tax Leakage and Border Tax Adjustment Concessions for Developing Countries' (2010–2011) 12(1) Vermont Journal of Environmental Law 149, 150. Truby makes proposals for a tax on dividends and corporate taxation. See also Yariv Brauner, 'International Trade and Tax Agreements May Be Coordinated, But Not Reconciled' (2005) 25 Virginia Tax Review 251, 253. Brauner argues that 'it is reasonable to expect that protectionism through the income tax regime will be undesirable from a domestic tax policy perspective'. This statement supports the idea that direct taxes are *a priori* less self-evident when it comes to the taxation of products.

[65] David F. Bradford, 'The X Tax in the World Economy' (2003) CEPS Working Paper No. 93, 3. See also Michael Devereux & Rita de la Feria, 'Designing and Implementing a Destination-Based Corporate Tax', CBT Annual Symposium, Oxford, 26 June 2013, available at <http://www.ceps.be/system/files/events/2013/04/P4_RitadelaFeria.pdf> (accessed 28 October 2015); Michael Devereux & Rita de la Feria, 'Designing and Implementing a Destination-Based Corporate Tax' (2014) Oxford Centre for Business Taxation, WP14/07. See also Alan Auerbach, Michael P. Devereux, Michael Keen & John Vella, 'Destination-Based Cash Flow Taxation' (2017) Oxford University Centre for Business Taxation, WP 17/01; Wolfgang Schön, 'Destination-Based Income Taxation and WTO Law: A Note' (2016) 03 Max Planck Institute for Tax Law and Public Finance (on 'destination-based taxation with border tax adjustments'), WP 16/03.

principle. He writes: 'Corresponding to charging value-added tax on imports is denying a deduction for business purchases from abroad in the X tax.'[66]

Although, in legal scholarship, it is rather uncontroversial that WTO law only allows adopting border adjustments in respect of indirect taxes,[67] a detailed legal analysis of WTO law provisions – not limited to the case of BTAs – may lead to the opposite conclusion, namely that WTO law does not limit the adoption of BTAs to indirect taxes but that BTAs may be designed in respect of direct taxes and *taxes occultes*. The next section first reviews the legal arguments in favour of the prevailing interpretation of BTAs' legal framework before explaining why these arguments may be criticised.[68]

5.2.1.1 Eligibility of direct taxes

5.2.1.1.1 BTAs on imports Concerning BTAs on imports, four main arguments support the traditional view that direct taxes are not eligible for adjustments.

5.2.1.1.1.1 ARGUMENTS IN FAVOUR OF BTAS IN RESPECT OF INDIRECT TAXES ONLY
First, reference is made to the conclusions of the GATT 1970 Report. This report suggests that the distinction between direct and indirect taxes is valid both for BTAs on exports and BTAs on imports.[69] A second and a third argument are grounded in the textual interpretation of GATT

---

66 Bradford, *supra* n. 65, 6. See also Daniel Shaviro, 'Replacing the Income Tax with a Progressive Consumption Tax' (2003) NYU Law School, Public Law Research Paper No. 70, Center for Law and Business Research Paper No. 03-18. Shaviro also refers to the Hall-Rabushka 'flat tax' proposal (Robert E. Hall & Alvin Rabushka, *The Flat Tax* (Hoover Institution Press, Stanford University 1995)). See also Schön, *supra* n. 65.

67 See GATT, Working Party on Border Adjustments, Note by the Secretariat, Meeting of 18 to 20 June 1968, 11 July 1968, L/3039, 3–4 (hereafter, 'GATT/L/3039'). See also WTO, Negotiating Group on Rules, Subsidies Disciplines Requiring Clarification and Improvement, Communication from the United States, 19 March 2003, TN/RL/W/78, 4.

68 See Jennifer E. Farrell, *The Interface of International Trade Law and Taxation* (26 IBFD Doctoral Series 2013), 45–51 and footnote 152; Gary Clyde Hufbauer, *Fundamental Tax Reform and Border Tax Adjustments* (Institute for International Economics 1996), 64. See also Paulo Penteado Neto, *International Trade Subsidy Rules and Tax and Financial Export Incentives: From Limitations on Fiscal Sovereignty to Development-inducing Mechanisms* (authorHouse 2012), 149.

69 GATT 1970 Report, *supra* n. 61, para. 14. See also para. 10.

provisions – as the expression 'taxes on products' is considered to refer to indirect taxes only[70] – and in the historical developments of BTAs. From Ricardo's theoretical contribution to the practical regulation of BTAs in bilateral treaties, adjustments were neither advocated nor adopted in respect of direct taxes.[71] A fourth argument, also related to BTAs' historical development, is taken from GATT legislative history. In a note of the Secretariat on 'the GATT rules on Border Tax Adjustments', reference was made to the Havana Charter, considering that '... it was recorded that "neither income taxes nor import duties fall within the scope of Article 18 (of the Havana Charter – Article III of the GATT) which is concerned solely with internal taxes on goods"'.[72]

5.2.1.1.1.2 COUNTERARGUMENTS: BTAS IN RESPECT OF DIRECT TAXES The arguments mentioned above can nevertheless be criticised to support non-traditional models of BTAs, which are not based on the distinction between 'direct' and 'indirect' taxes.

First, it can be argued that the OECD 1968 and 1970 Working Party reports should only 'be read as an authoritative statement' and not be assimilated to legal provisions.[73] In that sense, the value of the reports for

---

70 John H. Jackson, 'The General Agreement on Tariffs and Trade in United States Domestic Law' (1967) 66 Michigan Law Review 249; Servaas Van Thiel, 'General Report', in: Michael Land, Judith Herdin-Winter, Ines Hofbauer-Steffel (eds.), *WTO and Direct Taxation* (Linde Verlag 2005), 19. *Contra*: Reuven S. Avi-Yonah & Joel B. Slemrod, '(How) Should Trade Agreements Deal with Income Tax Issues?' (2002) 55(4) Tax Law Review 533, 536.

71 See Sidney Weintraub, 'Border Tax Adjustments and the GATT' (1964–1965) 17 Tax Executive 304, 305.

72 See GATT, Spec(68)55, *supra* n. 12, para. 12 quoting the Havana Reports 63. See also Van Thiel, *supra* n. 70, 19, quoting United Nations Conference on Trade and Employment, Third Committee: Commercial Policy Sub-Committee A (Articles 16, 17, 18, 19) Notes of the Twentieth Meeting held on Tuesday, 13 January 1948, E/CONF.2/C.3/A/W.32.

73 Hufbauer, *supra* n. 68, 57. See, however, Henrik Horn & Peter C. Mavroidis, 'Border Carbon Adjustments and the WTO' (2010) The Research Institute of Industrial Economics, Stockholm, Bruegel, Brussels, Centre for Economic Policy Research, London, 27–29. These two authors consider that

> 'there is doubt whether the WP report is a decision by the CONTRACTING PARTIES, and thus comes under the purview of Art. 1(b)(iv) GATT 1994, or whether it is part of the GATT *acquis*, and then comes under the purview of Art. XVI of the *Agreement Establishing the WTO*. No matter how it is classified, the WP report will have legal significance. If, however, it comes under the former it should be regarded as binding on all WTO Members,

determining whether only indirect taxes are eligible for BTAs, should not be overstated.

Second, the conclusion of the reports regarding the ineligibility of direct taxes should be read in the light of the definition of BTAs mentioned in the report. Indeed, the OECD 1968 Report analyses BTAs in light of the practice at the time of the report and subsequently uses this analysis in order to define the legal framework of BTAs.[74] As explained above, the analysis of national practices highlights that the destination principle characterises indirect taxes imposed on domestic and imported products.[75] From this perspective, the method used in the OECD report to analyse BTAs does not allow reflection on whether other types of taxes than indirect taxes could be eligible for BTAs.

Third, in addition to the weaknesses of the OECD 1968 Report for providing a full legal analysis of BTAs, the report also lacks clarity in its references to the destination principle, which lies at the heart of BTAs' definition. Indeed, the report bases the definition of BTAs on the destination principle, generally understood as a principle essential to indirect taxes, making it necessarily unsuitable for direct taxes to be considered for BTAs.[76] In other words, the definition of BTAs in the OECD report inherently implies the ineligibility of direct taxes for adjustments as soon as the destination principle is understood as an essential feature of indirect taxes, which seems to be (at least indirectly) done in the OECD report.

The main error of the OECD report is that it confuses two different understandings of the destination principle. The erroneous reasoning of the report may be summarised as follows.

On the one hand, the report seems to adopt the traditional tax-related definition of the destination principle: '... the goods may be subject to the taxes of the exporting country (the so-called country of origin principle) or to the taxes of the importing country (the country of

---

whereas if it comes under the latter it should be regarding as creating *legitimate expectations* that WTO practice will be guided by it'.

[74] See also OECD, Working Party No. 4 of the Council on Border Tax Adjustments, Second Draft Report to the Council, Note by the Secretary of the Working Party, Paris, 18 February 1966, C/WP4(66)3, paras. 23–24.

[75] On this point, see J. Andrew Hoerner, 'The Role of Border Tax Adjustments in Environmental Taxation: Theory and US Experience', Working Paper presented at the International Workshop on Market Based Instruments and International Trade, the Netherlands, March 1998, 4.

[76] Many authors have however developed proposals of 'destination-based income taxes' (e.g. Devereux & de la Feria, *supra* n. 65).

destination principle)'.[77] In other words, the report assumes that indirect taxes are based either on the destination or on the origin principle, depending on whether taxes are imposed in the country of destination (consumption country) or in the country of origin (production country).

On the other hand, the OECD 1968 Report seems to adopt a different (trade-based) definition that assimilates the destination principle to a mechanism allowing imported products to be taxed and exported products to be exempted from taxation. The report indeed characterises the destination principle as a principle 'which enable[s] exported products to be relieved of some or all of the tax charged in the exporting country in respect of similar domestic products sold to consumers on the home market' and 'which enable[s] imported products sold to consumers to be charged with some or all of the tax charged in the importing country in respect of similar domestic products'.[78] From this perspective, the destination principle functions as a rule that limits countries' taxing powers by defining the conditions under which a country may adopt BTAs.

The confusion between the two definitions has led to the general view that direct taxes should not be eligible for BTAs, assuming that direct taxes should be based on the origin principle.[79] This unfortunate assumption – made in the report and dominant in the literature – that direct taxes are guided by the origin principle is, however, based on false premises.[80] Indeed, in tax law, the origin and destination principles are traditionally described as legal principles that define how indirect taxes are implemented in practice. As a rule, these two principles do not characterise direct taxes. In other words, and under a traditional tax-based perspective, direct taxes fall outside the distinction between the origin and destination

---

77 OECD 1968 Report, *supra* n. 11, para. 5.

78 *Ibid.*

79 *Ibid.*

80 George Carlson, 'Origin Principle', in: Joseph J. Cordes, Robert D. Ebel & Jane G. Gravelle (eds.), *The Encyclopedia of Taxation & Tax Policy* (The Urban Institute Press 2005), 283–284; James E. Meade, *The Structure and Reform of Direct Taxation* (Routledge 2013; first published 1978), 173–174; Rosendahl, *supra* n. 1, 98. See also on the comparison between the origin and destination principles with the source and residence principles: Millar, 'Echoes of Source and Residence', *supra* n. 31, 6–7 ('origin taxation of supplies is equivalent to residence taxation of supplier's income'); Millar, 'Jurisdictional Reach of VAT', *supra* n. 31, 182–185. See also the very interesting analysis of Prof. Brauner in Brauner, *supra* n. 64, 306 ('Note that while "origin" is an important concept of indirect taxes, it is meaningless in the realm of income taxes').

principles. Direct taxes are traditionally governed by the residence and source principles.[81]

Though the origin principle and the source principle are often compared, these two principles should be distinguished. The origin and destination principles are traditionally aimed at defining the taxable event for indirect taxes: either production or consumption is taxed.[82] Based on the origin principle, taxation takes place where production is located as opposed to the place where consumption is located. In contrast, the source and residence principles do not define the taxable event but are rather proxies used to locate the place where income should be taxed.[83] In the case of corporate taxation, source and residence are often used as proxies for determining the country to which an enterprise owes 'economic allegiance'. Therefore, source and residence may be described as principles used to distribute income between countries.[84] Based on the source principle, taxation should also take place where 'production' is located, as opposed to the place where enterprises have their residence. In other words, the place of production is, under the source principle, a proxy (to be clarified by other proxies) used to represent the place of the economic allegiance of the enterprise. In contrast, under the origin principle that characterises indirect taxes, the operation of production *is* the rationale of the tax.

In addition to the source and residence principles, some authors have proposed reforming corporate taxes by defining a new proxy of economic allegiance. For example, Devereux & de la Feria have proposed adopting

---

[81] See the considerations in the Neumark Report (European Commission, EEC Report on Tax Harmonization, The Report of the Fiscal and Financial Committee (Neumark Report) and the Reports of the Sub-Groups A, B and C, unofficial translation by H. Thurston (IBFD 1963)), 76–78.

[82] John Black, Nigar Hashimzade & Gareth Myles, *A Dictionary of Economics* (OUP 2012), 106–107. See also Devereux & de la Feria, *supra* n. 65, 9–10.

[83] Peter Andrew Harris, *Corporate/Shareholder Income Taxation and Allocating Taxing Rights between Countries. A Comparison of Imputation Systems* (IBFD 1996), 276–277. See also Joachim Englisch, 'VAT/GST and Direct Taxes: Different Purposes', in: Michael Lang, Peter Melz & Eleonor Kristoffersson (eds.), *Value Added Tax and Direct Taxation: Similarities and Differences* (IBFD 2009), 23.

[84] See Brauner, *supra* n. 64, 282 (footnote 126) & 306. On the concept of 'economic allegiance', see Report on Double Taxation, submitted to the Financial Committee by Prof. Bruins, Prof. Senator Einaudi, Prof. Seligman and Sir Josiah Stamp, 5 April 1923, League of Nations (Geneva), Doc E.F.S.73 F.19.

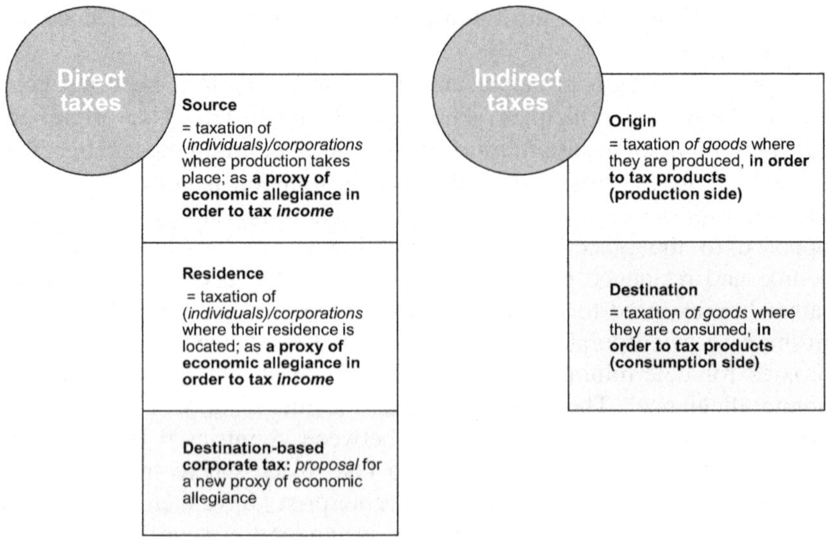

Figure 5.1 Distinctions between direct and indirect taxes

'destination-based corporate taxes'.[85] Despite the reference to the destination principle, such proposals should not be understood as the application of the traditional tax-based destination principle to direct taxes. Indeed, Devereux & de la Feria make clear that their analysis of 'a tax based in the place of the customer', which they call 'a destination-based tax', is not aimed at guaranteeing that the tax is levied in the country of consumption: their idea is rather to levy the tax 'in a place where the relevant activity is relatively immobile'.[86] In other words, their reference to the destination principle is only a way to describe their proposal for a new proxy of economic allegiance, in comparison with the traditional proxies that characterise direct taxes (Figure 5.1).[87]

By indirectly referring to the traditional fiscal understanding of the destination principle, BTAs' definition in the OECD 1968 Report automatically excludes direct taxes from its scope, not because direct taxes

---

[85] This proposal is comparable to the X-tax proposal discussed under Section 2.1. The X-tax is a proposal to apply the destination principle (under its international trade law definition) to a direct tax.

[86] Devereux & de la Feria, *supra* n. 65, 3.

[87] *Ibid.*, 11. See, however Bradford, *supra* n. 65. At the same time, their proposal – to a certain extent – implements the trade-based definition of the destination principle (imports could be taxed and exports left untaxed).

are based on the origin principle but simply because direct taxes are – traditionally – governed neither by the origin principle nor by the destination principle. Consequently, the question of whether direct taxes may be eligible for adjustments should be reconsidered, without any incorrect theoretical preliminary limitations.

A fourth counter-argument is based on the idea that the interpretation to be given to legal provisions surrounding BTAs should not remain static.[88] On the one hand, an historical analysis of BTAs proves that such interpretation has never been static. According to Hufbauer, the original distinction used to determine which taxes could be levied on imports was the one between 'product taxes' and 'general taxes'.[89] This distinction applied both to the provisions on BTAs and to the provisions on subsidies.[90] However, in 1960 the working party on subsidies seemed to understand the provisions on subsidies as distinguishing between 'indirect and direct taxes'.[91] Later, in 1968, the OECD report favoured the term 'consumption taxes' to describe 'all those taxes regarded as eligible for border adjustments'.[92] In 1970 the GATT Report switched again to the distinction between direct and indirect taxes.[93] The many changes in the concepts used to distinguish between eligible and ineligible taxes for BTAs illustrates that arguments in favour of a static interpretation of the distinction between direct and indirect taxes are not fully consistent. On the other hand, a dynamic interpretation would permit the inclusion of the new developments regarding the economic rationale of BTAs.[94] If,

---

[88] On static/dynamic interpretation methods, see Damien Neven & Joel P. Trachtman, 'Philippines – Taxes on Distilled Spirits: Like Products and Market Definition' (2013) 12(2) World Trade Review 297, 312–313. See WTO, Appellate Body Report, Korea – Taxes on Alcoholic Beverages, 18 January 1999, WT/DS75/AB/R; WT/DS84/AB/R (*Korea – Alcoholic Beverages*), para. 120. See also Isabelle Van Damme, *Treaty Interpretation by the WTO Appellate Body* (OUP 2009), chapter 6 'The Contextual Interpretation of the WTO Covered Agreements'.

[89] Gary Clyde Hufbauer, 'Tax Discipline in the WTO' (2010) 44(4) Journal of World Trade 763, 775.

[90] *Ibid.*

[91] Hufbauer, *supra* n. 89, 767, referring to GATT, L/1381 (*supra*, n. 50).

[92] OECD 1968 report, *supra* n. 11.

[93] GATT 1970 report, *supra* n. 61.

[94] *Contra:* Michael Lennard, 'The GATT 1994 and Direct Taxes: Some National Treatment and Related Issues', in: Michael Lang, Judith Herdin & Ines Hofbauer (eds.), *WTO and Direct Taxation* (2005 Linde Verlag), 73, 77. See also Joost Pauwelyn, 'The Nature of WTO Obligations' (2002) The Jean Monnet Center for International and Regional Economic Law & Justice, available

in Ricardo's time, direct taxes were not considered to be shifted into price, it is no longer the case today.[95] One of the reasons that can explain this change is that the distinction between direct taxes and indirect taxes was more clear-cut in Ricardo's time. John Stuart Mill, who is considered the father of the distinction, explained as follows:

> Taxes are either direct or indirect. A direct tax is one which is demanded from the very persons who, it is intended or desired, should pay it. Indirect taxes are those which are demanded from one person in the expectation and intention that he shall indemnify himself at the expense of another: such as the excise or customs.[96]

Mill's criterion is very much based on the intention of the legislator: an indirect tax is supposed to be a tax that has been designed by the legislator in such a way that the person – who is *intended* to be – liable to pay the tax is not the one who is asked to pay the tax.[97] A more objective criterion, which may also be derived from Mill, is to assess whether the taxpayer has the possibility of 'indemnify[ing] himself at the expense of another'.[98] This criterion is easy to apply in the case of the most common indirect taxes which existed in Mill's time. However, new types of direct and indirect taxes have been adopted in the 19th and 20th centuries.[99] For example, in the case of corporate income taxes, it might be difficult to determine who is the intended taxpayer and who actually

---

at <http://www.jeanmonnetprogram.org/archive/papers/02/020101-02.html> (accessed 28 October 2015), 'Interpreting the WTO Treaty: "contemporaneous" or "evolutionary" interpretation?').

95 The assumption that consumption taxes are 'always and fully shifted forward to the final consumer' is also 'obviously an inaccurate simplification' (Robert F. van Brederode, *Systems of General Sales Taxation: Theory, Policy and Practice* (Kluwer Law International 2009), 32 & 210). See also Gary Clyde Hufbauer, 'The Foreign Sales Corporation Drama: Reaching the Last Act?' (2002) International Economics Policy Briefs 1, 1.

96 John Stuart Mill, *Principles of Political Economy with Some of their Applications to Social Philosophy* (Longmans, Green and Co. 1848), available at http://www.econlib.org/library/Mill/mlP65.html (accessed 28 October 2015), book V, chapter III, para. 1.

97 Hufbauer, *supra* n. 68, 64–66. Prof. Wolfgang Schön seems to support the distinction between direct and indirect taxes based on the 'intent of the law' (see Schön, *supra* n. 63, 291–293).

98 Mill, *supra* n. 96, para. 1.

99 Victor Thuronyi, *Comparative Tax Law* (Kluwer Law International 2003), 54–57. See also Gary Clyde Hufbauer, 'The WTO as Tax Nanny', Center for Strategic Tax Reform's Tax Policy Wire, 25 April 2006, available at <http://www.cstr.org/commentaries/members/hufbauer.html> (accessed 25 August

supports the tax.[100] Indeed, corporations always – at least in theory – have the possibility of passing the tax to consumers by adjusting the price of the goods they produce (or the services they supply).[101]

In light of the evolution of tax systems, it could be argued that the distinction between direct and indirect taxes has lost its relevance and should be replaced by a distinction between taxes for which the taxpayer has the possibility of 'indemnify[ing] himself at the expense of another' (i.e. taxes which are passed on, at least partially, to the consumers) and taxes which necessarily fall exclusively on the intended taxpayer.[102] Based on this new distinction, any tax, as soon as the possibility exists for it to be passed through products' prices, could be considered eligible for adjustment.[103] Alternatively, it could be decided that any tax, as soon as it is proven that it has been passed, even partially, to the consumers, should be eligible for BTAs. BTAs would thus follow an economic rather than a legal understanding of the destination principle.[104] Against this suggestion, it could, however, be argued that not only taxation has

2014); Milton Leontiades, 'The Logic of Border Taxes' (1966) 19(2) National Tax Journal 173, 183. See also Michael Daly, 'WTO Rules on Direct Taxation' (2006) 29(5) The World Economy 527, 556. See also Farrell, *supra* n. 68, 51 ('In summation, the distinction between direct and indirect taxes remains convenient and practical, but is an outdated method to define the tax scope of the GATT').

[100] See also United Nations, Economic and Social Council, Second session of the preparatory Committee of the United Nations Conference on Trade and Employment, Verbatim Report Ninth Meeting of the Commission A Held on Thursday, 5 June 1947, Palais des Nations, Geneva, E/PC/T/A/PV/9, 18–19.

[101] Reuven S. Avi-Yonah, 'Corporations, Society and the State: A Defense of the Corporate Tax' (2004) 90(5) Virginia Law Review 1193, 1196; Steven A. Bank, 'Chapter 1: The Roots of Corporate Tax', *From Sword to Shield. The Transformation of the Corporate Income Tax, 1861 to Present* (OUP 2010); Steven A. Bank, *Anglo-American Corporate Taxation. Tracing the Common Roots of Divergent* Approaches (CUP 2011); Ken Messere, '20th Century Taxes and Their Future' (2002) 54(1) IBFD Bulletin 2; Edwin R.A. Seligman, *A Study of the History, Theory and Practice of Income Taxation at Home and Abroad* (The Macmillan Company 1911), available at <https://www.library.cornell.edu/> (accessed 21 January 2014).

[102] See IBFD, *Glossary* (Online Tax Research Platform).

[103] See Hufbauer, *supra* n. 68, 53 & 56. See WTO, Panel Report, *Argentina – Hides and Leather*, paras. 11.182–11.183. *Contra:* GATT, Panel Report, United States – restrictions on imports of tuna, 3 September 1991, DS21/R, BISD 39S/155, unadopted (*US – Tuna (Mexico)*, para. 5.13.

[104] On the relative impact of economic scholarship on legal developments, see van Brederode (*supra* n. 95, 210) who considers that '... economic truth has been replaced by perceived legal truth'.

changed, but also the rationale of BTAs. If, at Ricardo's time, the purpose of BTAs was to compensate for price shifting, it could be argued that, in the middle of the 20th century, BTAs were considered as an instrument of monetary policy in the context of a system of fixed exchange rates.[105] Under this hypothesis, BTAs would have lost their rationale in 1971 with the collapse of the fixed exchange rate system and no objective reason could now justify the need to apply BTAs in respect of any tax shifted into products' prices.

A fifth counter-argument may be derived from the fact that textual interpretation of the GATT is not as clear as it appears at first sight. It could indeed be argued that there is an asymmetry in the language of BTAs on imports and BTAs on exports.[106] The difference in language to be found in GATT Articles II:2(a), III:2 and XVI could be interpreted as an indication that Articles II:2(a) and III:2 are less restrictive than Article XVI (and the Ad Note to this article) as to the eligibility of taxes for BTAs. Indeed, Articles II:2(a) and III:2 refer to 'internal taxes imposed, *directly or indirectly*, to like domestic products' (which could indicate that direct taxes are also eligible for BTAs on imports) while the Ad Note to GATT Article XVI refers to 'duties or taxes *borne by* the like product when destined for domestic consumption'. This difference in language is reinforced by the fact that the language 'duties or taxes borne by the like product' was preferred in the Note to GATT Article XVI over the language that prevailed in the Havana Charter and which was much closer to the language of GATT Articles II:2(a) and III:2 ('duties or taxes imposed in respect of like products').[107] Hence, Hufbauer argues that 'corporate taxes equivalent to those paid by domestic manufacturers of like products' could be considered eligible for adjustments under GATT Articles II:2(a) and III:2.[108] He also points out that Article XVI of the Tokyo Round Code's Illustrative List of Export Subsidies (which was later used as a basis to draft the list mentioned in Annex I of the ASCM

---

[105] Leontiades, *supra* n. 99, 173–183. See Robert E. Baldwin, *Nontariff Distortions of International Trade* (George Allen & Unwin Ltd 1970), 88 & 96. See also the reference to the relationship between BTAs and the requirement of 'balance-of-payments equilibrium', e.g. in OECD, C(62)91, 2.

[106] Hufbauer, *supra* n. 68, 53–54. See, however, GATT 1970 Report, *supra* n. 61 ('GATT provisions on tax adjustment applied the principle of destination identically to imports and exports'). On the symmetry between BTAs on imports and exports, see also Demaret & Stewardson, *supra* n. 19, 30–31.

[107] GATT, Spec(68)55, *supra* n. 12, para. 29. *Contra*: GATT, L/3039, *supra* n. 67, 2. See also Rosendahl, *supra* n. 1, 95, footnote 35.

[108] Hufbauer, *supra* n. 68, 53–55.

and which excluded direct taxes from adjustments) should not be used as a legal ground to determine the taxes eligible for adjustments in respect of imports.[109] In his opinion, negotiators of the Tokyo Round Code on Subsidies and Countervailing Measures were only defining the eligibility criteria for BTAs on exports without considering the case of BTAs on imports.[110] A symmetrical interpretation of GATT provisions surrounding BTAs on imports and BTAs on exports would deny this fact.[111]

Finally, a last argument echoes the criticism that WTO law was not intended to constrain contracting parties as to the design of their direct taxes. Practice has, however, shown that direct taxes have been subject to the supervision of Panels and Appellate Bodies.[112] For example, it may be derived from the Panel report in *Argentina – Hides and Leather* that GATT Article III:2 puts conditions on the adoption of taxes on imported products used to compensate for the impact of domestic *direct* taxes.[113]

5.2.1.1.1.3 Eligibility of direct taxes for BTAs: practical consequences

The counter-arguments discussed above show that the common view that only indirect taxes are eligible for BTAs may be challenged. GATT provisions could indeed be interpreted in a broader way, opening the possibility for BTAs in respect of direct taxes. Despite this theoretical possibility, practical difficulties are nevertheless likely to limit the adoption of BTAs in respect of direct taxes.[114] If the distinction between the direct or indirect character of the tax is abandoned, the eligibility for BTAs should be based on other criteria, either the mere possibility to pass the burden of the tax to a third party or the evidence that the tax has effectively been economically passed into products' prices. In any case,

---

109 *Ibid.*, 55–56.

110 *Ibid.*

111 *Ibid.*

112 See WTO, Panel Report, *Argentina – Hides and Leather*; WTO, Panel Report, United States – Tax Treatment for 'Foreign Sales Corporations' – Recourse to Art. 21.5 of the DSU by the European Communities, 20 August 2001, WT/DS/108/RW (*US – FSC*) (concerning the compliance of an income tax with GATT Art. III:4); WTO, Panel Report, Indonesia – Certain Measures Affecting the Automobile Industry, 2 July 1998, WT/DS54/R, WT/DS55/R, WT/DS59/R, WT/DS64/R (*Indonesia – Autos*), para. 14.38. See also Daly, *supra* n. 99, 527–577.

113 WTO, Panel Report, *Argentina – Hides and Leather*, para. 11.159. See also Brauner, *supra* n. 64, 309–311.

114 Demaret & Stewardson, *supra* n. 19, 32; Schön, *supra* n. 63, 291. See also OECD, Trade and Environment: Processes and Production Methods (1994) OECD Documents 101.

BTAs will need to respect certain limits as to the tax burden that may be applied on imports. If the main rationale of BTAs remains the compensation of the tax burden imposed on domestic products, clear evidence should guarantee the non-excessive character of BTAs in light of their 'equivalent internal taxes'.

For both direct and indirect taxes, the economic effect of taxes on the price of domestic products is very difficult to predict. However, in the case of (non-cumulative) indirect taxes, the tax imposed on domestic products is clearly visible and usually easy to determine (though it does not mean that the effect of the tax on products' prices is identical to the amount of the tax legally imposed on the products). In the case of BTAs in the form of (non-cumulative) indirect taxes equivalent to 'internal indirect taxes', the evidence of 'equivalence' is therefore derived from the observation that the tax rate and tax base are equivalent. In other words, a presumption of 'equivalence' applies for indirect taxes regardless of their exact economic effect on products' prices.

In the case of BTAs in respect of direct taxes, the evidence of the 'equivalent and non-excessive character' of the taxes is much more difficult to prove. Indeed, in the case of direct taxes, the relationship between the tax and the product should first be established to allow for the adoption of BTAs. As it might be difficult to establish such relationship, the development of BTAs in respect of direct taxes is likely to be limited. This difficulty could explain why direct taxes have not been considered for BTAs in practice so far. Such an obstacle is, however, not insurmountable: cumulative indirect taxes have traditionally been considered eligible for BTAs despite the impossibility of guaranteeing a perfect equivalence between these taxes and their BTAs. Equivalence between taxes does not need (and cannot) be established with absolute certainty. Averaging has been an option for cumulative tax systems and may also offer a solution for the case of direct taxes. Moreover, with regard to the recent proposals in favour of destination-based corporate taxes (e.g. the proposal of Devereux and de la Feria), it is easier to establish a relationship between the tax and the products. Indeed, under these proposals, the tax is directly based, among other factors, on the sale of goods, which is not the case of traditional corporate income taxes.

5.2.1.1.2 BTAs on exports As to BTAs on exports, the most common argument in favour of the ineligibility of direct taxes for adjustments is based on the language of the ASCM. Indeed, one of the examples of prohibited export subsidies mentioned in the illustrative list of Annex I of the ASCM are BTAs on exports in respect of direct taxes.[115] In other words, adjustments in respect of direct taxes would be prohibited subsidies, falling under Article 3 of the ASCM. In contrast, it can be derived from Annex I that the (non-excessive) remission or the refund of indirect taxes will not be assimilated to a prohibited subsidy.[116]

The prohibition on adopting BTAs on exports in respect of direct taxes has been illustrated in the case law.[117] One famous example is the long-lasting dispute between the EU and the US regarding the US tax system allowing for the deferral of federal income tax on the export earnings of certain domestic companies.[118] In the *DISC* case, named after the 'domestic international sales corporation' legislation, the Panel considered that the US tax system could be assimilated to a partial exemption falling under the 1960 illustrative list of export subsidies, which was to be considered a prohibited subsidy under Article XVI:4 of the GATT.[119] The Panel and Appellate Body reached a similar conclusion in the subsequent *FSC* ('Foreign Sales Corporations') and *ETI* ('Extra-territorial Income Exclusion Act') cases.[120]

Against the view that only 'genuine' indirect taxes are eligible for BTAs on exports, two arguments should be mentioned. A first argument is related to the language of footnote 58 of the ASCM, which does not give a clear definition of the distinguishing features of direct and indirect taxes. Indeed, footnote 58 defines indirect taxes by reference to a list of examples. Consequently, uncertainty remains as to the taxes that are not explicitly listed in footnote 58.[121] The definition seems to classify as

---

[115] ASCM, Annex I, point (e). See also GATT, Spec(68)55, *supra* n. 12, paras. 30–31, where it is clearly stated that GATT Art. XVI does not allow for BTAs on exports in respect of direct taxes.

[116] See footnote 5 of the ASCM and WTO, Appellate Body Report, *US – FSC*, para. 93.

[117] See OECD 1994 note on Environmental BTAs, COM/ENV/EPOC/DAFFE/CFA(94)31, *supra* n. 1, para. 16.

[118] Starting from the *DISC* case in 1973: GATT, Panel Report, *US – DISC*.

[119] GATT, Panel Report, *US –DISC*, paras. 70–74.

[120] WTO, Panel Report, *US – FSC*; WTO, Appellate Body Report, *US – FSC*; WTO, Art. 21.5 Panel Report, *US – FSC*; WTO, Art. 21.5 Appellate Body Report, *US – FSC*, 14 January 2002, WT/DS108/AB/RW.

[121] On the difficulty of classifying taxes as direct or indirect, see Farrell, *supra* n. 68, 49; Hufbauer, *supra* n. 68, 64–65. On the classification of the Italian regional tax 'IRAP' (Imposta Regionale sulle Attività Produttive), see Carlo Garbarino, 'Hybrid Taxes and the Distinction between VST/GST and Direct Taxes: The Case of IRAP', in: Michael Lang, Peter Melz & Eleonor Kristoffersson (eds.), *Value Added Tax and Direct Taxation: Similarities and Differences*

indirect taxes 'all the taxes others than direct taxes' (i.e. all the taxes which are not mentioned in the limitative list of footnote 58) and 'all the taxes other than import charges'.[122] Second, Nedumpara challenges the view that BTAs on exports in respect of direct taxes should automatically be assimilated to a prohibited subsidy under the GATT and the ASCM.[123] He believes that the 1960 illustrative list of export subsidies did not create an absolute presumption of a practice that constitutes a prohibited subsidy. In the *DISC* case, both the US and the EU considered that the illustrative list established a non-absolute presumption of practices leading to 'bi-level pricing'.[124] A similar argument can be derived from the legislative history of Annex I of the ASCM, which dates back to the 1960s, when a working party on subsidies was established in order to analyse the steps to be taken in order to 'implement the provisions of paragraph 4 of Article XVI'.[125] A first list of measures 'generally … to be considered as subsidies in the sense of Article XVI:4' was adopted.[126] In other words, the list was intended to establish a rebuttable – non-absolute – presumption of the existence of an export subsidy. A last argument is based on the structure of the reasoning of the Panel in *FSC*. Nedumpara indeed considers that '… a careful review of the Appellate Body report in *US-FSC(I)*, indicates that an adjudicating body has to examine the elements of Article 1 of the SCM Agreement even in a dispute involving a claim under the Illustrative List'.[127] In other words, WTO law would not necessarily prohibit BTAs on exports made in

(IBFD 2009), 172–173 (Garbarino defines the IRAP as 'a hybrid tax': 'a hybrid of VAT (an indirect tax) and income tax (a direct tax)'); Alan Schenk & Olivier Oldman, *Value Added Tax: a Comparative Approach* (CUP 2006), 366.

[122] See Pauwelyn, *supra* n. 19, 478, footnote 80.

[123] Nedumpara, *supra* n. 64, 28–32.

[124] GATT, Panel Report, *US – DISC*, para. 72.

[125] GATT, Working Party on Subsidies, Membership and Terms of Reference, 5 November 1960, W.17/9.

[126] GATT, L/1381, *supra* n. 50, para. 5. See also the critical analysis made by Hufbauer of the *FSC* case: Gary Clyde Hufbauer, 'A Critical Assessment and an Appeal for Fundamental Tax Reform' (1999) Paper for the World Trade Organization Panel Report, Peterson Institute for International Economics, available at <http://www.iie.com/publications/papers/print.cfm?ResearchId=373&doc=pub#note2> (accessed 28 October 2015). Hufbauer considers that the *FSC* Panel and Appellate Body Reports did not respect the OECD Council understanding adopted in 1981 on the relationship between territorial tax system and GATT Art. XVI:4 (GATT, Tax Legislation, 18 December 1981, L/5271).

[127] See Pauwelyn, *supra* n. 19, 478, footnote 80. Nedumpara, *supra* n. 64, 32.

respect of taxes that fall under the category of direct taxes.[128] This argument may, however, be criticised considering that the Appellate Body stated in the *ETI* case that '[i]tem (e) of the Illustrative List identifies a particular measure which is deemed to be a prohibited export subsidy under Article 3.1(a)'.[129]

5.2.1.1.3 Eligibility of direct taxes for BTAs (imports & exports): interim conclusions The traditional approach interprets GATT provisions as permitting the adoption of BTAs only in respect of indirect taxes. This interpretation of WTO law provisions illustrates the dichotomy between legal and economic arguments. Law is based on fictions, assumptions and simplifications and may be applied detached from economic considerations.[130] The legal understanding of the destination principle is a clear example of the potential gap between law and economics. From a legal tax-based perspective, the destination principle refers to the proxies that are used to translate the idea that tax should be levied where consumption takes place. From a legal trade-based perspective, the destination principle suggests that, under certain circumstances (i.e. the conditions surrounding the adoption of BTAs), exports may be exempted and imports may be taxed. From an economic trade-based perspective, the destination principle refers to the idea that exports should be exempted and imports should be taxed following an economic rationale (i.e. the theories of the comparative and absolute advantage).

The common view that direct taxes are not eligible for BTAs may seem inherently contradictory. As for BTAs on imports, direct taxes are said to be ineligible because they are not shifted into products' prices where, as for BTAs on exports, direct taxes may not be exempted, rebated or reimbursed because such BTAs affect products' prices and could amount to a subsidy.[131] In other words, direct taxes would have no effect on domestic products' prices but, at the same time, the remission of direct taxes would have an impact on exported products' prices.[132] Despite the impression of a contradiction in the economic effects of

---

[128] See, however, the EU's views on the Illustrative List in WTO, Panel Report, *US – FSC*, paras. 4.638–4.639.

[129] WTO, Art. 21.5 Appellate Body Report, *US – FSC*, para. 130.

[130] Schenk & Oldman, *supra* n. 121, 5.

[131] Daly, *supra* n. 99, 555–556; Farrell, *supra* n. 68, 50, referring to GATT, L/3039, *supra* n. 67, para. 4; Hufbauer, *supra* n. 89, 770.

[132] See, on the question of direct taxes passed through prices, WTO, United States – Tax Treatment for 'Foreign Sales Corporations', Recourse to Arbitration by the United States under Art. 22.6 of the *DSU* and Art. 4.11 of the *SCM*

direct taxes, it could nevertheless be argued that the differences in economic impact are due to the fact that they are derived from two different situations: the imposition of direct taxes on imports and the exemption/rebate/refund of direct taxes on exports.

The legal analysis of the category of taxes that may be eligible for BTAs offers a first illustration of the diversity of interpretations of WTO law provisions surrounding BTAs. It also indirectly highlights that the issue is highly political: where the EU seems to prefer a restrictive approach to WTO law provisions surrounding BTAs (allowing for BTAs only in respect of indirect taxes), the US seems to reject the distinction between direct and indirect taxes (either in favour of a broader interpretation of WTO law provisions or in support of the repeal of the BTA regime). The US and EU positions are directly related to their respective tax regimes. The EU relies more broadly on BTAs for its VAT and excise duties system than does the US tax system. In addition to the dissensions between countries, legal scholarship is also greatly divided. The different views reflect different understandings and beliefs about the role of tax systems both at the national and international levels. For example, restrictive views on BTAs may be related to preferences for tax systems relying on indirect taxes or to a belief that tax sovereignty should be limited for the sake of free trade.

The various views on BTAs can be summarised in three categories. As explained before, the traditional view only considers BTAs in the form of *indirect* taxes in respect of *indirect* taxes. Two unorthodox views depart from this traditional view. On the one hand, it is argued that BTAs in the form of *indirect* taxes may be established to compensate for the economic effect of *direct* taxes. On the other hand, the most controversial view argues in favour of the possibility of adopting BTAs in the form of *direct* taxes to adjust for the economic effect of *direct* taxes.

5.2.1.2 Eligibility of *taxes occultes*

The question of the eligibility of *taxes occultes* is only relevant under the traditional view of BTAs, where the distinction between direct and indirect taxes is maintained. In the hypothesis where this distinction is abandoned, the issue of *taxes occultes* loses relevance as the decisive criterion for determining the eligibility of taxes for BTAs becomes the economic effect of the tax regardless of its design. Under the traditional view of BTAs, the issue of *taxes occultes* is, however, key for countries

Agreement, Decision of the Arbitrator, 30 August 2002, WT/DS108/ARB, paras. 6.51–6.52 and footnotes 97 & 106.

that wish to adopt BTAs in respect of 'hidden taxes' on products. The issue is politically sensitive and the interpretation of WTO law provisions surrounding *taxes occultes* has been very controversial. Neither the OECD 1968 Report nor the GATT 1970 Report give clear guidelines as to the compatibility of *taxes occultes* with GATT provisions. As already mentioned, the OECD 1968 Report defines the concept of *taxes occultes* as 'the hidden element of tax in an article, corresponding to the additional tax paid on any of these goods or services'.[133]

5.2.1.2.1 BTAs on imports in respect of taxes occultes The interpretation of WTO law provisions surrounding BTAs on imports in respect of *taxes occultes* is full of uncertainties. One important question pertains to which types of *taxes occultes* may be eligible for BTAs: 'Do GATT articles II:2(a) and III:2 allow adopting BTAs in respect of *any* taxes occultes or only in respect of taxes occultes on products incorporated in the final product?'[134] In the GATT 1970 Report, views are very much divided on the interpretation to be given to GATT Articles II:2(a) and III:2. On the one hand, the expression 'internal taxes and other internal charges' is understood as limiting the case of BTAs to 'taxes on the final product and on its components and ingredients … but not taxes on power consumed in manufacture'.[135] On the other hand, this same expression is interpreted in a broad way, including all possible types of taxes, by reference to the following expressions: 'taxes applied, directly or indirectly, to like domestic products' (in GATT Article III) and 'a charge equivalent to an internal tax … in respect of the like domestic product or in respect of an article from which the imported product has been manufactured or produced in whole or in part' (in GATT Article II:2(a)).[136] The legislative history of the GATT provides some evidence in favour of this broad view. In 1947, during the Second Session of the Preparatory Committee of the United Nations Conference on Trade and Employment, the US delegate noted that '[t]here are examples … , of a

---

[133] OECD 1968 report, *supra* n. 11, para. 19.

[134] GATT, Spec(68)55, *supra* n. 12, para. 14, quoting BISD, 3rd Supplement, page 210 (Working party review session).

[135] *Ibid.*, quoting Working party review sessions, BISD, 3rd Supplement, 210. See also ECOSOC, Second Session of the Preparatory Committee of the United Nations Conference on Trade and Employment, Ad Hoc Sub-Committee on Articles 14, 15 and 24, Note by the Secretariat on Articles 15 and 15A, 9 June 1947, E/PC/T/W/181 (in particular p. 3); GATT 1970 Report, *supra* n. 61, para. 14.

[136] *Ibid.*

tax, not a tax on a product as such but on the processing of the product, which are covered by the word "indirectly" here'.[137]

For now, uncertainties remain.[138] Usually, no distinction is made between GATT Articles II:2 and III:2, following the approach that these are 'overlapping provisions' (Section 5.1.2.1.1). However, under the hypothesis that the two provisions should be read independently, it could be considered that GATT Article III:2 is less restrictive than GATT Article II:2(a).[139] *Taxes occultes* falling under GATT Article III:2 – like, for example, the former cascade tax systems – would then be eligible for BTAs on imports, regardless of whether the inputs are incorporated or not in the final products. In contrast, BTAs on imports in respect of *taxes occultes* falling under GATT Article II:2(a) would only be permissible when the input is physically incorporated in the final products in order to comply with the literal reading of Article II:2(a).[140]

The wording in GATT Articles II:2(a) and III:2 is, however, not as clear cut as to allow for one single interpretation: 'Does the word "article" in GATT article II:2(a) refer to raw material, energy used in the

---

[137] ECOSOC, Second Session of the Preparatory Committee of the United Nations Conference on Trade and Employment, Ninth Meeting of Commission A Held on Thursday, 5 June 1947 at 2.30 P.M. in the Palais des Nations, Geneva, 5 June 1947, E/PC/T/A/PV/9 I, 19. See also GATT, L/3039, *supra* n. 67. Note that the US took a different perspective on the topic some years later: GATT, Spec(68)55, *supra* n. 12, para. 14, quoting BISD, 3rd Supplement, p. 210 (Working party review session), where the US supported a narrow interpretation of the concept, including 'only a tax levied on the final product competitive with the imported article'. See also Wen-Chen Shih, 'The Border Tax Adjustment Provisions of the GATT/WTO and their Implications on the Design of Energy and Carbon Tax' (2011) 14 International Trade and Business Law Review 53, 58–59.

[138] GATT Art. II:2(a). The French and Spanish versions do not help to interpret the text as the translations do not match perfectly. The French text reads as follows: 'un produit national similaire ou une marchandise qui a été incorporée dans l'article importé' and the Spanish version as follows: 'a un producto nacional similar o a una mercancía que haya servido, en todo o en parte, para fabricar el producto importado'.

[139] Pauwelyn, *supra* n. 19, 475; Trebilcock, Howse & Eliason, *supra* n. 16, 688, footnote 52.

[140] Note, however, that the Spanish version of Art. II:2(a) of the GATT does not support this interpretation. See Pauwelyn, *supra* n. 19, 479, footnote 84.

production process, labour forces?'[141] In the *Superfund* case, which is often used as evidence that *taxes occultes* may be border adjusted on imports,[142] the Panel was asked to examine three types of BTA. Among these three BTAs, one may be compared to a BTA in respect of a *taxe occulte*: the 'tax on certain imported substances produced or manufactured from taxable feedstock chemicals'. In the Panel report, the three types of BTA are analysed under GATT Article III:2. However, in the case of the 'tax on certain imported substances', reference is also made to GATT Article II:2(a).[143] As already mentioned, this special reference may be used as an argument in favour of a separate reading of GATT Articles III:2 and II:2(a). At the same time, the Panel report does not give much detail on whether the chemicals were incorporated or not into the products subject to the tax. This absence of details could be used as an argument in support of the possibility of adopting BTAs on imports in respect of *taxes occultes*, regardless of the incorporated character of the potential inputs concerned.

In *Canada – Periodicals*, reference was also made – at least implicitly – to the scope of *taxes occultes*, when Canada discussed the meaning of the word 'indirectly' in GATT Article III:2.[144] Canada argued that, because advertising services were not 'an input into the production of a good', the taxation of magazine advertising services should not have been analysed under GATT Article III:2 but under the GATS: 'the advertising services of a publisher are not, like labour in the production

---

[141] OECD 1994 note on Environmental BTAs, COM/ENV/EPOC/DAFFE/CFA(94)31, *supra* n. 1, para. 30: '... However, the concept of "article" remains somewhat ambiguous and again might refer to physical raw materials or to other inputs such as energy and labor'.

[142] See OECD, The Political Economy of Environmentally Related Taxes (2006), 101 ('true process-based BTA' referring to US taxes on petroleum).

[143] GATT, Panel Report, *US – Superfund*, para. 5.2.7. See also para. 3.2.5. with the reference made by the US to GATT Art. II:2(a).

[144] WTO, Panel Report, Canada – Certain Measures Concerning Periodicals, 14 March 1997, WT/DS31/R (*Canada – Periodicals*), para. 5.18. Another case, cited by Tracey Epps & Andrew James Green is *Argentina – Hides and Leather* (Tracey Epps & Andrew James Green, *Reconciling Trade and Climate: How the WTO Can Help Address Climate Change* (Edward Elgar Publishing 2010), 133). Epps & Green consider that *Argentina – Hides and Leather* is one of the two cases that 'have touched on the matter [of tax on inputs incorporated or exhausted in the production process], but only in a peripheral manner'. See WTO, Panel Report, *Argentina – Hides and Leather*, para. 11.183.

of a car, an input into the production of a good'.[145] Conversely, the US supported a broad interpretation of the term 'indirectly', arguing that 'neither the plain meaning of the term "indirectly" in Article III:2, nor the limited negotiating history concerning it, supports a restrictive meaning of that term. ... Advertisements affect a magazine's price, cost and competitive position as much as any input used in the production of a product.'[146] The Appellate Body rejected Canada's argument, considering that '... a periodical is a good comprised of two components: editorial content and advertising content. Both components can be viewed as having services attributes, but they combine to form a physical product – the periodical itself'.[147]

These cases do not offer a precise definition of the concept of *taxes occultes*. They do, however, highlight that there is scope for a broad interpretation of BTAs in respect of such taxes.

5.2.1.2.2 BTAs on exports in respect of taxes occultes Regarding GATT provisions surrounding BTAs in respect of exports, the literal reading of GATT Articles VI and XVI – which refer to 'tax borne by' – seems to allow for BTAs in respect of taxes on inputs.[148]

The 1960 illustrative list of prohibited exports did not contain any specific provisions on *taxes occultes*. Later, new developments came with the Tokyo Round and the Uruguay Round. The illustrative list of export subsidies in the Tokyo Round Subsidies Code referred to the remission, exemption and deferral of certain charges on 'goods that are physically incorporated in the exported product'.[149] In other words, BTAs in respect of *taxes occultes* would only have been permitted in case of inputs physically incorporated into the final product. During the Uruguay Round, a similar illustrative list of prohibited subsidies was added to the ASCM. However, the language used in Annex I of the ASCM differs from the wording used in the Tokyo Subsidies Code. Annex I of the

---

[145] WTO, Appellate Body Report, *Canada – Periodicals*, 4. Canada distinguished between 'inputs that are directly involved in the production or marketing of a good from services that are "end-products" in their own right'. See also Panel Report, *Canada – Periodicals*, paras. 3.43–3.56.

[146] Panel Report, *Canada – Periodicals*, para. 3.56; Appellate Body Report, *Canada – Periodicals*, 11.

[147] Appellate Body Report, *Canada – Periodicals*, 17.

[148] OECD 1994 note on Environmental BTAs, COM/ENV/EPOC/DAFFE/CFA(94)31, *supra* n. 1, paras. 30–33.

[149] Points (h) and (i) of the Annex (illustrative list of export subsidies). Duncan Brack, Michael Grubb & Windram Craig, *International Trade and Climate Change Policies* (Earthscan 2000), 85.

ASCM does not refer to 'goods that are physically incorporated ... in the exported product' (as in the Tokyo Code) but to 'inputs that are consumed in the production of the exported product', which footnote 61 of the ASCM defines as '... inputs physically incorporated, energy, fuels, and oil used in the production process and catalysts which are consumed in the course of their use to obtain the exported product'.[150] Authors have divergent opinions on the interpretation to be given to the change of language in the ASCM in comparison to the language used in the Tokyo Subsidies Code. The critical issue is whether the evolution of language broadens the scope of BTAs or not by allowing adjustments in respect of taxes imposed on inputs regardless of their incorporation into the final product.[151]

A first argument in favour of a restrictive interpretation of BTAs in respect of *taxes occultes* refers to the legislative history of the Tokyo Code and the ASCM.[152] This argument relates to the controversial legislative history of footnote 61 with the alleged opposition of the US to a literal interpretation of footnote 61. In support of this argument, reference is made to a letter sent by a US official to the President of the US Council for International Business.[153] According to this letter, the

---

150 Points (h) and (i) of the ASCM illustrative list of export subsidies, Annex I. See also Annex II ('Guidelines on consumption of inputs in the production process').

151 Hufbauer, *supra* n. 68, 49. See also Frank Biermann & Rainer Brohm, 'Implementing the Kyoto Protocol without the USA: The Strategic Role of Energy Tax Adjustments at the Border' (2005) 4(3) Climate Policy 289, 295–297; Frank Biermann & Rainer Brohm, 'Border Adjustments on Energy Taxes: A Possible Tool for European Policymakers in Implementing the Kyoto Protocol?' (2005) 74(2) Vierteljahrshefte zur Wirtschaftsforschung 249; J. Andrew Hoerner & Franck Muller, 'Carbon Taxes for Climate Protection in a Competitive World', paper prepared for the Swiss Federal Office for Foreign Economic Affairs, June 1996; Petersmann, *supra* n. 16, 147–148; Christian Pitschas, 'GATT/WTO Rules for Border Tax Adjustment and the Proposed European Directive Introducing a Tax on Carbon Dioxide Emissions and Energy' (1995) 24 Georgia Journal of International and Comparative Law 479.

152 Brack, Grubb & Craig, *supra* n. 149, 86–87, quoting the letter from D.M. Phillips, Assistant USTR for Industry, to A. Katz, President, US Council for International Business; Epps & Green, *supra* n. 144, 135–136. See also Demaret & Stewardson, *supra* n. 19, 29.

153 Demaret & Stewardson, *supra* n. 19, 30; Hufbauer, *supra* n. 68, 50; OECD, The Political Economy of Environmentally Related Taxes (2006), 106, footnote 13.

change of language was only aimed at referring to 'certain energy-intensive exports from a limited number of [developing] countries'.[154] The legal significance to be given to this letter in interpreting the ASCM is nevertheless more than debatable: as such, the letter is neither part of the negotiation history of the ASCM nor of footnote 61.

Brack et al. put forward a second argument in favour of a restrictive interpretation of WTO law provisions surrounding BTAs on exports.[155] They nuance the impact of the new wording in the ASCM as it should only refer to inputs subject to 'prior-stage cumulative indirect taxes'.[156] This view corresponds to the argument that GATT Article II:2(a) and Article III:2 should be read independently. In other words, for taxes integrated in an internal tax system (such as, for example, 'prior-stage cumulative indirect taxes'), taxes on inputs should be eligible for BTAs regardless of their incorporation into the final product. Conversely, for taxes that are not part of an internal tax system, BTAs in respect of *taxes occultes* should be limited to cases where inputs are incorporated into the final product. This second argument is not fully convincing. Where it is true that the text of Annex I to the ASCM, paragraph (h) clearly refers to 'prior-stage cumulative tax systems', the negotiation history of footnote 61 illustrates that the emphasis was put on the need to leave out the 'physical incorporation test'.[157]

---

[154] Hufbauer, *supra* n. 68, 50. See also OECD 1994 note on Environmental BTAs, COM/ENV/EPOC/DAFFE/CFA(94)31, *supra* n. 1, para. 35; WTO, WT/CTE/W/47, paras. 75–76.

[155] Brack, Grubb & Craig, *supra* n. 149, 85–86.

[156] *Ibid.*, 85. See, however, OECD 1994 note on Environmental BTAs, COM/ENV/EPOC/DAFFE/CFA(94)31, *supra* n. 1, para. 41, quoting GATT, Group on Environmental Measures and International Trade, Border Tax Adjustment, 11 January 1994, TRE/W/20, para. 34. Javier de Cendra also supports a broad reading of the annex to the ASCM: Javier de Cendra, 'Can Emissions Trading Schemes be Coupled with Border Tax Adjustments? An Analysis vis-à-vis WTO Law' (2006) 15(2) Review of European Community & International Environmental Law 131, 140; OECD, The Political Economy of Environmentally Related Taxes (2006) (this document also refers to Brack et al).

[157] WTO, Committee on Trade and Environment, Negotiating History of Footnote 61 of the Agreement on Subsidies and Countervailing Measures, 1 December 1995, WT/CTE/W/16, para. 10. According to Demaret and Stewardson, 'the gentleman's agreement is not recorded in public record to the knowledge of these authors' (Demaret & Stewardson, *supra* n. 19, 30). See also Schön, *supra* n. 63, 291 ('The subsidies agreement, however, now explicitly provides that these taxes can also be compensated (Annex I(h))'); Geert Van Calster, 'Climate Change Taxes, Emissions Trading, and International Trade Law', in: Marjan Peeters & Kurt Deketelaere (eds.), *EU Climate Change Policy:*

Under the hypothesis that preference is given to a strict interpretation of the ASCM, Pauwelyn suggests that the eligibility of *taxes occultes* on inputs not incorporated into the final products could be grounded on paragraph (g) of Annex I, which more generally refers to 'the production and distribution of exported products'.[158] However, such proposal calls into question the role of paragraph (h): 'Why would Annex I explicitly permit BTAs in respect of taxes on inputs as far as far as prior-stage cumulative indirect taxes are concerned (paragraph (h) of Annex I) while BTAs in respect of indirect input taxes are in any case permitted under paragraph (g)?' The reason behind the specific reference in paragraph (h) to 'prior-stage cumulative indirect taxes on goods or services used in the production of like products when sold for domestic consumption' may be explained in the light of the historical evolution of the illustrative list of export subsidies. Initially, paragraph (h) limited BTAs in respect of prior-stage cumulative indirect taxes on 'goods that are physically incorporated in the exported product'. In other words, the initial content of paragraph (h) did not oppose a broad interpretation of paragraph (g).[159] Under the hypothesis where paragraph (g) should be read in a broad way (allowing for BTAs in respect of *taxes occultes*, regardless of the incorporation into the final products), one may, however, wonder why paragraph (h) has not been cancelled from the annex of the ASCM. Indeed, if the objective of the change of language of paragraph (h) was to allow for a broader application of BTAs in respect of prior-stage cumulative indirect taxes, the broad language of paragraph (g) would have been sufficient to include these (prior-stage cumulative) indirect taxes.

Though the text of the ASCM could be interpreted to allow for BTAs in respect of any kind of *taxes occultes* (regardless of the incorporation of inputs into the final products), the practical implementation of such BTAs is likely to be complicated, if not impossible. The calculation of the amount of the adjustment is likely to be extremely difficult to determine

---

The Challenge of New Regulatory Initiatives (Edward Elgar Publishing 2006), 215–216. See also WTO, Negotiating Group on Rules, Verification system of duty rebate schemes and definition of inputs consumed under ASCM, Submission by India, 23 February 2011, TN/RL/GEN/153/Rev.2.

[158] Pauwelyn, *supra* n. 19, 479, footnote 85. See also Hoerner & Muller, *supra* n. 151, 36–37.

[159] *Contra*: Demaret & Stewardson, *supra* n. 19, 22–23.

in practice.[160] This difficulty is, however, not limited to taxes on inputs that are not incorporated into the final products. The implementation of BTAs in respect of any *taxes occultes* requires averaging. Averaging has also been used in the past in the case of BTAs in respect of cascade taxes and in the case of composite goods, for which it is necessary to average the ingredients present in the goods subject to tax.[161] Moreover, under the Tokyo Code, a 'normal allowance for waste' was made in the determination of BTAs on exports in respect of *taxes occultes* levied on goods that are physically incorporated in the exported product.[162] This 'allowance' was aimed at integrating 'that portion of a given input which does not serve an independent function in the production process, is not physically present in the final product (for reasons such as inefficiencies) and is not recovered, used nor sold by the same manufacturer'.[163] The determination of this 'normal allowance for waste' was also based on averaging.

5.2.1.3 Interim conclusions: eligibility of taxes for BTAs

The traditional views on BTAs usually consider that only indirect taxes are eligible for BTAs. These traditional views may, however, be challenged, both for BTAs on imports and BTAs on exports. Direct taxes may also have an economic effect on products' price, which calls into question the reasons why such taxes should be excluded from the regime of BTAs. The case of *taxes occultes* also highlights the lack of clarity that characterises BTAs' legal framework. No clear-cut conclusions have been reached so far as to the eligibility of *taxes occultes* for BTAs. Questions remain: 'Should BTAs be eligible for all types of *taxes occultes*?' or 'Should BTAs be limited to *taxes occultes* imposed on inputs that are incorporated into the imported and exported products that could subsequently be subject to BTAs?'

5.2.2 BTAs on Imports: The National Treatment (NT) Principle

In addition to the question as to which taxes may be eligible for adjustments, a second issue relates to the possibility for countries to apply differentiated BTAs on products. The NT principle indeed requires WTO

---

[160] OECD 1994 note on Environmental BTAs, COM/ENV/EPOC/DAFFE/CFA(94)31, *supra* n. 1, para. 42, 12.

[161] See GATT 1970 Report, *supra* n. 61, paras. 15–16.

[162] See point (h) of the Annex, Tokyo Subsidies Code. See also points (h) and (i) of the ASCM Annex I.

[163] GATT, Committee on Subsidies and Countervailing Measures, Guidelines on Physical Incorporation, 31 October 1985, SCM/68, point I, para. 4. See also ASCM, Annex II, para. 4.

members not to discriminate against foreign products from other members. In other words, this principle puts a limit on the extent to which countries may distinguish between domestic and imported products.

Under traditional views on BTAs, this question is mainly controversial for BTAs on imports. As for BTAs on exports, the implementation of a non-discrimination principle is *a priori* simple. Indeed, BTAs on exports allow for the remission or deferral of taxes on domestic products that are intended to be exported. These products are in principle always 'like products'.[164] Moreover, it is not difficult to ensure that the remission is 'not in excess' of the internal taxes as, under the traditional view, BTAs on exports take place through the remission of the tax. In the case of *taxes occultes* and, more generally, under the non-traditional view on BTAs, BTAs on exports nevertheless raise similar questions to the ones related to BTAs on imports.

Regarding BTAs on imports, GATT Article III:2 regulates the issue by requiring (1) that like imported products are not taxed excessively in comparison to domestic products (Article III:2, first sentence) and (2) that directly competitive or substitutable products are not subject to dissimilar taxation 'so as to afford protection to domestic production' (Article III:2, second sentence).[165] The analysis below follows the structure of GATT Article III:2, starting with the analysis of its first sentence and subsequently discussing its second sentence. This structure should, however, not be considered as a legal stand in favour of the view that GATT Article III:2, first and second sentences should be read separately.[166] This structure is simply used for practical reasons to

164 Note that footnote 46 of the ASCM gives a definition of the concept of 'like products'. This definition lacks precision however.

165 See also Ad Art. III, para. 2.

166 See e.g. Donald Regan's opinion. He considers that the two sentences should not necessarily be read separately and that the focus of the analysis should be on the protectionist character of the measure: Donald H. Regan, 'Regulatory Purpose in GATT Article III, TBT Article 2.1, the Subsidies Agreement, and elsewhere: *Hic Et Ubique*', in: Geert Van Calster & Denise Prévost (eds.), *Research Handbook on Environment, Health and the WTO* (Edward Elgar Publishing 2013), 43. *Contra*: Van den Bossche & Zdouc, *supra* n. 16, 356, quoting WTO, Appellate Body Report, *Canada – Periodicals*, para. 468 & WTO, Appellate Body Report, Japan – Taxes on Alcoholic Beverages, 4 October 1996, WT/DS8/AB/R, WT/DS10/AB/R, WT/DS11/AB/R (*Japan – Alcoholic Beverages II*), 24. See also Joost Pauwelyn, 'The Unbearable Lightness of Likeness', A Review of Mireille Cossy, 'Some Thoughts on the Concept of "Likeness" in the GATS' (2006), available at <SSRN: http://ssrn.com/abstract= 2030940> (accessed 28 October 2015); Marco M. Slotboom, 'Do Different

highlight the various views that have been expressed on GATT Article III:2, first and second sentences.

5.2.2.1 GATT Article III:2, first sentence

5.2.2.1.1 The concept of 'like products' One of the highly controversial issues surrounding the application of the NT principle concerns the possibility for countries to distinguish between products by means of BTAs. 'What allows two products to be considered "like products"?' 'On which basis may a legislator distinguish between products under WTO law?' These questions are at the heart of the NT principle.[167] A typical example of where these questions were raised is the case *Japan – Alcoholic Beverages II*, in which Japan was accused of differentiating between certain distilled products and Shochu, a Japanese alcoholic beverage.[168]

These questions have been discussed not only in the framework of BTAs but also in the context of regulatory adjustments on imported products.[169] Usually, the discussion focuses on the possibility of distinguishing between products based on criteria related to the process and production method (PPM) of the products.[170] Three main approaches may be distinguished.[171]

Treaty Purposes Matter for Treaty Interpretation? The Elimination of Discriminatory Internal Taxes in EC and WTO Law' (2001) 4(3) Journal of International Economic Law 557, 557, 566.

167 See Brauner, *supra* n. 64, 274.

168 See WTO, Appellate Body Report, *Japan – Alcoholic Beverages II*, 19–23.

169 Among the well-known cases, see GATT, Panel Report, United States – Restrictions on Imports of Tuna, 16 June 1994, DS29/R, unadopted (*US – Tuna (EEC)*); GATT, Panel Report, *US – Malt Beverages*; WTO, Appellate Body Report, *Japan – Alcoholic Beverages II*; WTO, Appellate Body Report, European Communities – Measures Affecting Asbestos and Products Containing Asbestos, 12 March 2001, WT/DS135/AB/R (*EC – Asbestos*).

170 Note that the question of whether PPMs can be considered to distinguish between products has also been analysed under GATT Art. XX. Here the analysis is, however, limited to GATT Art. III:2, first sentence as the objective is not to provide a general overview of how WTO law deals with the concept of PPM but to provide for an overview of the extent to which WTO law provisions *surrounding BTAs* allow for distinguishing between products based on PPMs. See also Amelia Porges & Joel P. Trachtman, 'Robert Hudec and Domestic Regulation: The Resurrection of Aim and Effects' (2003) 37(4) Journal of World Trade 783, 789–790 (they explain that 'aim and effects' can be examined under different provisions of the GATT, including Art. III and Art. XX).

171 These three approaches should be considered as 'ideal-type' along which the various tendencies to be found in the case law can be explained. Melischek

First, the most restrictive approach considers that differentiation is only possible in respect of products with different physical characteristics, on condition that the differentiation does not pursue a protectionist goal.[172] The protectionist intent of the legislator is assessed based on subjective or objective criteria.[173] The protectionist intent, however, plays no role when products are physically the same. Indeed, under this approach, when products are physically the same, it does not matter whether the differentiation is motivated by a protectionist objective or not. Physically 'like' products should never be subject to a differentiated tax system, regardless of the intent of the legislator. In other words, this approach very much limits the regulatory freedom of the legislator: products may only be differentiated when their physical characteristics are different.

Second, the least restrictive approach supports the possibility of differentiating between products based on any kind of regulatory purpose.[174] Under this approach, the concept of 'unlike products' is not limited to products which have different physical characteristics. Instead, any regulatory difference is to be considered as long as the measure does not have a protectionist purpose. The protectionist character is analysed

---

proposes a similar distinction. He indeed considers that 'the methodical approaches [to Art. III of the GATT] can be summarized into three distinct schools of thought: the traditional approach; the aims-and-effects test; and the "economics-based approach"' (Christian A. Melischek, 'Analytical Evolution from the Traditional to the Economic Approach', in *The Relevant Market in International Economic Law. A Comparative Antitrust and GATT Analysis* (CUP 2012), 67). I, however, do not fully agree with Melischek's analysis on the reasons explaining how these three approaches have evolved in the case law (see pp. 113 et al.). In my opinion, it is extremely difficult to determine which specific approach has been applied to a specific case. Usually, GATT/WTO case law is subject to various interpretations, which reflect aspects of more than one specific approach. See also Henrik Horn & J.H.H. Weiler, 'European Communities – Measures Affecting Asbestos and Asbestos-Containing Products' (2002) 2(S1) World Trade Review 14; Robert Howse, *The WTO System: Law, Politics & Legitimacy* (Cameron May 2007), 77–127.

172 It does not mean, however, that any difference related to a product's physical characteristics will make products 'unlike'. See Christiane R. Conrad, *Processes and Production Methods (PPMs) in WTO Law. Interfacing Trade and Social Goals* (OUP 2012), 487–488; Neven & Trachtman, *supra* n. 88, 303.

173 *Ibid.*

174 See i.a. Steve Charnovitz, 'GATT and the Environment: Examining the Issues' (1992) 4(3) International Environmental Affairs 203–233; Howse, *supra* n. 171, 90; Pauwelyn, *supra* n. 166, 4–5; Regan, *supra* n. 166, 41–78.

in light of the intent of the legislator, following a subjective analysis.[175] Although GATT Article III:2, first sentence does not include any explicit requirement regarding the protectionist purpose of the measure (in contrast to Article III:2, second sentence), this condition is supposed to be implicitly included in the concept of 'like products'.[176] According to Howse, '"Like" means roughly "not differing in any respect relevant to an actual non-protectionist policy" . ... in the context of a discussion of discrimination, what "like" standardly means is something like "not differing in any way which justifies different treatment"'.[177] A variation on this approach assumes that products can be distinguished based on any regulatory criterion, though regulatory distinctions related to the origin of the products will *a priori* be assimilated to a *de jure* or *de facto* discrimination.[178]

Third, a middle-ground approach consists in assessing 'likeness' between products based on economic considerations related to the competitive relationship between products, regardless of their physical characteristics and/or of the regulatory objectives pursued by the legislator.[179] Under this 'objective' approach, the regulatory freedom of the

---

[175] See Porges & Trachtman, *supra* n. 170, 790; Frieder Roessler, 'Beyond the Ostensible. A Tribute to Professor Robert Hudec's Insights on the Determination of the Likeness of Products Under the National Treatment Provisions of the General Agreement on Tariffs and Trade' (2003) 37(4) Journal of World Trade 771, 781.

[176] Howse, *supra* n. 171, 90. See also Donald H. Regan, 'Regulatory Purpose and "Like Products" in Article III:4 of the GATT (With Additional Remarks on Article III:2)' (2002) 36(3) Journal of World Trade 443, 444 & 446. See also Robert Howse & Donald Regan, 'The Product/Process Distinction – An Illusory Basis for Disciplining "Unilateralism" in Trade Policy' (2000) 11(2) European Journal of International Law 249.

[177] Howse, *supra* n. 171, 90.

[178] Robert E. Hudec, 'GATT/WTO Constraints on National Regulation: Requiem for an "Aim and Effects" Test' (1998) 32(3) The International Lawyer 619, 620. See Aaditya Mattoo & Arvind Subramanian, 'Regulatory Autonomy and Multilateral Disciplines: The Dilemma and a Possible Resolution' (1998) 1 Journal of International Economic Law 303. See also Regan, *supra* n. 176, 455; Roessler, *supra* n. 175, 772.

[179] See Emily Barrett Lydgate, 'Consumer preferences and the National Treatment Principle: Emerging Environmental Regulations Prompt a New Look at an Old Problem' (2011) 10(2) World Trade Review 165–188; Mattoo & Subramanian, *supra* n. 178, 13; Alan Swinbank, 'Like Products, Animal Welfare and the World Trade Organization' (2006) 40(4) Journal of World Trade 687, 706. This 'market-oriented approach' is criticised by Roessler, *supra* n. 175, 777–780. See also Neven & Trachtman and their proposal to base the evaluation

legislator is constrained by economic concerns. The legislator is only allowed to impose differentiated taxes on products that are considered different from an economic perspective. This approach may strongly constrain the adoption of differentiated taxes based on regulatory distinctions, making it *de facto* impossible for the legislator to use tax measures in order to change consumers' behaviour.[180] Products with the same physical characteristics are likely to fall under the category of 'like products' as, from an economic perspective, these products are more likely to be found in a competitive relationship.

The three approaches described above highlight three different ways of limiting the regulatory freedom of countries to differentiate between products and echo political considerations about the benefits and disadvantages of state regulation.[181] Two contradictory views may be distinguished.[182] They each reflect a different understanding of the extent

---

of 'discriminatory taxes' on an economic analysis, which they consider to be 'more sophisticated and precise' (Neven & Trachtman, *supra* n. 88, 325). Note that the approach of Neven & Trachtman can be considered as a 'third approach', which completely differs from the approach based on products' physical characteristics and the approach based on any regulatory distinctions. Under their approach, products are 'like' when an economic market analysis demonstrates that this is the case, regardless of products' physical characteristics and of the regulatory purpose pursued by the legislator. See also Alessandra Arcuri, 'Law and Economics of the SPS Agreement: A Critical Perspective', in: Geert Van Calster & Denise Prévost (eds.), *Research Handbook on Environment, Health and the WTO* (Edward Elgar Publishing 2013), 164 (on how the law and economics method may be used in the implementation of the SPS Agreement); Emch, *supra* n. 16, 415; Won-Mog Choi, *'Like Products' in International Trade Law – Towards a Consistent GATT/WTO Jurisprudence* (OUP 2003), 1–10; Jonell B. Goco, 'Non-Discrimination, "Likeness", and Market Definition in World Trade Organization Jurisprudence' (2006) 40(2) Journal of World Trade 315–340; Slotboom, *supra* n. 166, 576. See also the description of the economic analysis by Melischek, *supra* n. 171, 100 et al. with references to the case law where econometric analyses have been used.

180 See Emch, *supra* n. 16, 408.

181 See WTO, Appellate Body Report *Japan – Alcoholic Beverages II*, 15, point F. See Demaret & Stewardson, *supra* n. 19, 38–39; Hoerner, *supra* n. 75, 6; Hudec, *supra* n. 178, 633; Shannon Hudnall, 'Towards a Greener International Trade System' (1996) 29 Columbia Journal of Law and Social Problems 175, 177; Mattoo & Subramanian, *supra* n. 178, 3; Roessler, *supra* n. 175, 772.

182 The two approaches described below are taken as the two extremes of a large spectrum where middle-ground positions can be found in between. See also Bradly J. Condon, *Environmental Sovereignty and the WTO. Trade Sanctions and International Law* (Transnational Publishers 2006), 53 et al. (on the concept of 'like products' in GATT provisions).

to which states' taxing power should be limited.[183] First, the most restrictive approaches may be linked to political views in favour of a world trade system where regulatory requirements are preferably adopted through multilateral agreements, excluding unilateral state regulation.[184] Arguments related to transparency, legal certainty and simplicity are put forward in order to defend this position.[185] It is argued that non-objective regulatory distinctions (based on either 'non-physical' or 'non-economic' criteria) may be difficult to evaluate as such distinctions are subjective.[186] This view may also be linked to the belief that differences between products based on PPMs do not really matter and that producers (in particular producers located in other countries) should remain free to use the PPM they prefer.[187] Under this approach, non-objective regulatory distinctions between products are considered to lead to a reduction of (production) countries' freedom by giving the (consumption) countries a say in (production) countries' politics.[188] Second, the least restrictive approach – in contrast to the most restrictive approaches – may be linked to the political view that the WTO should not unduly constrain (consumption) states' ability in adopting regulations based on criteria that are not directly related to the physical characteristics of products.[189] This approach emphasises the need for (consumption) countries to be free to

---

[183] Alan Swinbank puts it as follows: 'It is argued that this reflects a schism in economic thinking between on the one hand a producer perspective, invoking the principle of comparative advantage, and on the other hand a consumer perspective emphasizing the primacy of consumer sovereignty' (Swinbank, *supra* n. 179, 689). See also Howse, *supra* n. 171, 109. Robert Howse distinguishes between the view that 'GATT creates a general right of market access' and the view that 'GATT creates no such general right of access, but creates only a negative right that access shall not be denied by rules that discriminate between countries'.

[184] See Melischek, *supra* n. 171, 129 & 237.

[185] See Swinbank, *supra* n. 179, 690, quoting Sir Leon Brittan.

[186] *Ibid.* See also Demaret & Stewardson, *supra* n. 19, 39; Melischek, *supra* n. 171, 119–128 (about the problem of the 'traditional approach'). See also Neven & Trachtman, *supra* n. 88, 303.

[187] See Swinbank, *supra* n. 179, 688 (where Swinbank argues that PPMs do matter).

[188] See Howse, *supra* n. 171, 108–113.

[189] See Regan, *supra* n. 176, 448. See also Hudec, *supra* n. 178, 626; Porges & Trachtman, *supra* n. 170, 784; Donald H. Regan, 'What Are Trade Agreements For? Two Conflicting Stories Told by Economists, with a Lesson for Lawyers' (2006) 9(4) Journal of International Economic Law 951, 964.

determine which products may be consumed on their territory.[190] Under this approach, PPMs are described as an inherent characteristic of the products.

The GATT and WTO case law is characterised by a chaotic mix of the two trends described above.[191] The scope of the concept of 'like products' – which appears in different provisions of the GATT – is usually described by reference to the image of an accordion, which can be opened more or less, from a narrow to a broader interpretation.[192] In this sense, the analysis of the 'likeness' between products should be made on a case-by-case basis.[193] Moreover, it is usually considered that the interpretation of the concept of 'like products' in GATT Article III:2, first sentence 'should be construed narrowly' in light of the broader category of 'directly competitive or substitutable products' referred to in GATT Article III:2, second sentence.[194] In other words, the category of 'like products' under GATT Article III:2 would be more limited than the category of 'like products' under GATT Article III:4. Despite this distinction, GATT and WTO members, when they face a dispute, often refer to cases based on GATT Article III:2 in disputes on GATT Article III:4 and conversely.

Panels and Appellate Bodies have enunciated various criteria in order to determine the 'likeness' or 'unlikeness' between products, usually

---

[190] Along the same line, authors argue that a restrictive reading of 'unlike products' limited to products which have different physical characteristics may lead to deregulation. See Robert Read, 'Process and Production Methods and the Regulation of International Trade', in: Nicholas Perdikis & Robert Read (eds.), *The WTO and the Regulation of International Trade. Recent Trade Disputes between the European Union and the United States* (Edward Elgar Publishing 2005), 245. See also Porges & Trachtman, *supra* n. 170, 798.

[191] This section does not aim to provide an exhaustive analysis of GATT & WTO law case law on Art. III:2. The objective is rather to highlight the various political views included in the interpretation of Panel and Appellate Body Reports.

[192] WTO, Appellate Body Report, *Japan – Alcoholic Beverages II*, 21; WTO, Appellate Body Report, *EC – Asbestos*, para. 96. See also Goco, *supra* 179, 324 (see the table listing all articles in which the concept of 'like products' appear in WTO law).

[193] GATT 1970 Report, *supra* n. 61, para. 18. See also GATT, Panel Report, Japan – Customs Duties, Taxes and Labelling Practices on Imported Wines and Alcoholic Beverages, 10 November 1987, L/6216, BISD 34S/83 (*Japan – Alcoholic Beverages I*), para. 5.6.

[194] WTO, Appellate Body Report, *EC – Asbestos*, para. 95; WTO, Appellate Body Report, *Japan – Alcoholic Beverages II*, 19–20.

referring to the criteria mentioned in the GATT 1970 Report.[195] These criteria include the product's physical properties, consumers' tastes and habits, the product's end-uses, the product's nature and quality, etc.[196] The case law suggests that none of these criteria plays a decisive role in the determination of the 'likeness' between products.[197] Overall, the case law does not offer any clear-cut answer as to the impact of regulatory criteria and the extent to which the legislative purpose of a disputed measure may be taken into account in order to consider that two products are 'unlike'.[198]

The question – of the possibility of differentiating between products based on regulatory criteria – has nevertheless been touched upon more specifically in some GATT and WTO cases. In 1992, in the case *US – Malt Beverages*, the Panel seemed to recognise member states' regulatory freedom in relation to GATT Article III:2, stating that

> [t]he purpose of Article III is thus not to prevent contracting parties from using their fiscal and regulatory powers for purposes other than to afford protection to domestic production. Specifically, the purpose of Article III is not to prevent contracting parties from differentiating between different

---

[195] See WTO, Appellate Body Report, *Japan – Alcoholic Beverages II*, 20–22; WTO, Panel Report, United States – Standards for Reformulated and Conventional Gasoline, 29 January 1996, WT/DS2/R (*US – Gasoline*), para. 6.8; WTO, Appellate Body Report, *EC – Asbestos*, paras. 101 & 133. See the critical analysis of Donald H. Regan (*supra* n. 176, 464–465). According to Barett Lydgate (*supra* n. 179, 166–167), 'Though it is not a mandatory aspect of Article III deliberation, of the 20 disputes that have fallen under Article III since the WTO's formation in 1995, 14 cite the BTA criteria ...'. See also Neven & Trachtman, *supra* n. 88, 312 ('The *Border Tax Adjustment* factors are precedent, not treaty language. And of course, precedent is not formally binding in WTO law').

[196] See GATT 1970 Report, *supra* n. 61, para. 18; OECD, Trade Principles and Concepts, 1995, OECD/DG(95)141, 10. According to Adrian Emch, all these factors are economic factors which refer to the market place (Emch, *supra* n. 16, 372–373).

[197] See, e.g. WTO, Appellate Body Report, *Japan – Alcoholic Beverages II*, 21. See also WTO, Appellate Body Report, Philippines – Taxes on Distilled Spirits, 21 December 2011, WT/DS396/AB/R, WT/DS403/AB/R (*Philippines – Distilled Spirits)*, para. 119.

[198] See OECD, Trade Principles and Concepts, 1995, OECD/DG(95)141, 11. See also Barett Lydgate, *supra* n. 179, 165 et al, spec. 169.

product categories for policy purposes unrelated to the protection of domestic production.[199]

Under this case law – commonly called the 'aims-and-effect' test – the Panel seemed to have recognised a large regulatory freedom to the legislator. This broad conception is commonly considered to have been reversed some years later by the 1996 Appellate Body report in the case *Japan –Alcoholic Beverages II*.[200] There is, however, no consensus on the interpretation of this report.[201] In two subsequent cases that did not directly concern GATT Article III:2 but Article III:4 and other WTO provisions, the US and the EU referred to the Panel report in *US – Malt Beverages* and recalled the regulatory freedom to distinguish between products, which had been made in relation to GATT Article III:2.

In *EC – Hormones*, the US recalled the Panel view, stating that 'Article III of GATT had been interpreted to permit governments to distinguish between otherwise like products for legitimate regulatory purposes'.[202] Similarly, the EU referred to the regulatory freedom to distinguish between products in the case *EC – Asbestos*.[203] In this case, the Appellate Body considered that products could be distinguished based on a regulatory distinction related to the health risks associated with the

[199] GATT, Panel Report, *US – Malt Beverages*, paras. 5.24–5.25. See also GATT, Panel Report, United States – Taxes on Automobiles, 11 October 1994, DS31/R, unadopted (*Taxes on Automobiles*), paras. 5.7 & 5.8.

[200] Schön, *supra* n. 63, 289, quoting Appellate Body Report, *Japan – Alcoholic Beverages II.*

[201] Some authors oppose the view that *Japan – Alcoholic Beverages* is a true reversal of the aims-and-effect test: Barett Lydgate, *supra* n. 179, 171–176; Howse, *supra* n. 171, 90 (footnote 23) & 97; Regan, *supra* n. 176, 471 & 477. See also WTO, Panel Report, *EC – Asbestos*, 18 September 2000, WT/DS135/R, para. 3.457. *Contra* Mireille Cossy, 'Determining "Likeness" under the GATS: Squaring the Circle?' (September 2006) World Trade Organization Staff Working Paper ERSD-2006-08, 16 & 24–25. See also WTO, Panel Report, *Argentina – Hides and Leather*, paras. 8.219–8.235 & paras. 11.133–11.138.

[202] WTO, Panel Report, EC Measures Concerning Meat and Meat Products (*Hormones*). Complaint by the United States, 18 August 1997, WT/DS26/R/USA (*EC – Hormones*), para. 4.249.

[203] WTO, Panel Report, *EC – Asbestos*, para. 3.458. See also WTO, Appellate Body Report, Dominican Republic – Measures Affecting the Importation and Internal Sale of Cigarettes, 25 April 2005, WT/DS302/AB/R (*Dominican Republic – Import and Sale of Cigarettes*), para. 96.

products concerned.[204] Since, however, the Appellate Body stated that health risks were to be examined 'under the existing criteria of physical properties, and of consumers' tastes and habits', it is nevertheless debatable whether this case supports the hypothesis that products may be differentiated based on PPMs.[205]

In *Argentina – Hides and Leather*, a case based on GATT Article III:2, the EU argued that a violation of Article III:2, first sentence could be established as soon as like imported products were taxed excessively. This view could be the expression of EU support for a restrictive interpretation of GATT Article III:2 (excluding product's differentiation based on regulatory criteria).[206] The EU's views were supported by the US as well by the Panel, which concluded that '... there is no requirement to establish, separately or otherwise, the presence of a protective application in order to show an infringement of Article III:2, first sentence'.[207] The *Argentina – Hides and Leather* case is nevertheless to be distinguished from cases where the defendant country argues that its disputed measure pursues a legitimate non-protectionist goal as a means to avoid the application of GATT Article III (III:2, first or second sentence or III:4). In this case, it was the complaining party (here, the EU) that considered that GATT Article III:2 did not require the protectionist character of the disputed measure to be proved.

In *US – Tuna II*, the regulatory objective of the disputed US measure was put forward so as to avoid the application of GATT Article III:4.[208] According to the US, GATT Article III:4 should be interpreted in light of

---

[204] WTO, Appellate Body Report, *EC – Asbestos*, para. 113.

[205] *Ibid.*, para. 113.

[206] WTO, Panel Report, *Argentina – Hides and Leather*, paras. 8.232–8.233. See WTO, Appellate Body Report, *EC – Bananas III*, para. 216. See also the reference to *Japan – Alcoholic Beverages* and *EC – Bananas III* in the following cases: WTO, Panel Report, Japan – Measures Affecting Consumer Photographic Film and Paper, 31 March 1998, WT/DS44/R (*Japan – Film*), paras. 10.370–10.371; WTO, Panel Report, Canada – Certain Measures Affecting the Automotive Industry, 11 February 2000, WT/DS139/R, WT/DS142/R (*Canada – Autos*), para. 10.78; WTO, Panel Report, Dominican Republic, Import and Sale of Cigarettes, 26 November 2004, WT/DS302/R (*Dominican Republic – Import and Sale of Cigarettes*), para. 7.202.

[207] WTO, Panel Report, *Argentina – Hides and Leather*, paras. 11.137–11.138. See also para. 9.3. for the US view. Please note that according to Regan, *supra* n. 176, 474, the case *Argentina – Hides and Leather* should be read in light of the fact that it concerned 'an origin-specific measure'.

[208] In addition to GATT Art. III:4, the case also touches upon the TBT Agreement.

the general objective of Article III to avoid protectionism.[209] Similarly, the EU argued that 'dolphin-safe' and 'non-dolphin-safe' tuna may potentially be considered unlike products based on consumers' preferences for 'dolphin-safe' tuna.[210] As the characteristic of being 'dolphin safe' clearly goes beyond the physical characteristics of tuna, the EU's argument can be understood as a claim for the recognition of regulatory distinctions, regardless of whether they are based on the physical characteristics of the products or not. Neither the Panel nor the Appellate Body analysed these claims under Article III:4.

Finally, in *Philippines – Taxes on Distilled Spirits*, a case under GATT Article III:2, first and second sentences, the Appellate Body stated as follows: 'While in the determination of "likeness" a Panel may logically start from the physical characteristics of the products, none of the criteria that a Panel considers necessarily has an overarching role in the determination of "likeness" under Article III:2 of the GATT 1994'.[211]

Considering the different cases mentioned above, no clear-cut conclusion can be drawn as to whether GATT Article III:2 permits regulatory distinctions based on criteria unrelated to products' physical characteristics. Although the common view is to consider such differentiation contrary to GATT Article III:2, the debate remains open.

5.2.2.1.2 The concept of 'taxes in excess' GATT/WTO case law suggests that, when likeness between products has been established, GATT Article III:2, first sentence requires that the tax imposed on imported products should not be in excess of the tax imposed on like domestic products. The excess is evaluated by comparing 'actual tax burdens rather than merely nominal tax burdens' and 'even the smallest amount of "excess" is too much'.[212] Differences in actual tax burdens may result from the way the tax is imposed. For example, in the case *Thailand – Cigarettes (Philippines)*, the Appellate Body considered that the excess

---

[209] WTO, Panel Report, United States – Measures Concerning the Importation, Marketing and Sale of Tuna and Tuna Products, 15 September 2011, WT/DS381/R, (*US–Tuna II (Mexico)*), para. 4.288. See also WTO, Appellate Body Report, United States – Measures Concerning the Importation, Marketing and Sale of Tuna and Tuna Products, 16 May 2012, WT/DS381/AB/R (*US – Tuna II (Mexico)*), para. 114.

[210] WTO, Panel Report, *US – Tuna II (Mexico)*, paras. 5.101–5.102.

[211] WTO, Appellate Body Report, *Philippines – Distilled Spirits*, para. 119. See also Neven & Trachtman, *supra* n. 88, 322.

[212] WTO, Panel Report, *Argentina – Hides and Leather*, para. 11.183; WTO, Panel Report, *Thailand – Cigarettes (Philippines)*, para. 7.495.

resulted from the fact that only resellers of imported cigarettes 'incur VAT liability as a consequence of failing to offset output tax'.[213] Finally, taxes in excess may not be justified by balancing 'more favourable tax treatment of imported products in some instances against less favourable treatment of imported products in other instances'.[214]

5.2.2.2 GATT Article III:2, second sentence[215]

5.2.2.2.1 The concept of 'directly competitive or substitutable' (DCS) products As is the case with GATT Article III:2, first sentence, the interpretation of GATT Article III:2, second sentence may be subject to three different approaches.

The first approach suggests that the concept of DCS products is a broader category than the concept of 'like products'.[216] In other words, 'unlike products' may fall under the category of DCS products.[217] Under this approach, the legislator is only allowed to adopt differentiated taxes on DSC products under the condition that these products are not subject to dissimilar taxation so as to afford protection to domestic products.

The second approach follows the logic of the least restrictive approach regarding the concept of likeness, emphasising the condition that the tax

---

213 WTO, Appellate Body Report, Thailand – Customs and Fiscal Measures on Cigarettes from the Philippines, WT/DS371/AB/R (*Thailand – Cigarettes (Philippines)*), 17 June 2011, para. 116. See also WTO, Panel Report, *Argentina – Hides and Leather*, para. 11. 183; WTO, Panel Report, *Thailand – Cigarettes (Philippines)*, para. 7.495.

214 WTO, Panel Report, *Argentina – Hides and Leather*, para. 11.260; GATT, Panel Report, United States – Measures Affecting the Importation, Internal Sale and Use of Tobacco, 4 October 1994, DS44/R, BISD 41S/131 (*US – Tobacco)*, para. 98.

215 See also Add Art. III, para. 2. Note that the relationship between the first and second sentences of GATT Art. III:2 has been analysed not only with regard to the condition of the 'protectionist intent', but also as to the sentence which should be analysed first. See Slotboom, *supra* n. 166, 567, quoting WTO, Panel Report, Korea – Taxes on Alcoholic Beverages, 17 September 1998, WT/DS75/R, WT/DS84/R (*Korea – Alcoholic Beverages*), para. 10.36.

216 See e.g. WTO, Panel Report, Chile – Taxes on Alcoholic Beverages, 15 June 1999, WT/DS87/R; WT/DS110/R (*Chile – Alcoholic Beverages*), para. 7.14. See also WTO, Appellate Body Report, *Japan – Alcoholic Beverages II*, 25, point H.2.(a).

217 WTO, Appellate Body Report, *Japan – Alcoholic Beverages II*, 25. See also GATT, Panel Report, *EEC – Animal Feed Proteins*, para. 4.2; WTO, Appellate Body Report, *Korea – Alcoholic Beverages*, para. 118. WTO, Appellate Body Report, *Philippines – Distilled Spirits*, paras. 148–149.

measure should only be forbidden when it 'afford[s] protection to domestic production'.[218] In other words, GATT Article III:2, first sentence and Article III:2, second sentence are read as one principle, which entails a (subjective) discrimination test.[219]

The third approach echoes the middle-ground approach on 'like products' described above. Under this approach, a purely economic analysis is preferred: the protectionist character of a measure is derived from an 'objective' analysis.[220] When products are found to be in a competitive relationship, the protectionist character of the measure is presumed as soon as objective elements indicate that taxation is 'dissimilar'. In other words, no great distinction is made between the first and second sentences of GATT Article III:2. Indeed, under both the first and the second sentences, the economic relationship between the two products is the decisive factor.

The significant difference between the three approaches described above lies in the role played by the protectionist purpose of the differentiated tax measure in assessing whether it infringes GATT Article III:2.[221] In other words, these three approaches to the concept of DCS products lead to different interpretations of the requirement according to which the measure should not be imposed 'so as to afford protection to domestic production'. In the hypothesis of an 'objective' analysis, the result will be the same as under the middle-ground approach on 'like products' described above. Indeed, when two DCS products are subject to dissimilar taxation, the measure is assumed to bear a protectionist intent. Consequently, the regulatory freedom of the legislator is significantly limited: differentiated tax measures are only permitted when no competitive relationship can be demonstrated between the products concerned.

---

218 Howse, *supra* n. 171, 97–98.

219 Pauwelyn, *supra* n. 166. See also Slotboom, *supra* n. 166, 566. Slotboom considers that 'the finding of the GATT panel in *Malt Beverages* effectively resulted in an elimination of a clear distinction between the test applicable to like products of the first sentence of Art. III:2 GATT and the test applicable to competitive products of the second sentence of that provision'.

220 See Melischek, *supra* n. 171, 104 et al.

221 In contrast, under GATT Art. III:2, first sentence, the three approaches differ in their understanding of the concept of 'likeness'. Indeed, where likeness is understood in a strict sense, the appreciation of the protectionist character of the measure can be disregarded. For example, differentiated taxes on products that do not differ in their physical characteristics will always be deemed incompatible with GATT Art. III:2, first sentence, regardless of the absence of the protectionist character of the measure.

The second ('subjective') approach offers the greatest regulatory freedom: under this approach, the real limit is that the legislator does not intend to protect domestic production. As explained above, the regulatory freedom left to the legislator is therefore significantly influenced by the approach – either objective or subjective – used to analyse the protectionist character of the disputed measure.

The case law on GATT Article III:2, second sentence has been subject to various interpretations, partly reflecting the models described above, though these theoretical models can never be found as such in the case law.

As for the concept of 'like products', the analysis should be made on a case-by-case basis.[222] In addition to the factors that are relevant for determining the 'likeness' between products (e.g. products' physical characteristics, common end-uses, etc.), other relevant factors include criteria related to the 'market place', such as cross-price elasticity of demand, potential and extant competitiveness, etc.[223] In some cases, the analysis of the case law seems to indicate a preference for an economic approach.[224] In the case of DCS products, it is nevertheless argued that it must also be proven that – as a separate condition – dissimilar taxation was made 'so as to afford protection to domestic production'.[225] The evaluation of the disputed measure must be made in light of the 'design, the architecture, and the revealing structure of the measure'.[226]

The case law is not clear as to the exact role of the intent of the legislator in the assessment of a potential violation of GATT Article III:2. In some cases, the intent of the legislator seems to be irrelevant to

---

[222] See, e.g., WTO, Panel Report, *Chile – Alcoholic Beverages*, para. 7.17; WTO, Appellate Body Report, *Japan – Alcoholic Beverages II*, 25–26, point H.2.(a).

[223] WTO, Appellate Body Report, *Japan – Alcoholic Beverages II*, 25, point H.2.(a). On the criterion of 'potential competition', see WTO, Appellate Body Report, *Korea – Alcoholic Beverages*, paras. 112–124. See also WTO, Panel Report, *Chile – Alcoholic Beverages*, paras. 7.30–7.79; WTO, Panel Report, *Mexico – Taxes on Soft Drinks*, paras. 4.44–4.49 & paras. 8.67–8.68; WTO, Appellate Body Report, *Philippines – Taxes on Distilled Spirits*, paras. 198–243. See also Howse, *supra* n. 171, 98.

[224] Melischek, *supra* n. 171, 186.

[225] WTO, Appellate Body Report, *Japan – Alcoholic Beverages II*, 30–31, point H.2.(c) and p. 32. See also WTO, Appellate Body Report, *Chile – Taxes on Alcoholic Beverages*, paras. 56–66, in particular para. 62.

[226] WTO, Appellate Body Report, *Japan – Alcoholic Beverages II*, 29.

proving that the measure does not 'afford protection to domestic products'. For example, in *Japan – Alcoholic Beverages II*, the Appellate Body stated as follows:

> This is not an issue of intent. It is not necessary for a panel to sort through the many reasons legislators and regulators often have for what they do and weigh the relative significance of those reasons to establish legislative or regulatory intent. If the measure is applied to imported or domestic products so as to afford protection to domestic production, then it does not matter that there may not have been any desire to engage in protectionism in the minds of the legislators or the regulators who imposed the measure.[227]

However, some other cases seem to recognise that legislative intent may play a role in the appreciation of the protectionist character of the measure.[228] For example, in *Chile – Alcoholic Beverages*, the Appellate Body seemed to consider that the intent of the legislators, 'to the extent that they are given objective expression in the statute itself', may be relevant.[229] Moreover, in the case *Canada – Periodicals*, clear references were made to statements of the government as a proof of the protectionist intent of the disputed measure.[230] This case was also referred to in *Mexico – Tax Measures on Soft Drinks* by the Panel, stating the following:

> The Appellate Body has cautioned against ascribing too much importance to the subjective legislative intent of legislators and regulators in the drafting of a particular measure, to determine whether the measure is applied so as to afford protection to domestic production, particularly when that declared

[227] WTO, Appellate Body Report, *Japan – Alcoholic Beverages II*, 27–29, point H.2.(c). See also WTO, Appellate Body Report, *Korea – Alcoholic Beverages*, para. 150. See also WTO, Appellate Body Report, *Chile – Alcoholic Beverages*, para. 71.

[228] According to Trebilcock, Howse & Eliason, *supra* n. 16, 153: 'In so doing, the Appellate Body notably brought considerations of objective regulatory purpose within its analysis of protective application, although it did not move to a pure intent-based test …'. See also Neven & Trachtman, *supra* n. 88, 309–311.

[229] WTO, Appellate Body Report, *Chile – Taxes on Alcoholic Beverages*, para. 62. Please note that in the analytical index on GATT Art. III:2, this case is presented as one example where the legislative intent was disregarded (para. 319: '… The Appellate Body again refused to accept explanations of policy objectives which were not ascertainable from the objective design, architecture and structure of the measure …', available at <http://www.wto.org/english/res_e/booksp_e/analytic_index_e/gatt1994_02_e.htm#article3C3civ> (accessed 15 January 2016). See Slotboom, *supra* n. 166, 575.

[230] WTO, Appellate Body Report, *Canada –Periodicals*, 30–32.

> intent is that protectionism was not an objective. However, the declared intention of legislators and regulators of the Members adopting the measure should not be totally disregarded, particularly when the explicit objective of the measure is that of affording protection to domestic production.[231]

No clear-cut conclusions can be derived from these different cases. One could nevertheless conclude that the case law accepts considering the legislative intent as evidence of the protectionist character of a measure (for example, in the case *Canada – Periodicals*) but not as evidence of the absence of this protectionist character (as could be derived from the case *Japan – Alcoholic Beverages II*).

5.2.2.2.2 The concept of 'dissimilar taxation' In contrast to the 'excess test' that applies to like products, the test for DCS products evaluates whether these products are 'not similarly taxed'. In *Japan – Alcoholic Beverages II*, the Appellate Body stated that 'to be "not similarly taxed", the tax burden on imported products must be heavier than on "directly competitive or substitutable" domestic products, and that burden must be more than *de minimis* in any given case'.[232] In other words, in the case of DCS products, it is not so that 'any amount of tax on imported products "in excess of" the tax on domestic "like products"' leads to the infringement of GATT Article III:2, second sentence.[233] As in the case of 'like products', dissimilar taxation cannot be justified by reference to more favourable treatment applied to imported products.[234]

5.3 INTERIM CONCLUSIONS

WTO law provisions surrounding BTAs present different legal issues.

A first issue concerns the definition of the legal provisions that apply to BTAs. Where BTAs on imports are primarily regulated by GATT Article II:2(a) and III:2, the legal framework surrounding BTAs on exports has very much evolved through the years from GATT provisions to the ASCM. Moreover, BTAs' legal framework raises questions as to the articulation of the different provisions that apply to BTAs. For example, questions arise as to the relationship between GATT Articles II:2(a) and III:2, which are the main legal grounds for BTAs on imports.

---

231 WTO, Panel Report, *Mexico – Taxes on Soft Drinks*, para. 8.91.

232 WTO, Appellate Body Report, *Japan – Alcoholic Beverages II*, 27, point H.2.(b).

233 *Ibid.*, 26, point H.2.(b).

234 WTO, Appellate Body Report, *Canada – Periodicals*, 29, B.(2).

A second issue pertains to the taxes that are eligible for BTAs. Though traditional views largely consider that BTAs should be limited to indirect taxes, BTAs' legal framework could be interpreted in a broad way, opening the door for BTAs in respect of direct taxes. The controversial case of *taxes occultes* also raises questions of eligibility. The interpretation of WTO law provisions in favour of a limited or broad scope for BTAs will necessarily influence the legal analysis surrounding environmental BTAs.

Finally, a third legal issue concerns the extent to which domestic tax systems that include BTAs may adopt differentiated taxes to pursue policy objectives. Again, where traditional views on WTO law provisions consider that tax differentiation should be strictly limited, less restrictive interpretations of WTO law provisions are also possible.

6. Legal framework of environmental BTAs

This chapter concentrates on the legal framework surrounding environmental BTAs, drawing attention to the peculiarities of environmental taxes in comparison to traditional BTAs.[1] The integration of environmental considerations into BTAs indeed raises additional legal questions, both within and beyond WTO law.

Environmental taxes differ from traditional taxes in three main aspects. First, environmental taxes – which are relatively new taxes – have not been explicitly classified under the categories of direct/indirect taxes. Consequently, under the traditional view on the eligibility of taxes for BTAs, the direct/indirect character of the environmental tax first needs to be determined. Second, environmental taxes are sometimes defined by reference to their specific purpose: the intent of the legislator is – or should be – to pursue (global) environmental objectives.[2] The environmental character of the legislative purpose of environmental taxes may be irreconcilable with the objective of traditional taxes. From a legal viewpoint, the environmental legal framework in which environmental taxes are implemented may clash with the international trade and tax framework of traditional BTAs. Third, in contrast to traditional taxes, the primary objective of environmental taxes is *a priori* not to raise revenue. Even more, the objective of environmental taxes may lead to the fact that no revenue is raised from the tax. Indeed, environmental taxes often aim at encouraging polluters to abandon their polluting conduct. Therefore,

---

[1] From an economic viewpoint, authors disagree on whether traditional BTAs and environmental BTAs are similar or not. See Ben Lockwood & John Whalley, 'Carbon Motivated Border Tax Adjustments: Old Wine in Green Bottles?' (2008) NBER Working Paper Series No. 14025; Christiane Kraus, *Import Tariffs as Environmental Policy Instruments* (Springer 2000); Jean-Marc Burniaux, Jean Chateau & Romain Duval, 'Is There a Case for Carbon-Based Border Tax Adjustment? An Applied General Equilibrium Analysis' (2010) 794 OECD Economics Department Working Papers.

[2] The EU seems to require as an additional condition that BTAs aim at mitigating *global* environmental issues (and not environmental issues limited to the national territory). See Chapter 2.

when this objective is fulfilled (namely when the polluting behaviour ceases), no tax can be raised due to the absence of tax event.

6.1 ENVIRONMENTAL BTAs UNDER WTO LAW SURROUNDING TRADITIONAL BTAs

Environmental BTAs are based on the same legal provisions as for traditional BTAs. For BTAs on imports, special attention should nevertheless be drawn to the different approaches concerning the relationship between GATT Articles II:2(a) and III:2. The hypothesis under which BTAs under the form of 'internal charges' should be distinguished from BTAs as 'border charges' may be more favourable for environmental BTAs. This hypothesis indeed provides for an independent legal ground for the adoption of *taxes occultes*. This peculiarity is particularly important as far as environmental BTAs are concerned since such BTAs are likely to be implemented in respect of environmental *taxes occultes* (Section 6.1.1.3). For example, the new excise-based model could benefit from such an approach, confirming the position taken by the Panel in the *Superfund* case.[3]

6.1.1 Eligible Taxes

The question of the eligibility of environmental taxes for BTAs is only relevant under the traditional views on BTAs. Indeed, under the unorthodox reading of BTA provisions, the direct or indirect nature of the tax no longer matters when it can be proven that the burden of the tax is shifted into products' prices (Chapter 5). Under the traditional view it is, however, necessary to determine whether environmental taxes fall under the category of direct or indirect taxes. As a side note, it could be argued that the difficulties in elaborating such classification may be an additional argument for leaving such classification out.

6.1.1.1 Distinction between consumption and production taxes

The OECD and GATT/WTO reports on environmental BTAs suggest that only product taxes – in contrast to production taxes – would be eligible for adjustments (Chapter 2). As explained above, the distinction between product and production taxes, is however, unclear.

---

[3] As explained above, the Panel in the Superfund case suggests that BTAs in respect of *taxes occultes* are grounded in GATT Art. II:2(a) (GATT, Panel Report, *US – Superfund*).

A first example of the blurred distinction between consumption and production taxes is the case of excise taxes that are usually classified in the category of consumption taxes but are legally defined through proxies related to production.

A second example relates to the US Superfund tax and its double adjustment. Indeed, the double adjustment that characterises the Superfund tax clearly calls into question the nature of the tax: 'Are the adjustments made in respect of domestic product/consumption taxes or in respect of domestic process/production taxes?' In the case of adjustment in respect of certain imported substances, the domestic tax on chemicals is considered through its effects on manufacturers, which could be interpreted as a signal that the tax is both a tax on consumption and a tax on production. Under the hypothesis of a tax on raw materials, on chemicals or on any intermediate components that may be used in and later transformed into other products, the distinction between production and consumption taxes seems confusing. The grey zone that sometimes exists between consumption and production taxes – and indirect and direct taxes – may be explained considering the dichotomy between the economic and legal definitions of consumption and production taxes. From a legal viewpoint, the distinction between consumption and production taxes is primarily a question of tax design: the tax is called a consumption tax as soon as it is designed as a tax that has been classified as a consumption tax. For example, the tax on chemicals (including the process-based adjustment) is considered a consumption tax because the tax has been designed as an excise tax, a tax that is traditionally considered to fall into the category of consumption taxes. From an economic viewpoint, a consumption tax is a tax that is meant to be paid by the final consumer in contrast to producers (who may also be – under certain circumstances – intermediate consumers, for example when they buy raw materials that they use to produce final goods).[4] In other words, from an economic perspective, the nature of process-based adjustments may be questioned: the tax on certain imported substances should be assimilated to a consumption tax only where the tax is meant to be shifted into products' prices so that the tax is borne by final consumers.

A third example is the US excise tax on ODC. As the Superfund tax, the ODC tax is designed as a tax on consumption.[5] The tax on imported

---

[4] To a certain extent, producers are indeed always consumers to the extent that they use (and so consume) raw materials, chemicals and intermediate products in the production process.

[5] See, however, Thomas A. Barthold, 'Issues in the Design of Environmental Excise Taxes' (1994) 8 Journal of Economic Perspectives 1, 141. Barthold points

products containing ODC is used to guarantee equality between domestic products and foreign products containing ODC, though domestically no tax is charged on the domestic products as such. Domestic products containing ODC are assumed to bear the costs related to the ODC tax, which was previously paid on the chemicals. This issue has been studied by economists from the perspective of the impact on competitiveness of environmental excise taxes imposed on intermediate products at the national level and on intermediate and final products at the import level.[6] From a legal viewpoint, the ODC tax (including the tax on imported products for which ODC had been used in the manufacture or production process) could be described as a general tax on chemicals, regardless of whether the tax is applied directly on the concerned chemicals or indirectly through the imposition of a tax on products for which the chemicals concerned have been used in the production process. However, because the ODC tax is applied on 'products ... if any ozone-depleting chemical was used as material in the manufacture or production of such product', the ODC tax has also been compared to a production/process tax.[7] Moreover, the legal regime of the exceptions to the ODC tax provides an additional argument in favour of defining the ODC tax as a combination of a consumption tax with a production tax. Indeed, exceptions to the tax are granted in order not to burden certain production processes that have no environmental impact.[8] For example, the 'use of any ozone-depleting chemical in the manufacture or production of any other chemical' is not taxed 'if the ozone-depleting chemical is entirely consumed in such use'.[9] This regime of exceptions goes against the idea

---

out that 'the "who" question [namely: "who pays the tax?"] is, in fact, a difficult question' (p. 145).

6 See James M. Poterba & Julio J. Rotemberg, 'Environmental Taxes on Intermediate and Final Goods When Both Can Be Imported' (1995) 2(2) International Tax and Public Finance 221. See also Barthold, *supra* n. 5; Steve McCorriston & Ian M. Sheldon, 'Market Access and WTO Border Tax Adjustments for Environmental Excise Taxes under Imperfect Competition' (2005) 7(4) Journal of Public Economic Theory 579–592.

7 Andrew J. Hoerner, 'The Role of Border Tax Adjustments in Environmental Taxation: Theory and US Experience', Working Paper presented at the International Workshop on Market Based Instruments and International Trade of the Institute for Environmental Studies, Amsterdam, the Netherlands, 19 March 1998, 12.

8 Andrew J. Hoerner, 'Taxing Pollution', in: Elizabeth Cook & Reynaldo Forte (eds.), *Ozone Protection in the United States: Elements of Success* (1996 World Resources Institute), 43.

9 26 US CODE §4682(d)(2)(A)(i). See also Hoerner, *supra* n. 8, 43.

that the ODC tax is a 'general tax on chemicals' as not all products for which the chemicals were used in the manufacturing/production process are subject to the tax.[10]

Due to the lack of clear distinction between consumption and production taxes, these categories cannot serve as a basis to determine environmental taxes' eligibility for adjustment. The traditional 'direct/indirect tax' distinction may better help in determining which taxes may be complemented by BTAs and which ones may not.

6.1.1.2 Traditional distinction between direct and indirect taxes

The traditional criterion used to determine whether a tax is eligible for adjustment is the distinction between direct and indirect taxes. Neither the OECD 1968 Report nor the GATT 1970 report discusses the case of environmental taxes or classifies them in one or the other category. Consequently, the categorisation of environmental taxes – as would be the case with any other non-traditional tax – should be based on the criteria used to distinguish between direct and indirect taxes.

As mentioned in Chapter 5, a first approach to determine the direct or indirect nature of a tax is based on a subjective interpretation of Mill's theory: 'indirect taxes are those which are demanded from one person in the expectation and intention that he shall indemnify himself at the expense of another'.[11] In other words, what matters is the intention of the legislator. Under this approach, environmental taxes will be classified as 'indirect taxes' as soon as their objective is to make consumers liable for the environmental costs related to consumption, regardless of the design of the tax.[12] This approach disregards the fact that the tax is (legally speaking) imposed on the producer, as soon as the tax is intended to be shifted into products' prices. From this perspective, this subjective approach seems to ignore the traditional division between direct and indirect taxes as far as 'unclassified' taxes are concerned.

---

[10] Prof. Milne rightly pointed out to me that this mechanism is justified by the environmental objective of the tax (given that in these cases, no emissions are released).

[11] John Stuart Mill, *Principles of Political Economy with some of their Applications to Social Philosophy* (Longmans, Green and Co. 1848), available at <http://www.econlib.org/library/Mill/mlP65.html> (accessed 28 October 2015).

[12] This approach is supported by Joost Pauwelyn, 'Carbon Leakage Measures and Border Tax Adjustments under WTO Law', in: Geert Van Calster & Denise Prévost (eds.), *Research Handbook on Environment, Health and the WTO* (2013 Edward Elgar Publishing), 479–480.

A second approach considers that, because environmental taxes do not fall in the classical distinction between direct and indirect taxes, they should *de facto* be assimilated to indirect taxes, following a literal reading of footnote 58 of Annex I to the ASCM.[13] Against this approach, it can be argued that the definitions included in footnote 58 should be limited to the Annex I of the ASCM and not be extended to other WTO law provisions.

A third opposite approach reflects a traditional reading of WTO law. Environmental taxes are deemed eligible for BTAs if they are based on the tax models that have traditionally been considered eligible for BTAs, such as VAT, excise duties, etc.[14] In other words, the distinction between direct and indirect taxes is based on the design of the tax. Taxes the design of which is comparable to traditional indirect taxes such as VAT, excise duties and sales taxes should be deemed eligible for BTAs. Other taxes should not. The Panel has indirectly supported this approach in the *Superfund* case, considering that 'the tax on certain chemicals, being a tax directly imposed on products, was eligible for border tax adjustment independent of the purpose it served'.[15] Though the Panel recognised that the objective of the tax on certain chemicals was related to the pollution released during production, the Panel seemed to support the view that the relevant criteria to distinguish between product and production taxes should not be based on the intent of the legislator but on the design of the tax, whether the tax is imposed on products or not.[16] This approach is restrictive as it strictly limits environmental BTAs to certain tax models while the peculiarities of environmental taxes imply that these models may not be suitable for achieving environmental goals.[17] In the climate

---

[13] *Ibid.*, footnote 80.

[14] Such approach would likely prevail when BTAs are considered an instrument of monetary policy or when a static interpretation of WTO law provision is favoured.

[15] GATT, Panel Report, *US – Superfund*, para. 5.2.8. See also, para. 5.2.4.

[16] The indirect recognition by the Panel that the Superfund tax was aimed at tackling pollution related to production is to be found in paragraph 5.2.5: 'Consequently, if a contracting party wishes to tax the sale of certain domestic products (*because their production pollutes the domestic environment*) and to impose a lower tax or no tax at all on like imported products (because their consumption or use causes fewer or no environmental problems), it is in principle free to do so. The General Agreement's rules on tax adjustment thus give the contracting party in such a case the possibility to follow the Polluter-Pays Principle, but they do not oblige it to do so' (emphasis added).

[17] See Jennifer Hillman, 'Changing Climate for Carbon Taxes, Who's Afraid of the WTO?' (2013) German Marshall Fund of the United States, 6–7.

debate, for example, most tax proposals focus on production taxes over product taxes.[18]

Except for environmental taxes on producers, the three approaches described above would permit BTAs in respect of all the models of environmental taxes described in Chapter 4.

6.1.1.3 *Taxes occultes*

There is no consensus as to the eligibility of *taxes occultes* for BTAs. As far as environmental taxes are concerned, authors defend both views.[19]

In the GATT 1970 Report, energy taxes were mentioned as an example of *taxes occultes* but no agreement was reached as to whether these taxes were eligible for adjustments. In comparison to the situation at the time of the GATT 1970 Report, the issue is nowadays much more significant considering the development of environmental taxes, which may often be described as *taxes occultes*. Therefore, the conclusion of the GATT 1970 Report that *taxes occultes* should not be further analysed due to the lack

---

[18] This could be explained by the dominant view that GHG emissions are calculated based on production and not based on consumption. As already mentioned, the IPCC reports and the UNFCCC illustrate the dominance of this view: GHG emissions per country are calculated based on the emissions derived from production in the country concerned and not based on the emissions linked to the consumption taking place in the country concerned. This conception may have an impact on the way environmental taxes are perceived: an environmental product tax, the tax rate of which varies according to a criterion that is usually seen as linked to production (as in the case of a criterion based on GHG emissions released during production) could arguably be assimilated to environmental production taxes. Here again, it appears particularly difficult to draw a distinction between product and production taxes. See also Mark L. Belleville, 'The Key Stone in the Carbon Tariff Wall: The Alberta Oil Sands and the Legality of Taxing Imports Based on Their Carbon Footprint' (2013) 43 Environmental Law 365, 375.

[19] See Frank Biermann & Rainer Brohm, 'Implementing the Kyoto Protocol without the USA: The Strategic Role of Energy Tax Adjustments at the Border' (2005) 4(3) Climate Policy 289, 293 et al; Paul Demaret & Raoul Stewarson, 'Border Tax Adjustments under GATT and EC Law and General Implications for Environmental Taxes' (1994) 28(4) Journal of World Trade Law 5, 26; Gary Clyde Hufbauer, Steve Charnovitz & Kim Jisun, *Global Warming and the World Trading System* (Peterson Institute for International Economics 2009), 46; Tracey Epps & Andrew James Green, *Reconciling Trade and Climate: How the WTO Can Help Address Climate Change* (Edward Elgar Publishing 2010), 132–133; Hoerner, *supra* n. 7; Henrik Horn & Peter C. Mavroidis, 'Border Carbon Adjustments and the WTO' (2010) The Research Institute of Industrial Economics, Stockholm, Bruegel, Brussels, Centre for Economic Policy Research, London; Pauwelyn, *supra* n. 12.

of practical importance of the issue is no longer true. Biermann and Brohm have argued that the development of environmental policies should permit a 'dynamic interpretation' to be given to WTO law provisions surrounding (environmental) BTAs.[20] As far as climate change is concerned, they believe that the UNFCCC negotiations process should lead WTO members to accept BTAs in respect of energy taxes.[21]

In the scholarship, the *Superfund* case is often mentioned as one concrete example of *taxes occultes* having been deemed eligible for BTAs.[22] The issue is indeed particularly relevant in the case of taxes copying the model of the Superfund and ODC taxes (such as, for example, the CO_2 tax model) or in the case of any tax applied on intermediate products.[23] In the *Superfund* case, the US made clear that the tax on certain imported substances was based on an idea close to the concept of *taxes occultes*: 'The Superfund Act thus imposed the same fiscal burden on imported and like domestic substances: Substances of domestic origin bore a fiscal burden corresponding to the tax on the chemicals used in their production.'[24] The Panel held that the US tax on certain imported substances was eligible for adjustments, which was 'in principle consistent with Article III:2, first sentence', subject to respect for the requirement of equivalence between the domestic tax on the chemicals and the BTAs on final products (compensating for the taxes on the chemicals used as intermediate products).[25]

The requirement of equivalence is the biggest (practical) challenge for the adoption of environmental BTAs in respect of environmental *taxes occultes*. However, the examples of the Superfund and ODC taxes illustrate that this challenge can be overcome by requesting importers to provide information about the intermediate products that have been used in the production process.

6.1.1.4 Environmental taxes or regulations?

The concept of BTAs has traditionally been limited to compensating tax measures in respect of tax instruments. In the literature, this tradition has

---

20 Biermann & Brohm, *supra* n. 19, 298.

21 *Ibid.*

22 See i.a. Pauwelyn, *supra* n. 12, 478–479; Biermann & Brohm, *supra* n. 19, 294–295.

23 See Duncan Brack, Michael Grubb & Windram Craig, *International Trade and Climate Change Policies* (Earthscan 2000), 84.

24 GATT, Panel Report, *US – Superfund*, para. 3.2.5.

25 *Ibid.*, paras. 5.2.9. & 5.2.10.

been maintained without questioning the possibility of adopting a mechanism comparable to BTAs in respect of (market-based) regulations. For example, many authors have assimilated cap and trade systems such as the EU ETS with taxes to argue that these market-based instruments were also eligible for BTAs.[26] This analysis – comparing the EU ETS to a tax – relies on the assumption that only taxes – in contrast to regulations – are eligible for BTAs.[27] Under this assumption, the eligibility of environmental taxes for BTAs may then be questioned given the strong regulatory character of environmental taxes.

As already mentioned, the relevance of this question is directly related to the assumption that BTAs are limited to tax instruments. This

---

[26] E.g. Javier de Cendra, 'Can Emissions Trading Schemes be Coupled with Border Tax Adjustments? An Analysis vis-à-vis WTO Law' (2006) 15(2) Review of European Community & International Environmental Law 131–145; Felicity Deane, 'The Border Adjustments of the Australian Clean Energy Package' (2014) 17 International Trade and Business Law Review 66–107; Valentina Durán Medina & Rodrigo Polanco Lazo, 'A Legal View on Border Tax Adjustments and Climate Change: A Latin American Perspective' (2011) 11(3) Sustainable Development Law & Policy 29; Felix Ekardt & Andrea Schmeichel, 'Border Adjustments, WTO Law and Climate Protection', in: Claudia Dias Soares, Janet Milne, Hope Ashiabor & Kurt Deketelaere (eds.), *Critical Issues in Environmental Taxation* (OUP 2010), 745; Carolyn Fischer & Alan K. Fox, 'Comparing Policies to Combat Emissions Leakage: Border Carbon Adjustments Versus Rebates' (2011) Resources for the Future Discussion Paper, 5; Roland Ismer & Karsten Neuhoff, 'Border Tax Adjustment: A Feasible Way to Support Stringent Emission Trading' (2007) 24(2) European Law Journal of Law and Economics 137; Pauwelyn, *supra* n. 12; Charles E. McLure, 'The GATT-Legality of Border Adjustments for Carbon Taxes and the Cost of Emissions Permits: A Riddle, Wrapped in a Mystery, inside an Enigma' (2011) 11 Florida Tax Review 221; Kommerskollegium (Swedish National Board of Trade), 'Climate and Trade Rules – Harmony or Conflict?' (2004) available at <http://www.kommers.se/Documents/dokumentarkiv/publikationer/2004/rapporter/report-climate-and-trade-rules.pdf> (accessed 3 November 2015); Jon M. Truby, 'Towards Overcoming the Conflict Between Environmental Tax Leakage and Border Tax Adjustment Concessions for Developing Countries' (2010–2011) 12(1) Vermont Journal of Environmental Law 149–183; Harro Van Asselt & Frank Biermann, 'European Emissions Trading and the International Competitiveness of Energy-intensive Industries: A Legal and Political Evaluation of Possible Supporting Measures' (2007) 35(1) Energy Policy 497. See also Stefen Nathaniel Zane, 'Leveling the Playing Field: The International Legality of Carbon Tariffs in the EU' (2011) 34(1) Boston College International & Comparative Law Review 199, 205–206. See however the detailed analysis of Kateryna Holzer, *Carbon-related Border Adjustment and WTO Law* (Edward Elgar Publishing 2014), 103–107.

[27] See Hufbauer, Charnovitz & Jisun, *supra* n. 19, 66.

assumption can, however, easily be criticised.[28] Tax and regulatory adjustments (usually called 'regulatory requirements') indeed present many similarities and the burden between (non-fiscal) market-based regulatory instruments and taxes is all but clear.[29] As far as imports are concerned, the same market-based measures may be applied on imports. Regarding exports, exemption or refund may be provided in respect of exported goods in a similar way as under BTAs.

Nevertheless, a good – traditional – reason for distinguishing between taxes and regulations is that these measures are not subject to the same legal provisions. At the national level, constitutional provisions surrounding the adoption of taxes usually provide for stronger guarantees than the provisions surrounding regulatory measures. As for border adjustments, WTO law does provide for specific rules regarding BTAs, which could suffice to explain the need to distinguish between tax and regulatory adjustments. However, since WTO law provisions surrounding regulatory adjustments present many similarities with those provisions surrounding BTAs – at least as far as imports are concerned – the relevance of the distinction may be criticised. In practice, it is indeed questionable whether the fiscal nature of a measure would influence the decision of the Panel or Appellate Body regarding its compatibility with WTO law. In various disputes related to regulatory measures, reference has been made to BTAs' provisions. For example, in the case *EC – Asbestos* the Appellate Body used the criteria mentioned in the GATT 1970 report to

---

[28] See Van Asselt & Biermann, *supra* n. 26, 501. See Pauwelyn, *supra* n. 12, 483. See also WTO, Appellate Body Report, *Japan – Alcoholic Beverages II*, 16.

[29] The distinction also seems to be particularly blurred in some documents of the UNCTAD and of the OECD. See e.g. UNCTAD, Trade and Development Board, Evolution of the international trading system and its trends from a development perspective, Note by the UNCTAD secretariat, fifty-ninth session, Geneva, 17–28 September 2012, TD/B/59/5, para. 16; OECD, Addressing International Competitiveness in a World of Non-Uniform Carbon Pricing: Lessons from a decade of OECD analysis, Policy Brief prepared by Bella Tonkonogy, November 2010. See also how the EU ETS – an example of a market-based instrument – relies on similar assumptions as the ones for traditional BTAs. In recital 25 of Directive 2009/29/EC, it is stated that proposals to deal with energy-intensive industry sectors should be based on 'the assessment of the inability of industries to pass on the cost of required allowances in product prices without significant loss of market share to installations outside the Community which do not take comparable action to reduce their emissions'. This assumption corresponds to the assumption of price shifting under BTA measures.

assess the likeness between the products under dispute.[30] As regards adjustments on imports, the NT principle contained in GATT Article III indeed applies to any measure, regardless of its regulatory or tax nature.[31] Though GATT Article III:2 only applies to taxes, the provisions of GATT Article III:1 and III:4 express a similar idea: imported products should not be subject to a discriminatory treatment.[32] Therefore, it is not fully relevant to ask whether a cap and trade system such as the EU ETS is a tax or a regulation in order to determine the eligibility of such a measure for adjustments. What matters is whether or not the application of the EU ETS discriminates against imported products in comparison to domestic products. As far as exports are concerned, WTO law seems to distinguish more clearly between taxes and regulatory adjustments. The ASCM is the main legal basis for determining whether exported products may be 'exempted' from national regulations. In contrast to BTAs in respect of indirect taxes, regulatory adjustments on the export side are not expressly mentioned in Annex I of the ASCM.[33] The fact that Annex I does not touch upon regulatory adjustments, however, does not mean that they are more likely to be assimilated to prohibited subsidies. On the contrary, the prohibited character of regulatory adjustments should be assessed against the definition of subsidies provided in the ASCM as well as the conditions to be met for a subsidy to be considered either a prohibited or an actionable subsidy.

As a general matter, though the design and the impact of regulatory and tax instruments may differ, their legal treatment may be comparable. The existence of specific provisions for adjustments in the form (and in respect) of taxes does not mean that regulatory adjustments should automatically be forbidden. These specific provisions could rather be

---

30 WTO, Appellate Body Report, *EC – Asbestos*, para. 109. See also WTO, Panel Report, *US – Gasoline*, para. 6.8. See also WTO, Appellate Body Report, *Japan – Alcoholic Beverages II*, 20–21.

31 See OECD 1994 note on Environmental BTAs, COM/ENV/EPOC/DAFFE/CFA(94)31, para. 47.

32 Authors argue that the test under GATT Arts. III:2 and III:4 presents some differences. See Reinhard Quick & Christian Lau, 'Environmentally Motivated Tax Distinctions and WTO Law. The European Commission's Green Paper on Integrated Product Policy in Light of the 'Like Product-' and 'PPM-' Debates' (2003) 6(2) Journal of International Economic Law 419, 436.

33 Pauwelyn, *supra* n. 12, 484. See also Luca Rubini, 'Subsidies for Emissions Mitigation under WTO Law', in: Geert Van Calster & Denise Prévost (eds.), *Research Handbook on Environment, Health and the WTO* (Edward Elgar Publishing 2013), 561–635.

understood in the light of the historical development of the GATT.[34] At the time of the drafting of the GATT, barriers in the form of regulations were less problematic than tax barriers. Furthermore, the GATT does not provide for a definition of the concept of tax. Authors usually apply the same definition as those that apply at national level or refer to the definition of the OECD.[35] As such, nothing, however, forbids a broader definition.

6.1.2 National Treatment Principle

The extent to which WTO members may implement environmental BTAs is directly related to the interpretation of the NT test. As discussed above, a range of approaches exist, from restrictive to permissive ones.[36]

Many of the models described in Chapter 4 differentiate between products based on differences related to the pollution released during production processes (or based on a 'pollution factor', used to indicate the pollution associated with a product through its entire lifecycle). As soon as the legislator aims at tackling pollution released during production, environmental tax models are used to differentiate between products that are likely to be physically the same and to be in a competitive relationship. For example, the model proposed by De Camillis and Goralczyk[37] clearly distinguishes between products which are *a priori* 'like products'. In their tax models, the VAT rate imposed on a product should be calculated by taking into account the environmental performance of the product subject to the tax with the 'reference environmental performance of the product'. Such differentiated tax measures could be deemed contrary to the NT principle, under a restrictive approach.

---

34 See Horn & Mavroidis, *supra* n. 19, 40–41.

35 Deane, *supra* n. 26, 191–196; Pauwelyn, *supra* n. 12; de Cendra, *supra* n. 26, 135; Zane, *supra* n. 26, 205–206.

36 A liberal approach was expressed in an OECD report of 1995 (OECD, Trade principles and concepts, 1995, OECD/DG(95)141). See also GATT, TRE/W/20, para. 24; OCDE, OCDE/GD(97)137; OECD 1994 note on Environmental BTAs, COM/ENV/EPOC/DAFFE/CFA(94)31. See also Congress of the United States, Office of Technology Assessment, Trade and Environment. Conflicts and Opportunities, Washington DC, Government Printing Office, May 1992, OTA-BP-ITE-94.

37 Camillo De Camillis & Malgorzata Goralczyk, 'Towards Stronger Measures for Sustainable Consumption and Production Policies: Proposal of a New Fiscal Framework Based on a Life Cycle Approach' (2013) 18(1) International Journal of Life Cycle Assessment 263–272.

The excise duty-based models as well as the CAT model are probably less problematic. As for models based on excise duty systems, an argument in favour of their compatibility with WTO law could merely refer to the examples of the Superfund and ODC taxes. If such taxes have already been accepted in the past, there would be no reason to find them incompatible with WTO law. Under the CAT model, the tax is calculated by multiplying the rate by a polluting factor (instead of a price factor as under traditional VAT models). The peculiarity of the CAT model is that it differentiates between all products and not only between a limited number of categories between 'polluting' and 'non-polluting' products. From this perspective, the CAT model may be more easily acceptable. Indeed, the only difference from traditional VAT models is that the price is replaced (fully or not) by a polluting factor. Consequently, it could be argued that the CAT model does not create a bigger differentiation between products than the traditional VAT models: two products that are identical from the viewpoint of their physical characteristics may also differ in price (as they may differ regarding their polluting factor) and thus be subject to different taxes. A price factor is, however, not completely comparable with a polluting factor. The advantage of a price factor is that it *a priori* entails neutrality and objectivity. Therefore, it could only be argued that VAT discriminates against imported products based on a price factor when imports are usually more expensive than domestic products. On the contrary, the polluting factor is more sensitive to differences between countries. For example, production processes in developing countries are arguably more polluting, which would systematically lead to higher taxation of imports from these countries and could be considered a discrimination.[38] Moreover, as soon as the environmental factor takes into consideration the pollution deriving from transportation, imported products will *a priori* get a higher 'polluting score' as products from abroad are necessarily subject to longer transport distances. A similar issue would appear under the environmental VAT model. For example, under Albrecht's proposal, 'international travelling foodstuff' should be divided into three categories: (1) sustainable (local production, low use of pesticides), (2) high transportation costs, (3) high use of pesticides (not sustainable).[39] Such a classification would likely be

---

[38] Kommerskollegium (Swedish National Board of Trade), *supra* n. 26, 28.

[39] Johan Albrecht, 'The Use of Consumption Taxes to Re-launch Green Tax Reforms' (2006) 26(1) International Review of Law and Economics 88–103.

contrary to the NT principle since imported products would necessarily be subject to a higher rate.[40]

This argument could nevertheless be tempered in light of current (traditional) VAT systems, which include certain expenses in the taxable amount that could *de facto* lead to discrimination against imported products. For example, the EU VAT Directive provides that 'the taxable amount shall include ... incidental expenses, such as commission, packing, transport and insurance costs'.[41] Given that transport costs are likely to be systematically higher in the case of imported products, a violation of the NT principle could also be invoked in the case of traditional VAT systems.

Under the approach that differentiation based on products' production process should be authorised, the legislator will face practical difficulties in determining the amount of the tax to be levied on imported products (Chapter 4, Section 4.3.1). Where traditional BTAs are calculated on products' prices, environmental BTAs are to be calculated taking into account an environmental factor. In contrast to prices, which represent transparent and easily accessible data, the environmental value of products may be much more challenging to determine. Importers could be asked to provide the necessary information to calculate the environmental factor of imported products.

Given that WTO law forbids imported products from being subjected to higher tax rates than 'like' or 'directly competitive and substitutable' products, the implementation of environmental BTA models should preferably not rely on complicated and costly certification systems.[42] For the same reasons, WTO members should preferably choose a voluntary certification system, leaving the possibility that imported products' environmental value be assessed on the basis of a standard method.[43]

In the hypothesis of no or insufficient information, the determination of the environmental factor could be based on averaging by assuming that the product has been made using the 'predominant method of production' in the implementing country or the 'best available technique'. In any case, to comply with WTO law requirements on BTAs, the calculation of the environmental factor should not lead to the 'excessive' taxation of

---

[40] See the arguments made in WTO, Panel Report, *Canada – Autos*, especially in para. 10.24.

[41] See Art. 86, para. 1(b) of the EU VAT Directive 2006/112/EC.

[42] See GATT Arts. III:2, III:4, VIII:4(f), Ad Art. VIII, para. 2. See also the provisions of the TBT agreement (*infra*).

[43] Obligatory certification systems could be found contrary to GATT Art. III. Legal issues could also arise with regard to the TBT.

imported products or to protectionism.[44] For this reason, averaging based on the 'predominant method of production' in the implementing country may be criticised as it could lead to higher taxes imposed on imported products without justification (e.g. in the case where imported products are produced in a way that is less polluting than the 'predominant method of production'). Where the assessment is based on the predominant method of production in the exporting country, the environmental character of imported products would be defined on a country-specific basis, which would likely be contrary to GATT Article I. Assessments based on the best available technique are more likely to be compatible with WTO law provisions surrounding BTAs given that this does not lead to any type of discrimination against imported products. However, from an environmental viewpoint, this assessment method is likely to benefit imported products that have been produced in a highly polluting way (since their environmental value is nevertheless assessed based on the 'best available technique').

6.1.3 MFN Principle (GATT Article I)

The MFN principle requires that BTAs are imposed on imported products regardless of the country of import.[45] As already mentioned, many of the proposals in favour of environmental BTAs nevertheless limit the application of BTAs in respect of imported products from those countries where no similar environmental regulations exist.[46] By imposing different taxes on imported products based on their origin, these proposals clash not only with the traditional concept of BTAs, but also with the MFN principle. Indeed, to comply with the requirements of GATT Article I,

---

44 GATT, Panel Report, *US – Superfund*, para. 5.2.9.

45 GATT Art. I.

46 See WTO, Preparatory Committee, Preparatory Committee for the Sub-Committee on Trade and Environment, Report of the Meeting held on 15–16 September 1994, Note by the Secretariat, 10 October 2004, PC/SCTE/M/3/rev.1, para. 33 (Korea's representative). See also Wolfgang Schön, 'World Trade Organization Law and Tax Law' (2004) 58(7) IBFD Bulletin 283–296; See Alessandra Arcuri, 'Law and Economics of the SPS Agreement: A Critical Perspective', in: Geert Van Calster & Denise Prévost (eds.), *Research Handbook on Environment, Health and the WTO* (Edward Elgar Publishing 2013), 182. Note that the MFN requirement could be found contrary to the requirement of GATT Art. XX. See Gavin Goh, 'The World Trade Organization, Kyoto and Energy Tax Adjustments at the Border' (2004) 38(3) Journal of World Trade 395, 420.

products should not be differentiated based on country-specific conditions.[47] Examples of tax differentiation based on country-specific conditions include tax models where transportation costs are included in the assessment of the environmental character of imported products. Such taxes could be deemed to amount to a violation of GATT Article I, given that exporting countries located further away from the importing country could be discriminated against.[48] GATT Article I therefore implies that BTAs may not be implemented so as to take into consideration differences between WTO members' environmental policies.[49] In the past, countries have nevertheless designed environmental taxes based on such country-specific differentiation. Such is the case, to a certain extent, for the exemption regime of the ODC tax, which provides for the exemption of the tax on certain imported products under the condition that these chemicals are 'imported from any country which is a signatory to the Montreal Protocol on Substances that Deplete the Ozone Layer'.[50] Though the US ODC tax has not been questioned under WTO law, this provision seems to contradict the MFN principle. Indeed, WTO law in principle forbids distinguishing between countries while this type of exemption makes a clear distinction between the countries that are part of the Montreal Protocol and those that are not.

The other side of the coin of GATT Article I is that BTAs may be imposed regardless of the policy framework of third countries. Under the traditional concept of BTAs, it does not matter whether the implementation of BTAs leads to double taxation due to the fact that third countries

---

[47] See also Paul-Erik Veel, 'Carbon Tariffs and the WTO: An Evaluation of Feasible Policies' (2009) Journal of International Economic Law 749, 796; Benjamin M. Eichenberg, 'Greenhouse Gas Regulation and Border Tax Adjustments: The Carrot and the Stick' (2008) 3(2) Golden Gate University Environmental Law Journal 283–364, 352.

[48] Traditional tariffs could offer an argument in favour of the inclusion of transport cost since the transaction value of imported products may include transportation costs. See Art. 8, para. 2(a) of the Agreement on Implementation of Art. VI of the General Agreement on Tariffs and Trade 1994. See also at the EU level, Art. 71, para. 1(e)(i) of Regulation (EU) No. 952/2013 of the European Parliament and of the Council of 9 October 2013 laying down the Union Customs Code, 10 October 2013, OJ L269/1.

[49] Schön, *supra* n. 46, 287. See also Pauwelyn, *supra* n. 12, footnote 121; GATT, Industrial Pollution Control and International Trade, Note by the GATT Secretariat, 9 June 1971, L/3538, 14.

[50] 26 US CODE §4682(d)(1).

use an origin-based tax system.[51] Similarly, it should not matter for environmental BTAs whether other environmental regulations have been imposed in third countries on the imported products. Though, at first sight, this restriction may seem to counter the environmental objective of BTAs, it does not, however, make environmental BTAs meaningless. Indeed, although the concept of BTAs does not directly allow environmental differences between countries to be taken into account, differences related to the level of internalisation of the pollution associated with a product can nevertheless be considered through BTAs. Instead of differentiating between products on the basis of the country from which the products are imported, environmental BTAs could be designed in order to tax products on the basis of the extent to which the pollution associated with the product has already been internalised, regardless of whether this internalisation took place due to the high level of environmental policies in the exporting country or due to internal policies put in place by private actors, for example the enterprises producing the products subject to BTAs (Section 4.3.1).

6.2 ENVIRONMENTAL BTAs UNDER OTHER (WTO AND NON-WTO) RELEVANT LEGAL PROVISIONS

Besides the traditional legal grounds surrounding BTAs, additional WTO and non-WTO legal provisions may be relevant to assess the compatibility of environmental BTAs. Under WTO law, GATT Article XX is one of these provisions. Other examples of potentially relevant WTO provisions are the Agreement on Agriculture, the Agreement on Technical Barriers to Trade (TBT) and the Agreement on the Application of Sanitary and Phytosanitary Measures (SPS). The TBT agreement, for example, could be relevant for those models of environmental BTAs the tax design of which requires certification of the environmental character of products (such as through product categories that permit a distinction between 'environmentally friendly' and 'non-environmentally friendly' products).[52] This section focuses on GATT Article XX as it is the most relevant provision and as it has been one of the legal grounds by scholars

---

[51] Schön, *supra* n. 46, p. 291. In the *Superfund* case the US did not take into consideration whether similar environmental measures had been adopted in other countries.

[52] See Ross Astoria, 'Design of an International Trade Law Compliant Carbon Border Tax Adjustment' (2015–2016) 6 Arizona Journal of Environmental Law & Policy 491, 525–528.

analysing environmental BTAs (Section 6.2.1). In addition to WTO law, principles of environmental, tax and international public law could either support or put into question the adoption of environmental BTAs (Section 6.2.2).

6.2.1 Other WTO Relevant Legal Provisions: GATT Article XX

In legal scholarship, GATT Article XX has often been described as a key legal provision to permit the adoption of environmental BTAs.[53] The role of GATT Article XX – as a general exceptions provision – should, however, remain limited to the hypothesis whereby environmental BTAs violate the traditional legal grounds on which they rely.

GATT Article XX is *not* a specific legal basis for BTAs but a legal ground for *any* trade measure that pursues one of the goals listed in this provision. Most proposals for environmentally related measures based on GATT Article XX should not be called BTAs as these measures do not share the legal grounds of traditional BTAs. The fact that these trade-related measures may share some characteristics with traditional BTAs, such as, for example, their implementation through taxes, is insufficient. Rather than being compared to BTAs, these measures should be framed based on other trade-related measures such as customs duties.

---

[53] See e.g. Eichenberg, *supra* n. 47, 329–334; Ekardt & Schmeichel, *supra* n. 26, 737, 748; Goh, *supra* n. 46, 413–422; Pauwelyn, *supra* n. 12, 496–505; Harro van Asselt, Thomas Brewer & Michael Mehling, 'Addressing Leakage and Competitiveness in US Climate Policy. Issues Concerning Border Adjustment Measures' (2009) Climate Strategies Working Paper, 52–57; Ryan Vanden Brink, 'Competitiveness Border Adjustments in US Climate Change Proposals Violate GATT: Suggestions to Utilize GATT's Environmental Exceptions'(2010) 21 Colorado Journal of International Environmental Law and Policy 85, 105–115; Zhu Zhu, Eum-sup Lee & Kim Sun-ok, 'A Discussion on the Legitimacy of Carbon Tariffs under the WTO' (2011) 10 International Conference on Sociality and Economics Development IPEDR 221; Zane, *supra* n. 26, 209–224. See also the reference to GATT Art. XX in the Belgian Senate Proposal for the introduction of green and social customs duties: Belgium, Sénat, Proposition de résolution demandant l'instauration au niveau européen de droits sociaux et environnementaux dans le Code des douanes communautaire, déposée par M. Jacky Morael et consorts, Session de 2012–2013, 11 October 2012, No. 5-1807/1, 5.

6.2.1.1 The role of GATT Article XX under WTO law

6.2.1.1.1 GATT Article XX vis-à-vis GATT general provisions GATT Article XX – GATT general exceptions provision – allows WTO members to adopt certain measures that would otherwise be contrary to other GATT provisions. In other words, GATT Article XX gives priority to certain policy objectives over other GATT provisions. Among the objectives listed in GATT Article XX, three could serve to justify measures aimed at fostering environmental goals: GATT XX, paragraph a ('measures necessary to protect public morals'), GATT XX, paragraph b ('measures necessary to protect human, animal or plant life or health') and GATT XX, paragraph g ('measures relating to the conservation of exhaustible natural resources if such measures are made effective in conjunction with restrictions on domestic production or consumption').

Given that Article XX is a general exceptions provision, it only applies where a measure is found contrary to other GATT provisions. This explains the interaction that exists between the interpretation given to other GATT provisions and the application of GATT Article XX.[54] For example, in the case of environmental BTAs, a restrictive interpretation of GATT traditional provisions surrounding BTAs on imports (mainly GATT Articles I, II:2(a) and III:2) implies that GATT Article XX may play a significant role as a potential legal ground for environmental BTAs. In contrast, an interpretation that leaves space to base environmental BTAs on GATT Articles I, II:2(a) and III:2 reduces the role of GATT Article XX in justifying environmental BTAs. In this regard, the *effet utile* of GATT Article XX is sometimes used as an argument in favour of a restrictive reading of GATT Articles I, II:2(a) and III:2: 'If GATT article III only prohibits protectionist measures, what would then be the objective of GATT article XX?'[55] However, a broad reading of GATT Article III does not necessarily make GATT Article XX *inutile* ('useless'). Authors consider that GATT Article XX would keep its *effet utile*, both in the case of a violation of GATT Article III as well as in the case of a violation of other GATT provisions.[56]

First, GATT Article XX has its own conditions of application, which are independent from the conditions surrounding other GATT provisions. Consequently, environmental border taxes justified on the basis of GATT

[54] See Robert Howse & Donald Regan, 'The Product/Process Distinction – An Illusory Basis for Disciplining "Unilateralism" in Trade Policy' (2000) 11(2) European Journal of International Law 249–289.

[55] See e.g. Quick & Lau, *supra* n. 32, 454.

[56] See i.a. Howse & Regan, *supra* n. 54, 266.

Article XX do not need to meet the conditions surrounding environmental BTAs (as mentioned in GATT Article III:2 for BTAs on imports). Even more, environmental BTAs could be found incompatible with GATT Article XX because they were primarily designed to respect other legal provisions.[57]

Second, in contrast to GATT general provisions, the burden of proof under GATT Article XX primarily relies on the defendant, not the complainant. In other words, the defendant should submit a *prima facie* case that the measure is to be justified under GATT Article XX.[58]

Third, the choice to base environmental BTAs on GATT Article XX gives a political reading of WTO law that assumes that environmental BTAs *a priori* violate GATT general provisions, meaning that such taxes could only be adopted on an exception basis. In contrast, when environmental BTAs are based on GATT Articles I, II, III or other general provisions, the political reading of the GATT reflects an approach to WTO law that is less restrictive and more open to non-trade values.

6.2.1.1.2 GATT Article XX vis-à-vis other GATT (& GATS) exceptions provisions In the framework of environmental BTAs, GATT Article XX is the most generally mentioned exceptions provision. Article XX is, however, not the only provision that allows WTO members to adopt measures that would otherwise contradict other GATT provisions.[59] WTO law indeed contains other types of exceptions: GATT Article XIX ('safeguards'), GATT Article XXI ('security exceptions'), GATT Article XXIV ('customs unions and free trade areas') and Article IX of the Marrakesh Agreement establishing the WTO ('waiver'). These provisions are nevertheless unlikely to serve as justification grounds for environmental BTAs. First, WTO members are unlikely to be able to rely on GATT Article XIX, given that this article only permits members to suspend, withdraw or modify their concessions when 'as a result of unforeseen developments … any product is being imported into [their] territory in such increased quantity and under such conditions as to cause

---

[57] On the relationship between GATT Arts. I and XX, see Holzer, *supra* n. 26, 173, quoting van Asselt, Brewer & Mehling, *supra* n. 53, 55.

[58] WTO, Panel Report, *EC – Asbestos*, paras. 8.177–8.183. See also WTO, Panel Report, *US – Gasoline*, 38 & 44; WTO, Appellate Body Report, *US – Gasoline*, 29 April 1996, WT/DS2/AB/R, 22–23.

[59] Rüdiger Wolfrum, 'Article XX GATT [Introduction]', in: Rüdiger Wolfrum, Peter-Tobias Stoll & Holger P. Hestermeyer (eds.), *WTO – Trade in Goods*, Max Planck Commentaries on World Trade Law (Martinus Nijhoff Publishers 2011, Vol. 5), 455–456.

or threaten serious injury to domestic producers ...'.[60] In the hypothesis where environmental BTAs were adopted (although the reason for their adoption may relate to the protection of domestic industry), the threat or serious injury to domestic producers would derive from the adoption of domestic environmental policy, which cannot be considered an 'unforeseen development'.[61] Second, GATT Article XXI is unlikely to serve as a legal ground for the adoption of environmental BTAs given that environmental issues are in principle not considered a security issue.[62] In the future it is, however, not impossible that environmental global challenges would be assimilated to security challenges. For now, energy policies indeed already include security considerations. Third, authors have referred to GATT Article XXIV as a legal instrument to adopt environmental BTAs at a bilateral level in the case where trade partners do not find agreement on the harmonisation of environmental standards.[63] Such a proposal would nevertheless face the same legal uncertainty as environmental BTAs adopted outside a Regional Trade Agreement (RTA), although trade partners could be less likely to challenge such a system.[64] Fourth, Article IX of the Marrakesh Agreement establishing the WTO allows contracting parties to waive a GATT obligation under exceptional circumstances. For example, a waiver was granted in the framework of the Kimberley Process Certification Scheme for Rough Diamonds in 2003.[65] Article IX is unlikely to permit the adoption of controversial measures such as environmental BTAs given that waivers are usually

---

[60] GATT Art. XIX:1(a).

[61] See, however, Meinhard Doelle, 'Climate Change and the WTO: Opportunities to Motivate State Action on Climate Change through the World Trade Organization' (2004) 13(1) Review of European Community & International Environmental Law 85, 101.

[62] See Felicity Deane, *Emissions Trading and WTO Law. A Global Analysis* (Edward Elgar Publishing 2015), 86–88. Regarding the interpretation of GATT XXI, Deane also refers to UN, Economic and Social Council, Second Session for the Preparatory Committee of the United Nations Conference on Trade and Employment, Thirty-Third Meeting of Commission A held on Thursday, 24 July 1947, Palais des Nations, Geneva, E/PC/T/A/PV/33, 21.

[63] See Holzer, *supra* n. 26, 289–292. Note that when Holzer speaks about PTAs, she does not refer to 'preferential trade arrangements' but to 'preferential trade agreements'. In a similar way, Leal-Arcas proposes integrating environmental clauses into RTAs (Rafael Leal-Arcas, *Climate Change and International Trade* (Edward Elgar Publishing 2013), 363–418.

[64] Holzer, *supra* n. 26, 292.

[65] WTO, Waiver concerning Kimberley Process Certification Scheme for Rough Diamonds, Decision of 15 May 2003, 27 May 2003, WT/L/518.

adopted by consensus (or at least three-quarters of the members should agree with the decision).

Under the GATS, Article XIV plays a similar role as GATT Article XX, which means that this article will serve to justify violations to the GATS. One interesting characteristic of GATS Article XIV is that it provides an exception to GATS MFN principle in the hypothesis where a measure leads to a differentiated treatment, which is 'the result of an agreement on the avoidance of double taxation or provisions on the avoidance of double taxation in any other international agreement or arrangement by which the member is bound'.[66] No similar exception exists in the GATT. This means that environmental BTAs that would only be imposed vis-à-vis products from countries that have not yet adopted environmental taxes would not be justified under the GATT, even though the differentiated treatment could be aimed at avoiding double taxation with tax treaty partner countries that have already implemented environmental taxes.

6.2.1.1.3 GATT Article XX vis-à-vis other WTO Agreements (ASCM, TBT, SPS) The question arises as to whether WTO members may rely on GATT Article XX to justify measures – including environmental BTAs – that would otherwise violate other WTO law provisions.

Regarding the TBT, some scholars suggest that a legitimate regulatory objective could justify measures that would otherwise be found contrary to the TBT, *de facto* interpreting the TBT as if it implicitly integrated a provision similar to GATT Art. XX.[67]

Following the case law in *China – Raw Materials*, GATT Article XX should nevertheless only apply in relation to agreements that contain an

---

66 Art. XIV(e) GATS.

67 See Gabrielle Marceau & Joel P. Trachtman, 'A Map of the World Trade Organization Law of Domestic Regulation of Goods: The Technical Barriers to Trade Agreement, the Sanitary and Phytosanitary Measures Agreement, and the General Agreement on Tariffs and Trade' (2014) 48(2) Journal of World Trade 351, 364 & 409–410. See also WTO, Appellate Body Report, United States – Certain Country of Origin Labelling (COOL) Requirements, 29 June 2012, WT/DS384/AB/R, WT/DS386/AB/R (*US – COOL*), para. 271; WTO, Appellate Body Report, United States – Measures Affecting the Production and Sale of Clove Cigarettes, 4 April 2012, WT/DS406/AB/R (*US – Clove Cigarettes*), para. 109; WTO, Panel Report, European Communities – Measures Prohibiting the Importation and Marketing of Seal Products, 25 November 2013, WT/DS400/R, WT/DS401/R (*EC – Seal Products*), para. 7.634. See also Erich Vranes, *Trade and the Environment: Fundamental Issues in International Law, WTO Law, and Legal Theory* (OUP 2009), 304–305.

explicit reference to this provision.[68] Article 8 of the ASCM provides a list of non-actionable subsidies, which could be seen as a form of exceptions provision for subsidies that pursued certain goals (i.a. 'assistance to disadvantaged regions', 'assistance to promote adaptation of existing facilities to new environmental requirements …').[69] WTO members may nevertheless no longer rely on this provision as it was only in effect for a period of five years, ending in December 1999.[70] Uncertainties therefore remain as to whether WTO members may rely on GATT Article XX to justify measures violating the ASCM.

6.2.1.2 GATT Article XX: conditions of application

In *US – Gasoline,* the Appellate Body stated that GATT Article XX only applies when the disputed measures meet a two-tiered test.[71] First, the measures should fall into one of the policy goals categories as defined in paragraphs (a) to (j) of GATT Article XX. In the case of environmental BTAs, the objectives listed in GATT paragraphs (a), (b) and (g) are the most relevant.[72] Second, the measures should respect the requirement

---

[68] WTO, Appellate Body Report, China – Measures Related to the Exportation of Various Raw Materials, 30 January 2012, WT/DS394/AB/R, WT/DS395/AB/R, WT/DS398/AB/R (*China – Raw Materials*), para. 303; WTO, Appellate Body Report, China – Measures Affecting Trading Rights and Distribution Services for Certain Publications and Audiovisual Entertainment Products, 21 December 2009, WT/DS363/AB/R (*China – Publications and Audiovisual Products*), paras. 229–230. See also Deane, *supra* n. 62, 172; Stefan Lorenzmeier, 'WTO and Human Rights', in: Norman Weiß & Jean-Marc Thouvenin (eds.), *The Influence of Human Rights on International Law* (Springer 2015), 158–159; Marceau & Trachtman, *supra* n. 67, 351–432; Stefan Zleptnig, *Non-Economic Objectives in WTO Law. Justification Provisions of GATT, GATS, SPS and TBT Agreements* (Martinus Nijhoff Publishers 2010), 1214.

[69] On the application of GATT Art. XX in relation to the ASCM, see Christopher Tran, 'Using GATT, Art XX to Justify Climate Change Measures in Claims under the WTO Agreements' (2010) 27 Environmental and Planning Law Journal 346, 354 & 356–358. See Pauwelyn, *supra* n. 12, 496 (footnote 127).

[70] See Art. 31 of the ASCM.

[71] WTO, Appellate Body Report, *US – Gasoline*, 22. See also WTO, Panel Report, European Communities – Conditions for the Granting of Tariff Preferences to Developing Countries, WT/DS246/R, 1 December 2003 (*EC – Tariff Preferences*), paras. 7.195–7.199; WTO, Korea – Measures Affecting Imports of Fresh, Chilled and Frozen Beef, 11 December 2000, WT/DS161/AB/R, WT/DS169/AB/R (*Korea – Various Measures on Beef)*, para. 164.

[72] GATT Art. XX(d) is not analysed here as it is very unlikely that this provision could serve to justify environmental BTAs. See Susanne Reyes-Knoche & Katrin Arend, 'Article XX lit. d GATT', in: Rüdiger Wolfrum, Peter-Tobias

defined in the chapeau of GATT Article XX, which states as follows: 'Subject to the requirement that such measures are not applied in a manner which would constitute a means of arbitrary or unjustifiable discrimination between countries where the same conditions prevail, or a disguised restriction on international trade …'.[73]

6.2.1.2.1 The objectives defined under GATT Article XX(a), (b) and (g)
The different models of environmental BTAs described in chapter 4 pursue a variety of objectives. Even though environmental BTAs may not be primarily based on an environmental rationale (e.g. the environmental BTAs grounded on the economic theories of Ricardo or Smith), they always pursue, at the very least, secondarily, environmental goals.

Four categories of environmental objectives – often interconnected – may be distinguished. First, environmental BTAs may aim at guaranteeing that environmental costs are internalised. Second, environmental BTAs may allow protecting countries regulatory power to adopt environmental taxes or regulations at the national level: without the adoption of environmental BTAs, countries would be discouraged from maintaining their environmental regulatory framework. Third, environmental BTAs may be used to encourage other countries to adopt a higher level of environmental policy framework. A fourth reason is the prevention of pollution leakage and pollution haven. This fourth reason is directly linked to the three other objectives.

This section analyses whether environmental BTAs may fall under GATT Article XX(a), (b) and (g).

6.2.1.2.1.1 GATT ARTICLE XX(A) GATT Article XX(a) concerns 'measures necessary to protect public morals'. This article is not often referred to in relation to measures aimed at environmental protection. A broad interpretation of the concept of 'public morals' could, however, allow some environmental issues to be tackled.[74] For example, in the case *EC – Seal Products* the Panel analysed 'EU public moral concerns on seal welfare' under GATT Article XX(a).[75]

Stoll & Anja Seibert-Fohr (eds.), *WTO – Technical Barriers and SPS Measures* (Koninklijke Brill 2007), 125.

73 GATT Art. XX.

74 See Steve Charnovitz, 'The Moral Exception in Trade Policy' (1998) 38 Virginia Journal of International Law 689, 697.

75 See WTO, Panel Report, European Communities – Measures Prohibiting the Importation and Marketing of Seal Products, 25 November 2013,

The moral aspects may seem more explicit in the case of the welfare of seals than in relation to other global environmental challenges (e.g. the protection of biodiversity, the protection of ecosystems by mitigating climate change). However, environmental protection may in fact always be grounded in a moral rationale. Many different reasons are put forward to explain that human beings need to protect the environment, from economic (i.e. the argument that the economic impact of environmental damage costs more than the costs related to *ex ante* environmental protection) to ethical reasons. For example, from a religious viewpoint, it could be argued that the environment must be protected for its own sake. As part of the environment, human beings should take care of nature. Up to now, this moral approach on environmental protection has not gained much influence in international arenas. At the UN level, the economic approach towards environmental protection seems very influential: the new concept of 'green economy' is only one example of the impact of economic views on the field of environmental protection. The case law surrounding GATT Article XX(a), however, recognises that member states 'should be given some scope to define and apply for themselves the concepts of "public morals"'.[76] In other words, the 'content of these concepts for Members can vary in time and space, depending upon a range of factors, including prevailing social, cultural, ethical and religious values'.[77] Therefore, some WTO members, when a moral perspective on environmental matters prevails within their legal framework, could refer to GATT Article XX(a) as a ground of justification in relation to environmental measures that otherwise would violate other GATT provisions.

Aside from the definition of the goal of the contested measure, an additional requirement for a measure to fall under GATT Article XX(a) is that the measure should be considered *necessary* to protect public morals. According to consistent case law, the necessity test implies '"a process of

---

WT/DS400/R, WT/DS401/R (*EC – Seal Products*), paras. 7.625–7.639. See also Laura Nielsen, *The WTO, Animals and PPMs* (Martinus Nijhoff Publishers 2007).

[76] WTO, Panel Report, United States – Measures Affecting the Cross-border Supply of Gambling and Betting Services, 10 November 2004, WT/DS285/R (*US – Gambling*), para. 6.461.

[77] See WTO, Panel Report, China – Measures Affecting Trading Rights and Distribution Services for Certain Publications and Audiovisual Entertainment Products, 12 August 2009, WT/DS363/R (*China – Publications and Audiovisual Products*), para. 7.759. In this case, the Panel refers to the interpretation of GATS Art. XIV(a) – which corresponds to GATT Art. XX within the GATS framework – as mentioned in *US – Gambling* (para. 6.461).

weighing and balancing" of "all the relevant factors, particularly the extent of the contribution to the achievement of a measure's objective and its trade restrictiveness, in the light of the importance of the interests or values at stake"'.[78] Moreover, the necessity test also requires comparing 'the measure with its possible alternatives, which may be less restrictive while providing an equivalent contribution to the achievement of the objective pursued'.[79] In the *EC – Seal Products* case, the Panel considered that, in order to assess whether the EU measure contributed to the objective defined under GATT Article XX(a), a 'genuine relationship of ends and means between the objective pursued and the measure at issue' should exist. The Panel considered that the EU seal regime contributed to the EU objective of reduction of global demand for seal products and helped '... the EU public avoid being exposed to seal products on the EU market that may have been derived from seals killed inhumanely'.[80]

Environmental BTAs aimed at internalising environmental costs could fall under GATT Article XX(a) based on the reasoning applied by the Panel in the *EC – Seal Products* case: such measures would aim at avoiding the EU public being exposed to products that may have been derived from production processes that do not internalise environmental costs. In contrast, environmental BTAs aimed at guaranteeing WTO members' possibility to adopt environmental taxes would unlikely meet the conditions of GATT Article XX(a). The objective to 'avoid that domestic legislator be discouraged to adopt environmental policies' is unlikely to be considered an objective of public morals. Regarding environmental BTAs aimed at encouraging other countries to adopt higher levels of environmental policies, it could be argued that such models contribute to the objective of limiting the offer of products from countries with low levels of environmental protection. An argument against such models would, however, be that the tax does not contribute

---

[78] WTO, Panel Report, *EC – Seal Products*, para. 7.630. See also WTO, Appellate Body Report, Brazil – Measures Affecting Imports of Retreaded Tyres, 3 December 2007, WT/DS332/AB/R (*Brazil – Retreaded Tyres*), paras. 210–212; WTO, Appellate Body Report, *Dominican Republic – Import and Sale of Cigarettes*, paras. 69–70; WTO, Appellate Body Report, United States – Measures Affecting the Cross-border Supply of Gambling and Betting Services, 7 April 2005, AT/DS285/AB/R (*US – Gambling*), paras. 305–306. On the interpretation of the balancing test, see Donald H. Regan, 'The meaning of "necessary" in GATT Article XX and GATS Article XIV: the myth of cost-benefit balancing' (2007) 6(3) World Trade Review 347.

[79] WTO, Panel Report, *EC – Seal Products*, para. 7.630.

[80] *Ibid.*, para. 7.637.

to this objective since it does not ban the products from environmentally unfriendly countries but merely subjects them to higher taxes. Indeed, unless tariffs are so high that trade stops, higher tariffs do not prevent trade between countries. In other words, a tariff policy based on environmental considerations may not pass the 'necessity' test of GATT Article XX given that other measures than tariffs could be used to achieve the same goals. In the case of environmental BTAs, the necessity test could indeed be problematic since less strict alternatives exist (e.g. negotiations at the international level; the exemption of highly polluting enterprises, etc.).

The question of whether measures that are based on PPMs may meet the necessity test under GATT Article XX(a) is also highly controversial. Some authors believe that such measures would lack a connection to the objective of protecting public morals in addition to being extra-territorial.[81] A counter-argument may, however, be based on the reasoning of the Panel in the case *EC – Seal Products*, namely that a country should be able to legislate so that its citizens are not exposed to products that would be contrary to public morals. Given that most of the models of environmental BTAs are based on PPMs, this debate has a significant impact on the compatibility of environmental BTAs with WTO law.[82]

6.2.1.2.1.2 GATT ARTICLE XX(B) GATT Article XX(b) concerns 'measures necessary to protect human, animal or plant life or health'. In contrast to GATT XX(a), this article more explicitly relates to environmental issues. Nevertheless, questions arise as to whether this provision covers any type of environmental measures or whether it should be interpreted in a more restrictive way.[83] The language of GATT Article XX(b) only refers to the protection of human, animal or plant life or health and not to the protection of the environment in general.[84] Consequently, it is uncertain that environmental BTAs aimed at the

---

81 See Wenzel, 'Article XX lit. a GATT', in: Rüdiger Wolfrum, Peter-Tobias Stoll & Holger P. Hestermeyer (eds.), *WTO – Trade in Goods*, Max Planck Commentaries on World Trade Law (Martinus Nijhoff Publishers 2011, Vol. 5), 486–490. See also Daniel C.K. Chow & Thomas J. Schoenbaum, *International Trade Law: Problems, Cases and Materials* (Wolters Kluwer Law & Business 2013), 508.

82 See Holzer, *supra* n. 26, 154.

83 See Krista Nadakavukaren Schefer, *Social Regulation in the WTO. Trade Policy and International Legal Development* (Edward Elgar Publishing 2010), 170–172.

84 Wenzel, *supra* n. 81, 479; Stoll & Strack, 'Article XX lit. b GATT', in: Rüdiger Wolfrum, Peter-Tobias Stoll & Holger P. Hestermeyer (eds.), *WTO –*

general objective of internalising environmental costs would fall under GATT Article XX(b).

In the cases *US – Gasoline* and *Brazil – Retreaded Tyres* references to global environmental issues – such as air or climate change – suggest that GATT Article XX(b) may be read in a broad way. In *US – Gasoline* the Panel analysed 'a policy to reduce air pollution resulting from the consumption of gasoline' under GATT Article XX(b).[85] In *Brazil – Retreaded Tyres* the Appellate Body made an indirect reference to the issue of climate change in analysing the question of whether Brazil's import ban on retreaded tyres met the objective under GATT Article XX(b). Indeed, the Appellate Body recognised that 'the results obtained from certain actions – for instance, measures adopted to attenuate global warming and climate change … can only be evaluated with the benefit of time'.[86] Therefore, the necessity test could 'consist of quantitative projections in the future, or qualitative reasoning based on a set of hypotheses that are tested and supported by sufficient evidence'.[87]

The same reasoning as that described above in relation to GATT Article XX(a) should apply as far as the necessity test is concerned: 'Does the measure contribute to the achievement of the objective laid down in GATT Article XX(b) in the light of the interests at stake?'[88] If so, 'Are there other reasonably available less trade restrictive alternatives to achieve the objective?'[89] In the case *EC – Tariff Preferences* the Panel considered that the EU drug regime was not 'necessary', taking into account the reasonable available alternatives that the European Communities could have used in order to achieve the objectives of the drug arrangements.[90] Among these alternatives, the Panel referred to the possibility of providing 'financial and technical assistance, combined with multilaterally negotiated tariff reductions'.[91] A similar argument could be used to reject the use of GATT Article XX(b) in order to justify environmental BTAs. For example, it could be argued that environmental

Trade in Goods, Max Planck Commentaries on World Trade Law (Martinus Nijhoff Publishers 2011, Vol. 5), 507.

85 WTO, Panel Report, *US – Gasoline*, para. 6.21.

86 WTO, Appellate Body Report, Brazil – Measures Affecting Imports of Retreaded Tyres, 3 December 2007, WT/DS332/AB/R (*Brazil – Retreaded Tyres*), para. 151. See, however, WTO, Panel Report, *Brazil – Retreaded Tyres*, para. 7.46.

87 WTO, Appellate Body Report, *Brazil – Retreaded Tyres*, para. 151.

88 *Ibid*, para. 182.

89 *Ibid.*, para. 156.

90 WTO, Panel Report, *EC – Tariff Preferences*, paras. 7.221–7.223.

91 *Ibid.*, para. 7.223.

BTAs are not the 'least WTO-inconsistent' alternative to foster environmental protection. Moreover, in the case *US – Gasoline*, the Panel suggested that less trade-restrictive measures could not be ruled out because they were not as easy to implement.[92] Countries should therefore carefully design their environmental BTAs and avoid designing the tax in a more trade-restrictive way, even when the objective is to make its application easier from an administrative viewpoint. For example, a tax based on the carbon content of products could be easier to administer when the carbon content of imported products is defined by reference to predetermined average carbon amounts than when the carbon content of imported products is assessed based on a carbon certificate submitted by exporters. From a trade perspective, however, the second method could be considered less restrictive and therefore more likely to be justified under GATT Article XX(a) or Article XX(b).

Environmental BTAs aimed at avoiding that the legislator be discouraged from adopting or maintaining environmental policies at the domestic level could also face difficulties in meeting the necessity test. In the case of energy taxes, it could be argued that less restrictive alternatives exist, for example exemptions for energy-intensive industries.[93] Finally, in a similar way as under GATT Article XX(a), environmental BTAs aimed at encouraging other countries to adopt higher levels of environmental policies would likely fall short of the necessity test. Such BTAs would not contribute to the objective of limiting the consumption of products from polluting countries since such tax measures do not ban the products from 'environmentally unfriendly countries' but merely subjects them to higher levels of taxes.[94]

In a similar way as under GATT Article XX(a), the question arises as to whether PPM measures may fall under GATT Article XX(b). The arguments put forward are pretty much the same as under GATT Article XX(a). As such, the question is highly political and reflects the preference given either to a 'freer' or 'fairer' trade. Moreover, the debate relies

---

92 WTO, Panel Report, *US – Gasoline*, para. 6.26.

93 This argument could nevertheless be criticised since exemption measures do not permit the same goal to be pursued as environmental BTAs imposed on imported products.

94 Moreover, the measure would likely fall short of the requirements under the chapeau of GATT Art. XX (*infra*). The nexus between the objective of the measures and the products concerned would also likely be considered too loose (see WTO, Appellate Body Report, United States – Import Prohibition of Certain Shrimp and Shrimp Products, 12 October 1998, WT/DS58/AB/R (*US – Shrimp*), para. 133).

on (political) arguments concerning the prohibition on infringing other countries' sovereignty by adopting extraterritorial measures based on PPMs.[95]

6.2.1.2.1.3 GATT ARTICLE XX(G) GATT Article XX(g) pertains to 'measures relating to the conservation of exhaustible natural resources if such measures are made effective in conjunction with restrictions on domestic production or consumption'. This provision is often referred to in conjunction with GATT Article XX(b) in cases related to environmental issues.

As for GATT Article XX(b), the wording of GATT Article XX(g) has been subject to discussion. In *US – Shrimp* the Appellate Body favoured a dynamic interpretation of the expression 'exhaustible natural resources', considering that this expression 'must be read by a treaty interpreter in the light of contemporary concerns of the community of nations about the protection and conservation of the environment'.[96] The question remains, however, as to whether measures aimed at mitigating global environmental challenges such as climate change or measures aimed at the general objective of internalisation of environmental costs may fall under GATT Article XX(g).[97] The *US – Shrimp* case does not solve this issue as the legal question that was at stake was to determine whether the terms 'exhaustible natural resources' could include 'living natural resources' such as sea turtles. This legal question does not help to answer the question as to whether measures to mitigate climate change could be covered by GATT Article XX(g). The facts in the cases *US – Taxes on Automobiles* and *US – Gasoline* more directly relate to the issue of climate change. In these cases, the disputed measures concerning the conservation of carbon fuels (*US – Taxes on Automobiles)* and the

---

[95] See GATT, Panel Report, *US – Tuna (EEC)*, paras. 5.31–5.33 & para. 5.38 (unadopted). See the comments made by Schefer, *supra* n. 83, 184. See also Sharizal Mohd Zin & Ashraf U. Sarah Kazi, 'An analysis of customary international law and the importance of dispute settlement: a study of environmental law exceptions under Article XX' (2011) 7(1) Macquarie Journal of International and Comparative Environmental Law 39.

[96] WTO, Appellate Body Report, *US – Shrimp*, para. 129. See also para. 130.

[97] See Matz-Lück & Wolfrum, 'Article XX lit. g GATT', in: Rüdiger Wolfrum, Peter-Tobias Stoll & Holger P. Hestermeyer (eds.), *WTO – Trade in Goods*, Max Planck Commentaries on World Trade Law (Martinus Nijhoff Publishers 2011, Vol. 5), 550–551. See also Eichenberg, *supra* n. 47, 343–344.

conservation of clean air (*US – gasoline)* were analysed under GATT Article XX(g).[98]

In contrast to GATT Article XX(a) and XX(b), GATT Article XX(g) does not include a necessity test. Under GATT Article XX(g), the measures should *relate* to the conservation of exhaustible natural resources. In the case law, the 'relationship requirement' between the measure at stake and the objective of conservation of exhaustible natural resources has been interpreted to mean that the measure 'should be primarily aimed at'[99] the conservation of exhaustible natural resources or that there should exist a 'close and genuine relationship of ends and means'.[100] Although this 'relationship requirement' seems less strict than the necessity requirement, the question also arises under GATT Article XX(g) as to whether measures based on PPMs would meet this requirement or whether such measures would be deemed not to have a 'close and genuine relationship with the goal of conservation of exhaustible natural resources'.[101] In that regard, environmental BTAs aimed at preventing pollution leakage – including those aimed at avoiding that the legislator be discouraged from adopting or maintaining environmental policies at the domestic level as well as environmental BTAs aimed at encouraging other countries to adopt higher levels of environmental policies – could fall short of this test. It could indeed be argued that these measures are not primarily aimed at an environmental objective but are rather based on economic considerations.[102]

In addition to the 'relationship requirement', GATT Article XX(g) finally requires that the 'measures are made effective in conjunction with restrictions on domestic production or consumption'. In *US – Gasoline* the Appellate Body considered that this requirement meant that 'the measures concerned impose restrictions, not just in respect of imported gasoline but also with respect to domestic gasoline'.[103] In contrast to the NT principle under GATT Article III, the GATT Article XX(g) requirement seems to be less restrictive: the idea is that an 'even-handedness'

---

[98] GATT, Panel Report, *US – Taxes on Automobiles*, para. 3.314; WTO, Panel Report, *US – Gasoline*, paras. 6.36–6.37.

[99] GATT, Panel Report, Canada – Measures affecting exports of unprocessed herring and salmon, 22 March 1988, L/6268, BISD 35S/98 (*Canada – Herring and Salmon)*, para. 4.6; WTO, Appellate Body Report, *US – Gasoline*, 19.

[100] WTO, Appellate Body Report, *US – Shrimp*, para. 129. See also paras. 136–137.

[101] See GATT, *US – Tuna (EEC)*, para. 5.26.

[102] See McLure, *supra* n. 26, 272.

[103] WTO, Appellate Body Report, *US – Gasoline*, paras. 20–21.

should exist in the imposition of a measure.[104] This requirement should not be a problem in the framework of environmental BTAs, whose objective is to complement domestic environmental policies.

6.2.1.2.2 GATT Article XX chapeau In addition to the requirements derived from GATT Article XX, paragraphs (a) to (j), the disputed measures should meet the requirement laid down in the chapeau of this provision.[105] Measures only benefit from the exception provision of GATT Article XX when they are not 'applied in a manner which would constitute a means of arbitrary or unjustifiable discrimination between countries where the same conditions prevail, or a disguised restriction on international trade'.[106] The case law surrounding GATT Article XX provides examples of measures that have been found in violation of the chapeau. These examples help in establishing some good practices in relation to GATT Article XX.

First, WTO members should favour cooperation over trade-restrictive measures.[107] When a country has the possibility of negotiating a bilateral or multilateral agreement instead of adopting a trade-restrictive measure, it should do so. Since the best option to mitigate global environmental challenges is always through international cooperation, this requirement could be a problem in the case of environmental BTAs. In the *US – Shrimp* case the Appellate Body considered that the fact that 'the United States negotiated seriously with some, but not with other Members' had an unjustifiable discriminatory effect, in particular with regard to the resulting unilateral character of the US import ban.[108] Countries that wish to adopt environmental BTAs should therefore seriously negotiate with all members concerned.

Second, WTO members should take into account the extent to which trade-restrictive measures would affect foreign producers.[109] In other words, WTO members should avoid measures with a 'coercive effect on the specific policy decisions made by foreign governments', namely

---

[104] *Ibid.* The Appellate Body also notes that '... the second clause of Article XX(g) speaks disjunctively of "domestic production *or* consumption"'.

[105] See Lorand Bartels, 'The Chapeau of Article XX GATT: A New Interpretation' (2014) University of Cambridge, Legal Studies Research Paper Series No. 40.

[106] GATT Art. XX, chapeau.

[107] WTO, Appellate Body Report, *US – Gasoline*, 28; WTO, Appellate Body Report, *US – Shrimp*, paras. 171–172.

[108] WTO, Appellate Body Report, *US – Shrimp*, para. 172.

[109] WTO, Appellate Body Report, *US – Gasoline*, para. 28.

measures that require other members to adopt 'essentially the same policy' as they apply domestically.[110] With regard to environmental BTAs, countries should make sure that taxes are not designed in such a way that exporting countries are obliged to follow certain PPMs in order to benefit from the lowest tax rates. The design of the tax should allow enough flexibility for foreign producers and exporters to develop their own PPMs and benefit from the lowest tax rates as soon as the environmental impact corresponds to the levels that open the door to the application for these lowest tax rates. Similarly, the certification procedure should not arbitrarily discriminate against exporters.[111]

Third, WTO members should pay attention to the coherence of their legal framework.[112] In *Brazil – Retreaded Tyres* the Panel considered that the import ban was applied in a discriminatory manner because Mercosur members were exempt from the ban. The Appellate Body considered that the import ban amounted to arbitrary or unjustifiable discrimination under the chapeau of GATT Article XX because the Mercosur exemption had 'no rational connection' to the objectives pursued by the import ban.[113] Consequently, countries that wish to adopt environmental BTAs should also pay attention to the coherence of their tax system. Preferably, they should avoid their tax system including measures that encourage polluting behaviour.[114]

The reference in the chapeau to 'countries where the same conditions prevail' suggests that GATT Article XX allows the justification of differentiated taxes that could otherwise be contrary to GATT Article I. Therefore, environmental BTAs designed in such a way that developing countries would face lower taxes could be deemed compatible with the chapeau of GATT Article XX.[115] Even more, equal treatment of unequal situations could be considered contrary to the requirement of the chapeau

---

110 WTO, Appellate Body Report, *US – Shrimp*, para. 161.

111 *Ibid.*, paras. 180–184.

112 A lack of coherence could also imply that a measure is not deemed 'necessary'. See GATT, Panel Report, Thailand – Restrictions on importation of internal and internal taxes on cigarettes, 7 November 1990, DS10/R, BISD 37S/200 (*Thailand – Cigarettes*), para. 81.

113 WTO, Appellate Body Report, *Brazil – Retreaded Tyres*, paras. 227–229.

114 See Simonetta Zarrilli, 'Domestic Taxation of Energy Products and Multilateral Trade Rules: Is This a Case of Unlawful Discrimination?' (2003) 37(2) Journal of World Trade 359, 385.

115 See Hillman, *supra* n. 17, 15. See also Holzer, *supra* n. 26, 173; McLure, *supra* n. 26, 276.

of GATT Article XX. This requirement differs from the MFN principle under GATT Article I, which requires that all countries benefit from the same treatment.[116]

6.2.2 Other Non-WTO Relevant Legal Provisions

Aside from WTO law, other legal branches should be considered in the legal analysis of environmental BTAs, including principles of international public law, environmental law and tax law. The impact of environmental, tax and international public law may be both positive and negative, though negative impacts may often be tempered. As this section addresses a variety of legal issues, the objective is not to propose an exhaustive analysis of the principles of international public law, environmental law and tax law that could limit the possibility of adopting environmental BTAs. The goal of this section is rather to quickly review some of the arguments that could be used to support or criticise proposals in favour of environmental BTAs.[117]

6.2.2.1 Issues of international public law

The debate surrounding environmental BTAs usually features arguments related to international public law. Environmental BTAs are described as unilateral, extraterritorial measures that would infringe principles of international public law such as the sovereignty principle. A closer look at principles of international public law, however, illustrates that they do not forbid the adoption of environmental BTAs. The argument that unilateral measures should be avoided is based on a political statement – or, at most, on soft law principles – rather than on binding principles of international public law. In other words, international public law does not serve as a legal basis for arguments against the adoption of environmental BTAs.

---

[116] See WTO, Appellate Body Report, *US – Shrimp*, para. 165. See also Holzer, *supra* n. 26, 169–173; McLure, *supra* n. 26, 276; Veel, *supra* n. 47, 790.

[117] For a broad overview on these issues, see i.a. Geert van Calster, *International & EU Trade Law. The Environmental Challenge* (Cameron May 2000), 199–303.

6.2.2.1.1 'Unilateral', 'extraterritorial' measures under international public law[118] Models of environmental BTAs are unilateral measures, which do not result from an international agreement.[119] Even though international non-binding agreements recommend avoiding the adoption of unilateral measures that may affect third countries, no binding principle of international public law generally prohibits the adoption of unilateral measures, even though some MEAs recommend mitigating global environmental issues at the international level rather than unilaterally.[120]

Aside from their unilateral character, environmental BTAs are often described as 'extraterritorial measures' due to the fact that their design may include references to situations that took place abroad, which are assumed to lead to extraterritorial effects.[121] In comparison to the legal claims regarding the unilateral nature of environmental BTAs, the claims regarding their extraterritorial character are more controversial.[122] So far, no clear rules permit a definition of which measures fall under the category of 'extraterritorial measures' that are contrary to international public law.[123] References to the extraterritorial character of environmental BTAs usually imply that such measures would violate the

---

[118] This section has been inspired by Alice Pirlot, 'Environmental Border Tax Adjustments (BTAs): A Critical Analysis', in: Jan De Bruyne, Michaël de Potter de ten Broeck & Isabelle Van Hiel (eds.), *Policy Within and Through Law* (Maklu 2015), 107–120.

[119] See Christiane R. Conrad, *Processes and Production Methods (PPMs) in WTO Law. Interfacing Trade and Social Goals* (OUP 2012), 108–109.

[120] See WTO, Panel Report, *US – Shrimp*, para. 7.61. Bradly J. Condon & Tapen Sinha, *The Role of Climate Change in Global Economic Governance* (OUP 2013), 41–50, spec. 46.

[121] *Contra:* see the authors mentioned by Vranes, *supra* n. 67, 159–160. See also the very interesting contributions of Nollkaemper and Van Calster: André Nollkaemper, 'Rethinking States' Rights to Promote Extra-territorial Environmental Values', in: Friedl Weiss, Erik M.G. Denters, Paul J.I.M. de Waart (eds.), *International Economic Law With a Human Face* (Kluwer Law International 1998), 175–202; Geert Van Calster, 'Amerikanen, eskimo's en konijnen – extraterritorialiteit en milieuwetgeving', in: Kurt Deketelaere, Michael Faure & Gaëtan Verhoosel (eds.), *Grensoverschrijdende milieuproblemen: uitdagingen voor de nationale en internationale rechtsorde* (Intersentia 1998), 112–123.

[122] See Nollkaemper, *supra* n. 121, 177.

[123] See Cedric Ryngaert, 'Jurisdiction in International Law. United States and European Perspectives', Ph.D. Dissertation, Katholieke Universiteit Leuven, 12 February 2007, available at <https://lirias.kuleuven.be/bitstream/1979/911/2/doctoraat.pdf> (accessed 2 November 2015), 19–20. See also Francesco Francioni, 'Chapter VI. Extraterritorial Application of Environmental Law', in: Karl Matthias Meessen (ed.), *Extraterritorial Jurisdiction in Theory and Practice*

territoriality principle under international public law. Measures that apply to extraterritorial situations or that have extraterritorial effects are however not *per se* incompatible with international public law.[124]

Under international public law, one of the main legal issues surrounding the adoption of environmental BTAs may be summarised as follows: 'Is a state, under international public law, allowed to adopt taxes on imported products that are defined – at least partially – based on situations that took place abroad?' This question amounts to the scope of states' prescriptive jurisdiction under international public law. No clear answer exists and the literature is divided into two main views.[125]

Under least restrictive views, states are free to adopt any type of legislation, including 'extraterritorial legislation'. Even though states may not be able to enforce legislation beyond their own territory, their possibility to prescribe extraterritorial rules should not be restricted.[126] As environmental BTAs are imposed on imported products, which, by definition, are found on the territory of the implementing country, countries would not face difficulties in enforcing such taxes. Indeed, countries would not have to enforce BTAs on other states' territory.

In contrast, under the most restrictive views, states should not be able to regulate extraterritorial matters. Jurisdiction should be limited to matters with which a state has a sufficient connection, for example a territorial connection (i.e. the so-called 'territorial nexus').[127] Environmental BTAs could be considered to lack territorial connection with the

---

(Kluwer Law International 1996), 122; André Müller, Christoph Böhringer, Thomas Cottier, Kateryna Holzer & René Matteotti, 'Border Tax Adjustments. Can Energy and Carbon Taxes be Adjusted at the Border?' (2013) Ecoplan, World Trade Institute, Universität Zürich, 81.

[124] See Ryngaert, *supra* n. 123, 19–20. See also the concept of 'territorial extension' used by Scott: Joanne Scott, 'The New EU "Extraterritoriality"' (2014) 51(5) Common Market Law Review 1343. See also Joanne Scott, 'Territorial Sovereignty and Territorial Extension in an Inter-Connected World', in: Richard Rawlings, Peter Leyland & Alison Young (eds.), *Sovereignty and the Law: Domestic, European and International Perspectives* (OUP 2013), 269–285; Joanne Scott, 'Extraterritoriality and Territorial Extension in EU Law' (2004) 62(1) American Journal of Comparative Law 87, 90.

[125] Ryngaert, *supra* n. 123, 32–33.

[126] Cedric Ryngaert refers to the Lotus case (Ryngaert, *supra* n. 123, 35). See Permanent Court of International Justice, Affaire du 'Lotus', Publications of the Permanent Court of International Justice, Series A. No. 10, 7 September 1927, 18–19.

[127] See e.g. WTO, Submission by New Zealand, Item 1: The relationship between the provisions of the multilateral trading system and trade measures for

importing countries given that they apply to imported products, taking into account how products have been processed and produced abroad.[128] Indeed, the tax would be designed in such a way that products would be taxed according to their overall environmental impact, including their environmental effects derived from production activities in third countries. For this reason, the territorial link between environmental BTAs and the implementing country could be considered insufficient. Under this view, environmental BTAs would be described as taxes on producers rather than as taxes on products. Counter-arguments could, however, support the view that environmental BTAs have sufficient territorial connection with the implementing country. On the one hand, BTAs are imposed on imported products when they are located on the territory of the implementing country, which shows that a sufficient territorial connection exists between the products and the implementing country.[129] On the other hand, the fact that environmental BTAs aim to mitigate global pollution, which is a transnational issue that affects the international community as a whole, would also contribute to the nexus that exists between such taxes and the implementing country.[130] These counter-arguments would support the claim that possible extraterritorial effects of environmental BTAs do not make these taxes incompatible with principles of international public law.

The two views described above reflect two conflicting views on the concept of territorial sovereignty.[131] Given the cross-border character of

---

environmental purposes including those pursuant to multilateral environmental agreements (MEAs), 15 February 1996, WT/CTE/W/20, para. 80. See Bradly J. Condon, *Environmental Sovereignty and the WTO. Trade Sanctions and International Law* (Transnational Publishers 2006), 247.

[128] See Amelia Porges & Joel P. Trachtman, 'Robert Hudec and Domestic Regulation: The Resurrection of Aim and Effects' (2003) 37(4) Journal of World Trade 783, 798.

[129] See Conrad, *supra* n. 119, 106–113 & 275–281.

[130] See Nielsen, *supra* n. 75, 328: '… the notion of common concern in relation to biodiversity can establish such nexus; i.e., all countries, all humans, have a legitimate interest in the preservation of biological diversity, which *per se* gives them an interest strong enough to justify the utilization of NPR-PPMs'.

[131] There is no single definition of the concept of territorial sovereignty. See i.a. Tanja E. Aalberts, *Constructing Sovereignty between Politics and Law* (Routledge 2012); John H. Jackson, *Sovereignty, the WTO, and Changing Fundamentals of International Law* (CUP 2006); Richard Joyce, *Competing Sovereignties* (Routledge 2012); John H. Jackson, 'Sovereignty: Outdated Concept or New Approaches', in: Wenhua Shan, Penelope Simons & Dalvinder Singh (eds.), *Redefining Sovereignty in International Economic Law* (Hart

most environmental issues, the claim of one state to regulate polluting activities on its territory may clash with the claim of other states to exercise exclusive competence on their territory.[132] Therefore, arguments in favour of the adoption of environmental BTAs may indirectly give preference to the sovereignty of the importing country.[133] The importing country is free to define the design on its taxes on imported products, regardless of whether it could affect the exporting country.[134] Indeed, environmental BTAs could have extraterritorial effects in exporting countries by encouraging producers to produce in a more environmentally friendly way or 'oblige' exporting countries to adopt stricter environmental regulations in relation to production so as to avoid the products they export being subject to high tax burdens.[135] In contrast,

---

Publishing 2008); Stephen D. Krasner, *Sovereignty: Organized Hypocrisy* (Princeton University Press 1999). One definition often referred to is one found in the Island of Palmas case (Netherlands, USA):

> Territorial sovereignty, as has already been said, involves the exclusive right to display the activities of a State. This right has as corollary a duty: the obligation to protect within the territory the rights of other States, in particular their right to integrity and inviolability in peace and in war, together with the rights which each State may claim for its nationals in foreign territory.

(UN, Island of Palmas case (Netherlands, USA), 4 April 1928, Report of International Arbitral Awards, Vol. II, 839).

[132] Gunther Handl, 'Territorial Sovereignty and the Problem of Transnational Pollution' (1975) 69 American Journal of International Law 50, 55. See also Joseph A. Camilleri & Jim Falk, *The End of Sovereignty? The Politics of a Shrinking and Fragmenting World* (Edward Elgar Publishing 1992), 185; Conrad, *supra* n. 119, 106–108; Francioni, *supra* n. 123, 132; Ramon Jeffery, *The Impact of State Sovereignty on Global Trade and International Taxation* (Kluwer Law International 1968, 1999), 20–21; Fiona Macmillan, *WTO and the Environment* (Sweet & Maxwell 2001), 9; Ryngaert, *supra* n. 123, 19–20; Edith Brown Weiss, 'Environment and Trade as Partners in Sustainable Development: A Commentary' (1992) 86(4) The American Journal of International Law 728, 730.

[133] On this topic, see Douglas A. Kysar, 'Preferences for Processes: The Process/Product Distinction and the Regulation of Consumer Choice' (2004) 118(2) Harvard Law Review 525–641 (see the reference to the 'sovereignty of consumers').

[134] See Martha J. Rutsel Silvestre, 'Extraterritorial Taxation in International Law', in: Karl M. Meessen (ed.), *Extraterritorial Jurisdiction in Theory and Practice* (Kluwer Law International 1996), 23.

[135] This does not mean that the tax will be targeted at products from certain countries in violation of the MFN principle. BTAs could tax imported products based on their emission level, which has not yet been internalised (either based

arguments against the adoption of environmental BTAs with extraterritorial effects give priority to the sovereignty of the exporting country. In this hypothesis, the importing country is forbidden to adopt taxes on imported products that are based on extraterritorial elements, such as the way a product has been produced, given that such taxes could have extraterritorial effects.[136] When preference is given to the sovereignty of exporting countries, the regulatory freedom of countries to tax consumption based on environmental considerations is much limited.

Overall, good arguments exist to defend the view that environmental BTAs are not contrary to international public law, even though they may have extraterritorial effects. So far, the case law has not openly ruled on the question of whether or not environmental BTAs would violate principles of international public law due to their possible extraterritorial effects. However, non-fiscal environmental measures with extraterritorial effects have been analysed by the WTO Appellate Body and the ECJ.[137] In the *US – Shrimp* case the Appellate Body referred to the nexus between the US and turtles that are protected by a US ban on imports of certain shrimps, considering that 'there is a sufficient nexus between the migratory and endangered marine populations involved and the United States for purposes of Article XX(g)'.[138] Moreover, at the EU level, the ECJ has ruled on the extraterritorial character of the inclusion of the aviation sector into the EU ETS. In this case, the ECJ considered that the measure did not infringe the principle of territoriality or the sovereignty of third states as the aircrafts that would fall under the EU ETS 'are physically in the territory of one of the Member States of the European Union and are thus subject on that basis to the unlimited jurisdiction of the European Union'.[139] In her opinion on this case, Advocate General Kokott emphasised that the fact that a measure takes

---

on the domestic legislation of the exporting country or based on a personal statement of the exporting enterprise).

[136] See Müller, Böhringer, Cottier, Holzer & Matteotti, *supra* n. 123, 82. See also Geert Van Calster, 'Animal Welfare, the EU and the World Trade Organization – Member States' Sovereignty between a Rock and a Hard Place?', in: Anton Vedder (ed.), *The World Trade Organisation and Concerns Regarding Animals and Nature* (Wolf Legal Publishers 2003), 61–85 (see the conclusion).

[137] The two cases analysed below are also analysed by Condon & Sinha, *supra* n. 120, 41–50.

[138] WTO, Appellate Body Report, *US – Shrimp*, para. 133. See however, GATT, *US – Tuna (EEC)*, para. 5.24.

[139] ECJ, *The Air Transport Association of America and Others*, 21 December 2011, Case C-366/10, para. 125. See also Opinion of Advocate General Kokott delivered on 6 October 2011 in case C-366/10, para. 148.

account of 'events that take place ... on the territory of third countries' does not make it 'extraterritorial'.[140]

6.2.2.1.2 Exceptions under international public law International public law provides for circumstances under which a state may adopt measures that would otherwise violate its international obligations. In other words, under the hypothesis that environmental BTAs would be found contrary to international public law, such taxes could still be justified if their adoption relates to one of the circumstances that preclude their wrongfulness.[141]

Among these circumstances, countermeasures could serve to support the adoption of environmental BTAs under the hypothesis that such taxes would otherwise be considered contrary to international public law.[142] States are indeed allowed to adopt non-forcible countermeasures in response to violations of obligations of international public law.[143] In the case of environmental BTAs, it could be difficult to prove that the absence of environmental action by third countries amounts to an 'international wrongful act'.[144] One possibility, however, would be to argue that countermeasures in the form of environmental BTAs may be adopted as a response to countries' violation of the principle of good neighbourliness (in Latin *sic utere tuo ut alienum non laedas*).[145] The *sic*

---

140 Opinion of Advocate General Kokott delivered on 6 October 2011 in case C-366/10, para. 147.

141 See UN GA, Responsibility of States for internationally wrongful acts, 12 December 2001, A/RES/56/83.

142 See e.g. Holzer, *supra* n. 26, 157–158.

143 See Sarah H. Cleveland, 'Human Rights Sanctions and the World Trade Organization', in: Francesco Francioni (ed.), *Environment, Human Rights and International Trade* (Hart Publishing 2001), 199, 210.

144 In relation to climate change, see Hendrik A. Strydon, 'The Legal Principles Relating to Climate Change', Encyclopedia of Life Support System, available at <http://www.eolss.net/sample-chapters/c14/E1-36-10-00.pdf> (accessed 2 November 2015). See also Jaye Ellis, 'Liability for International Environmental Harm' (2013) Oxford Bibliographies, available at http://www.oxfordbibliographies.com/view/document/obo-9780199796953/obo-9780199796953-0017.xml (accessed 2 November 2015).

145 See Art. 74 of the UN Charter, Principle 21 of the Stockholm declaration (UN, Report of the United Nations Conference on the Human Environment, Stockholm, 5–16 June 1972, A/CONF.48/14/Rev.1). See also Holzer, *supra* n. 26; Michael Jeffery QC, 'Environmental Imperatives in a Globalised World: The Ecological Impact of Liberalising Trade' (2007) 7 Macquarie Law Journal 25, 47; John Snape & Jeremy de Souza, *Environmental Taxation Law: Policy, Contexts & Practice* (Ashgate Publishing 2006), 192.

utere tuo principle – which means that states should use their property without injuring that of other states – has indeed often been referred to in cases related to transboundary pollutions (e.g. water pollution in watercourses that flow into different countries).[146] A similar argument could be made in relation to global environmental challenges when countries do not respect their commitments under MEAs or refuse to take adequate action to mitigate global environmental issues.[147] In 2012 a group of small island states requested an advisory opinion of the ICJ on the environmental obligations of states to avoid GHG emissions being emitted under its jurisdiction leading to damage in other states.[148] Even though the small island states have not been able to submit the question to the ICJ, it illustrates the support of some countries for the recognition of climate obligations under international public law. Finally, aside from the case of countermeasures, necessity could provide another ground for precluding the wrongfulness of environmental BTAs under international public law.[149] Necessity refers to exceptional situations 'where the only way a State can safeguard an essential interest threatened by a grave and imminent peril is, for the time being, not to perform some other international obligation of lesser weight or urgency'.[150] For example, the Russian government invoked necessity in support of a decree to protect

---

146 Aaron Schwabach, 'Transboundary Environmental Harm and State Responsibility: Customary International Law', Encyclopedia of Life Support Systems, available at <http://www.eolss.net/sample-chapters/c14/e1-36-02-02.pdf> (accessed 2 November 2015). Schwabach refers to three cases: the *Trail Smelter* arbitration case, the ICJ *Corfu Channel* case and the *Lac Lanoux* arbitration.

147 See Ottavio Quirico, 'Primary Sovereign Rights or Secondary Environmental Duties? Critical International Law Issues Raised by the Extraterritorial Application of the EU Emission Trading System in the Aviation Sector', in: Christine Bakker & Francesco Francioni (eds.), *The EU, the US and Global Climate Governance* (Ashgate Publishing 2014), 152–156.

148 See UN, Press Conference on Request for International Court of Justice Advisory Opinion on Climate Change, available at <http://www.un.org/press/en/2012/120203_ICJ.doc.htm> (accessed 2 November 2015). See also Douglas A. Kysar, 'Climate Change and the International Court of Justice' (2013) Yale Law School, Public Law Research Paper No. 315.

149 See Art. 25 of UN GA, Responsibility of States for internationally wrongful acts, 12 December 2001, A/RES/56/83.

150 See UN Articles on the Responsibility of States for Internationally Wrongful Acts, UN Legislatives Series (2012), ST/LEG/SER.B/25, available at <http://legal.un.org/legislativeseries/documents/Book25/Book25.pdf> (accessed 3 December 2015), Commentary Art. 25, para. 1, 167.

fur seals in the high seas.[151] With regard to global environmental challenges, it is unlikely that this ground is accepted as a justification for the adoption of environmental BTAs. Indeed, necessity only permits preclusion of the wrongful character of an act when it 'is the only way for the State to safeguard an essential interest against a grave and imminent peril'.[152] Despite the significant negative impact of global environmental issues, it is unlikely that such issues are considered to amount to 'imminent peril'.

6.2.2.2 Principles of environmental law

In addition to international trade law, international environmental law also contributes to the legal framework surrounding environmental BTAs.[153] Summarising, international environmental law plays a two-fold role in relation to environmentally related trade-restrictive measures, including environmental BTAs.

On the one hand, it confirms principles enunciated under international trade law by emphasising that environmental measures should not create new barriers to trade. In this case, international environmental law rejects the use of trade-restrictive measures to achieve environmental goals. In other words, environmental protection should be pursued through non-restrictive trade measures, such as, for example, MEAs or domestic regulations. On the other hand, international environmental law supports the adoption of environmental BTAs by reinforcing the argument that such taxes comply with GATT Article XX. MEAs indeed illustrate that a consensus exists on the need to protect some of the environmental issues that environmental BTAs aim at solving.

These two contradictory effects of international environmental law on the legal analysis of trade-restrictive measures highlight the two differing ideological perspectives on the relationship between environmental and trade policies. Environmental and international trade law may be seen

---

151 *Ibid.* Commentary, Art. 25, para. 6, 169.

152 Art. 25.1(a) of UN Articles on Responsibility of States for Internationally Wrongful Acts.

153 On the expression 'international environmental law', see Snape & de Souza, *supra* n. 145, 184. See also Winfried Lang, 'UN-Principles and International Environmental Law' (1999) 3 Max Planck UNYB 157; Nicolas Jan Schrijver, 'Sovereignty Over Natural Resources: Balancing Rights and Duties in an Interdependent World', Proefscrift Rijksuniversiteit Groningen, 2 March 1995, 218. For a broad overview on environmental principles, see Nicolas de Sadeleer, *Environmental Principles. From Political Slogans to Legal Rules* (OUP 2002).

either as mutually supportive (trade and environmental policies reinforce each other) or as representing conflicting values (environmental protection has a negative impact on international trade and vice versa).[154]

6.2.2.2.1 Limits to the adoption of environmental BTAs MEAs sometimes contain provisions that limit the possibility of adopting environmentally related trade-restrictive measures. These provisions often copy the language to be found in some provisions of the GATT or WTO agreements. They limit the possibilities for adopting environmental BTAs and influence their design by adding to the conditions that environmental BTAs should fulfil.

A first limit to be found in many MEAs is the requirement that environmental policies should not result in unnecessary restrictions to trade. Agenda 21 – the non-binding action plan that came out of the UN Conference on Environment and Development in 1992 – states as follows: 'Trade policy measures for environmental purposes should not constitute a means of arbitrary or unjustifiable discrimination or a disguised restriction on international trade.'[155] Similarly, the Kyoto Protocol provides that parties 'shall strive to implement policies and measures ... in such a way as to minimize adverse effects, including the adverse effects of climate change, effects on international trade, and social, environmental and economic impacts on other Parties ...'.[156]

Some MEAs also require countries to avoid unilateral action to mitigate environmental issues that are not limited to their territory, encouraging them to prefer international cooperation.[157] A first example is found in the Convention on Biological Diversity. Article 5 of the

---

[154] See John H. Jackson, 'World Trade Rules and Environmental Policies: Congruence or Conflict?' (1992) 49 Washington and Lee Law Review 1227; Jeffery, *supra* n. 145, 27; Kati Kulovesi, 'Climate Change and Trade: At the Intersection of Two International Legal Regimes', in: E.J. Hollo et Michael Mehling (eds.), *Climate Change and the Law* (Springer 2013), 419. See also Ernst-Ulrich Petersmann, 'International Trade Law and International Environmental Law: Environmental Taxes and Border Tax Adjustment in WTO Law and EC Law', in: Richard L. Revesz, Phillipe Sands & Richard B. Stewart (eds.), *Environmental Law, the Economy, and Sustainable Development* (CUP 2000), 150.

[155] UN, Agenda 21, points 2.22 (i) & 39.3(d). See also Principle 12 of the Rio Declaration.

[156] Art. 2.3. of the UN Kyoto Protocol to the United Nations Framework Convention on Climate Change, 1998 (hereafter, 'Kyoto Protocol').

[157] UN, Agenda 21. points 2.22 (i) and 39.3(d). See also Principle 12 of the Rio Declaration.

Convention reads as follows: 'Each Contracting Party shall, as far as possible and as appropriate, cooperate with other Contracting Parties, directly or, where appropriate, through competent international organizations, in respect of areas beyond national jurisdiction and on other matters of mutual interest, for the conservation and sustainable use of biological diversity.'[158] The UN Convention on the Law of the Sea offers a second example of a provision that encourages international action.[159] Article 118 of the Convention indeed requires states to 'cooperate with each other in the conservation and management of living resources in the areas of the high seas'.[160] A third example is Article 2(2) of the Kyoto Protocol, which requires parties to 'pursue limitation or reduction of emissions of greenhouse gases not controlled by the Montreal Protocol from aviation and marine bunker fuels, working through the International Civil Aviation Organization and the International Maritime Organization, respectively'.

In the EU aviation case, the ECJ was asked to determine whether the inclusion of the aviation sector into the EU rules on emissions trading was contrary to Article 2(2) of the Kyoto Protocol (because the EU had taken action unilaterally and not through the International Civil Aviation Organization).[161] The ECJ did not give a direct answer to the question, considering that Article 2(2) of the Kyoto Protocol was not 'unconditional and sufficiently precise so as to confer on individuals the right to rely on it'.[162] According to Advocate General Kokott, Article 2(2) of the Kyoto Protocol 'confines itself to regulating certain legal relationships between the Contracting Parties to the Kyoto Protocol'.[163] In other words, this article would not offer any procedural guarantee to individuals.[164] The aviation case supports the view that international agreements giving preference to cooperation over unilateral action have limited legal effect. As Advocate General Kokott pointed out in the aviation case,

---

158 Art. 5, UN Convention on Biological Diversity 1992.

159 See Steve Charnovitz, 'Environmental Trade Sanctions and the GATT: An Analysis of the Pelly Amendment on Foreign Environmental Practices' (1994) 9(3) American University International Law Review 751, 803: 'On the high seas, UNCLOS may be read as suggesting that conservation measures must be multilateral'.

160 Art. 118, UN Convention on the Law of the Sea, Part VII, Art. 118.

161 ECJ, *The Air Transport Association of America and Others*, 21 December 2011, Case C-366/10, para. 45.

162 *Ibid.*, para. 77.

163 Opinion of Advocate General Kokott, delivered on 6 October 2011 in Case C-366/10, para. 86.

164 *Ibid.*, para. 86.

such provisions have an institutional nature that does not create substantive rights. Therefore, it could easily be argued that they do not limit the possibility of states to adopt unilateral environmentally related trade measures. This conclusion finds support in the *US – Shrimp* case, which recognised the possibility for a WTO member to 'legitimately require, as a condition of access of certain products to its market, that exporting countries commit themselves to a regulatory programme deemed comparable to its own'.[165] However, based on the reasoning of the Appellate Body in *US – Shrimp*, WTO members should preferably make sure that they negotiate seriously with other WTO members before they adopt unilateral measures, such as environmental BTAs. Indeed, in the *US – Shrimp* case the Appellate Body considered that the fact that the US had not seriously negotiated with all WTO members exporting shrimps to the US amounted to an unjustifiable discrimination.[166]

A second limit to be found in many MEAs is the Common but Differentiated Responsibilities (CBDR) principle.[167] As its name indicates, this principle recognises a common responsibility to all in protecting the environment but also acknowledges that this responsibility should be shared, taking account of differences between states. In other words, developing and least-developed countries should not bear the same burden of responsibility as developed countries.[168]

Since the CBDR principle could be considered in conflict with MFN and NT principles, the question arises as to whether it applies to environmental BTAs and, if this is the case, whether it limits the adoption of such taxes (and to what extent).[169] Developing countries could indeed

---

[165] WTO, Art. 21.5 Panel Report, *US – Shrimp*, para. 5.103. See also WTO, Art. 21.5 Appellate Body Report, *US – Shrimp*, para. 124.

[166] WTO, Appellate Body Report, *US – Shrimp*, paras. 171–172. See Marceau & Trachtman, *supra* n. 67, 393.

[167] See Principle 7 of the Rio Declaration; Art. 3(1) of the UNFCCC; Art. 10 of the Kyoto Protocol. See also Duncan French, 'Developing States and International Environmental Law: The Importance of Differentiated Responsibilities' (2000) 49(1) The International and Comparative Law Quarterly 35–60; Shufan Sung, 'Border Tax Adjustments and Developing Countries: A Perspective from China' (2016) 21 Annual Survey of International & Comparative Law 149–176; Long Yingfeng, 'Challenges to China from Carbon Tax Border Adjustment under Global Climate Change and China's Answer' (2015) 3 China Legal Science 61, 72–76.

[168] See Gillian Moon, 'Trade and Equality: A Relationship to Discover' (2009) 12(3) Journal of International Economic Law 617–642.

[169] See Sarah Davidson Ladly, 'Border Carbon Adjustments, WTO-law and the Principle of Common but Differentiated Responsibilities' (2012) 12(1)

invoke this principle to contest the imposition of environmental BTAs on their products. Developed countries could, however, consider that the CBDR principle does not apply: environmental BTAs are not necessarily a means to increase the environmental responsibility borne by other countries. As long as environmental BTAs are not targeted at products from one specific country, it could always be argued that such taxes do not affect countries but producers or consumers. For example, environmental BTAs could be considered a legal instrument used to guarantee that domestic consumers bear the environmental costs of all the products they consume, regardless of where they are produced. Environmental BTAs are not necessarily a 'sanction' against exporting countries used to oblige them to taking their share of responsibility in respect to pollution derived from production. Moreover, developed countries could argue that the CBDR principle is a principle of soft law with no binding effect.[170] Following this argument, from a practical viewpoint, developing countries would not be able to introduce a complaint against a policy measure of a developed country that is deemed to be in violation of the CBDR principle under the assumption that this principle is an instrument of soft law. So far, MEAs have not established specific judicial bodies to settle disputes involving environmental matters.[171] Existing bodies such as the WTO dispute settlement system or the ICJ are not better prepared to recognise a violation of a principle of a soft law nature, such as the CBDR principle. Regarding the ICJ, it is unlikely that the Court would

---

International Environmental Agreements 63–84. See also the questions raised by Cosbey in Aaron Cosbey, 'Border Carbon Adjustment: Questions and Answers (But More of the Former)' (2009) Background paper produced for the 2009 International Trade Experts' Meeting (Toronto), available at <https://www.iisd.org/pdf/2009/bali_bcas_questions_answers.pdf> (accessed 2 November 2015), 8–9.

[170] Ladly, *supra* n. 169, 73; Pananya Larbprasertporn, 'The Interaction Between WTO Law and the Principle of Common but Differentiated Responsibilities in the Case of Climate-Related Border Tax Adjustments' (2014) 6(1) Goettingen Journal of International Law 145, 149–150. See also Jutta Brunnée & Stephen J. Toope, *Legitimacy and Legality in International Law. An Interactional Account*, Cambridge Studies in International and Comparative Law (CUP 2010), 152. See, however, the reasoning of Goyal on the concept of sustainable development in Anupam Goyal, *The WTO and International Environmental Law: Towards Conciliation* (OUP 2006), 52–61.

[171] See Dionysa-Theodora Avgerinopoulou, 'The Role of the International Judiciary in the Settlement of Environmental Disputes and Alternative Proposals for Strengthening International Environmental Adjudication', paper prepared for the 'Global Environmental Governance: the Post-Johannesburg Agenda', Yale Center for Environmental Law and Policy, 23–25 October 2003.

apply the CBDR principle, given that a soft law principle does not fall under the sources of law that the Court applies to decide disputes.[172] Furthermore, the Court is *a priori* only competent for 'cases which the parties refer to it', meaning that the defendant (i.e. the developed country accused of a violation of the CBDR principle) should accept the jurisdiction of the ICJ.[173] Regarding WTO dispute settlement bodies, a similar reasoning applies. Even though in the *US – Shrimp* case the Article 21.5 Panel Report contains a direct reference to the CBDR principle, this case did not, as such, find a violation of the principle. The concluding remarks of the case read as follows:

> The Panel urges Malaysia and the United States to cooperate fully in order to conclude as soon as possible an agreement which will permit the protection and conservation of sea turtles to the satisfaction of all interests involved and taking into account the principle that States have common but differentiated responsibilities to conserve and protect the environment.[174]

Therefore, the CBDR principle could be considered as a principle that should only have an effect on international environmental negotiations (in that developing countries should not be required to bear the same responsibility as developed countries) and not on domestic environmental policies adopted unilaterally. In other words, under this hypothesis, the CBDR principle would have no effect on the tax design of environmental BTAs.

Aside from the arguments against the application of the CBDR principle to environmental BTAs, many authors nevertheless consider that this principle would limit their adoption. References to the CBDR principle in the literature surrounding environmental BTAs may be understood as an indirect recognition of the binding effect of this

---

172 Art. 38, para. 1 of the Statute of the International Court of Justice. See also Harmut Hillgenberg, 'A Fresh Look at Soft Law' (1999) 10(3) European Journal of International Law 499–515. See however Xiaoqin Zhu & Jinlong He, 'International Court of Justice's Impact on International Environmental Law: Focusing on the *Pulp Mills* Case' (2012) 23(1) Yearbook of International Environmental Law 106, 109.

173 Art. 36 of the Statute of the International Court of Justice.

174 WTO, Art. 21.5 Panel Report, *US – Shrimp*, para. 7.2. On the role of non-binding principles in the interpretation of WTO law, see Isabelle Van Damme, *Treaty Interpretation by the WTO Appellate Body* (OUP 2009), 369.

principle, most likely as a customary principle of international law.[175] Under this assumption – where the CBDR is considered part of the legal framework surrounding environmental BTAs – the CBDR would limit their adoption in two different ways, depending on whether tax models that differentiate between developed and developing countries are considered to violate the WTO law non-discrimination principle. Under the first hypothesis, the GATT non-discrimination principle is interpreted in such a way that it allows differences between developed and developing countries to be taken into account. Although WTO law clearly recognises the need to take into account the specific situation of developing countries, it is doubtful that GATT Article I could be interpreted as permitting differentiation between developed and developing countries outside of the application of specific regimes such as under the enabling clause.[176] Some authors, however, consider that the reference to 'arbitrary or unjustifiable discrimination' under GATT Article XX permits differences to be taken between developed and developing countries.[177] Under this hypothesis, WTO law would not constrain countries in designing proposals in favour of environmental BTAs that explicitly implement the CBDR principle. For example, products from developing countries could be exempted from environmental BTAs or subject to a lower rate. Second, in the case where WTO law is interpreted more strictly, as generally prohibiting differentiation between developed and developing countries, countries wishing to adopt environmental BTAs would face difficulties in complying both with the WTO law non-discrimination principle as well as with the CBDR principle. One proposal could be to design BTAs so that they apply both to products from developed as well as to products from developing countries (following the MFN principle) while allocating the tax revenue to an international fund dedicated to projects taking place in developing countries.[178]

---

[175] Art. 38, para. 1(c) of the Statute of the International Court of Justice. See, for example, the direct reference to the CBDR principle in recital 25 of Directive 2009/29/EC.

[176] Larbprasertporn, *supra* n. 170, 152–153 & 162–163.

[177] Ladly, *supra* n. 169, 79. She also refers to Pauwelyn (Joost Pauwelyn, 'US Federal Climate Policy and Competitiveness Concerns: the Limits and Options of International Trade Law' (2007) Nicholas Institute for Environmental Policy Solutions, Duke University, NI WP 07-02, 39). *Contra:* Larbprasertporn, *supra* n. 170, 165–169.

[178] See Frank Biermann, Frédéric Böhm, Rainer Brohm, Susanne Dröge & Harald Trabold, 'The Polluter Pays Principle under WTO Law: The Case of National Energy Policy Instruments' (2003) Environmental Research of the Federal Ministry of the Environment, Nature Conservation and Nuclear Safety,

Third, besides the CBDR principle, general principles of environmental law such as the polluter-pays principle could also limit the design of environmental BTAs by requiring that the tax be designed in such a way that the person who economically supports the tax burden is the 'polluter'.[179] The Rio Declaration contains a direct reference to this principle, stating that 'National authorities should endeavour to promote the internalization of environmental costs and the use of economic instruments, taking into account the approach that the polluter should, in principle, bear the cost of pollution, with due regard to the public interest and without distorting international trade and investment'.[180] Similarly, the polluter-pays principle has been integrated into the TFEU, recognising that 'the environmental damage should as a priority be rectified at source and that the polluter should pay'.[181] The legal impact of the polluter-pays principle is nevertheless likely to be limited due to the difficulties in putting it into practice. At most, the polluter-pays principle could serve as an additional argument to determine whether an environmental tax is contrary to EU or WTO law. For example, in the *Tatu* case the ECJ referred to the polluter-pays principle to make clear that the Romanian legislator could have designed its pollution tax on motor vehicles in a non-discriminatory way, which would also have been consistent with the polluter-pays principle.[182] In the *US Superfund* case,

Research Report 201 19 107, 40; Robyn Eckersley, 'The Politics of Carbon Leakage and the Fairness of Border Measures' (2010) 24(4) Ethics & International Affairs 367, 388.

179 See e.g. the reference to the polluter-pays principle in Clara Brandi, 'Trade and Climate Change: Environmental, Economic and Ethical Perspectives on Border Carbon Adjustments' (2013) 16(1) Ethics, Policy and Environment 79–93. At the same time, the polluter-pays principle has been used as a basis for justifying the adoption of environmental cross-border taxes. See de Sadeleer, *supra* n. 153, 44–49; Kurt Deketelaere, 'Naar een Europese Milieufiscaliteit. Het gebruik van fiscale instrumenten in het Europese Milieubeleid', Ph.D. dissertation, Katholieke Universiteit Leuven, 11 January 1995, 244; Holzer, *supra* n. 26, 56; Margaret A. Young, 'Principle 12. The Environment and Trade', in: Jorge E. Viñuales (ed.), *The Rio Declaration on Environment and Development: A Commentary* (OUP 2015), 345.

180 Principle 16 Rio Declaration.

181 Art. 191, para. 2 TFEU. See also Art. 192, para. 5 TFEU.

182 ECJ, *Ioan Tatu v. Statul român prin Ministerul Finanţelor şi Economiei, Direcţia Generală a Finanţelor Publice Sibiu, Administraţia Finanţelor Publice Sibiu, Administraţia Fondului pentru Mediu and Ministerul Mediului*, 27 January 2011, C-402/09, para. 60. See also the reference to the polluter-pays principle in ECJ, *European Commission v. Federal Republic of Germany*, 11 September 2014, C-525/12.

however, the Panel explicitly refused to apply the polluter-pays principle, stating as follows:

> The General Agreement's rules on tax adjustment thus give the contracting party in such a case the possibility to follow the Polluter-Pays Principle, but they do not oblige it to do so.
>
> 5.2.6 The mandate of the Panel is to examine the case before it 'in the light of the relevant GATT provisions' (paragraph 1.4 above). The Panel therefore did not examine the consistency of the revenue provisions in the Superfund Act with the environmental objectives of that Act or with the Polluter-Pays Principle.[183]

On the one hand, it can easily be argued that the polluters-pays principle is insufficiently precise to lead to any specific legal consequences or create binding obligations.[184] 'How to determine who is the polluter with regards to products' environmental impact?';[185] 'Should the consumers or the producers be held responsible?' In the hypothesis that the *consumers* should be held responsible, 'how to design the tax so as to make sure that the tax is indeed financially supported by the consumers?' In the hypothesis that the *producers* should be held responsible, 'how to make sure that they pay the tax and do not pass its costs to the consumers?' Moreover, in the specific case of global environmental issues, an additional (country-related) dimension makes it difficult to apply the polluter-pays principle: 'Which country should be held responsible for the pollution, the environmental damage, etc.?'[186] Finally, similar questions as under the CBDR principle would also arise as to whether the

---

[183] GATT, Panel Report, *US – Superfund*, paras. 5.2.5. & 5.2.6.

[184] See i.a. the analysis of de Sadeleer in the framework of EU law: Nicolas de Sadeleer, 'The Polluter-pays Principle in EU Law – Bold Case Law and Poor Harmonisation' (2012) Pro Natura: Festskrift Til H.C. Bugge, 405–419, available at <http://www.tradevenvironment.eu/uploads/papers/de%20Sadeleer.pdf> (accessed 15 November 2015). See also Dominic Roser & Luke Tomlinson, 'Trade Policies and Climate Change: Border Carbon Adjustments as a Tool for a Just Global Climate Regime' (2014) Ancilla Iuris 223, available at <http://www.anci.ch/_media/beitrag/ancilla2014_223_roser-tomlinson.pdf> (accessed 4 December 2015), 235–238.

[185] See de Sadeleer, *supra* n. 184, 38–42.

[186] See Richard A. Westin, *Environmental Tax Initiatives and Multilateral Trade Agreements: Dangerous Collisions* (Kluwer Law International 1997), 115, footnote 404, referring to OECD, Recommendation of the Council on Guiding Principles concerning International Economic Aspects of Environmental Policies, adopted by the Council at its 293rd Meeting, 26 May 1972, Annex (the polluter-pays principle would not apply to the case of 'trans-frontier pollution').

pollution-pays principle requires a distinction to be made between developed and developing countries.[187] On the other hand, as is the case with the CBDR principle, no specific international jurisdictional body exists to settle disputes related to general principles such as the polluter-pays principle. Even though Panels and the Appellate Body may take into account principles of environmental law to settle WTO disputes, the role of the polluter-pays principle in the design of environmental BTAs should not be overstated.[188]

6.2.2.2.2 Support for the adoption of environmental BTAs MEAs may not only have a limitative effect on the adoption of environmental BTAs. Indeed, they may also have a positive impact on such taxes by supporting a less restrictive reading of WTO law provisions surrounding their adoption, confirming the references in the preamble of the WTO Agreement to the need to 'protect and preserve the environment'.[189]

First, MEAs may be used as an argument in favour of the application of GATT Article XX. Indeed, the existence of MEAs may serve as an indication of both the need to protect the environment as well of the absence of 'arbitrary or unjustifiable discrimination'.[190] On the one hand, MEAs may participate in the recognition that the international community has reached a consensus on the necessity to act for mitigating certain environmental issues. For example, the UNFCCC, the Convention on Biodiversity and the UN Convention to Combat Desertification highlight the international consensus on the need to deal with these global environmental challenges. In the case where a WTO member adopts trade-restrictive measures that *a priori* violate WTO law general provisions, the presence of MEAs may facilitate the recognition that these measures fall under GATT Article XX. In the case *EC – Asbestos*,

---

[187] Brandi, *supra* n. 179.

[188] See Peter Van den Bossche, Nico Schrijver & Gerrit Faber, 'Unilateral Measures Addressing Non-trade Concerns' (2007) Study for the Ministry of Foreign Affairs of the Netherlands (The Hague), 196–199. See also Gabrielle Marceau, 'Conflicts of Norms and Conflicts of Jurisdictions. The Relationship between the WTO Agreement and MEAs and other Treaties' (2001) 35(6) Journal of World Trade 1081–1131; Joost Pauwelyn, 'The Role of Public International Law in the WTO: How Far Can We Go?' (2001) 95 American Journal of International Law 535.

[189] See i.a. Goh, *supra* n. 46, 420. See also Goyal, *supra* n. 170, 355–396.

[190] See Stoll & Strack, 'GATT XX. General Exceptions (b)', in: Rüdiger Wolfrum, Peter-Tobias Stoll & Holger P. Hestermeyer (eds.), *WTO – Trade in Goods*, Max Planck Commentaries on World Trade Law (Martinus Nijhoff Publishers 2011, Vol. 5), 517. *Contra:* Charnovitz, *supra* n. 159, 798.

for example, the Panel and Appellate Body both referred to the international recognition of the health risks posed by chrysotile asbestos fibres.[191] In addition to the evidence of an international consensus on the need to protect the environment, MEAs may, on the other hand, help to prove that environmental measures (including environmental BTAs) do not lead to 'unjustifiable or arbitrary discrimination'.[192] Indeed, in the *US – Shrimp* case the Article 21.5 Panel and Appellate Body considered the 'serious, good faith efforts made by the United States to negotiate an international agreement' in reaching the conclusion that the US trade-restrictive measures concerning the import of shrimps were 'now applied in a manner that no longer constitutes a means of unjustifiable or arbitrary discrimination'.[193]

Second, environmental BTAs may be included in a MEA in the same way as trade sanctions have been included in the Montreal Protocol or the Convention on International Trade in Endangered Species of Wild Fauna and Flora (CITES).[194] Such inclusion of environmental BTAs into an MEA could have an impact on their compatibility under WTO law. So far, the relationship between international trade law and trade-restrictive measures included in MEAs is, however, not clear cut.[195] Case law is non-existent.[196] In practice, the absence of case law could indicate that countries are less likely to contest the legality of trade-restrictive measures that are included in an MEA. This hypothesis is certainly true for countries that are party to the MEA but could also be true for countries that are not party to the agreement. From a legal perspective, MEAs are

---

191 WTO, Appellate Body Report, European Communities – Measures Affecting Asbestos and Products Containing Asbestos, 18 September 2000, WT/DS135/AB/R (*EC – Asbestos*), para. 162; WTO, Panel Report, para. 8.188.

192 Goyal, *supra* n. 170, 86–87.

193 WTO, Art. 21.5 Panel Report, *US – Shrimp*, para. 5.137; WTO, Art. 21.5 Appellate Body Report, *US – Shrimp*, para. 134.

194 See Deane, *supra* n. 62, 42: '... it was suggested that the non-compliance trading procedures proposed under the Montreal Protocol would be justified by the GATT exceptions'. See also, IISD & UNEP, 'Chapter 5.10 (MEAs and the WTO)', *Environment and Trade. A Handbook*, available at <https://www.iisd.org/trade/handbook/5_10.htm> (accessed 13 November 2015).

195 See WTO, Committee on Trade and Environment, Special Session, Multilateral environmental agreements (MEAs) and WTO rules: proposals made in the committee on trade and environment (CTE) from 1995–2002, Note by the secretariat, 23 May 2002, TN/TE/S/1.

196 James K.R. Watson, *The WTO and the Environment. Development of Competence beyond Trade* (Routledge 2013), 131.

nevertheless unlikely to take precedence over WTO law in the case of a dispute between a country that is both a WTO and MEA member and a country that is a member of the WTO.[197] Article 30(4) of the Vienna Convention would not allow giving precedence to an MEA in the case where such MEA contains an environmental BTA that violates WTO law.[198] For this reason, the inclusion of environmental BTAs in an MEA may only have a limited impact on the interpretation of GATT Article XX when a country that is not party to the MEA considers that such taxes violate WTO law general provisions.[199]

6.2.2.3 Principles of tax law[200]

As for environmental law principles, the question arises as to the extent to which tax law principles constrain the adoption of environmental BTAs. Indeed, various tax principles guide the adoption of new taxes. In some countries, these principles have a constitutional value (e.g. the ability-to-pay principle). In others, they only have a recommendatory character.

6.2.2.3.1 Principles in domestic tax laws Principles of tax law – either recognised in the constitution or generally accepted – usually constrain the adoption of taxes.[201] Consequently, these general principles also apply to environmental BTAs, regardless of their cross-border nature.[202] In most countries, they include both procedural principles and substantive principles.

A first procedural principle is the principle of legality. This principle requires that taxes are imposed by law and not by administrative

---

[197] Holzer, *supra* n. 26, 35–36; de Sadeleer, *supra* n. 153, 348–349; Van den Bossche, Schrijver, Faber, *supra* n. 188, 192–196. See also Appellate Body Report, *US – Gasoline*, 17; See WTO, Panel Report, *EC – Approval and Marketing of Biotech Products*, paras. 7.49–7.96.

[198] See Van den Bossche, Schrijver & Faber, *supra* n. 188, 194.

[199] *Ibid.*, 193–194.

[200] For a broad overview of tax law principles, see Cécile Brokelind (ed.), *Principles of Law: Function, Status and Impact in EU Tax Law* (IBFD 2014).

[201] See Michael Rodi & Hope Ashiabor, 'Legal Authority to Enact Environmental Taxes', in: Janet E. Milne & Mikael Skou Andersen (eds.), *Handbook of Research on Environmental Taxation* (Edward Elgar Publishing 2012), 59.

[202] Only a few tax principles are analysed here. Many other principles exist in domestic tax laws. They could also affect the adoption of environmental BTAs.

regulations.[203] In other words, in countries where this principle applies, environmental BTAs should be adopted by law. A second example of procedural principles is the non-retroactivity principle that generally forbids the retroactive effect of tax laws.[204]

Substantive principles include the ability-to-pay principle, the equality principle and the non-discrimination principle, and the prohibition of double and confiscatory taxation. The ability-to-pay principle has been the most discussed in relation to environmental taxes as this principle is not always easy to reconcile with the objectives pursued by environmental taxes.[205] One important objective of environmental taxes is indeed to internalise environmental costs by making polluters pay for these costs, following the polluter-pays principle.[206] As its name indicates, the ability-to-pay principle requires individuals to pay taxes according to their ability, which may not easily correspond to the idea that individuals pay taxes according to how much they pollute. Even though the ability-to-pay principle is recognised in the constitutions of some countries, it may be subject to various interpretations, leaving more or less space to the adoption of environmental taxes.[207] Progressive income taxes are one of the best examples of taxes that reflect the ability-to-pay principle: the more an individual earns, the heavier the tax burden. Consumption taxes are also usually considered to comply with the ability-to-pay principle: the act of consumption is evidence of the ability to pay.[208] A similar argument could be used with regard to environmental BTAs given that such taxes are imposed on products in the same way as consumption

---

[203] Victor Thuronyi, *Comparative Tax Law* (Kluwer Law International 2003), 70–71.

[204] *Ibid.*, 76.

[205] See Federica Pitrone, 'Environmental Taxation from a Legal Perspective: In Search of a Balance Between Environmental Goals and Tax Fairness', Ph.D. dissertation, Luiss Guido Carli University, February 2014, 138–157.

[206] See e.g. Industrial Economics, Incorporated, 'Economic Impacts of Superfund Taxes', report prepared for the Office of Policy Analysis, the Office of Policy, Planning and Evaluation, the US Environmental Protection Agency, February 1994, point 5-4: '... fairness in the context of environmental taxes is often measured by the degree to which the tax system adheres to the principle, "the polluter pays"'.

[207] See Stephen Utz, 'Ability to Pay' (2001–2002) 23 Whittier Law Review 867–950. See also Pedro M. Herrera, 'Legal Limits on the Competence of Governments in Spain', in: Janet Milne, Kurt Deketelaere, Larry Kreiser & Hope Ashiabor (eds.), *Critical Issues in Environmental Taxation. International and Comparative Perspectives* (OUP 2008), 112–117.

[208] See Pitrone, *supra* n. 205, 144.

taxes. Counter-arguments exist however. Environmental BTAs that differentiate between products based on their environmental impact (e.g. the emissions intensity of products) could also lead to a situation where people with less ability to pay would be subject to a higher tax burden.[209]

6.2.2.3.2 Environmental taxes with a cross-border character Some general tax principles, such as the principle of fiscal sovereignty and the prohibition of double taxation, are more directly related to the case of environmental BTAs.

First, the principle of fiscal sovereignty – which is inherently related to the concepts of 'extraterritoriality' and 'sovereignty' under international public law[210] – should not be a barrier against the adoption of environmental BTAs but rather a 'catalyst'.[211] The principle of fiscal sovereignty supports the design of a tax system that integrates considerations related to other jurisdictions (in either the tax base, the tax rate or other elements of the tax system). The principle of fiscal sovereignty indeed confirms the fiscal competence of a country to adopt environmental BTAs given the clear connection between imported products and the importing country.[212] Consequently, the adoption of environmental BTAs based on PPMs should not be controversial under international tax law.

Second, the prohibition of double taxation is sometimes used to argue that countries cannot impose environmental BTAs on imported products the environmental cost of which has already been internalised in other

---

209 *Ibid.*, 145.

210 See Silvestre, *supra* n. 134, 21. See also Joachim English, John Vella & A. Yevgenyeva, 'The Financial Transaction Tax Proposal under the Enhanced Cooperation Procedure: Legal and Practical Considerations' (2013) 2 British Tax Review 223; Ryngaert, *supra* n. 123, 18–19.

211 It is true that WTO law puts limits on members' fiscal sovereignty. Under international tax law, however, fiscal sovereignty is an attribute of the states that confirm their possibility to freely adopt taxes (see the references to this concept by WTO Panels and Appellate Bodies: Graham Cook, *A Digest of WTO Jurisprudence on Public International Law Concepts and Principles* (CUP 2015), 263–265 ('sovereignty and taxation').

212 See, on the concept of fiscal sovereignty and fiscal territoriality, Otto Marres, 'The Principle of Territoriality and Cross-Border Loss Compensation' (2011) 39(3) Intertax 112–125; Allison Christians, 'Sovereignty, Taxation and Social Contract' (2009) 18 Minnesota Journal of International Law 99, 109, footnote 30; Klaus Vogel, *Klaus Vogel on Double Taxation Conventions: A Commentary to the OECD-, UN- and US Model Conventions for the Avoidance of Double Taxation on Income and Capital* (Kluwer Law International 1997).

countries.[213] Such an argument is, however, based on a misunderstanding of the concept of double taxation and the principle that forbids it. First, the prohibition of double taxation only applies in countries that recognise this principle. Second, when it is recognised, the principle usually concerns situations of (juridical) double taxation within one jurisdiction, and not cross-border situations of (economic) double taxation (which could be the case for environmental BTAs).[214] In other words, principles related to the prohibition of double taxation do not forbid double taxation that takes place because two or more countries each impose taxes on the same taxpayer or the same economic activity. It is true that, as far as direct taxes are concerned, double taxation conventions permit situations of double taxation to be avoided by allocating taxing rights between countries.[215] It is also true that situations of double taxation are rare as far as indirect taxes are concerned because most countries have adopted the destination principle, according to which taxation should take place in the country of consumption.[216] Despite the global use of double taxation treaties and destination-based indirect tax systems, most authors do not believe in a principle of 'single taxation' as far as cross-border transactions are concerned. Avi-Yonah, however, claims that such a tax principle exists under international tax law, meaning that 'income from cross-border transactions should be subject to tax once, that is, not more than once but also not less than once'.[217] Unless the 'single tax

---

213 See e.g. the reference to double taxation in Holzer, *supra* n. 26, 172.

214 See e.g. the recognition of this principle at the Belgian level: Belgium, Cass., 30 November 1950, *Pas.,* 1951, I, 191; Belgium, Cass., 16 October 1997. See also IBFD Glossary, concept of 'double taxation'.

215 See Klaus Vogel, 'Double Tax Treaties and Their Interpretation' (1986) 4 Berkeley Journal of International Law 1. See also, as far as EU law is concerned, Marjaana Helminen, 'Chapter 17: The Principle of Elimination of Double Taxation under EU Law – Does it Exist?', in: Cécile Brokelind (ed.), *Principles of Law: Function, Status and Impact in EU Tax Law* (IBFD 2014), 391–412. Double tax treaties could nevertheless have a significant impact on the compatibility of proposals in favour of BTAs in respect of direct taxes.

216 Patricia Brandstetter, *'Taxes Covered': A Study of Article 2 of the OECD Model Tax Conventions* (IBFD 2011), 94. See also the efforts to avoid double taxation as regards VAT/GST by means of the OECD, *International VAT/GST Guidelines.*

217 Reuven S. Avi-Yonah, 'Commentary (Response to article by H. David Rosenbloom)' (2000) 53(2) Tax Law Review 167, 169; Reuven S. Avi-Yonah, 'International Tax as International Law' (2007) Public Law and Legal Theory Research Paper No. 41, 11–12 and 15. *Contra:* David H. Rosenbloom, 'Cross-Border Arbitrage: The Good, the Bad and the Ugly' (2007) The Tax Magazine 115; David H. Rosenbloom, 'The David R. Tillinghast Lecture. International Tax

principle', as defined by Avi-Yonah, is followed, countries would not be constrained under international tax law to exempt from environmental BTAs imported products that have already been subject to environmental regulations or taxes in other countries.

6.3 INTERIM CONCLUSIONS

Various legal questions arise from the peculiar nature of environmental taxes in comparison to non-environmentally specific taxes under WTO law.

First, environmental taxes question the traditional distinctions used to determine which taxes are eligible for BTAs and which are not. For example, the distinction between consumption and production taxes is easily blurred in the case of environmental taxes, given that such taxes are usually imposed on products but, at the same time, are based on criteria related to the production process. Similarly, environmental taxes are not easily classified in the traditional categories of direct and indirect taxes. Moreover, the regulatory purpose of environmental taxes makes the distinction between fiscal and regulatory measures less clear than it appeared at first sight.

Second, the analysis of environmental BTAs' compatibility with WTO law highlights the significant impact of WTO law's interpretation of the extent to which countries will be able or not to adopt environmental BTAs. Models of environmental BTAs will more or less easily comply with GATT Article III:2, depending on the approach chosen to interpret the NT test (including the concept of 'likeness'). Indeed, environmental BTAs may distinguish between products based on their production process, which is not always related to physical characteristics of products. Models of environmental BTAs are likely to violate the NT principle in the case where differentiations based on PPMs are not recognised.

Third, the MFN principle recalls that environmental BTAs should not differentiate between products based on criteria related to other WTO members. Indeed, BTAs may not serve to impose differentiated taxes on imported products based on conditions concerning the environmental policies that have been put in place in other WTO member states.

Arbitrage and the "International Tax System"' (1999–2000) 53 Tax Law Review 137. See also Yariv Brauner, 'An International Tax Regime in Crystallization' (2003) 56 Tax Law Review 259, 291–292.

Fourth, in the literature surrounding environmental BTAs, reference is often made to GATT Article XX as a key provision to support the compatibility of such taxes with WTO law. Even though this provision is obviously relevant for the legal analysis of any environmentally trade-related measure (including environmental BTAs), the role of GATT Article XX should not be overestimated. On the one hand, the role of GATT Article XX is limited because some models of environmental BTA taxes may not fulfil all the conditions surrounding its application. Countries may face difficulties in proving that certain environmental BTAs aim to fulfil the objective mentioned in GATT Article XX(a), (b), (g) and meet the necessity test or the 'relationship requirement' of the chapeau. On the other hand, GATT Article XX should only be envisaged when environmental BTAs are found contrary to WTO law general provisions. Environmental BTAs may be designed to maximise their chances to be found compatible with WTO law general provisions. In these cases, GATT Article XX is not needed to justify their adoption. From this perspective, the limited role of GATT Article XX does not imply that environmental BTAs cannot be adopted under WTO law.

Aside from WTO law, other legal branches may also contribute to the legal framework of environmental BTAs. In the literature, some of these legal grounds have usually been put forward as arguments against the development of such environmental taxes. The legal analysis of environmental law provisions, principles of tax law, and principles of international public law illustrate that these other legal branches largely support the adoption of environmental BTAs. Arguments related to the extraterritoriality of environmental BTAs, despite their appealing political character, do not find strong legal grounds in international public law. Similarly, references to the prohibition of double taxation are politically appealing but not strongly based on international tax law principles. The greatest support for the adoption of environmental BTAs are MEAs given that they may have a favourable impact on the interpretation of WTO law provisions surrounding environmental BTAs.

Conclusion

This work discussed environmental BTAs, a topic at the crossroads between international trade law, tax law and environmental law. This conclusion highlights how this book contributes to bringing some coherence to the legal literature surrounding environmental BTAs. The objective is not to give a detailed overview of the interim conclusions that have already been summarised after each of the six chapters and are schematically presented in Table C.1. Rather, this conclusion puts forward the methodological value-added of this book for further research on related topics; its overall substantive results and, finally, its role for legislators and non-state actors interested by the topic.

AN ACTIVE AND CRITICAL APPROACH TO WTO LAW

This research has been inspired by the critical legal studies that require us to be 'active' vis-à-vis the legal phenomenon. Indeed, one of the main roles of critical legal studies is to question legal rules by stepping back from their (so-called) objective nature.[1] This 'active' approach to WTO law allowed us to deconstruct the topic of environmental BTAs, going back to the history of tariffs and BTAs. This historical perspective was used as a tool to highlight the evolving role of (environmental) BTAs and how interpretations of WTO law provisions have changed (sometimes in an incoherent way) over the years.[2] This method of critical legal studies has served to point out the indeterminate character of the international (trade) law surrounding the phenomenon of environmental BTAs. The mainstream interpretations of WTO law should not be considered the

---

[1] Mark Kelman, *A Guide to Critical Legal Studies* (Harvard University Press 1987), 295.

[2] See Gregory C. Shaffer, 'The Nexus of Law and Politics: The WTO's Committee on Trade and Environment', in: Richard H. Steinberg (ed.), *The Greening of Trade Law* (Rowman & Littlefield Publishers 2002), 114.

'unique' method to determine whether WTO law permits the adoption of environmental BTAs. Aside from the interpretations of WTO law that broadly prevail in the literature, alternative views are possible. For example, the view that only indirect taxes should be eligible for adjustment is broadly accepted in legal scholarship. A critical analysis of the WTO law provisions surrounding BTAs, however, highlights that GATT Articles II:2(a) and III:2 could leave space for BTAs in respect of *taxes occultes* and direct taxes.

This critical approach is not only useful for the analysis of existing legal provisions, but also permits us to shed light on the political values that are at stake in the case of legal instruments at the proposal stage. Regan compares these political values to 'pre-dispositions' that necessarily come up in the analysis of prospective legal instruments, such as BTAs: 'Because the legal issues are so uncertain, people's views about them are inevitably influenced by their underlying prejudices and predispositions concerning PPMs. The Border Tax Adjustment provisions in particular seem to function as a Rorschach blot for revealing people's pre-dispositions'.[3]

A critical approach helps us to be conscious of these (political) predispositions, allowing us to give a full account of the diversity of legal interpretations that may apply to measures at the proposal stage. This 'active' approach indeed permits us to distance ourselves from the topic of environmental BTAs to assess the ideological values on which such taxes rely. Environmental BTAs are an economic instrument, the practical implementation of which requires us to 'put a price' on the environment. The arguments in favour of environmental BTAs are primarily grounded in economic theories, which favour environmental taxes over environmental regulations. Stakeholders who are still undecided over the need to adopt environmental BTAs should be aware of these theoretical grounds. Moreover, political actors should always make clear from what perspective they envisage the adoption of environmental BTAs. A diversity of objectives may be pursued through BTAs from economic objectives to the internalisation of environmental costs on a broad basis in order to mitigate global environmental challenges.

---

[3] Donald H. Regan, 'How to Think about PPMs (and Climate Change)', in: Thomas Cottier et al. (eds.), *International Trade Regulation and the Mitigation of Climate Change. World Trade Forum* (CUP 2009), 101.

Finally, the critical approach to environmental BTAs opens up the discussion to non-legal fields and suggests using interdisciplinarity carefully. The same concept can be used in different ways, depending on the field. Environmental BTAs provide a good example of what could be called in linguistics 'false friends'. Economic studies that discuss 'environmental border taxes' sometimes deal with taxes that would rather be called 'tariffs' by legal scholars. From this perspective, stakeholders should always refer to economic analyses on the economic effects of environmental BTAs with great caution, paying attention to potential incoherencies in the use of concepts.

A research method inspired by critical legal studies could be useful to analyse other legal instruments, including legal measures that are still at the proposal stage, as is the case with the environmental BTAs. In environmental law, a critical approach could be used to assess other market-based instruments such as, for example, habitat banking, a 'biodiversity compensation mechanism'.[4] In tax law, a critical approach could help assess proposals for tax reforms, such as the recent Base Erosion and Profit Shifting (BEPS) project at the OECD level. An historical analysis of the BEPS project and its rhetoric would permit a better understanding of the dynamic (and ideological values) behind the project.[5] In WTO law, a critical approach could be used to further analyse GATT provisions (as Hudec has already done excellently in his critical article on the interaction between GATT Articles I and III) or the interaction between WTO law and labour standards.[6]

---

[4] Eftec, IEEP et al., 'The use of market-based instruments for biodiversity protection – The case of habitat banking – Technical report', available at <http://ec.europa.eu/environment/enveco/pdf/eftec_habitat_technical_report.pdf> (accessed 14 December 2015), 3.

[5] Jogarajan has provided historical analysis of today's tax issues, such as tax evasion. See e.g. Sunita Jogarajan, 'The Drafting of the 1925 League of Nations Resolutions on Tax Evasion', in: Peter Harris & Dominic de Cogan, *Studies in the History of Tax Law*, (Hart 2015, Vol. 7), 253–292.

[6] Robert E. Hudec, '"Like Product": The Differences in Meaning in GATT Article I and III', in: Thomas Cottier & Petros C. Mavroidis (eds.), *Regulatory Barriers and the Principle of Non-Discrimination in World Trade Law* (The University of Michigan Press 2000), 101–123.

THE SUBSTANTIVE VALUE OF THIS BOOK: BRINGING SOME COHERENCE TO THE LEGAL LITERATURE

This research brings some coherence to the legal literature surrounding environmental BTAs from three main perspectives.

First, this research clarifies the main objectives that can be pursued through (environmental) BTAs. It provides a typology of the rationale behind such taxes, highlighting that BTAs are instruments for neutralising the economic effects of domestic taxes on products' prices (following the theory of the comparative advantage and the theory of the absolute advantage). Based on the theory of the legitimate absolute advantage, BTAs could also be used as an instrument to internalise environmental costs. In contrast, BTAs are not the most suitable instrument for neutralising the effects of the differences in environmental protection levels with third countries. In other words, BTAs should neither be used to level the playing field with third countries nor to sanction 'environmentally unfriendly' countries. Research on the rationale behind environmental BTAs points out that such taxes cannot be defined by a unique environmental objective.

Second, this book provides an overview of how environmental factors may be integrated into the design of BTAs. The research makes it clear that environmental BTAs cannot be described as a unique tax model. Instead various tax models are possible. Excise duty-based models should be distinguished from VAT-based models and other models based on retail sales taxes. Excise duty models include traditional environmental excise duty models, models based on the US Superfund and ODC taxes and CO_2 tax models. VAT-based models include what has been named the 'CAT' – carbon added tax – and the 'environmental VAT'. This research highlights that stakeholders in favour of environmental BTAs should always make clear which tax models they have in mind when they advocate in favour of such taxes.

Third, this book proposes a critical analysis of the WTO law provisions surrounding environmental BTAs, which offers an overview of the diversity of perspectives on the interpretation of these provisions. The research goes beyond traditional views of the environmental BTAs' legal framework in an attempt to give an account of the whole spectrum of opinions regarding the environmental dimension of border taxation, from the interpretations that are most in favour of unregulated trade to the interpretations that are most open to (environmental) regulatory freedom. The research also discusses in detail some of the legal issues that have not yet been thoroughly analysed. The book examines the legal grounds of BTAs on imported products, the interactions between GATT Article II:2(a) and GATT Article III:2, the eligibility of direct taxes and *taxes occultes* for BTAs. Finally, the book analyses BTAs' legal framework beyond WTO law, opening the discussion to other legal fields: principles of public international law, environmental law and tax law. Overall, this book shows that international (trade) law leaves scope to develop the environmental dimension of BTAs.

THE CALL TO POLITICAL ACTORS AND OTHER STAKEHOLDERS

This book, apart from its technical legal analysis, also carries a message to political actors, legislators and other stakeholders. This message is the following: 'do not use environmental BTAs as an excuse to refuse adopting higher standards of environmental protection at the domestic level'. As recognised in the Paris Agreement, global environmental challenges, such as climate change, are 'an urgent and potentially irreversible threat to human societies and the planet', which requires effective policy action.[7] As Pauwelyn rightly states with regard to climate change: 'People should stop using the WTO as an excuse not to tackle climate change. ... the WTO should not stop your efforts, but merely guide them as one relevant factor amongst many other, arguably more important, criteria such as cost-effectiveness, administrative feasibility and risk of circumvention'.[8]

WTO law indeed leaves scope to adopt environmental BTAs if such taxes are considered necessary to complement domestic environmental policies. Two hypotheses may be distinguished: either legislators do not find it necessary to adopt environmental BTAs (in this case, environmental BTAs should in no case be used as an excuse not to act at the domestic level to mitigate global environmental challenges) or they find it useful (and in this hypothesis, they should take steps to design environmental BTAs that meet the objectives that they wish to pursue).

---

[7] UN, Conference of the Parties, Adoption of the Paris Agreement, Proposal by the President, Draft decision -/CP.21, 12 December 2015, FCCC/CP/2015/L.9/Rev.1 (preamble).

[8] Joost Pauwelyn, Testimony Before the Subcommittee on Trade of the House on Ways and Means, 24 March 2009, 2.

Political actors should avoid proposing to adopt environmental BTAs (such as, for example, border carbon taxes) when those proposals later appear to be mere declarations of intent because of the alleged risks of incompatibility with WTO law. These declarations of intent are, at best, political tools used as 'carrot and stick' diplomacy vis-à-vis third countries. At worse, such declarations sound like lame excuses not to take (regulatory) environmental action at the domestic level.

Professor Deketelaere has expressed before his fear that environmental taxation would remain a rhetorical exercise rather than a concrete tax policy in favour of environmental protection.[9] This book will hopefully help the rhetoric of environmental BTAs to either disappear from political discourse, replaced by concrete action at the domestic level, or be turned into reality, allowing for higher levels of environmental protection both at the domestic and cross-border levels.

Table C.1 Overview

	(Environmental) BTAs
Traditional rationale	• Ricardian theory of comparative advantage • Smith theory of absolute advantage
Best-suited environmental rationale	• Revised Ricardian theory of comparative advantage • Revised theory of absolute advantage → level playing field • Theory of the legitimate absolute advantage (not always suited to the concept of BTAs)
Tax design and tax models	• Excise-based models: 'traditional' and models based on Superfund/ODC taxes • VAT-based models: 'CAT' and 'environmental VAT' • Models based on the retail sales tax • Other models
Valuation and environmental proxies	• Averaging based on predominant method of production or best available technique OR • Actual environmental features

[9] Kurt Deketelaere, 'European Environmental Tax Policy: Proposal for a Policy Vision and a Legal Framework' (1996) European Environmental Law Review 9, 15: 'So, we should hope that we will not have to add the concept "European environmental tax law" to the list of hollow and grandiloquent environmental policy terms of the European Community.'

Table C.1 (continued)

	(Environmental) BTAs
Risks of abuse and solutions	• Risks: abuse in relation to 'environmental value' and products' classification • Solutions: anti-circumvention measures; well-defined certification system; specific task force
Allocation of revenue	• Similar to domestic environmental taxes: environmental tax reforms (reduction of labour taxes) • Earmarking • Allocation to an international fund
Main legal grounds under WTO law	• GATT Arts. I; II:2(a) & III:2 • ASCM (BTAs on exports)
Legal issues under WTO law	• Are domestic environmental taxes *indirect* taxes? Are direct taxes eligible for BTAs? • Are *taxes occultes* eligible for BTAs? • NT (& MFN) principle: possibility to distinguish products based on PPMs? • GATT Art. XX: environmental objective that falls under Arts. XX(a), XX(b) or XX(g)? Does it respect the chapeau?
Interactions with other legal branches	A. International public law: • Unilateral character? Extraterritoriality? B. Environmental law: • Polluter-pays principle & CBDR principle: unlikely to be an obstacle • Role of MEAs in supporting the adoption of environmental cross-border taxes C. Tax law: • Principle of fiscal sovereignty & prohibition of double taxation: unlikely to be an obstacle

Bibliography

This bibliography only contains references to secondary sources (books, chapters in edited collections, articles, working papers and Ph.D. dissertations).

1. BOOKS

Aalberts, Tanja E., *Constructing Sovereignty between Politics and Law* (Routledge 2012).

Asakura, Hironori, *World History of the Customs and Tariffs* (WCO 2003).

Bakker, Anuschka, *Tax and the Environment: A World of Possibilities* (IBFD 2009).

Baldwin, Robert E., *Nontariff Distortions of International Trade* (George Allen & Unwin Ltd 1970).

Bank, Steven A., *From Sword to Shield. The Transformation of the Corporate Income Tax, 1861 to Present* (OUP 2010).

Bank, Steven A., *Anglo-American Corporate Taxation. Tracing the Common Roots of Divergent Approaches* (CUP 2011).

Bermejo, Roberto, *Handbook for a Sustainable Economy* (Springer 2014).

Bethlehem, Daniel, McRae, Donald & Neufeld, Rodney, *The Oxford Handbook of International Trade Law* (OUP 2009).

Bhala, Raj, *International Trade Law: Interdisciplinary Theory and Practice* (Lexis Law Publishing 2008).

Black, John, Hashimzade, Nigar & Myles, Gareth, *A Dictionary of Economics* (OUP 2012).

Bonin, Holger, *Generational Accounting. Theory and Application* (Springer 2001).

Brack, Duncan, Grubb, Michael & Craig, Windram, *International Trade and Climate Change Policies* (Earthscan 2000).

Brandstetter, Patricia, *'Taxes Covered': A Study of Article 2 of the OECD Model Tax Conventions* (IBFD 2011).

Brokelind, Cécile (ed.), *Principles of Law: Function, Status and Impact in EU Tax Law* (IBFD 2014).

Brunnée, Jutta & Toope, Stephen J., *Legitimacy and Legality in International Law. An Interactional Account,* Cambridge Studies in International and Comparative Law (CUP 2010).

Camilleri, Joseph A. & Falk, Jim, *The End of Sovereignty? The Politics of a Shrinking and Fragmenting World* (Edward Elgar Publishing 1992).

Choi, Won-Mog, *'Like Products' in International Trade Law – Towards a Consistent GATT/ WTO Jurisprudence* (OUP 2003).

Chow, Daniel C.K. & Schoenbaum, Thomas J., *International Trade Law: Problems, Cases and Materials* (Wolters Kluwer Law & Business 2013).

Condon, Bradly J., *Environmental Sovereignty and the WTO. Trade Sanctions and International Law* (Transnational Publishers 2006).

Condon, Bradly J. & Sinha, Tapen, *The Role of Climate Change in Global Economic Governance* (OUP 2013).

Conrad, Christiane R., *Processes and Production Methods (PPMs) in WTO Law. Interfacing Trade and Social Goals* (OUP 2012).

Cook, Graham, *A Digest of WTO Jurisprudence on Public International Law Concepts and Principles* (CUP 2015).

de la Feria, Rita, *The EU VAT System and the Internal Market* (IBFD 2009).

de Sadeleer, Nicolas, *Environmental Principles. From Political Slogans to Legal Rules* (OUP 2002).

De Schutter, Olivier, *Trade in the Service of Sustainable Development. Linking Trade to Labour Rights and Environmental Standards* (Hart Publishing 2015).

Deane, Felicity, *Emissions Trading and WTO Law. A Global Analysis* (Edward Elgar Publishing 2015).

Ecker, Thomas, *A VAT/GST Model Convention* (IBFD Doctoral Series 2013).

Eicher, Theo S., Mutti, John H. & Turnovsky, Michelle H., *International Economics* (Routledge 2009).

Eisenstein, Louis, *The Ideologies of Taxation* (Harvard University Press 2000; first published by Roland Press Co. 1961).

Epps, Tracey & Green, Andrew James, *Reconciling Trade and Climate: How the WTO Can Help Address Climate Change* (Edward Elgar Publishing 2010).

Farrell, Jennifer E., *The Interface of International Trade Law and Taxation* (26 IBFD Doctoral Series 2013).

Faure, Michael, *L'analyse économique du droit de l'environnement* (Bruylant 2007).

Folsom, Ralph, *Principles of International Trade* (West Academic Publishing 2014).

Franchetti, Matthew J. & Apul, Defne, *Carbon Footprint Analysis: Concepts, Methods, Implementation, and Case Studies* (CRC Press 2012).

Gale, Robert, Barg, Stephan & Gillies, Alexander, *Green Budget Reform: An International Casebook of Leading Practices* (Earthscan 1995).

Gomes, Leonard, *The Economics and Ideology of Free Trade: A Historical Review* (Edward Elgar Publishing 2003).

Goyal, Anupam, *The WTO and International Environmental Law: Towards Conciliation* (OUP 2006).

Grando, Michelle T., *Evidence, Proof, and Fact-Finding in WTO Dispute Settlement* (OUP 2009).

Grapperhaus, Ferdinand H.M., *Tax Tales from the Second Millennium* (IBFD 2009).

Hall, Robert E. & Rabushka, Alvin, *The Flat Tax* (Hoover Institution Press, Stanford University 1995).

Harris, Peter Andrew, *Corporate/Shareholder Income Taxation and Allocating Taxing Rights between Countries. A Comparison of Imputation Systems* (IBFD 1996).

Healy, John C. & Schadewald, Michael S., *2012 Multistate Corporate Tax Guide Vol. II (Sales/Use Tax)* (CCH Wolters Kluwer Business 2012).

Herbain, Charlène Adline, *VAT Neutrality* (Promoculture Larcier 2015).

Holzer, Kateryna, *Carbon-Related Border Adjustment and WTO Law* (Edward Elgar Publishing 2014).

Howse, Robert, *The WTO System: Law, Politics & Legitimacy* (Cameron May 2007).

Hufbauer, Gary Clyde, *Fundamental Tax Reform and Border Tax Adjustments* (Institute for International Economics 1996).

Hufbauer, Gary Clyde, Charnovitz, Steve & Kim, Jisun, *Global Warming and the World Trading System* (Peterson Institute for International Economics 2009).

Infanti, Anthony C. & Crawford, Bridget J. (eds.), *Critical Tax Theory: An Introduction* (CUP 2009).

Jackson, John H., *Sovereignty, the WTO, and Changing Fundamentals of International Law* (CUP 2006).

Jeffery, Ramon, *The Impact of State Sovereignty on Global Trade and International Taxation* (Kluwer Law International 1968, 1999).

Joyce, Richard, *Competing Sovereignties* (Routledge 2012).

Kelman, Mark, *A Guide to Critical Legal Studies* (Harvard University Press 1987).

Klöpffer, Walter & Grahl, Birgit, *Life Cycle Assessment (LCA): A Guide to Best Practice* (Wiley 2014).

Krasner, Stephen D., *Sovereignty: Organized Hypocrisy* (Princeton University Press 1999).
Kraus, Christiane, *Import Tariffs as Environmental Policy Instruments* (Springer 2000).
Lang, Michael, Herdin, Judith & Hofbauer, Ines (eds.), *WTO and Direct Taxation* (Linde Verlag 2005).
Lang, Michael, Herdin-Winter, Judith & Hofbauer-Steffel, Ines (eds.), *The Relevance of WTO Law for Tax Matters* (Linde Verlag 2006).
Leal-Arcas, Rafael, *Climate Change and International Trade* (Edward Elgar Publishing 2013).
Lester, Simon, Mercurio, Bryan & Davies, Arwel, *World Trade Law: Text, Materials and Commentary* (Hart 2012).
Macmillan, Fiona, *WTO and the Environment* (Sweet & Maxwell 2001).
Maneshi, Andrea, *Comparative Advantage in International Trade. A Historical Perspective* (Edward Elgar Publishing 1998).
McConville, Mike & Chui, Wing Hong, *Research Methods for Law* (Edinburgh University Press 2007).
Meade, James E., *The Structure and Reform of Direct Taxation* (Routledge 2013; first published 1978).
Melischek, Christian A., *The Relevant Market in International Economic Law. A Comparative Antitrust and GATT Analysis* (CUP 2012).
Mill, John Stuart, *Principles of Political Economy with Some of their Applications to Social Philosophy* (Longmans, Green and Co. 1848), available at <http://www.econlib.org/library/Mill/mlP65.html>.
Milne, Janet E. & Andersen, Mikael Skou (eds.), *Handbook of Research on Environmental Taxation* (Edward Elgar Publishing 2012).
Neto, Paulo Penteado, *International Trade Subsidy Rules and Tax and Financial Export Incentives: From Limitations on Fiscal Sovereignty to Development-inducing Mechanisms* (authorHouse 2012).
Nielsen, Laura, *The WTO, Animals and PPMs* (Martinus Nijhoff Publishers 2007).
Pigou, Arthur C., *The Economics of Welfare* (Macmillan 1930), available at <http://www.econlib.org/library/NPDBooks/Pigou/pgEW.html>.
Qureshi, Asif H., *Interpreting WTO Agreements* (CUP 2015).
Ricardo, David, *On the Principles of Political Economy and Taxation* (John Murray 1817).
Ricardo, David, *On Protection to Agriculture* (London William Clowes John Murray, Albermarle-Street 1822).
Ricardo, David, *The Works and Correspondence of David Ricardo* (Pamphlets and Papers 1815–1823, ed. Piero Sraffa with the Collaboration of M.H. Dobb, Liberty Fund 2005, Vol. 4), available at <http://oll.libertyfund.org/title/205/38614/885295>.

Sadowsky, Marilyne, *Droit de l'OMC, droit de l'Union européenne et fiscalité directe* (Larcier 2013).

Schefer, Krista Nadakavukaren, *Social Regulation in the WTO. Trade Policy and International Legal Development* (Edward Elgar Publishing 2010).

Schenk, Alan & Oldman, Olivier, *Value Added Tax: A Comparative Approach* (CUP 2006).

Seligman, Edwin R.A., *A Study of the History, Theory and Practice of Income Taxation at Home and Abroad* (The Macmillan Company 1911), available at <https://www.library.cornell.edu/>.

Sinn, Hans-Werner, *The New Systems Competition* (Blackwell 2003).

Smith, Adam, *An Inquiry into the Nature and Causes of the Wealth of Nations* (Edwin Cannan, Methuen & Amp, 1776 Library of Economics and Liberty 1904), available at <http://www.econolib.org/library/Smith/smWN13.htlm>.

Snape, John & de Souza, Jeremy, *Environmental Taxation Law: Policy, Contexts and Practice* (Ashgate Publishing 2006).

Steichen, Alain, *Manuel de droit fiscal. Droit fiscal général* (Saint Paul 2006).

Terra, Ben J.M. & Wattel, Peter J., *European Tax Law* (Wolters Kluwer 2012).

Terra, Ben & Kajus, Julie, *A Guide to the European VAT Directives. Introduction to European VAT 2012* (IBFD 2013, Vol. 1).

Thuronyi, Victor, *Comparative Tax Law* (Kluwer Law International 2003).

Trebilcock, Michael, Howse, Robert & Eliason, Antonia, *The Regulation of International Trade* (4th edn. Routledge 2013).

van Brederode, Robert F., *Systems of General Sales Taxation: Theory, Policy and Practice* (Kluwer Law International 2009).

Van Calster, Geert, *International and EU Trade Law. The Environmental Challenge* (Cameron May 2000).

Van Damme, Isabelle, *Treaty Interpretation by the WTO Appellate Body* (OUP 2009).

Van den Bossche, Peter & Zdouc, Werner, *The Law and Policy of the World Trade Organization* (CUP 2013).

van Schaik, Louise G., *EU Effectiveness and Unity in Multilateral Negotiations. More than the Sum of Its Parts?* (Palgrave Macmillan 2013).

Vogel, Klaus, *Klaus Vogel on Double Taxation Conventions: A Commentary to the OECD-, UN- and US Model Conventions for the Avoidance of Double Taxation on Income and Capital* (Kluwer Law International 1997).

Vranes, Erich, *Trade and the Environment: Fundamental Issues in International Law, WTO Law, and Legal Theory* (OUP 2009).
Watson, James K.R., *The WTO and the Environment. Development of Competence beyond Trade* (Routledge 2013).
Westin, Richard A., *Environmental Tax Initiatives and Multilateral Trade Agreements: Dangerous Collisions* (Kluwer Law International 1997).
Wold, Chris, Gaines, Sanford & Block, Greg, *Trade and the Environment. Law and Policy* (Carolina Academic Press 2005).
Wolfrum, Rüdiger, Stoll, Peter-Tobias & Hestermeyer, Holger P. (eds.), *WTO – Trade in Goods, Max Planck Commentaries on World Trade Law*, Vol. 5 (Martinus Nijhoff Publishers 2011).
Zleptnig, Stefan, *Non-Economic Objectives in WTO Law. Justification Provisions of GATT, GATS, SPS and TBT Agreements* (Martinus Nijhoff Publishers 2010).

2. CHAPTERS IN EDITED COLLECTIONS

Arcuri, Alessandra, 'Law and Economics of the SPS Agreement: A Critical Perspective', in: Geert Van Calster & Denise Prévost (eds.), *Research Handbook on Environment, Health and the WTO* (Edward Elgar Publishing 2013), 164–206.
Antimiani, Alessandro, Costantini, Valeria, Martini, Chiara, Salvatici, Luca & Tommasino, Maria Cristina, 'Carbon Leakage and Trade Adjustment Policies', in: Valeria Costantini & Massimiliano Mazzanti (eds.), *The Dynamics of Environmental and Economic Systems. Innovation, Environmental Policy and Competitiveness* (Springer 2013), 25–43.
Brown, Catherine & Mintz, Jack, 'On the Relationship between International Tax Neutrality and Non-Discrimination Clauses under Tax Treaties for Source-Based Taxes', in: Michael Lang, Pasquale Pistone et al. (eds.), *Tax Treaties: Building Bridges between Law and Economics* (IBFD 2010), 581–605.
Carlson, George, 'Origin Principle', in: Joseph J. Cordes, Robert D. Ebel & Jane G. Gravelle (eds.), *The Encyclopedia of Taxation & Tax Policy* (The Urban Institute Press 2005), 283–284.
Charnovitz, Steve, 'Article I and Annex A SPS', in: Rüdiger Wolfrum, Peter-Tobias Stoll & Anja Seibert-Fohr (eds.), *WTO – Technical Barriers and SPS Measures* (Koninklijke Brill 2007), 375–391.
Cleveland, Sarah H., 'Human Rights Sanctions and the World Trade Organization', in: Francesco Francioni (ed.), *Environment, Human Rights and International Trade* (Hart Publishing 2001), 199–261.

Cnossen, Sijbren, 'Commentary on "Value Added Tax and Excises"', in: Stuart Adam et al (eds.), *Dimensions of Tax Design. The Mirrlees Review* (OUP 2010), 370–386.

Cottier, Thomas & Shariff, Nashina, 'International Trade and Climate Change', in: Geert Van Calster & Denise Prévost (eds.), *Research Handbook on Environment, Health and the WTO* (Edward Elgar Publishing 2013), 413–447.

Crawford, Ian, Keen, Michael & Smith, Stephen, 'Value Added Tax and Excises', in: Stuart Adam et al (eds.), *Dimensions of Tax Design. The Mirrlees Review* (OUP 2010), 275–362.

Ekardt, Felix & Schmeichel, Andrea, 'Border Adjustments, WTO Law and Climate Protection', in: Claudia Dias Soares, Janet Milne, Hope Ashiabor & Kurt Deketelaere (eds.), *Critical Issues in Environmental Taxation* (OUP 2010), 737–760.

Ekins, Paul & Speck, Stefan, 'Impacts on Competitiveness: What Do We Know from Modeling?', in: Janet E. Milne & Mikael Skou Andersen (eds.), *Handbook of Research on Environmental Taxation* (Edward Elgar Publishing 2012), 377–396.

Englisch, Joachim, 'VAT/GST and Direct Taxes: Different Purposes', in: Michael Lang, Peter Melz & Eleonor Kristoffersson (eds.), *Value Added Tax and Direct Taxation: Similarities and Differences* (IBFD 2009), 1–34.

Francioni, Francesco, 'Chapter VI. Extraterritorial Application of Environmental Law', in: Karl Matthias Meessen (ed.), *Extraterritorial Jurisdiction in Theory and Practice* (Kluwer Law International 1996), 122–146.

Fullerton, Don, 'Why Have Separate Environmental Taxes?', in: James M. Poterba (ed.), *Tax Policy and the Economy* (MIT Press 1996, Vol. 10), 33–70.

Garbarino, Carlo, 'Hybrid Taxes and the Distinction between VST/GST and Direct Taxes: The Case of IRAP', in: Michael Lang, Peter Melz & Eleonor Kristoffersson (eds.), *Value Added Tax and Direct Taxation: Similarities and Differences* (IBFD 2009), 169–184.

Helminen, Marjaana, 'Chapter 17: The Principle of Elimination of Double Taxation under EU Law – Does It Exist?', in: Cécile Brokelind (ed.), *Principles of Law: Function, Status and Impact in EU Tax Law* (IBFD 2014), 391–412.

Herrera, Pedro M., 'Legal Limits on the Competence of Governments in Spain', in: Janet Milne, Kurt Deketelaere, Larry Kreiser & Hope Ashiabor (eds.), *Critical Issues in Environmental Taxation. International and Comparative Perspectives* (OUP 2008), 111–123.

Hoerner, J. Andrew, 'Taxing Pollution', in: Elizabeth Cook & Reynaldo Forte (eds.), *Ozone Protection in the United States: Elements of Success* (World Resources Institute 1996), 39–54.

Hudec, Robert E., '"Like Product": The Differences in Meaning in GATT Article I and III', in: Thomas Cottier & Petros C. Mavroidis (eds.), *Regulatory Barriers and the Principle of Non-Discrimination in World Trade Law* (The University of Michigan Press 2000), 101–123.

Jackson, John H., 'Sovereignty: Outdated Concept or New Approaches', in: Wenhua Shan, Penelope Simons & Dalvinder Singh (eds.), *Redefining Sovereignty in International Economic Law* (Hart Publishing 2008), 3–26.

Jogarajan, Sunita, 'The Drafting of the 1925 League of Nations Resolutions on Tax Evasion', in: Peter Harris & Dominic de Cogan, *Studies in the History of Tax Law* (Hart 2015, Vol. 7), 253–292.

Kulovesi, Kati, 'Climate Change and Trade: At the Intersection of Two International Legal Regimes', in: E.J. Hollo et Michael Mehling (eds.), *Climate Change and the Law* (Springer 2013), 441–445.

Lassudrie-Duchêne, Bernard & Ünal-Kesenci, Deniz, 'L'avantage comparatif, notion fondamentale et controversée', *L'Economie Mondiale en 2002* (La découverte 2001), 90–104.

Lennard, Michael, 'The GATT 1994 and Direct Taxes: Some National Treatment and Related Issues', in: Michael Lang, Judith Herdin & Ines Hofbauer (eds.), *WTO and Direct Taxation* (Linde Verlag 2005), 73–101.

Lipsey, Robert E., 'Measuring International Trade in Services', in: Marshall B. Reinsdorf & Matthew J. Slaughter (eds.), *International Trade in Services and Intangibles in the Era of Globalization* (University of Chicago Press 2009), 27–70.

Lorenzmeier, Stefan, 'WTO and Human Rights', in: Norman Weiß & Jean-Marc Thouvenin (eds.), *The Influence of Human Rights on International Law* (Springer 2015), 147–166.

Metcalf, Gilbert E., 'Life Cycle versus Annual Perspectives on the Incidence of a Value Added Tax', in: James M. Poterba (ed.), *Tax Policy and the Economy* (MIT Press 1994, Vol. 8).

Millar, Rebecca, 'Jurisdictional Reach of VAT', in: Richard Krever (ed.), *VAT in Africa* (Pretoria University Law Press 2008), 175–214.

Nollkaemper, André, 'Rethinking States' Rights to Promote Extraterritorial Environmental Values', in: Friedl Weiss, Erik M.G. Denters & Paul J.I.M. de Waart (eds.), *International Economic Law with a Human Face* (Kluwer Law International 1998), 175–201.

Pauwelyn, Joost, 'Carbon Leakage Measures and Border Tax Adjustments under WTO Law', in: Geert Van Calster & Denise Prévost (eds.), *Research Handbook on Environment, Health and the WTO* (Edward Elgar Publishing 2013), 448–506.

Peters, Cees, 'International Tax Neutrality and Non-Discrimination: Plea for a More Explicit Dialogue between the State and the Market', in: Michael Lang, Pasquale Pistone et al. (eds.), *Tax Treaties: Building Bridges between Law and Economics* (IBFD 2010), 607–628.

Petersmann, Ernst-Ulrich, 'International Trade Law and International Environmental Law: Environmental Taxes and Border Tax Adjustment in WTO Law and EC Law', in: Richard L. Revesz, Phillipe Sands & Richard B. Stewart (eds.), *Environmental Law, the Economy, and Sustainable Development* (CUP 2000), 127–155.

Pirlot, Alice, 'Environmental Border Tax Adjustments (BTAs): A Critical Analysis', in: Jan De Bruyne, Michaël de Potter de ten Broeck & Isabelle Van Hiel (eds.), *Policy Within and Through Law* (Maklu 2015), 107–120.

Quirico, Ottavio, 'Primary Sovereign Rights or Secondary Environmental Duties? Critical International Law Issues Raised by the Extraterritorial Application of the EU Emission Trading System in the Aviation Sector', in: Christine Bakker & Francesco Francioni (eds.), *The EU, the US and Global Climate Governance* (Ashgate Publishing 2014), 143–160.

Read, Robert, 'Process and Production Methods and the Regulation of International Trade', in: Nicholas Perdikis & Robert Read (eds.), *The WTO and the Regulation of International Trade. Recent Trade Disputes between the European Union and the United States* (Edward Elgar Publishing 2005), 239–266.

Regan, Donald H., 'How to Think about PPMs (and Climate Change)', in: Thomas Cottier et al. (eds.), *International Trade Regulation and the Mitigation of Climate Change. World Trade Forum* (CUP 2009), 97–123.

Regan, Donald H., 'Regulatory Purpose in GATT Article III, TBT Article 2.1, the Subsidies Agreement, and Elsewhere: Hic et Ubique', in: Geert Van Calster & Denise Prévost (eds.), *Research Handbook on Environment, Health and the WTO* (Edward Elgar Publishing 2013), 41–78.

Reyes-Knoche, Susanne & Arend, Katrin, 'Article XX lit. d GATT', in: Rüdiger Wolfrum, Peter-Tobias Stoll & Anja Seibert-Fohr (eds.), *WTO – Technical Barriers and SPS Measures* (Koninklijke Brill 2007), 125.

Rodi, Michael & Ashiabor, Hope, 'Legal Authority to Enact Environmental Taxes', in: Janet E. Milne & Mikael Skou Andersen (eds.), *Handbook of Research on Environmental Taxation* (Edward Elgar Publishing 2012), 59–81.

Rodi, Michael, Schlegelmich, Kai & Mehling, Michael, 'Designing Environmental Taxes in Countries in Transition: a Case Study of

Vietnam', in: Janet E. Milne & Mikael Skou Andersen (eds.), *Handbook of Research on Environmental Taxation* (Edward Elgar Publishing 2012), 122–138.

Rubini, Luca, 'Subsidies for Emissions Mitigation under WTO Law', in: Geert Van Calster & Denise Prévost (eds.), *Research Handbook on Environment, Health and the WTO* (Edward Elgar Publishing 2013), 561–635.

Scott, Joanne, 'Territorial Sovereignty and Territorial Extension in an Inter-Connected World', in: Richard Rawlings, Peter Leyland & Alison Young (eds.), *Sovereignty and the Law: Domestic, European and International Perspectives* (OUP 2013), 269–285.

Shaffer, Gregory C., 'The Nexus of Law and Politics: The WTO's Committee on Trade and Environment', in: Richard H. Steinberg (ed.), *The Greening of Trade Law* (Rowman & Littlefield Publishers 2002), 81–114.

Silvestre, Martha J. Rutsel, 'Extraterritorial Taxation in International Law', in: Karl M. Meessen (ed.), *Extraterritorial Jurisdiction in Theory and Practice* (Kluwer Law International 1996), 19–38.

Soares, Claudia Dias, 'Earmarking Revenues from Environmentally Related Taxes', in: Janet E. Milne & Mikael Skou Andersen (eds.), *Handbook of Research on Environmental Taxation* (Edward Elgar Publishing 2012), 102–121.

Speck, Stefan, Summerton, Philip, Lee, Daniel & Wiebe, Kirsten, 'Chapter 5. Environmental Taxes and ETRs in Europe: The Current Situation and a Review of the Modelling Literature', in: Stefan Speck & Paul Ekins (eds.), *Environmental Tax Reform (ETR): A Policy for Green Growth* (Oxford Scholarship Online 2011), 99–130.

Stiglitz, Joseph, 'Sharing the Burden of Saving the Planet: Global Social Justice for Sustainable Development: Lessons from the Theory of Public Finance', in: Joseph Stiglitz & Mary Kaldor (eds.), *The Quest for Security: Protection without Protectionism and the Challenge of Global Governance* (Columbia University Press 2013), 161–204.

Terra, Ben J.L., 'Chapter 8, Excises', in: Victor Thuronyi (ed.), *Tax Law Design and Drafting* (IMF 1996).

Van Calster, Geert 'Amerikanen, eskimo's en konijnen – extraterritorialiteit en milieuwetgeving', in: Kurt Deketelaere, Michael Faure & Gaëtan Verhoosel (eds.), *Grensoverschrijdende milieuproblemen: uitdagingen voor de nationale en internationale rechtsorde* (Intersentia 1998), 111–129.

Van Calster, Geert, 'Animal Welfare, the EU and the World Trade Organization – Member States' Sovereignty between a Rock and a Hard Place?', in: Anton Vedder (ed.), *The World Trade Organisation and Concerns Regarding Animals and Nature* (Wolf Legal Publishers 2003), 61–85.

Van Calster, Geert, 'Topsy-turvy: the European Court of Justice and Border (Energy) Tax Adjustments – Should the WTO Follow Suit?', in: Janet Milne, Kurt Deketelaere, Larry Kreiser & Hope Ashiabor (eds.), *Critical Issues in Environmental Taxation: International and Comparative Perspectives* (OUP 2003), 311–341.

Van Calster, Geert, 'Climate Change Taxes, Emissions Trading, and International Trade Law', in: Marjan Peeters & Kurt Deketelaere (eds.), *EU Climate Change Policy. The Challenge of New Regulatory Initiatives* (Edward Elgar Publishing 2006), 205–219.

Van Thiel, Servaas, 'General Report', in: Michael Land, Judith Herdin-Winter, Ines Hofbauer-Steffel (eds.), *WTO and Direct Taxation* (Linde Verlag 2005), 13–47.

Vanberg, Viktor J., 'Competition among Governments: The State's Two Roles in a Globalized World', in: Young Back Choi (ed.), *Institutional Economics and National Competitiveness* (Routledge 2012), 24–43.

Williams, David, 'Chapter 6, Value-Added Tax', in: Victor Thuronyi (ed.), *Tax Law Design and Drafting* (IMF 1996).

Young, Margaret A., 'Principle 12. The Environment and Trade', in: Jorge E. Viñuales, *The Rio Declaration on Environment and Development: A Commentary* (OUP 2015).

Zee, Howell H., 'Inter-jurisdictional Sharing of the VAT', in: Richard Krever (ed.), *VAT in Africa* (Pretoria University Law Press 2008), available at <http://www.pulp.up.ac.za/pdf/2008_04/2008_04.pdf> 161–174.

Zhou, Xin, 'Chapter 14: Environmentally Extended Multi-Region Input-Output Model: Sharing Responsibility Across the Globe', in: Joy Murray & Richard Wood (eds.), *The Sustainability Practitioner's Guide to Input-Output Analysis* (Common Ground Publishing 2010), 165–176.

3. ARTICLES

Albrecht, Johan, 'The Use of Consumption Taxes to Re-launch Green Tax Reforms' (2006) 26(1) International Review of Law and Economics 88–103.

Aldrich, John, 'The Discovery of Comparative Advantage' (2004) 26(3) Journal of the History of Economic Thought 379–399.

Altman, Andrew, 'Legal Realism, Critical Legal Studies, and Dworkin' (1986) 15(3) Philosophy & Public Affairs 205–235.

Andersen, Mikael Skou, 'Denmark/Sweden – Reflections on the Scandinavian Model: Some Insights into Energy-Related Taxes in Denmark and Sweden' (2015) 55(6) European Taxation 235–244.

Astoria, Ross, 'Design of an International Trade Law Compliant Carbon Border Tax Adjustment' (2015–2016) 6 Arizona Journal of Environmental Law & Policy 491–534.

Avi-Yonah, Reuven S., 'Commentary (Response to Article by H. David Rosenbloom)' (2000) 53(2) Tax Law Review 167–175.

Avi-Yonah, Reuven S., 'Corporations, Society and the State: A Defense of the Corporate Tax' (2004) 90(5) Virginia Law Review 1193–1255.

Avi-Yonah, Reuven S. & Slemrod, Joel B., '(How) Should Trade Agreements Deal with Income Tax Issues?' (2002) 55(4) Tax Law Review 533–554.

Avi-Yonah, Reuven S. & Uhlmann, David M., 'Combating Global Climate Change: Why a Carbon Tax Is a Better Response to Global Warming Than Cap and Trade' (2009) 28(1) Stanford Environmental Law Journal 3–50.

Babiker, Mustafa H. & Rutherford, Thomas F., 'The Economic Effects of Border Measures in Subglobal Climate Agreements' (2005) 26(4) The Energy Journal 99–125.

Barrett, John A., 'The Global Environment and Free Trade: A Vexing Problem and a Taxing Solution' (2001) 76(4) Indiana Law Journal 829–887.

Barthold, Thomas A., 'Issues in the Design of Environmental Excise Taxes' (1994) 8 Journal of Economic Perspectives 1.

Baumol, William J. & Oates, Wallace E., 'The Use of Standards and Prices for Protection of the Environment' (1971) 73(1) Swedish Journal of Economics 42–54.

Bednar-Friedl, Birgit, Schinko, Thomas & Steininger, Karl W., 'The Relevance of Process Emissions for Carbon Leakage: A Comparison of Unilateral Climate Policy Options With and Without Border Carbon Adjustment' (2012) 34 Energy Economics 168–180.

Belleville, Mark L., 'The Key Stone in the Carbon Tariff Wall: The Alberta Oil Sands and the Legality of Taxing Imports Based on Their Carbon Footprint' (2013) 43 Environmental Law 365–416.

Bhagwati, Jagdish, 'Trade Liberalisation and "Fair Trade" Demands: Addressing the Environmental and Labour Standards Issues' (1995) 18(6) The World Economy 745–759.

Biermann, Frank & Brohm, Rainer, 'Border Adjustments on Energy Taxes: A Possible Tool for European Policymakers in Implementing the Kyoto Protocol?' (2005) 74(2) Vierteljahrshefte zur Wirtschaftsforschung 249–258.

Biermann, Frank & Brohm, Rainer, 'Implementing the Kyoto Protocol without the USA: The Strategic Role of Energy Tax Adjustments at the Border' (2005) 4(3) Climate Policy 289–302.

Bird, Richard M. & Gendron, Pierre-Pascal; 'Sales Taxes in Canada: the GST-HST-QST-RST "System"' (2009–2010) 63 Tax Law Review 517–582.

Blough, Roy, 'The Adjustment Process and the International Role of the Dollar' (1969) 24(2) The Journal of Finance 345–359.

Böhringer, Christoph, Balistreri, Edward J. & Rutherford, Thomas F., 'The Role of Border Carbon Adjustment in Unilateral Climate Policy: Overview of an Energy Modeling Forum Study' (EMF 29) (2012) 34 Energy Economics 97–110.

Bongartz, Matthias, 'Trade in Goods Subject to Excise Duties which Have Been Released for Consumption in other Member States. Analysis with Reference to Directive 2008/118/EC and German Excise Law' (2012) 6(2) World Customs Journal 19–28.

Bracken, Joseph M. 'Zenith Radio Corp. v. United States: Countervailing Duty – Application to Nonexcessive Remission of Indirect Taxes' (1979) 4(2) Maryland Journal of International Law 221–230.

Brandi, Clara, 'Trade and Climate Change: Environmental, Economic and Ethical Perspectives on Border Carbon Adjustments' (2013) 16(1) Ethics, Policy and Environment 79–93.

Brauner, Yariv, 'An International Tax Regime in Crystallization' (2003) 56 Tax Law Review 259–328.

Brauner, Yariv, 'International Trade and Tax Agreements May Be Coordinated, But Not Reconciled' (2005) 25 Virginia Tax Review 251–311.

Brown, Karen, Fellows, Mary Louise & Crawford, Bridget, 'The Past, Present, and Future of Critical Tax Theory: A Conversation' (2012) 10(59) Pittsburgh Tax Review 13–49.

Calvacanti, Clóvis, 'Conceptions of Ecological Economics: Its Relationship with Mainstream and Environmental Economics' (2010) 24(68) Estudos Avançados 53–67.

Caron, Justin, 'Estimating Carbon Leakage and the Efficiency of Border Adjustments in General Equilibrium – Does Sectoral Aggregation Matter?' (2012) 34 Energy Economics 111–126.

Charnovitz, Steve, 'GATT and the Environment: Examining the Issues' (1992) 4(3) International Environmental Affairs 203–233.

Charnovitz, Steve, 'Environmental Trade Sanctions and the GATT: An Analysis of the Pelly Amendment on Foreign Environmental Practices' (1994) 9(3) American University International Law Review 751–807.

Charnovitz, Steve, 'The North American Free Trade Agreement: Green Law or Green Spin?' (1994–1995) 26 Law and Policy in International Business 1–77.
Charnovitz, Steve, 'The Moral Exception in Trade Policy' (1998) 38 Virginia Journal of International Law 689–746.
Christian, Amy C., 'Designing a Carbon Tax: The Introduction of the Carbon-Burned Tax (CBT)' (1991–1992) 10 UCLA Journal of Environmental Law and Policy 221–281.
Christians, Allison, 'Sovereignty, Taxation and Social Contract' (2009) 18 Minnesota Journal of International Law 99–153.
Clarke, Harry, 'Carbon Leakages, Consumption Tax Bases and International Climate Change Agreements' (2010) 29(2) Economic Papers: A Journal of Applied Economics and Policy 156–68.
Clarke, Harry, 'Some Basic Economics of Carbon Taxes' (2011) 44(2) The Australian Economic Review 123–136.
Cnossen, Sijbren, 'A VAT Primer for Lawyers, Economists, and Accountants' (2011) Tax Analysts 23–51.
Conconi, Paola & Wouters, Jan, 'Appellate Body Report, India – Additional and Extra–Additional Duties on Imports from the United States (WT/DS360/AB/R, adopted on 17 November 2008)' (2010) 9(1) World Trade Review 239–263.
Courchene, Thomas J. & Allan, John R., 'Climate Change: The Case for a Carbon Tariff/Tax' (March 2008) 29(3) Policy Options 59–64.
Courchene, Thomas J. & Allan, John R., 'Missing the Bigger Picture: A Response to McLure's View of the Carbon-Added Tax' (2011) Policy Options 75.
Daly, Michael, 'WTO Rules on Direct Taxation' (2006) 29(5) The World Economy 527–557.
Das, Kasturi, 'Can Border Carbon Adjustments Be WTO-Legal?' (2011) 8(3) Manchester Journal of International Economic Law 65–97.
De Camillis, Camillo & Goralczyk, Malgorzata, 'Towards Stronger Measures for Sustainable Consumption and Production Policies: Proposal of a New Fiscal Framework Based on a Life Cycle Approach' (2013) 18(1) International Journal of Life Cycle Assessment 263–272.
de Cendra, Javier, 'Can Emissions Trading Schemes Be Coupled with Border Tax Adjustments? An Analysis vis-à-vis WTO Law' (2006) 15(2) Review of European Community & International Environmental Law 131–145.
Deketelaere, Kurt, 'European Environmental Tax Policy: Proposal for a Policy Vision and a Legal Framework' (1996) European Environmental Law Review 9–15.
Deketelaere, Kurt, 'European Environmental Tax Law and Policy: Greenspeak!' (2000) 123 Water, Air, and Soil Pollution 361–377.

de Sadeleer, Nicolas, 'The Polluter-pays Principle in EU Law – Bold Case Law and Poor Harmonisation' (2012) Pro Natura: Festskrift Til H.C. Bugge, 405–419, available at <http://www.tradevenvironment.eu/uploads/papers/de%20Sadeleer.pdf>.

De Schutter, Olivier, 'Les Critical Legal Studies au pays du droit international public' (1992) 22 Droit & Société 585–605.

De Schutter, Olivier, 'Trade in the Service of Climate Change Mitigation: The Question of Leakage' (2014) 5 Journal of Human Rights and the Environment 65–102.

Deane, Felicity, 'The Border Adjustments of the Australian Clean Energy Package' (2014) 17 International Trade and Business Law Review 66–107.

Demaret, Paul & Stewardson, Raoul, 'Border Tax Adjustments under GATT and EC Law and General Implications for Environmental Taxes' (1994) 28(4) Journal of World Trade Law 5–65.

Desta, Melaku Geboye, 'The GATT/WTO System and International Trade in Petroleum: An Overview' (2003) 21 Journal Energy & Natural Resources Law 385–398.

Doelle, Meinhard, 'Climate Change and the WTO: Opportunities to Motivate State Action on Climate Change through the World Trade Organization' (2004) 13(1) Review of European Community & International Environmental Law 85–103.

Duff, David G., 'Carbon Taxation in British Columbia' (2008–2009) 10 Vermont Journal of Environmental Law 87–107.

Dziubla, Robert, 'Zenith Radio Corp v. United States: The Demise of Congressionally Mandated Countervailing Duties' (1979) 1 Northwestern Journal of International Law & Business 318–337.

Eckersley, Robyn, 'The Politics of Carbon Leakage and the Fairness of Border Measures' (2010) 24(4) Ethics & International Affairs 367–393.

Eichenberg, Benjamin M., 'Greenhouse Gas Regulation and Border Tax Adjustments: The Carrot and the Stick' (2008) 3(2) Golden Gate University Environmental Law Journal 283–364.

Eichner, Thomas & Pethig, Rüdiger, 'Unilateral Consumption-based Carbon Taxes and Negative Leakage' (2015) 40 Resource and Energy Economics 127–142.

Elliott, Joshua, Foster, Ian, Kortum, Samuel, Munson, Todd, Cervantes, Fernando Pérez & Weisbach, David, 'Trade and Carbon Taxes' (2010) 100 American Economic Review: Papers & Proceedings 465–469.

Emch, Adrian, 'Same Same But Different? Fiscal Discrimination in WTO Law and EU Law: What Are "Like" Products?' (2005) 32(4) Legal Issues of Economic Integration 369–415.

English, Joachim, Vella, John & Yevgenyeva, Anzhela, 'The Financial Transaction Tax Proposal under the Enhanced Cooperation Procedure: Legal and Practical Considerations' (2013) 2 British Tax Review 223–259.

Feaver, Donald & Sheehy, Benedict, 'Climate Policy and Border Adjustment Regulation: Designing a Coherent Response' (2012) 13 Melbourne Journal of International Law 792–817.

Fox, William F. & Luna, Leann, 'Subnational Taxing Options: Which Is Preferred, a Retail Sales Tax or a VAT?' (2002–2003) 21(1) Journal of State Taxation 875–884.

Fox, William F. & Luna, Leann, 'How Broad Should State Sales Tax Bases Be? A Review of the Empirical Literature' (2013) Tax Analysts.

French, Duncan, 'Developing States and International Environmental Law: The Importance of Differentiated Responsibilities' (2000) 49(1) The International and Comparative Law Quarterly 35–60.

Gersman, Paul, 'Value-Added Tax' (1965) 19 The OECD Observer 39.

Ghosh, Madanmohan, Deming, Luo, Muhammad, Shahid Siddiqui & Yunfa, Zhu, 'Border Tax Adjustments in the Climate Policy Context: CO_2 versus Broad-based GHG Emission Targeting' (2012) 34 Energy Economics 154–167.

Gillespie, Alexander, 'The Contradiction between Comparative Advantage in International Trade and Environmental Protection' (1995) 3 Waikato Law Review 127–136.

Goco, Jonell B., 'Non-Discrimination, "Likeness", and Market Definition in World Trade Organization Jurisprudence' (2006) 40(2) Journal of World Trade 315–340.

Godar, Javier, Persson, U. Martin, Tizado, E. Jorge & Meyfroidt, Patrick, 'Towards More Accurate and Policy Relevant Footprint Analyses: Tracing Fine-scale Socio-environmental Impacts of Production to Consumption' (2015) 112 Ecological Economics 25–35.

Goh, Gavin, 'The World Trade Organization, Kyoto and Energy Tax Adjustments at the Border' (2004) 38(3) Journal of World Trade 395–423.

Goulder, Lawrence H. 'Environmental Taxation and the Double Dividend: A Reader's Guide' (1995) 2 International Tax and Public Finance 157–183.

Gros, Daniel & Egenhofer, Christian, 'The Case for Taxing Carbon at the Border' (2011) 11 Climate Policy 1262–1268.

Handl, Gunther, 'Territorial Sovereignty and the Problem of Transnational Pollution' (1975) 69 American Journal of International Law 50–76.

Havel, Brian F. & Mulligan, John Q., 'The Triumph of Politics: Reflections on the Judgment of the Court of Justice of the European Union

Validating the Inclusion of Non-EU Airlines in the Emissions Trading Scheme' (2012) 37(1) Air & Space Law 3–33.
Hellerstein, Walter, 'State Sales Tax Reform in the United States: The Streamlined Sales Tax Project' (2005) (59)5 IBFD Bulletin 170–184.
Hellerstein, Walter, 'Recent Developments in US Subnational State Taxation with International Implications' (2008) 62(2) IBFD Bulletin 77, 85–86.
Helm, Dieter, Hepburn, Cameron & Ruta, Giovanni, 'Trade, Climate Change, and the Political Game Theory of Border Carbon Adjustments' (2012) 28(2) Oxford Review of Economic Policy 368–394.
Hillgenberg, Harmut, 'A Fresh Look at Soft Law' (1999) 10(3) European Journal of International Law 499–515
Hillman, Jennifer, 'Changing Climate for Carbon Taxes, Who's Afraid of the WTO?' (2013) German Marshall Fund of the United States 1–17.
Horn, Henrik & Mavroidis, Petros C., 'To B(TA) or Not to B(TA)? On the Legality and Desirability of Border Tax Adjustments from a Trade Perspective' (2011) 34(11) The World Economy 1911–1937.
Horn, Henrik & Weiler, J.H.H., 'European Communities – Measures Affecting Asbestos and Asbestos-Containing Products' (2002) 2(S1) World Trade Review 14–40.
Howse, Robert & Regan, Donald, 'The Product/Process Distinction – An Illusory Basis for Disciplining "Unilateralism" in Trade Policy' (2000) 11(2) European Journal of International Law 249–289.
Howse, Robert & Trebilcock, Michael J., 'The Fair Trade–Free Trade Debate: Trade, Labor, and the Environment' (1996) 16(1) International Review of Law and Economics 61–79.
Hudec, Robert E., 'GATT/WTO Constraints on National Regulation: Requiem for an "Aim and Effects" Test' (1998) 32(3) The International Lawyer 619–649.
Hudnall, Shannon, 'Towards a Greener International Trade System' (1996) 29 Columbia Journal of Law and Social Problems 175–215.
Hufbauer, Gary Clyde, 'Tax Discipline in the WTO' (2010) 44(4) Journal of World Trade 763–777.
Ireland, Robert, 'Implications for Customs of Climate Change Mitigation and Adaptation Policy Options: A Preliminary Examination' (2010) 4(2) World Customs Journal 21–36.
Irfanoglu, Zeynep Burcu, Sesmero, Juna P. & Golub, Alla, 'Potential of Border Tax Adjustments to Deter Free Riding in International Climate Agreements' (2015) 10 Environmental Research Letters.
Jackson, John H., 'The General Agreement on Tariffs and Trade in United States Domestic Law' (1967) 66 Michigan Law Review 249–332.

Jackson, John H., 'World Trade Rules and Environmental Policies: Congruence or Conflict?' (1992) 49 Washington and Lee Law Review 1227–1278.

Jeffery QC, Michael, 'Environmental Imperatives in a Globalised World: The Ecological Impact of Liberalising Trade' (2007) 7 Macquarie Law Journal 25–51.

Johnson, Harry & Krauss, Mel, 'Border Taxes, Border Tax Adjustments, Comparative Advantage, and the Balance of Payments' (1970) 3(4) The Canadian Journal of Economics 595–602.

Judy, Martha L. & Probst, Katherine N., 'Superfund at 30' (2009–2010) 11 Vermont Journal of Environmental Law 191–247.

Kander, Astrid, Jiborn, Magnus, Moran, Daniel D. & Wiedmann, Thomas O., 'National Greenhouse-gas Accounting for Effective Climate Policy on International Trade' (2015) 5 Nature Climate Change 431–435.

Keen, Michael, 'VAT, Tariffs, and Withholding: Border Taxes and Informality in Developing Countries' (2008) 92(10) Journal of Public Economics 1892–1906.

Kuik, Onno & Hofkes, Marjan, 'Border Adjustment for European Emissions Trading: Competitiveness and Carbon Leakage' (2010) 38(4) Energy Policy 1741–1748.

Kulovesi, Kati, 'Addressing Sectoral Emissions outside the United Nations Framework Convention on Climate Change: What Roles for Multilateralism, Minilateralism and Unilateralism?' (2012) 21(3) Review of European Community & International Environmental Law 193–203.

Kysar, Douglas A., 'Preferences for Processes: The Process/Product Distinction and the Regulation of Consumer Choice' (2004) 118(2) Harvard Law Review 525–641.

Ladly, Sarah Davidson, 'Border Carbon Adjustments, WTO-law and the Principle of Common but Differentiated Responsibilities' (2012) 12(1) International Environmental Agreements 63–84.

Lang, Winfried, 'UN-Principles and International Environmental Law' (1999) 3 Max Planck UNYB 157–172.

Larbprasertporn, Pananya, 'The Interaction Between WTO Law and the Principle of Common but Differentiated Responsibilities in the Case of Climate-Related Border Tax Adjustments' (2014) 6(1) Goettingen Journal of International Law 145–170.

Leontiades, Milton, 'The Logic of Border Taxes' (1966) 19(2) National Tax Journal 173–183.

Low, Patrick, Marceau, Gabrielle & Reinaud, Julia, 'The Interface between the Trade and Climate Change Regimes: Scoping the Issue' (2012) 46(3) Journal of World Trade 485–544.

Lydgate, Emily Barrett, 'Consumer Preferences and the National Treatment Principle: Emerging Environmental Regulations Prompt a New Look at an Old Problem' (2011) 10(2) World Trade Review 165–188.

Mani, Muthukumara S, 'Environmental Tariffs on Polluting Imports. An Empirical Study' (1996) 7(4) Environmental and Resource Economics 391–411.

Marceau, Gabrielle, 'Conflicts of Norms and Conflicts of Jurisdictions. The Relationship between the WTO Agreement and MEAs and other Treaties' (2001) 35(6) Journal of World Trade 1081–1131.

Marceau, Gabrielle & Trachtman, Joel P., 'The Technical Barriers to Trade Agreement, the Sanitary and Phytosanitary Measures Agreement, and the General Agreement on Tariffs and Trade. A Map of the World Trade Organization Law of Domestic Regulation of Goods' (2002) 36(2) Journal of World Trade 811–881.

Marceau, Gabrielle & Trachtman, Joel P., 'A Map of the World Trade Organization Law of Domestic Regulation of Goods: The Technical Barriers to Trade Agreement, the Sanitary and Phytosanitary Measures Agreement, and the General Agreement on Tariffs and Trade' (2014) 48(2) Journal of World Trade 351–432.

Marres, Otto, 'The Principle of Territoriality and Cross-Border Loss Compensation' (2011) 39(3) Intertax 112–125.

Mason, Charles F., Barbier, Edward B. & Umanskaya, Victoria I., 'On the Strategic Use of Border Tax Adjustments as a Second-best Climate Policy Measure' (2015) 20(4) Environment and Development Economics 539.

Mastromarco, Dan R., 'U.S. International Tax Reform? Define "Reform" for Me' (2006) 43(6) Tax Notes International 481–496.

Mattoo, Aaditya & Subramanian, Arvind, 'Regulatory Autonomy and Multilateral Disciplines: The Dilemma and a Possible Resolution' (1998) 1 Journal of International Economic Law 303–322.

Mattoo, Aaditya, Subramanian, Arvind, van de Mensbrugghe, Dominique & He, Jianwu, 'Trade Effects of Alternative Carbon Border-tax Schemes' (2013) 149 Review of World Economics 587–609.

McAusland, Carol & Najjar, Nouri, 'Carbon Footprint Taxes' (2014) 61(1) Environmental and Resource Economics 37–70.

McCorriston, Steve & Sheldon, Ian M., 'Market Access and WTO Border Tax Adjustments for Environmental Excise Taxes under Imperfect Competition' (2005) 7(4) Journal of Public Economic Theory 579–592.

McLure, Charles E., 'Panel Discussion: Alternative Tax Policies for the Future in Light of the Current Economic and Budget Outlook' (1989) 4(3) Journal of Accounting, Auditing & Finance 388.

McLure, Charles E., 'Rethinking State and Local Reliance on the Retail Sales Tax: Should We Fix the Sales Tax or Discard It?' (2000) Brigham Young University Law Review 77–137.
McLure, Charles E., 'Globalization, Tax Rules and National Sovereignty' (2001) 55(8) Bulletin for International Taxation 328–341.
McLure, Charles E, 'EU and US Sales Taxes in the Digital Age: A Comparative Analysis' (2002) 56(4) IBFD Bulletin 135–145.
McLure, Charles E., 'The Carbon-Added Tax: A CAT that Won't Hunt' (2010) Policy Options 62–66.
McLure, Charles E., 'The Carbon-Added Tax: An Idea Whose Time Should Never Come' (2010) 3 Carbon & Climate Law Review 250–259.
McLure, Charles E., 'The GATT-Legality of Border Adjustments for Carbon Taxes and the Cost of Emissions Permits: A Riddle, Wrapped in a Mystery, Inside an Enigma' (2011) 11 Florida Tax Review 221–294.
McLure, Charles E., 'Could VAT Techniques Be Used To Implement Border Carbon Adjustments?' (2012) 66(8) Bulletin for International Taxation 436–446.
Medina, Valentina Durán & Lazo, Rodrigo Polanco, 'A Legal View on Border Tax Adjustments and Climate Change: A Latin American Perspective' (2011) 11(3) Sustainable Development Law & Policy 29–66.
Messere, Ken, '20th Century Taxes and Their Future' (2002) 54(1) IBFD Bulletin 2–29.
Metcalf, Gilbert E. & Weisbach, David, 'The Design of a Carbon Tax' (2009) 33 Harvard Environmental Law Review 499–556.
Milne, Janet E., 'Carbon Taxes in the United States: The Context for the Future' (2008–2009) 10 Vermont Journal of Environmental Law 1–30.
Monjon, Stéphanie & Quirion, Philippe, 'A Border Adjustment for the EU ETS: Reconciling WTO Rules and Capacity to Tackle Carbon Leakage' (2011) 11(5) Climate Policy 1212–1225.
Moon, Gillian, 'Trade and Equality: A Relationship to Discover' (2009) 12(3) Journal of International Economic Law 617–642.
Neven, Damien & Trachtman, Joel P., 'Philippines – Taxes on Distilled Spirits: Like Products and Market Definition' (2013) 12(2) World Trade Review 297–326.
Oates, Wallace E., 'Green Taxes: Can We Protect the Environment and Improve the Tax System at the Same Time?' (1995) 61(4) Southern Economic Journal 915–922.
Pauwelyn, Joost, 'The Role of Public International Law in the WTO: How Far Can We Go?' (2001) 95 American Journal of International Law 535–578.

Pitschas, Christian, 'GATT/WTO Rules for Border Tax Adjustment and the Proposed European Directive Introducing a Tax on Carbon Dioxide Emissions and Energy' (1995) 24 Georgia Journal of International and Comparative Law 479–500.

Porges, Amelia & Trachtman, Joel P., 'Robert Hudec and Domestic Regulation: The Resurrection of Aim and Effects' (2003) 37(4) Journal of World Trade 783–799.

Poterba, James M. & Rotemberg, Julio J., 'Environmental Taxes on Intermediate and Final Goods When Both Can Be Imported' (1995) 2(2) International Tax and Public Finance 221–228.

Quick, Reinhard & Lau, Christian, 'Environmentally Motivated Tax Distinctions and WTO Law. The European Commission's Green Paper on Integrated Product Policy in Light of the 'Like Product-' and 'PPM-' Debates' (2003) 6(2) Journal of International Economic Law 419–458.

Regan, Donald H., 'Regulatory Purpose and "Like Products" in Article III:4 of the GATT (With Additional Remarks on Article III:2)' (2002) 36(3) Journal of World Trade 443–478.

Regan, Donald H., 'What Are Trade Agreements For? Two Conflicting Stories Told by Economists, with a Lesson for Lawyers' (2006) 9(4) Journal of International Economic Law 951–988.

Regan, Donald H., 'The Meaning of "Necessary" in GATT Article XX and GATS Article XIV: The Myth of Cost-benefit Balancing' (2007) 6(3) World Trade Review 347–369.

Rodi, Michael, 'Ecological Tax Reform in Germany' (2000) 54(8) IBFD Bulletin 486–494.

Roessler, Frieder, 'Beyond the Ostensible. A Tribute to Professor Robert Hudec's Insights on the Determination of the Likeness of Products Under the National Treatment Provisions of the General Agreement on Tariffs and Trade' (2003) 37(4) Journal of World Trade 771–781.

Roessler, Frieder, 'Comment. India – Additional and Extra-Additional Duties on Imports from the United States' (2010) 9(1) World Trade Review 265–272.

Roland Ismer & Karsten Neuhoff, 'Border Tax Adjustment: A Feasible Way to Support Stringent Emission Trading' (2007) 24(2) European Law Journal of Law and Economics 137–164.

Rosenbloom, David H., 'The David R. Tillinghast Lecture. International Tax Arbitrage and the "International Tax System"' (1999–2000) 53 Tax Law Review 137–166.

Rosenbloom, David H., 'Cross-Border Arbitrage: The Good, the Bad and the Ugly' (2007) The Tax Magazine 115–118.

Rosendahl, Roger W., 'Border Tax Adjustments: Problems and Proposals' (1970) 2 Law & Policy in International Business 85–146.

Ruffin, Roy J., 'David Ricardo's Discovery of Comparative Advantage' (2002) 34(4) History of Political Economy 727–748.
Sakai, Marco & Barrett, John, 'Border Carbon Adjustments: Addressing Emissions Embodied in Trade' (2016) 92 Energy Policy 102–110.
Sakmar, Susan L., 'Bringing Energy Trade into the WTO: The Historical Context, Current Status, and Potential Implications for the Middle East Region' (2008) 18 Indiana International & Comparative Law Review 89–111.
Schenk, Alan, 'Value Added Tax: Does this Consumption Tax Have a Place in the Federal Tax System?' (1987) 7(2) Virginia Tax Review 207–301.
Schön, Wolfgang, 'World Trade Organization Law and Tax Law' (2004) 58(7) IBFD Bulletin 283–296.
Schumacher, Reinhard, 'Adam Smith's Theory of Absolute Advantage and the Use of Doxography in the History of Economics' (2012) 5(2) Erasmus Journal for Philosophy and Economics 54–80.
Scott, Joanne, 'Extraterritoriality and Territorial Extension in EU Law' (2004) 62(1) American Journal of Comparative Law 87–125.
Scott, Joanne, 'The New EU "Extraterritoriality"' (2014) 51(5) Common Market Law Review 1343–1380.
Sewalk, Stephen, 'A Carbon Tax with Reinvestment Is WTO Compatible' (2013–2014) 25(2) Fordham Environmental Law Review 338–392.
Shih, Wen-Chen, 'The Border Tax Adjustment Provisions of the GATT/WTO and their Implications on the Design of Energy and Carbon Tax' (2011) 14 International Trade and Business Law Review 53–84.
Slotboom, Marco M., 'Do Different Treaty Purposes Matter for Treaty Interpretation? The Elimination of Discriminatory Internal Taxes in EC and WTO Law' (2001) 4(3) Journal of International Economic Law 557–579.
Springmann, Marco, 'A Look Inwards: Carbon Tariffs versus Internal Improvements in Emissions-Trading Systems' (2012) 34 Energy Economics 228–239.
Sundelson, J. Wilner, 'Budgetary Principles' (1935) 50(2) Political Science Quarterly 236–263.
Sung, Shufan, 'Border Tax Adjustments and Developing Countries: A Perspective from China' (2016) 21 Annual Survey of International & Comparative Law 149–176.
Swinbank, Alan, 'Like Products, Animal Welfare and the World Trade Organization' (2006) 40(4) Journal of World Trade 687–711.
Thorndike, Joseph J., 'Early Proposals for an American VAT' (2009) Tax Analysts.

Tran, Christopher, 'Using GATT, Art XX to Justify Climate Change Measures in Claims under the WTO Agreements' (2010) 27 Environmental and Planning Law Journal 346–359.

Truby, Jon M., 'Towards Overcoming the Conflict between Environmental Tax Leakage and Border Tax Adjustment Concessions for Developing Countries' (2010–2011) 12(1) Vermont Journal of Environmental Law 149–183.

Truby, Jon, 'Extraterritoriality or an Illegal Tax? A Challenge to the Inclusion of Aviation in the EU Emissions Trading Scheme' (2012) 14(4) Environmental Law Review 301–306.

Tushnet, Mark, 'Critical Legal Studies: A Political History' (1990–1991) 100 Yale Law Journal 1515–1544.

Unger, Roberto Mangabeira, 'The Critical Legal Studies Movement' (1983) 96(3) Harvard Law Review 561–675.

Utz, Stephen, 'Ability to Pay' (2001–2002) 23 Whittier Law Review 867–950.

Van Asselt, Harro & Biermann, Frank, 'European Emissions Trading and the International Competitiveness of Energy-intensive Industries: A Legal and Political Evaluation of Possible Supporting Measures' (2007) 35(1) Energy Policy 497–506.

van Brederode, Robert F., 'Introduction to the US State Sales and Use Taxes' (2007) 18(4) International VAT Monitor 270–276.

van Brederode, Robert F., 'The Metamorphosis of US Corporate Income Tax into a Value Added Income Tax' (2008) 19(4) International VAT Monitor 266–274.

van Brederode, Robert F., 'Towards a Federal Sales Tax in the United States?' (2008) International VAT Monitor 114–120.

Vanden Brink, Ryan, 'Competitiveness Border Adjustments in US Climate Change Proposals Violate GATT: Suggestions to Utilize GATT's Environmental Exceptions' (2010) 21 Colorado Journal of International Environmental Law and Policy 85–122.

Veel, Paul-Erik, 'Carbon Tariffs and the WTO: An Evaluation of Feasible Policies' (2009) Journal of International Economic Law 749–800.

Viard, Alan D., 'Use Tax Collection on Interstate Sales: The Need for Federal Legislation' (2012) 66(9) Tax Analysis State Tax Notes 657–667.

Vogel, Klaus, 'Double Tax Treaties and Their Interpretation' (1986) 4 Berkeley Journal of International Law 1.

Weintraub, Sidney, 'Border Tax Adjustments and the GATT' (1964–1965) 17 Tax Executive 304–320.

Weiss, Edith Brown, 'Environment and Trade as Partners in Sustainable Development: A Commentary' (1992) 86(4) The American Journal of International Law 728–735.

Weitzel, Matthias, Hübler, Michael & Peterson, Sonja, 'Fair, Optimal or Detrimental? Environmental vs. Strategic Use of Border Carbon Adjustment' (2012) 34 Energy Economics 198–207.
Wirsenius, Stefan, Hedenus, Frederik & Mohlin, Kristina, 'Greenhouse Gas Taxes on Animal Food Products: Rationale, Tax Scheme and Climate Mitigation Effects' (2011) 108(1–2) Climate Change 159–184.
X, 'State Sales Tax Reform in the United States: The Streamlined Sales Tax Project' (2005) 59(5) IBFD Bulletin 176–181.
Yingfeng, Long, 'Challenges to China from Carbon Tax Border Adjustment under Global Climate Change and China's Answer' (2015) 3 China Legal Science 61–86.
Zane, Steven Nathaniel, 'Leveling the Playing Field: The International Legality of Carbon Tariffs in the EU' (2011) 34 Boston College International and Comparative Law Review 199–225.
Zarrilli, Simonetta, 'Domestic Taxation of Energy Products and Multilateral Trade Rules: Is This a Case of Unlawful Discrimination?' (2003) 37(2) Journal of World Trade 359–394.
Zelenak, Lawrence, 'Taking Critical Tax Theory Seriously' (1997) 76 North Carolina Law Review 1521–1580.
Zhu, Xiaoqin & He, Jinlong, 'International Court of Justice's Impact on International Environmental Law: Focusing on the Pulp Mills Case' (2012) 23(1) Yearbook of International Environmental Law 106–130.
Zin, Sharizal Mohd & Kazi, Ashraf U. Sarah, 'An Analysis of Customary International Law and the Importance of Dispute Settlement: A Study of Environmental Law Exceptions under Article XX' (2011) 7(1) Macquarie Journal of International and Comparative Environmental Law 39–80.

4. WORKING PAPERS, CONFERENCE PAPERS, ARTICLES, TECHNICAL REPORTS, ETC.

Aldy, Joseph E., Ley, Eduardo & Parry, Ian, 'A Tax-Based Approach to Slowing Global Climate Change' (2008) 26 Resources for the Future 3.
Altamirano, Juan-Carlos & Vielle, Marc, 'Climate Policies and Competitiveness: Options for Border Adjustment Measures' (2011) NCCR Climate and École Polytechnique Fédérale de Lausanne.
Altshuler, Rosanne, 'The GATT-Legality of Border Adjustments for Carbon Taxes and the Cost of Emissions Permits', Prepared for the ATPI Conference on US Energy Taxes, 15–16 October 2009.
Auerbach, Alan, Devereux, Michael P., Keen, Michael & Vella, John, 'Destination-Based Cash Flow Taxation' (2017) Oxford University Centre for Business Taxation, WP 17/01.

Avgerinopoulou, Dionysa-Theodora, 'The Role of the International Judiciary in the Settlement of Environmental Disputes and Alternative Proposals for Strengthening International Environmental Adjudication', paper prepared for the 'Global Environmental Governance: the Post-Johannesburg Agenda', Yale Center for Environmental Law and Policy, 23–25 October 2003.

Avi-Yonah, Reuven S., 'International Tax as International Law' (2007) Public Law and Legal Theory Research Paper No. 41.

Bartels, Lorand, 'The Inclusion of Aviation in the EU ETS. WTO Law Considerations' (2012) 6 Trade and Sustainable Energy Series, International Centre for Trade and Sustainable Development.

Bartels, Lorand, 'The Chapeau of Article XX GATT: A New Interpretation' (2014) University of Cambridge, Legal Studies Research Paper Series No. 40.

Biermann, Frank, Böhm, Frédéric, Brohm, Rainer, Dröge, Susanne & Trabold, Harald, 'The Polluter Pays Principle under WTO Law: The Case of National Energy Policy Instruments' (2003) Environmental Research of the Federal Ministry of the Environment, Nature Conservation and Nuclear Safety, Research Report 201 19 107.

Boeters, Stefan & Bollen, Johannes, 'Fossil Fuel Supply, Leakage and the Effectiveness of Border Measures in Climate Policy' (2012) 215 CPB Netherlands Bureau for Economic Policy Analysis.

Bovenberg, A. Lans & Horne, Jocelyn P, 'Taxes on Commodities. A Survey', in: George Kopits (ed.), *Tax Harmonization in the European Community: Policy Issues and Analysis* (1992) 34 IMF Occasional Papers.

Bradford, David F., 'The X Tax in the World Economy' (2003) CEPS Working Paper No. 93.

Branger, Frédéric & Quirion, Philippe, 'Would Border Carbon Adjustments Prevent Carbon Leakage and Heavy Industry Competitiveness Losses? Insight from a Meta-analysis of Recent Economic Studies' (2013) CIRED Working Paper Series No. 52.

Bueb, Julien, Richieri Hanania, Lilian & Le Clézio, Alison, 'Border Adjustments Mechanisms. Elements for Economic, Legal, and Political Analysis' (2016) 20 WIDER Working Paper.

Burniaux, Jean-Marc, Chateau, Jean, Duval, Romain & Jamet, Stéphanie, 'The Economics of Climate Change Mitigation: Policies and Options for the Future', OECD Economics Department Working Paper No. 658, 17 December 2008, ECO/WKP(2008)66.

Burniaux, Jean-Marc, Chateau, Jean & Duval, Romain, 'Is There a Case for Carbon-Based Border Tax Adjustment? An Applied General Equilibrium Analysis' (2010) 794 OECD Economics Department Working Papers.

Carlson, N., Hufbauer, G.C. & Krauss, M.B., 'Destination Principle Border Tax Adjustments for the Corporate Income and Social Security Taxes' (1976) OTA Paper 20.

Cnossen, Sijbren, 'Key Questions in Considering a Value-Added Tax for Central and Eastern European Countries' (1991) 91/69 IMF Working Paper 1–45.

Cnossen, Sijbren, 'Three VAT Studies' (2010) 90 CPB Netherlands Bureau for Economic Policy Analysis.

Condon, Madison & Ignaciuk, Ada, 'Border Carbon Adjustment and International Trade. A Literature Review' (2013) 06 OECD Trade and Environment Working Papers, OECD Publishing.

Copenhagen Economics, Reduced VAT for Environmentally Friendly Products (2008) DG Taxud, Final Report.

Cosbey, Aaron, 'Border Carbon Adjustment: Questions and Answers (But More of the Former)' (2009) Background paper produced for the 2009 International Trade Experts' Meeting (Toronto), available at <https://www.iisd.org/pdf/2009/bali_bcas_questions_answers.pdf>.

Cosbey, Aaron, Droege, Susanne, Fischer, Carolyn, Reinaud, Julia, Stephenson, John, Weischer, Lutz & Wooders, Peter, 'A Guide for the Concerned: Guidance on the Elaboration and Implementation of Border Carbon Adjustment' (2012) 3 Entwined Policy Report.

Cossy, Mireille, 'Determining "Likeness" under the GATS: Squaring the Circle?' (September 2006) World Trade Organization Staff Working Paper ERSD-2006-08.

Cottier, Thomas, Espa, Ilaria, Hirsbrunner, Simon, Holzer, Kateryna & Payosova, Tetyana, 'Differential Taxation of Electricity. Assessing the Compatibility with WTO Law, EU Law and the Swiss-EEC Free Trade Agreement', legal opinion established for the Federal Finance Administration, the Swiss Federal Office of Energy and the State Secretariat for Economic Affairs, 18 April 2014, available at <http://www.wti.org/research/publications/735/differential-taxation-of-electricity-assessing-the-compatibility-with-wto-law-eu-law-and-the-swiss-eec-free-trade-agreement/>.

Cottier, Thomas, Espa, Ilaria & Holzer, Kateryna, 'Renewable Electricity Tax Exemptions and Trade Remedies under International Law. An Assessment of Policy Space under WTO Law, the Swiss-EU FTA and EU Law', Confédération Suisse, 8 March 2015.

Courchene, Thomas J., 'Climate Change, Competitiveness and Environmental Federalism: The Case for a Carbon Tax' (2008) Background document for an Address to the Canada 2020 Speakers' Series.

de la Feria, Rita & Krever, Richard, 'Ending VAT Exemptions: Towards a Post-Modern VAT' (2012) Oxford University Centre for Business Taxation, WP 12/28.

de la Feria, Rita, 'EU VAT Rate Structure: Towards Unilateral Convergence?', WP 13/05 Oxford University Centre for Business Taxation, Saïd Business School, available at <http://www.sbs.ox.ac.uk/sites/default/files/Business_Taxation/Docs/Publications/Working_Papers/Series_13/WP1305.pdf>.

De Oliveira Rodrigues, Monica, 'Case Study: Most-Favoured-Nation Treatment and National Treatment in the GATT and the GATS and the Differentiated Tax Treatment as National Policy on Climate Change in Brazil' (2013) Revista Con-texto 39, available at <http://papers.ssrn.com/sol3/papers.cfm?abstract_id=2307330>.

Devereux, Michael & de la Feria, Rita, 'Designing and Implementing a Destination-Based Corporate Tax', CBT Annual Symposium, Oxford, 26 June 2013, ppt available at <http://www.ceps.be/system/files/events/2013/04/P4_RitadelaFeria.pdf>.

Devereux, Michael & de la Feria, Rita, 'Designing and Implementing a Destination-Based Corporate Tax' (2014) Oxford Centre for Business Taxation, WP14/07.

Dhar, Biswajit, 'The European Union's Proposed Carbon Equalisation System: Some Implications for India's Exports' (2014) 191 Research and Information System for Developing Countries.

Dhar, Biswajit & Das, Kasturi, 'The European Union's Proposed Carbon Equalization System: Can It Be WTO Compatible?' (2009) 156 Research and Information System for Developing Countries.

Due, John H., 'Excise Taxes' (1994) 1251 World Bank Policy Research Working Paper 1–38.

Duff, David G. & MacDonald, Margaret, 'Towards a Destination-Based Carbon Tax', 14th Global Conference on Environmental Taxation, Kyoto, 17–19 October 2013.

Dunmore, John C., 'Competitiveness and Comparative Advantage of US Agriculture', Paper presented at the 1986 National Public Policy Education Conference, Denver, Colorado, 16 September 1986.

Eftec, IEEP et al., 'The Use of Market-based Instruments for Biodiversity Protection – The Case of Habitat Banking – Technical Report', available at <http://ec.europa.eu/environment/enveco/pdf/eftec_habitat_technical_report.pdf>.

Ellis, Jaye, 'Liability for International Environmental Harm' (2013) Oxford Bibliographies, available at <http://www.oxfordbibliographies.com/view/document/obo-9780199796953/obo-9780199796953-0017.xml>.

Farmanfarmaian, Salman, 'The Case for CATS (Carbon Added Taxes) – Tackling Environmental Externalities in a Global Economy' (2008) Salman's blog available at <https://docs.google.com/document/d/1rejuqJLf3OsswX5JIxy944ULPPV4tKpcIoEOLQtgDQU/edit)>.

Fischer, Carolyn & Fox, Alan K., 'Comparing Policies to Combat Emissions Leakage: Border Carbon Adjustments versus Rebates' (2011) Resources for the Future Discussion Paper 09-02-REV.

Fullerton, Don, Leicester, Andrew & Smith, Stephen, 'Environmental Taxes' (2008) 14197 National Bureau of Economic Research 440.

Gale, William G. & Harris, Benjamin H., 'Proposal 10: Creating an American Value-Added Tax' (2013) The Hamilton Project, Brookings Institution, 1.

Gerstetter, Christiane, Görlach, Benjamin, Stoessel, Susanah, Ivanoca, Maria, Cavalieri, Sandra, Tedsen, Elizabeth & Bar-On, Haran, 'Rio+20: Financial Resources for Improved International Environmental Governance' (May 2012) Project No. (FKZ) 3711 19 104 on behalf of the German federal environment agency.

Gros, Daniel & Egenhofer, Christian, 'Climate Change and Trade. Taxing Carbon at the Border?' (2010) Centre for European Policy Studies.

Gupta, Satya Dev, 'Comparative Advantage and Competitive Advantage: An Economics Perspective and a Synthesis' (2009), available at <http://economics.ca/2009/papers/0534.pdf>.

Heine, Dirk, Norregaard, John & Parry, Ian W.H., 'Environmental Tax Reform: Principles from Theory and Practice to Date' (2012) IMF, WP/12/180.

Hoerner, J. Andrew, 'The Role of Border Tax Adjustments in Environmental Taxation: Theory and US Experience', Working Paper presented at the International Workshop on Market Based Instruments and International Trade of the Institute for Environmental Studies, Amsterdam, the Netherlands, March 1998.

Hoerner, J. Andrew & Muller, Franck, 'Carbon Taxes for Climate Protection in a Competitive World', paper prepared for the Swiss Federal Office for Foreign Economic Affairs, June 1996.

Horn, Henrik & Mavroidis, Peter C., 'Border Carbon Adjustments and the WTO' (2010) The Research Institute of Industrial Economics, Stockholm, Bruegel, Brussels, Centre for Economic Policy Research, London.

Horn, Henrik & Mavroidis, Petros C., 'Border Carbon Adjustments and the WTO', study part of the ENTWINDED – Environment and Trade in a World of Interdependence – project, 14 March 2010.

Hufbauer, Gary Clyde, 'A Critical Assessment and an Appeal for Fundamental Tax Reform' (1999) Paper for the World Trade Organization Panel Report, Peterson Institute for International Economics, available at <http://www.iie.com/publications/papers/print.cfm?ResearchId=373&doc=pub#note2> (accessed 28 October 2015).

Hufbauer, Gary Clyde, 'The Foreign Sales Corporation Drama: Reaching the Last Act?' (2002) International Economics Policy Briefs 1.

Hufbauer, Gary Clyde, 'The WTO as Tax Nanny', Center for Strategic Tax Reform's Tax Policy Wire, 25 April 2006, available at <http://www.cstr.org/commentaries/members/hufbauer.html>.

Hufbauer, Gary Clyde & Grieco, Paul L.E., 'Reforming the US Corporate Tax' (2005) Peterson Institute for International Economics.

IISD & UNEP, 'Chapter 5.10 (MEAs and the WTO)', *Environment and Trade. A Handbook*, available at <https://www.iisd.org/trade/handbook/5_10.htm>.

Industrial Economics, Incorporated, 'Economics Impacts of Superfund Taxes', report prepared for the Office of Policy Analysis, the Office of Policy, Planning and Evaluation and the US Environmental Protection Agency, February 1994.

Infanti, Anthony C. & Crawford, Bridget J., 'Critical Tax Theory: An Introduction' (2009) 4 University of Pittsburgh Legal Studies Research Paper.

Jaeger, William K., 'Environmental Taxation and the Double Dividend', paper prepared for the Internet Encyclopedia of Ecological Economics.

Kommerskollegium (Swedish National Board of Trade), 'Climate and Trade Rules – harmony or conflict?' (2004) available at <http://www.kommers.se/Documents/dokumentarkiv/publikationer/2004/rapporter/report-climate-and-trade-rules.pdf>.

Kopits, Geroge, 'Overview', in: George Kopits, *Tax Harmonization in the European Community: Policy Issues and Analysis* (1992) IMF Occasional Papers.

Kopits, George, *Tax Harmonization in the European Community: Policy Issues and Analysis* (1992) 34 IMF Occasional Papers.

Kortum, Sam & Weisbach, David, 'Border Adjustments for Carbon Emissions: Basic Concepts and Design' (2016) Resources for the Future.

Kotchen, Matthew J., Metcalf, Gilbert E. & Pizer, William A., 'The Case for the Green Climate Fund', The Hill, 6 March 2015, available at <http://thehill.com/opinion/op-ed/243974-the-case-for-the-green-climate-fund>.

Kysar, Douglas A., 'Climate Change and the International Court of Justice' (2013) Yale Law School, Public Law Research Paper No. 315.

Lanzi, Elisa, Mullaly, Damian, Château, Jean & Dellink, Rob, 'Addressing Competitiveness and Carbon Leakage Impacts Arising from Multiple Carbon Markets: A Modelling Assessment' (2013) OECD Environment Working Paper No. 58, ENV/WKP(2013)5.

Laurent, Eloi & Le Cacheux, Jacques, 'An Ever Less Carbonated Union? Towards a Better European Taxation Against Climate Change' (2009) 74 Notre Europe, Studies & Research.

Laurent, Eloi & Le Cacheux, Jacques, 'Taxe carbone: TCA contre CO2' (2009) 311 Lettre de l'OFCE 1–4.
Laurent, Eloi & Le Cacheux, Jacques, 'Réforme de la Fiscalité du Carbone dans l'Union européenne. Les options en présence' (2011) 16(1) Revue de l'OFCE 393–08.
Lockwood, Ben & Whalley, John, 'Carbon Motivated Border Tax Adjustments: Old Wine in Green Bottles?' (2008) NBER Working Paper Series No. 14025.
Long, Bill L., 'International Environmental Issues and the OECD 1950–2000: An Historical Perspective' (2000) OECD Publishing.
Manders, Tom & Veenendaal, Paul, 'Border Tax Adjustments and the EU-ETS. A Quantitative Assessment' (2008) 171 Centre Planning Bureau (CPB) Document.
McAusland, Carol & Najjar, Nouri, 'The WTO Consistency of Carbon Footprint Taxes' (2013) available at at <http://people.landfood.ubc.ca/carol.mcausland/The%20WTO%20Consistency%20of%20Carbon%20Footprint%20Taxes.pdf>.
McGuigan, Janet Stone, 'The Potential Economic Impact of Environmental Liability: The American and European Contexts' (2000) Study for the European Commission.
McKibbin, Warwick J. & Wilcoxen, Peter J., 'The Economic and Environmental Effects of Border Tax Adjustments for Climate Policy' (2008–2009) Brookings Trade Forum 1–34.
Metcalf, Gilbert E., 'Tax Reform and Environmental Taxation' (2005) NBER Working Paper No. 11665.
Millar, Rebecca, 'Echoes of Source and Residence in VAT Jurisdictional Rules' (2009) 09/44 Legal Studies Research Paper 1–34.
Milne, Janet, 'Mining the Air and Minding the Consequences: A Dark Cloud Tax', presentation at the 16th Global Conference on Environmental Taxation, 23–26 September 2015, University of Technology Sydney.
Müller, André, Böhringer, Christoph, Cottier, Thomas, Holzer, Kateryna & Matteotti, René, 'Border Tax Adjustments. Can Energy and Carbon Taxes be Adjusted at the Border?' (2013) Ecoplan, World Trade Institute, Universität Zürich.
Müller, Benito, 'To Earmark or Not to Earmark? A Far-reaching Debate on the Use of Auction Revenue from (EU) Emissions Trading' (November 2008) Oxford Institute for Energy Studies, EV 43.
Nedumpara, James J., 'Lessons Learned from DISC/FSC/ETI Disputes: Reshaping the Quest Towards a GATT/WTO Friendly Corporate Tax Reform in the United States' (2011) O.P. Jindal Global University, Research Paper No. 10.

Newman, John, 'Climate Change Policy and Iron and Steel Industry', OECD Steel Committee (2010) DSTI/SU(2010)17.

Oosterhuis, Frans et al., 'The Use of Differential VAT Rates to Promote Changes in Consumption and Innovation', Final Report commissioned by the European Commission, DG Environment, 25 June 2008, available at <http://ec.europa.eu/environment/enveco/taxation/pdf/vat_final.pdf>.

Pauwelyn, Joost, 'The Nature of WTO Obligations' (2002) The Jean Monnet Center for International and Regional Economic Law & Justice, available at <http://www.jeanmonnetprogram.org/archive/papers/02/020101-02.html> (accessed 28 October 2015).

Pauwelyn, Joost, 'The Unbearable Lightness of Likeness', A Review of Mireille Cossy, 'Some Thoughts on the Concept of "Likeness" in the GATS' (2006), available at SSRN: <http://ssrn.com/abstract=2030940> (accessed 28 October 2015).

Pauwelyn, Joost, 'US Federal Climate Policy and Competitiveness Concerns: the Limits and Options of International Trade Law' (2007) Nicholas Institute for Environmental Policy Solutions, Duke University, NI WP 07-02.

Pauwelyn, Joost, Testimony Before the Subcommittee on Trade of the House on Ways and Means, 24 March 2009.

Peterson, Everett B. & Schleich, Joachim, 'Economic and Environmental Effects of Border Tax Adjustments' (2007) Working paper sustainability and innovation S1.

Poitier, Michel & Tébar Less, Cristina, Joint Working Party on Trade and Environment, 'Trade and Environment at the OECD: Key Issues since 1991', Working Paper on Trade and Environment, No. 2008-01, COM/TAD/ENV/JWPTE(2007)38/FINAL, 17.

Reinaud, Julia, 'Issues Behind Competitiveness and Carbon Leakage. Focus on Heavy Industry' (2008) OECD/IEA.

Roser, Dominic & Tomlinson, Luke, 'Trade Policies and Climate Change: Border Carbon Adjustments as a Tool for a Just Global Climate Regime' (2014) Ancilla Iuris 223, available at <http://www.anci.ch/_media/beitrag/ancilla2014_223_roser-tomlinson.pdf>.

Sampford, Charles, 'Global Transparency: Fighting Corruption for a Sustainable Future: From National Integrity Systems to Global Integrity Systems' commissioned conference discussion paper for 13th IACC, Athens, November 2008.

Sampford, Charles, 'Reconceiving the Good Life – the Key to Sustainable Globalisation' (2009), Good Life Conference, Griffith University, Brisbane, 12 February 2009, available at <http://eprints.qut.edu.au/43380/1/Sampford-Reconceiving-the-Good-Life-HL.pdf>.

Schön, Wolfgang 'Destination-Based Income Taxation and WTO Law: A Note' (2016) 03 Max Planck Institute for Tax Law and Public Finance WP 16/03.

Schwabach, Aaron, 'Transboundary Environmental Harm and State Responsibility: Customary International Law', Encyclopedia of Life Support Systems, available at <http://www.eolss.net/sample-chapters/c14/e1-36-02-02.pdf>.

Shaviro, Daniel, 'Replacing the Income Tax with a Progressive Consumption Tax' (2003) NYU Law School, Public Law Research Paper No. 70, Center for Law and Business Research Paper No. 03-18.

Siggel, Eckhard, 'The Many Dimensions of Competitiveness' (2007) CESifo Venice Summer Institute.

Smith, Stephen, 'Environmental Taxes and Competitiveness: An Overview of Issues, Policy Options, and Research Needs', OECD paper, 11 June 2003, COM/ENV/EPOC/DAFFE/CFA(2001)90/REV1.

Stephenson, John & Upton, Simon, 'Competitiveness, Leakage, and Border Adjustment: Climate Policy Distractions?', Round Table on Sustainable Development, 22–23 July 2009, SG/SD/RT(2009)3.

Stewart, Terence P., Salonen, Eric P. & McDonough, Patrick J., 'More Than 50 Years of Trade Rule Discrimination on Taxation: How Trade With China Is Affected' (2007) Trade Lawyers Advisory Group, 24.

Stiglitz, Joseph E., 'Sharing the Burden of Saving the Planet: Global Social Justice for Sustainable Development. Lessons from the Theory of Public Finance', Paper presented at the International Economic Association meetings, Istanbul, June 2009, available at <http://academiccommons.columbia.edu/catalog/ac%3A126988>.

Strydon, Hendrik A., 'The Legal Principles Relating to Climate Change', Encyclopedia of Life Support System, available at <http://www.eolss.net/sample-chapters/c14/E1-36-10-00.pdf>.

Toder, Eric, Nunns, Jim & Rosenberg, Joseph, 'Using a VAT to Reform the Income Tax' (2012) Tax Policy Center/PEW Charitable Trusts.

Trachtman, Joel P., 'WTO Law Constraints on Border Tax Adjustments and Tax Credit Mechanisms to Reduce the Competitive Effects of Carbon Taxes' (2016) Resources for the Future.

van Asselt, Harro, Brewer, Thomas & Mehling, Michael, 'Addressing Leakage and Competitiveness in US Climate Policy. Issues Concerning Border Adjustment Measures' (2009) Climate Strategies Working Paper.

Van den Bossche, Peeter, Schrijver, Nico & Faber, Gerrit, 'Unilateral Measures Addressing Non-trade Concerns' (2007) Study for the Ministry of Foreign Affairs of the Netherlands (The Hague).

Winchester, Niven, Paltsev, Sergey & Reilly, John, 'Will Border Carbon Adjustments Work?' (2010) 184 MIT Joint Program on the Science and Policy of Global Change.

Wooders, Peter, 'Border Carbon Adjustments and Free Allowances in the Steel Sector', OECD Steel Committee meeting, 6–7 May 2010, DSTI/SU/SC(2010)8.

Wooders, Peter & Cosbey, Aaron, 'Climate-linked Tariffs and Subsidies: Economic Aspects (Competitiveness & Leakage)', background paper written for the conference 'Climate Change, Trade and Competitiveness: Issues for the WTO', 16–18 June 2000.

World Bank, 'Five Years after Rio. Innovations in Environmental Policy' (1997) Environmentally Sustainable Development Studies and Monographs Series No. 18.

Zhang, Zhong Xiang, 'Competitiveness and Leakage Concerns and Border Carbon Adjustments' (2012) CCEP Working Paper 1208.

Zhu, Zhu, Lee, Eum-sup & Kim, Sun-ok, 'A Discussion on the Legitimacy of Carbon Tariffs under the WTO' (2011) 10 International Conference on Sociality and Economics Development IPEDR 221.

5. PH.D. DISSERTATIONS

Deketelaere, Kurt, 'Naar een Europese Milieufiscaliteit. Het gebruik van fiscale instrumenten in het Europese Milieubeleid', Ph.D. dissertation, Katholieke Universiteit Leuven, 11 January 1995.

Pitrone, Federica, 'Environmental Taxation from a Legal Perspective: In Search of a Balance Between Environmental Goals and Tax Fairness', Ph.D. dissertation, Luiss Guido Carli University, February 2014.

Ryngaert, Cedric, 'Jurisdiction in International Law. United States and European Perspectives', Ph.D. Dissertation, Katholieke Universiteit Leuven, 12 February 2007, available at <https://lirias.kuleuven.be/bitstream/1979/911/2/doctoraat.pdf>.

Schrijver, Nicolas Jan, 'Sovereignty Over Natural Resources: Balancing Rights and Duties in an Interdependent World', Proefscrift Rijksuniversiteit Groningen, 2 March 1995.

Index